Quantum Computing with Python

Hands-on quantum programming with Qiskit, Cirq, and AWS Braket

Dr. Muralidhar Kurni

Ramesh Krishnamaneni

Dr. Srinivasa K.G.

www.bpbonline.com

First Edition 2026

ISBN: 978-93-78543-609

Dedicated to

The curious minds shaping the future of quantum computing

Foreword

In 2016, **IBM** put the first **5-qubit quantum computer** in the cloud. Today, it seems like one of the **90+ quantum hardware companies** announces a tens-of-millions-of-dollars investment round every week. Once a month or so, some Special Purpose Acquisition Company (SPAC) tells the world it is bringing a private quantum company public.

Are there yet? Do we have **quantum computers** that are simple to use? Can any programmer or coder use a standard high-level software development kit to develop applications and easily take advantage of the promised **quantum computational power**?

Unfortunately, no.

Instead, we need to enlarge our workforce's knowledge so they can take advantage of this **new paradigm** as it continues to develop over the coming years. We must educate them on the basics of **quantum computing coding**. This includes the **basic gates**, or operations, that are the building blocks of **quantum circuits**. We combine **quantum circuits** into **quantum applications** and then integrate them with **classical processing** to **develop solutions**.

While powerful **quantum libraries** like **Qiskit, Cirq, PennyLane, and Braket** provide useful tools for constructing these circuits and applications, it is still necessary to learn **quantum computing programming from the bottom up**. **That's where this book comes in**.

Quantum computing is a **very different paradigm** from **classical coding and programming**, the kind used since the 1960s to first write mainframe, then minicomputer, client-server, personal computer, laptop, mobile, Internet of Things, web, cloud, and many other platform applications. The best coder for these classical scenarios is not necessarily a great, or even a good, **quantum programmer**.

This book provides a **unique perspective** on **quantum coding**. By offering many examples and **algorithms** and showing how they can be implemented in **different ways**, the reader learns more than from a **single approach**. To use a cooking analogy, the reader learns not just a few strict recipes to follow, but also how to make delicious dishes with the selection of ingredients available today.

If that made you hungry, or at least curious about how to become a **quantum master chef**, then **jump right into this book**. **Your diligence and practice** will both **satisfy your curiosity** about this **critical new technology** and help you prepare to become an **important member** of the new **quantum software workforce**.

Robert S. Sutor, Ph.D.
Founder & CEO, Sutor Group Intelligence and Advisory
Former Vice President, IBM Quantum Ecosystem Development
Author of *"Dancing with Qubits"*
New York, USA
https://sutorgroupintelligenceandadvisory.com/

About the Authors

- **Dr. Muralidhar Kurni** has more than 25 years of experience in teaching, research, and academic leadership, and is currently serving as an associate professor in the department of computer science and engineering and as dean of **Research & Development (R&D)** at Anantha Lakshmi Institute of Technology & Sciences (Autonomous), Anantapuramu, India. He holds a Ph.D. in computer science and engineering from JNTUA and has completed postdoctoral research at the University of South Florida, USA. His areas of expertise include AI, ML, high-performance computing, and quantum computing. A Senior Member of IEEE and an **International Engineering Educator (IGIP)**, he has authored and edited several books with leading publishers. He has published extensively in reputed SCIE and Scopus-indexed journals. Through his teaching, research, and workshops, he has consistently focused on making complex computing concepts accessible, with a strong emphasis on Python-based learning and practical quantum computing education.

- **Ramesh Krishnamaneni** has over 18 years of experience in software engineering, cloud architecture, and emerging technologies, and has played key roles as a solutions architect at IBM. He has led and delivered enterprise-scale solutions across IBM Cloud, AWS, Azure, and Red Hat OpenShift, enabling organizations to build scalable and intelligent systems. His expertise spans high-performance computing, AI, and quantum computing, with a strong focus on practical implementation using Python-based frameworks such as Qiskit and Cirq. He holds an M.S. in Software Systems from BITS Pilani and has completed advanced training in AI and ML from the University of Texas at Austin. He has contributed to research and technical work in AI-driven analytics, IoT, and advanced computing domains, and actively explores how to integrate quantum computing into real-world applications through modern programming approaches.

- **Dr. Srinivasa K.G.** has over two decades of experience in teaching, research, and academic leadership, and is currently serving as professor of data science and AI and dean (academics) at DSPM IIIT-Naya Raipur, India. He holds a Ph.D. in computer science from Bangalore University and has served at several reputed institutions, including NITTTR Chandigarh, MSRIT Bangalore, and CBP Government Engineering College, New Delhi. A Senior Member of IEEE and ACM, he has authored numerous books and published more than 150 research papers in international journals and conferences. His expertise includes AI, high-performance computing, and emerging quantum technologies. He is a recipient of prestigious awards, including the AICTE Career Award, ISTE Best Research Award, IEI Young Engineer Award, and the BOYSCAST Fellowship from the department of science and technology, government of India. He actively contributes to advancing research and education in next-generation computational systems, including quantum computing.

About the Reviewers

- **Anusha Dasarakothapalli** is a principal software engineer at Amazon, in the applied AI services organization, specializing in distributed systems, large-scale data and streaming platforms, and AI-driven software infrastructure. She has over 10 years of experience designing and operating mission-critical cloud services and developer platforms used at global scale. Her work focuses on building reliable, high-performance systems for data streaming, storage, and intelligent software development workflows. Throughout her career, Anusha has contributed to systems spanning real-time streaming platforms, large-scale storage services such as Amazon S3, Amazon S3 Glacier, Amazon **Managed Streaming for Apache Kafka** (**MSK**), and observability frameworks for modern AI-enabled software development. Her work currently focuses on developing next-generation agentic solutions for software development teams powered by AI. In addition to her engineering work, Anusha actively contributes to the broader technology community by participating in technical reviews, evaluating innovative research and engineering work, and supporting the advancement of emerging technologies in distributed systems and AI-driven software development.

- **Rajkumar Kuppuswami** is a manager–data scientist at Applied Materials in the United States and a Ph.D. researcher in data science, specializing in AI, machine learning, and advanced analytics. He is currently focused on applying AI-driven solutions to enterprise challenges including semiconductor supply chain optimization, global trade analytics, and data-driven decision intelligence. His work involves building scalable analytics platforms, predictive models, and intelligent automation systems that help organizations transform data into strategic insights. Rajkumar is particularly interested in emerging technologies such as generative AI, agentic AI, and immersive digital technologies that are shaping modern business ecosystems. Alongside his industry work, he actively contributes to the research and technology community through academic collaborations, editorial and advisory roles, and participation in conferences and innovation initiatives. He is passionate about exploring how artificial intelligence, data science, and immersive technologies can create measurable business value while supporting responsible and ethical AI adoption across industries.

Acknowledgements

- **Dr. Muralidhar Kurni** would like to thank his mother Smt. P. Sanjeevamma; Shri M. Ramesh Naidu, Vice Chairman of Anantha Lakshmi Institute of Technology & Sciences (Autonomous), and his friends, Dr. Mujeeb Shaik Mohammed, Mr. K. Somasena Reddy, and his students K. Shahir Basha and K. Anusha, for their wholehearted support in completing this book.

- **Ramesh Krishnamaneni** would like to express heartfelt gratitude to his family for their constant encouragement and support throughout this journey. He also would like to thank his mentors, Gajendra Sanil, Pradeep Mansey, Neil De Lima, Dhruv Rajput, and Neeraj Kaushik, for their invaluable help, feedback, and motivation during the development of this book.

- **Dr. Srinivasa K. G.** would like to thank Prof. Om Prakash Vyas, Vice Chancellor & Director, IIIT Naya Raipur, for his kind encouragement to publish this book. He would also like to thank all the faculty members of IIIT Naya Raipur for their wholehearted support in publishing this book.

Preface

Quantum computing is rapidly emerging as one of the most transformative technologies of the modern era, with the potential to address problems that are beyond the capabilities of classical systems. From optimization and cryptography to **artificial intelligence** (**AI**) and scientific simulation, quantum computing is redefining how complex computational challenges are approached. Despite its growing importance, the subject often appears abstract and mathematically intensive, making it difficult for many learners to engage with it effectively.

This book is written with a clear objective: to make quantum computing accessible, practical, and implementable with Python. Drawing from our combined experience in teaching, research, and industry, we have presented the concepts in a structured and intuitive manner, supported by hands-on examples and real-world applications. The focus is not limited to theoretical understanding; instead, the book emphasizes learning through implementation using widely adopted frameworks such as Qiskit, Cirq, and AWS Braket.

The content is carefully organized to guide readers from foundational principles to advanced applications. Each chapter builds progressively, enabling readers to move from understanding core quantum concepts to developing practical quantum programs and projects. This book is intended for students, educators, developers, and researchers who wish to build a strong foundation in quantum computing and apply it in real-world scenarios.

Chapter 1: Introduction to Quantum Computing –This chapter introduces the fundamental concepts of quantum computing and explains how it differs from classical computing. It provides an overview of key principles, such as superposition and entanglement, and the relevance of quantum computing to solving complex real-world problems.

Chapter 2: Qubits and Quantum States –This chapter explores the building blocks of quantum computing, focusing on qubits and their representation. It explains quantum states, the Bloch sphere, and Dirac notation, helping readers understand how information is stored and manipulated in quantum systems.

Chapter 3: Quantum Gates and Circuits –This chapter introduces quantum gates and their role in manipulating qubits. It explains single-qubit and multi-qubit gates, as well as the construction of quantum circuits, enabling readers to understand how quantum operations are designed and executed.

Chapter 4: Quantum Algorithms –This chapter presents foundational quantum algorithms, including Grover's and Shor's algorithms. It explains their working principles and demonstrates how quantum approaches can outperform classical methods for specific computational problems.

Chapter 5: Quantum Hardware and Noise –This chapter explores the practical aspects of quantum computing by discussing quantum hardware technologies and their limitations. It introduces concepts such as noise, decoherence, and error mitigation, helping readers understand real-world challenges in quantum systems.

Chapter 6: Getting Started with Python for Quantum Computing – This chapter provides the necessary Python foundation for quantum programming. It introduces essential libraries, tools, and environments for effectively implementing quantum algorithms and simulations.

Chapter 7: Programming with Qiskit from IBM –This chapter focuses on Qiskit, one of the most widely used quantum computing frameworks. It guides readers through building, simulating, and executing quantum circuits, including running programs on real quantum hardware.

Chapter 8: Quantum Utility and Qiskit Patterns -This chapter discusses the concept of quantum utility and how quantum systems can deliver practical value. It introduces structured programming patterns in Qiskit to help design efficient, scalable quantum workflows.

Chapter 9: Programming with Cirq -This chapter introduces Cirq, a framework designed for quantum circuit design and simulation. It explains how to model quantum systems, simulate noise, and develop circuits aligned with near-term quantum hardware.

Chapter 10: Programming with AWS Braket –This chapter explores AWS Braket, a cloud-based quantum computing service. It demonstrates how to access multiple quantum hardware providers and build hybrid workflows using cloud infrastructure.

Chapter 11: Variational and Hybrid Algorithms with Python –This chapter introduces hybrid quantum-classical algorithms such as the **variational quantum eigensolver** (**VQE**) and **Quantum Approximate Optimization Algorithm** (**QAOA**). It explains how these approaches enable practical problem-solving on current quantum devices.

Chapter 12: Quantum Cryptography and Security –This chapter covers the fundamentals of quantum cryptography, including quantum key distribution. It explains how quantum principles can be used to secure communication systems and introduces concepts such as the BB84 protocol.

Chapter 13: Quantum Machine Learning –This chapter explores the intersection of quantum computing and ML. It introduces quantum data encoding, hybrid models, quantum neural networks, and practical implementation approaches.

Chapter 14: Quantum Simulation Projects –This chapter focuses on simulation-based applications of quantum computing. It demonstrates how quantum systems can model physical and chemical processes using practical examples and Python-based frameworks.

Chapter 15: End-to-end Mini Projects – This chapter provides hands-on mini projects that integrate concepts learned throughout the book. It includes applications such as quantum search, optimization, and classification, helping readers apply their knowledge in real-world scenarios.

Chapter 16: Artificial Intelligence and Quantum Computing –This chapter examines the convergence of AI and quantum computing. It highlights how the two fields complement each other and explores hybrid approaches to solving complex computational problems.

Chapter 17: Road Ahead for Quantum Computing –This chapter discusses future directions in quantum computing, including scalability, emerging technologies, and industry trends. It provides insights into the evolving ecosystem and prepares readers for advancements in quantum technologies.

Appendix: AI-assisted Programming for Quantum Computing –This appendix introduces the use of AI-assisted tools in quantum programming. It explains how tools such as code assistants can support circuit design, debugging, and optimization, enabling faster development and improved productivity in quantum workflows.

Code Bundle and Coloured Images

Please follow the link to download the
Code Bundle and the ***Coloured Images*** of the book:

https://rebrand.ly/1jtd0i3

The code bundle for the book is also hosted on GitHub at
https://github.com/bpbpublications/Quantum-Computing-with-Python.
In case there's an update to the code, it will be updated on the existing GitHub repository.

We have code bundles from our rich catalogue of books and videos available at https://github.com/bpbpublications. Check them out!

Errata

We take immense pride in our work at BPB Publications and follow best practices to ensure the accuracy of our content to provide an indulging reading experience to our subscribers. Our readers are our mirrors, and we use their inputs to reflect and improve upon human errors, if any, that may have occurred during the publishing processes involved. To let us maintain the quality and help us reach out to any readers who might be having difficulties due to any unforeseen errors, please write to us at: errata@bpbonline.com

Your support, suggestions and feedback are highly appreciated by the BPB Publications' Family.

Piracy

If you come across any illegal copies of our works in any form on the internet, we would be grateful if you would provide us with the location address or website name. Please contact us at business@bpbonline.com with a link to the material.

If you are interested in becoming an author

If there is a topic that you have expertise in, and you are interested in either writing or contributing to a book, please visit www.bpbonline.com. We have worked with thousands of developers and tech professionals, just like you, to help them share their insights with the global tech community. You can make a general application, apply for a specific hot topic that we are recruiting an author for, or submit your own idea.

Reviews

Please leave a review. Once you have read and used this book, why not leave a review on the site that you purchased it from? Potential readers can then see and use your unbiased opinion to make purchase decisions. We at BPB can understand what you think about our products, and our authors can see your feedback on their book. Thank you!

For more information about BPB, please visit www.bpbonline.com.

Join our Discord space

Join our Discord workspace for latest updates, offers, tech happenings around the world, new releases, and sessions with the authors:

https://discord.bpbonline.com

Table of Contents

CHAPTER 1
Introduction to Quantum Computing

Introduction

Quantum computing marks a paradigm shift in how information is processed and understood. While classical computers rely on deterministic logic using **binary digits** (**bits**) that exist as 0 or 1, quantum computers harness the laws of quantum mechanics: superposition, entanglement, and interference, to evaluate many possibilities simultaneously. This capability enables them to address problems that grow exponentially in complexity, far beyond the reach of even the most powerful supercomputers.

This chapter introduces the foundational differences between classical and quantum computing, tracing the evolution of computation and the emerging need for quantum approaches. It explores the rise of global quantum missions and industrial ecosystems that unite governments, research institutions, and technology companies in building quantum infrastructure and standards.

Real-world applications are examined across domains such as cryptography, optimization, **machine learning** (**ML**), and computational chemistry, illustrating how quantum algorithms achieve selective advantages over classical methods. The chapter concludes by emphasizing the pivotal role of Python, the unifying language of quantum programming, which connects theoretical models to practical experimentation through frameworks like *Qiskit*, *Cirq*, and *PennyLane*.

By bridging scientific theory with practical implementation, this chapter lays the groundwork for understanding how classical and quantum systems can coexist in hybrid architectures, shaping the future of computation.

Structure

This chapter covers the following topics:

- Classical vs. quantum computing
- Global quantum missions and industry ecosystem
- Quantum computing applications in cryptography optimization machine learning
- Role of Python in quantum programming

Objectives

This chapter introduces the foundational concepts that distinguish quantum computing from classical computation. Readers will understand how principles such as superposition, entanglement, and interference enable new ways of processing information beyond binary logic. The chapter also explores the global quantum ecosystem, highlighting key national missions, industry collaborations, and research initiatives driving innovation. Through real-world applications in cryptography, optimization, ML, and chemistry, readers will see how quantum algorithms deliver selective computational advantages. Finally, the chapter presents Python as the core programming interface for quantum systems, enabling seamless development with frameworks such as Qiskit, Cirq, and PennyLane. By the end, readers will gain a holistic understanding of quantum principles, current global progress, and the essential tools needed to begin practical exploration of quantum programming.

Classical vs. quantum computing

Classical computing processes information using binary logic, bits that exist as 0 or 1, executed through deterministic operations. While this model has powered decades of technological progress, it struggles with problems that scale exponentially. Quantum computing, by contrast, leverages superposition, entanglement, and interference to process many possibilities simultaneously, offering a fundamentally different approach to computation.

The evolution of computing

Computing, at its essence, is the systematic processing of information using well-defined instructions to produce meaningful results. From early mechanical calculators to modern supercomputers, classical computing has been the dominant paradigm for more than seven decades. It transformed every scientific, industrial, and social domain by automating arithmetic, data management, and decision-making processes.

The classical computer operates on a simple but compelling idea representing and manipulating information using bits. Each bit exists in one of two states, 0 or 1, encoded physically as low/high voltages, magnetic polarity, or optical pulses. Millions (and now billions) of transistors are integrated to form processors that execute logical instructions with deterministic precision. This paradigm has underpinned the digital revolution, enabling innovations ranging from spreadsheets and social networks to spacecraft navigation and deep learning systems.

However, the relentless growth of computational demand in simulating molecular systems, optimizing supply chains, or training trillion-parameter AI models is revealing the inherent limits of classical computation. Problems whose complexity grows exponentially with input size are rapidly beyond the reach of even the most advanced supercomputers. This challenge has sparked interest in an alternative model: quantum computing, inspired by the laws governing atomic and subatomic particles.

Deterministic logic and linear scaling in classical computing

A classical computer can be formally modeled as a system that manipulates strings of bits through a finite sequence of operations known as **logic gates**. Each gate implements a Boolean function such as *AND*, *OR*, *NOT*, or *XOR*, converting specific input patterns into predictable outputs. Larger computations are built by chaining these gates into circuits executed step-by-step by a processor.

Core characteristics of classical computing: The following table summarizes these characteristics, emphasizing their deterministic behavior and resource-bounded scalability:

Property	Description
Determinism	Every computation follows a fixed sequence of logical transformations; identical inputs always yield identical outputs.
Discrete state space	A register of n bits can represent exactly one of 2^n possible configurations at any instant.
Irreversible operations	Many logic gates lose information (e.g., an AND gate cannot reconstruct its inputs from an output of 0), producing heat and energy loss.
Scalability constraints	To explore all 2^n states, a classical computer must process them sequentially or use massive parallelism, quickly exhausting memory and time.

***Table 1.1**: Core characteristics of classical computing*

While classical computers are extraordinarily versatile, they struggle with tasks that involve state-space explosion, such as simulating quantum interactions, solving NP-hard optimization problems, or factoring large integers. In these domains, runtime grows exponentially with problem size, making exact solutions computationally prohibitive.

Harnessing the laws of quantum mechanics in quantum computing

Quantum computing represents a radical re-imagining of computation, replacing deterministic bits with **quantum bits (qubits)** governed by the principles of superposition, entanglement, and interference. Instead of processing information sequentially, a quantum computer exploits the inherent parallelism of quantum mechanics to evaluate many possibilities simultaneously.

The quantum bit

A qubit is the fundamental unit of quantum information. Unlike a bit, which is strictly 0 or 1, a qubit can exist in a superposition of both states:

$$|\psi\rangle = \alpha|0\rangle + \beta|1\rangle,$$

Where α and β are complex probability amplitudes satisfying $|\alpha|^2 + |\beta|^2 = 1$..

Upon measurement, the qubit collapses probabilistically to $|0\rangle$ or $|1\rangle$, with respective probabilities $|\alpha|^2$ and $|\beta|^2$. This probabilistic nature introduces an entirely new computational dimension—one that allows quantum algorithms to explore vast state spaces in parallel.

Superposition and parallelism

In a register of n qubits, the system can simultaneously represent 2^n possible classical states. For example, 3 qubits can encode 8 values at once. When properly manipulated, this collective superposition allows specific algorithms to process an exponential number of possibilities in a single computational step, a property that underlies quantum speed-up.

Correlated information beyond-classical limits through entanglement

Entanglement is a uniquely quantum correlation in which the state of one qubit cannot be described independently of another. Once qubits become entangled, measuring one immediately influences the other, regardless of distance. This interconnected behavior allows quantum systems to store and process joint information rather than treating qubits individually.

In quantum computing, entanglement is a core computational resource that enables coordinated manipulation of an exponentially large state space. It supports phenomena such as quantum teleportation, superdense coding, and strengthens quantum error correction by distributing information across multiple qubits. Algorithms like Grover's search and Shor's factoring also rely on entangled states to explore and evaluate many possibilities simultaneously.

Overall, entanglement provides the beyond-classical correlations that give quantum computers their distinctive computational power.

Interference and measurement

Quantum computations leverage interference—the constructive and destructive combination of probability amplitude, to amplify correct outcomes and suppress incorrect ones. A well-designed algorithm orchestrates these interference patterns so that measurement yields the desired answer with high probability.

Quantum gates and circuits

Just as classical logic gates form the building blocks of digital circuits, quantum gates manipulate qubits through unitary transformations. Each gate is reversible and preserves total probability, reflecting the conservation principles of quantum mechanics.

Figure 1.1 shows how classical and quantum gates operate on bits and qubits, highlighting the difference between deterministic and quantum state transformations:

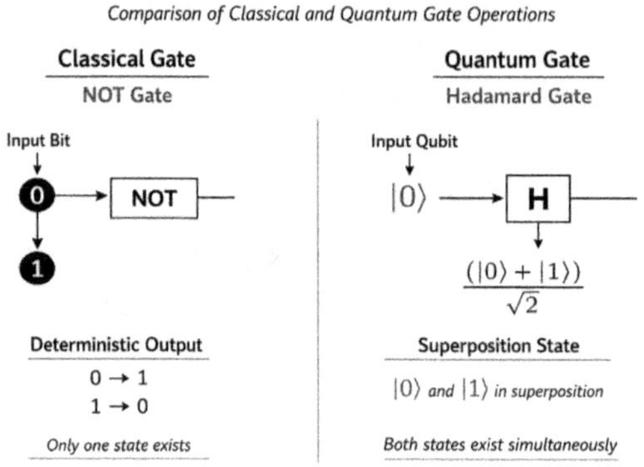

Figure 1.1: *Classical NOT gate vs. quantum Hadamard gate operation*

The comparison highlights the shift from deterministic binary operations to quantum state manipulation. Classical gates act on fixed bits, while quantum gates operate on qubits and enable superposition. Later chapters demonstrate how such gates can be used to form quantum circuits using frameworks such as *Qiskit*, *Cirq*, and *AWS Braket*.

The following table summarizes some fundamental quantum gates and their functions:

Quantum gate	Circuit symbol	Symbolic action	Primary function
Hadamard (H)	[H]	(	0⟩ → (
Pauli-X (NOT)	[X]	(	0⟩ ↔
CNOT (CX)	●—⊕	Conditional NOT	Generates entanglement between two qubits
Phase / Rotation Gates	[R]	(R_x(θ), R_z(φ))	Rotates the qubit state on the Bloch sphere
Measurement	[M]	(	ψ⟩ →

Table 1.2: *Fundamental quantum gates and their functions*

Figure 1.2 shows the standard circuit symbols used to represent common quantum gates in circuit diagrams:

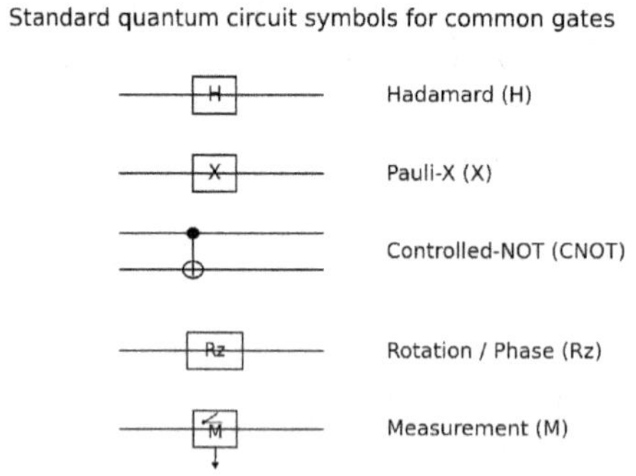

Figure 1.2: *Standard circuit symbols for common quantum gates*

In quantum circuit diagrams, qubits are represented as horizontal wires, and gate operations are applied along these wires using standardized symbols. Single-qubit gates appear as labeled boxes, while multi-qubit gates use control dots and connecting lines to indicate conditional operations. Quantum circuits are sequences of such gates applied to one or more qubits, allowing quantum states to evolve through a series of controlled transformations. Because these operations are reversible, information is not destroyed but evolves coherently until the final measurement. Modern quantum software frameworks such as Qiskit, Cirq, and AWS Braket provide Python-based tools for constructing, visualizing, and executing these circuits, topics that will be explored in later chapters.

Contrasting paradigms

While both classical and quantum computers are designed to process information, they are built on fundamentally different physical and mathematical principles. Classical systems rely on deterministic logic and binary representation, whereas quantum systems exploit superposition, entanglement, and probabilistic computation.

The following table contrasts the two paradigms, highlighting their distinctive characteristics, strengths, and limitations:

Aspect	Classical computing	Quantum computing
Basic unit	Bit (0 or 1)	Qubit ($\|0\rangle$, $\|1\rangle$, or a superposition of both)
Information representation	Fixed binary states	Complex-valued probability amplitudes
Computation type	Deterministic, sequential	Probabilistic, parallel through superposition
Logic model	Irreversible Boolean gates	Reversible unitary transformations
Correlation	Independent bits	Entangled multi-qubit states
Strengths	Mature technology; universal applicability	Exponential parallelism; quantum advantage on select problems
Limitations	Exponential scaling; resource bottlenecks	Fragility to noise; limited qubit counts (**Noisy Intermediate-Scale Quantum** (**NISQ**) era)

***Table 1.3**: Comparison between classical and quantum computing paradigms*

This comparison highlights the complementary nature of the two paradigms.

Classical computers remain unmatched for general-purpose tasks, data storage, and control operations, while quantum computers promise speed-ups for a restricted but profoundly important class of problems—including factoring, unstructured search, quantum simulation, and optimization.

Synergy between quantum and classical computing

The near-term vision of computation is hybrid. **Quantum processing units** (**QPUs**) handle subtasks that exploit quantum parallelism, while classical **central processing units** (**CPUs**) and **graphical processing units** (**GPUs**) handle control, optimization, and post-processing. This collaboration defines the NISQ era, characterized by devices containing tens to hundreds of qubits with limited coherence times but sufficient capability to explore meaningful applications.

Hybrid workflows already exist in practice:

- Variational algorithms such as **variational quantum eigensolver** (**VQE**) and **Quantum Approximate Optimization Algorithm** (**QAOA**) alternate between quantum circuit evaluations and classical optimizers.
- Quantum simulators leverage classical resources for noise modeling and circuit transpilation.
- Cloud platforms integrate both worlds, as seen in *IBM Quantum Runtime* and *AWS Braket Hybrid Jobs*.

Figure 1.3 illustrates the hybrid quantum–classical optimization loop commonly used in variational algorithms such as VQE and QAOA:

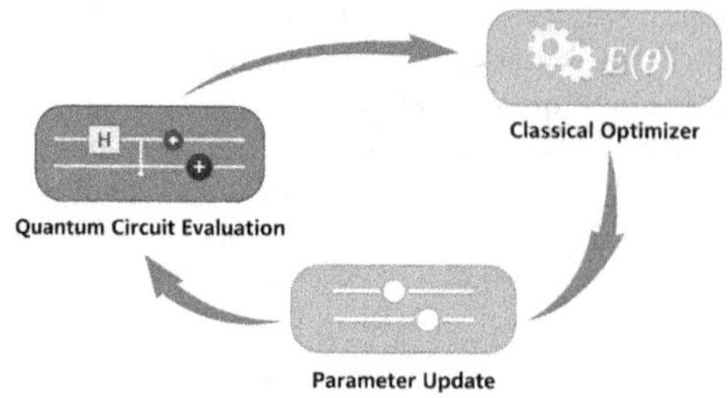

Figure 1.3: *Hybrid quantum–classical optimization loop*

Such synergy will persist even in future fault-tolerant systems, ensuring that classical and quantum processors co-evolve rather than compete.

While current quantum devices operate within the NISQ era, researchers are steadily working toward the development of fault-tolerant quantum computers capable of performing longer and more reliable computations. Achieving this goal requires significant advances in quantum error correction, scalable hardware architectures, and improved qubit stability. Although the exact timeline remains uncertain, many industry and academic estimates suggest that practical fault-tolerant quantum systems may begin to emerge in the mid-to-late 2030s. Until then, hybrid quantum–classical approaches are expected to remain the primary framework for exploring and developing real-world quantum applications.

Looking ahead

As transistor miniaturization approaches physical limits, quantum computing offers an alternative trajectory for computational growth. Rather than relying on faster clock speeds or parallel processors, it introduces a fundamentally new way to encode and transform information. The field is transitioning from laboratory prototypes to cloud-accessible systems operated by *IBM*, *Google*, *IonQ*, and *Rigetti*—a phase where theoretical elegance meets experimental validation.

Global quantum missions and industry ecosystem

Quantum computing has rapidly evolved from a theoretical pursuit into a strategic global enterprise. Nations and industries worldwide are investing heavily to secure leadership in this emerging technology, recognizing its potential to revolutionize communication security, data processing, and scientific discovery. The 2020s mark a decisive shift from isolated research efforts to coordinated national quantum missions and industrial collaborations, shaping a vibrant international ecosystem.

The global quantum revolution

Quantum computing has transcended the boundaries of laboratory research to become a strategic frontier for nations and corporations worldwide. Much like the early days of classical computing and the space race, today's quantum revolution is driven by a shared vision—harnessing the peculiar laws of quantum mechanics to achieve computational capabilities far beyond current limits.

Governments, research institutions, and technology enterprises are investing billions to establish leadership in quantum hardware, software, communication, and cryptography. This ecosystem extends across disciplines-physics, computer science, electrical engineering, and materials science, reflecting a true convergence of knowledge.

The significance of these initiatives is twofold:

- **National security and economic competitiveness**: Quantum technologies promise breakthroughs in secure communications, logistics optimization, and materials innovation, domains with direct geopolitical and industrial implications.

- **Scientific discovery**: By simulating nature's quantum systems directly, these machines could accelerate discoveries in chemistry, biology, and energy sciences.

As the 2020s unfold, the quantum race is defined by a blend of collaboration and competition, with academia, startups, and technology giants contributing to a vibrant, rapidly evolving global landscape.

Strategic quantum initiatives

Many nations have launched comprehensive quantum missions to build infrastructure, develop talent, and stimulate industrial ecosystems. The following are notable examples that collectively represent the world's leading efforts toward quantum readiness:

- **United States: National Quantum Initiative (NQI) Act**:

  Enacted in 2018, the U.S. NQI provides a structured roadmap for advancing quantum information science.

  It established partnerships among federal agencies such as the **Department of Energy** (DOE), **National Institute of Standards and Technology** (NIST), and **National Science Foundation** (NSF) to support:

  - Quantum research centers focusing on computing, networking, and sensing.
  - Public–private collaborations to translate academic research into scalable technologies.
  - Standardization and cybersecurity frameworks for quantum-safe encryption.

  The U.S. ecosystem is further strengthened by corporate programs—*IBM Quantum*, *Google Quantum AI*, *Microsoft Azure Quantum*, and *Amazon Braket*—which offer global cloud access to quantum processors, promoting an open research culture.

- **European Union: Quantum Flagship Program**

  The EU Quantum Flagship, launched in 2018 with a budget exceeding €1 billion, coordinates research across member states in four domains: communication, computing, simulation, and sensing/metrology.

  Its objectives include:

  - Establishing quantum internet testbeds using **quantum key distribution** (QKD).
  - Supporting industrial prototypes and startups in the quantum technology sector.
  - Building pan-European research infrastructure, notably through the *Quantum Technology Innovation Hubs*.

  Europe's coordinated approach emphasizes both academic excellence and industrial scalability, aiming to integrate quantum technology into mainstream digital transformation strategies by the early 2030s.

- **China: National Laboratory for Quantum Information Sciences**

  China has made significant investments in quantum communication and computing, anchored by its National Laboratory for Quantum Information Sciences in *Hefei*. Its landmark achievements include:

  - The *Micius* satellite, which conducted the world's first quantum-encrypted intercontinental communication experiment.
  - Development of superconducting and photonic quantum processors, demonstrating quantum advantage in specific tasks.
  - Strong integration between national defense, telecommunications, and academic research ecosystems.

  China's emphasis on quantum sovereignty reflects its strategy to secure long-term dominance in information security and advanced manufacturing.

- **India: National Quantum Mission (NQM)**

  Launched in April 2023, India's NQM is a major government initiative aimed at fostering indigenous capabilities in quantum computing, communication, sensing, and materials.

The mission's key goals include:

- Establishing four thematic hubs across premier institutions for focused **research and development (R&D)**.
- Developing 20–1000 qubit quantum computers using various physical platforms (superconducting, photonic, and ion-trap).
- Building a national quantum communication network leveraging QKD for secure data transfer.
- Creating a skilled quantum workforce through targeted academic programs and international collaborations.

India's NQM aligns with its *Digital India* and *Atmanirbhar Bharat* (self-reliant India) initiatives, positioning the country as a regional hub for quantum innovation.

- **Other global programs**:

  Beyond the major national missions in the United States, Europe, China, and India, several other countries have launched strategic quantum initiatives to strengthen their positions in the global innovation landscape. These programs emphasize regional strengths, ranging from silicon-based qubit fabrication to quantum communication networks, and foster collaboration between universities, industries, and government research bodies.

  The following table highlights prominent quantum technology initiatives currently driving advancements across different regions:

Country/Region	Initiative	Key focus areas
Japan	Quantum Technology Innovation Strategy	Quantum computers, sensors, and secure communication under government–industry alliances.
Canada	National Quantum Strategy (2022)	Research funding, commercialization pathways, and startup incubation (notably *Xanadu, D-Wave*).
Australia	**Centre for Quantum Computation and Communication Technology (CQC2T)**	Silicon-based qubits and quantum error correction.
United Kingdom	**National Quantum Technologies Programme (NQTP)**	Applications in secure communication, imaging, and timing; major university–industry collaboration.
Singapore	**Centre for Quantum Technologies (CQT)**	Regional leadership in quantum communication and photonics.

***Table 1.4**: Selected international quantum initiatives and their focus areas*

Together, these programs demonstrate that quantum capability is now a key metric of national innovation strength, akin to space or AI leadership in previous decades.

The industry and research ecosystem

The progress of quantum technology depends on the synergy between academia, startups, corporations, and funding agencies:

- **Academic and research institutions**: Universities and national laboratories drive the theoretical foundations and hardware experimentation essential to the field. Institutions such as *MIT, Stanford, University of Oxford, Tsinghua University*, and *IISc Bangalore* contribute to innovations in superconducting circuits, trapped ions, topological qubits, and photonic integration.

  Their roles extend beyond research—they serve as training grounds for the next-generation of quantum engineers and algorithm developers.

- **Startups and quantum innovators**: Quantum innovation is increasingly powered by agile startups that complement the efforts of large corporations.

  Examples:

  - **IonQ**: Specializing in trapped-ion hardware with high fidelity and cloud accessibility.
  - **Rigetti Computing**: Developing modular superconducting qubit systems for hybrid cloud use.
  - **Xanadu**: Advancing photonic quantum computing and the open-source library PennyLane for **quantum ML** (**QML**).
  - **Pasqal and QuEra**: focusing on neutral atom architectures with scalable control mechanisms.

  These startups form the experimental edge of the ecosystem, often collaborating directly with universities and cloud providers.

- **Established tech corporations**: Major technology companies are investing heavily in full-stack quantum ecosystems that integrate hardware, middleware, and developer tools. These companies are transforming quantum computing from a purely experimental pursuit into a cloud-accessible computational service, enabling global participation in algorithm development and benchmarking.

  The following table summarizes the key industrial initiatives and their distinctive contributions to the quantum landscape:

Company	Platform/Initiative	Key contributions
IBM	IBM Quantum/Qiskit	Open-source SDK, cloud hardware access, and the quantum utility benchmarking initiative.
Google	Quantum AI/Cirq/Sycamore	Demonstration of quantum supremacy; focus on error correction and scalable architectures.
Amazon	AWS Braket	Cloud integration offering multi-vendor quantum backends and hybrid quantum–classical workflows.
Microsoft	Azure Quantum	Unified development environment supporting multiple hardware partners and the Q# language.
Intel	Horse Ridge Chip and Cryo-CMOS	Hardware innovations for scalable qubit control and integration with classical systems.

***Table 1.5**: Leading technology corporations and their quantum computing initiatives*

  These platforms not only provide access to real quantum processors but also cultivate communities of learners, researchers, and developers—making quantum computing increasingly democratized.

- **Venture capital and funding landscape**: Venture capital investment in quantum startups has increased significantly since 2020, reflecting growing confidence in the field's long-term potential. Global funding exceeded $2.5 billion in 2023, with major investment rounds supporting companies such as *IonQ*, *PsiQuantum*, and *D-Wave*. Industry analyses, including reports from the *McKinsey Global Institute*, highlight this surge as a key indicator of accelerating commercial interest in quantum technologies. Governments also act as strategic investors, providing grants and co-funding mechanisms through innovation councils and defense research agencies. This dual public–private model accelerates both academic discovery and commercial translation, enabling faster transitions from laboratory prototypes to viable products.

Collaboration and standardization efforts

Quantum technologies thrive in collaborative ecosystems. International organizations and alliances are emerging to ensure interoperability, ethical use, and security standards.

Key global initiatives include:

- **Quantum Economic Development Consortium (QED-C)**: U.S.-led consortium fostering public–private partnerships.
- **European Telecommunications Standards Institute (ETSI) Quantum Safe Working Group**: Establishing encryption and QKD interoperability standards.
- **IEEE Quantum Initiative**: Promoting standards for benchmarking, circuit design, and education.
- **ISO/IEC JTC 1 quantum information technology (QIT)**: Advancing international consensus on terminology, quality assurance, and system testing.

These efforts are critical for creating trust, transparency, and compatibility across platforms, paving the way for the commercial quantum internet and global-scale applications.

Outlook on a converging ecosystem

The global quantum landscape is characterized by rapid technological evolution and unprecedented international participation. What began as isolated national projects has evolved into a multinational collaborative ecosystem where shared testbeds, open-source software, and cloud-based platforms accelerate discovery.

The next decade will likely witness:

- Error-corrected quantum processors exceeding 1,000 qubits, as anticipated in several industry roadmaps, including projections from IBM Quantum and other major quantum computing initiatives.
- Hybrid AI–quantum applications integrated into cloud services.
- Quantum networking and secure communication infrastructure connecting continents.
- Widespread adoption of open-source frameworks such as Qiskit, Cirq, and PennyLane in academic curricula.

Quantum computing is no longer a distant aspiration; it is becoming an essential component of digital transformation strategies and scientific innovation pipelines worldwide.

The momentum built by these global missions and industry collaborations sets the stage for the next section, where we explore real-world applications in cryptography, optimization, ML, and chemistry, the domains that first showcase quantum advantage.

Quantum computing applications in cryptography optimization ML

Quantum computing's practical value emerges not from replacing classical systems entirely, but from solving specific problems that are intractable for classical architectures. Its ability to exploit superposition, entanglement, and interference enables exponential gains in select domains where computation scales combinatorially or interactions are inherently quantum-mechanical.

Introduction from theory to quantum advantage

The power of quantum computing lies not in universal superiority over classical computers, but in its selective superiority, its ability to outperform classical methods for specific classes of problems. These are typically tasks where solution spaces grow exponentially, interactions are inherently quantum-mechanical, or probabilistic interference can be exploited to find optimal outcomes faster.

Over the past two decades, several application domains have emerged as testbeds for demonstrating quantum advantage:

- Cryptography and cybersecurity
- Optimization and operations research
- ML and data analysis
- Computational chemistry and materials science

Each field illustrates how quantum principles translate into tangible computational benefits, particularly in the NISQ era.

Quantum cryptography and cybersecurity

The emergence of quantum computing is reshaping the foundations of cybersecurity. As quantum systems grow in capability, they simultaneously threaten classical encryption and introduce new, physics-based methods for securing information.

The following list discusses how quantum computing threatens classical encryption and how quantum principles enable secure communication:

- **Breaking classical encryption**: Modern digital security relies on mathematical problems presumed to be intractable for classical computers. Algorithms such as RSA and **Elliptic Curve Cryptography** (**ECC**) rely on the difficulty of integer factorization and discrete logarithm problems.

  However, Shor's algorithm (1994) demonstrated that a sufficiently large quantum computer could factor integers and compute discrete logarithms in polynomial time—a task that would take classical supercomputers millions of years. If executed on a fault-tolerant machine with thousands of logical qubits, Shor's algorithm could render much of today's public-key cryptography obsolete. For example, estimates suggest that breaking widely used RSA-2048 encryption would require on the order of several thousand logical qubits (roughly 4,000 or more) along with large numbers of physical qubits for error correction, highlighting the significant technological gap between current NISQ devices and cryptographically relevant quantum computers.

  This looming threat has catalyzed the field of **post-quantum cryptography** (**PQC**)—the development of classical algorithms resistant to quantum attacks—and accelerated interest in quantum-safe standards, led by NIST and ETSI initiatives.

- **Quantum-secure communication**: While quantum computing endangers classical cryptography, quantum mechanics also offers intrinsically secure alternatives. QKD uses the principles of superposition and measurement collapse to detect eavesdropping attempts. In protocols such as *BB84*, any interception disturbs the quantum state, revealing an intrusion to both communicating parties. *Figure 1.4* shows the photon polarization states used in the BB84 protocol:

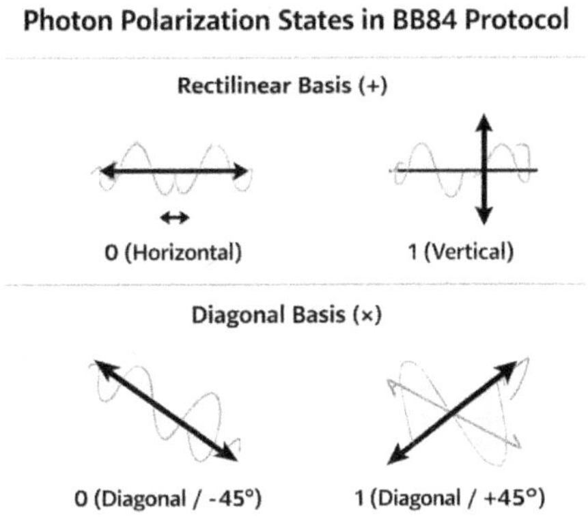

Figure 1.4*: Photon polarization states in the BB84 protocol*

Several countries, including China, India, and EU Quantum Flagship members, are already deploying quantum communication networks that use entangled photon pairs to distribute cryptographic keys over fiber-optic and satellite links securely. These systems mark the beginning of the quantum internet, where information is protected not by computational complexity but by the laws of physics themselves.

Quantum optimization and combinatorial problems

Optimization problems pervade logistics, finance, manufacturing, and network design. Classical algorithms, such as simulated annealing, linear programming, or greedy heuristics, often become inefficient for large, high-dimensional search spaces. Quantum computing introduces a fundamentally different search mechanism: exploiting superposition to explore multiple configurations simultaneously and interference to amplify optimal solutions.

This section introduces the key concepts of the QAOA and its applications across various industries.

- **QAOA**: Developed by *Farhi et al. (2014)*, QAOA is a hybrid quantum–classical algorithm particularly suited to the NISQ era. It alternates between two operators:
    - A problem Hamiltonian encoding the cost function (e.g., Max-Cut, portfolio optimization).
    - A mixing Hamiltonian that explores neighboring configurations.

  A classical optimizer iteratively tunes the circuit parameters to minimize the cost function. *Figure 1.5* shows the hybrid optimization loop used in QAOA:

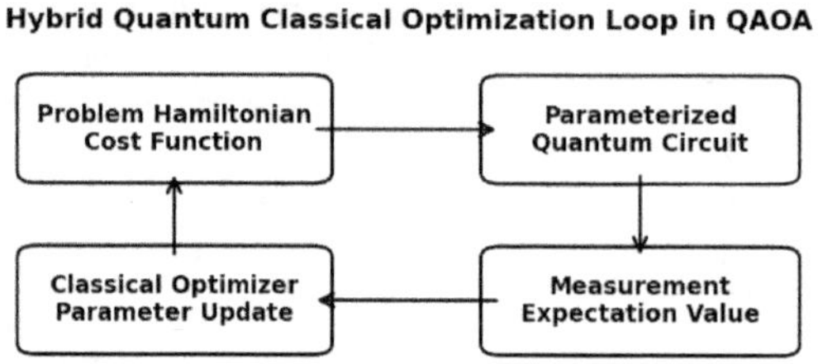

***Figure 1.5**: Hybrid optimization loop in QAOA*

  QAOA demonstrates how a quantum processor can enhance combinatorial optimization without requiring full error correction.

- **Applications and industry impact**: Quantum optimization has begun to influence a variety of real-world domains, particularly where classical methods struggle to find global optima within exponentially large search spaces. By leveraging hybrid quantum–classical algorithms such as the QAOA and VQE, industries are exploring more efficient solutions to complex scheduling, resource allocation, and decision-making challenges.

The following table illustrates representative sectors and example problems where quantum approaches are already demonstrating potential benefits:

Domain	Example problem	Quantum approach
Logistics and supply chain	Vehicle routing, warehouse scheduling	Hybrid QAOA or quantum annealing (D-Wave)
Finance	Portfolio optimization under risk constraints	QAOA with mean–variance Hamiltonian
Energy grid	Optimal power flow and unit commitment	Quantum gradient descent and VQE-based formulations
Manufacturing	Resource allocation and layout optimization	Ising model mapping with QAOA

***Table 1.6**: Representative domains and quantum approaches in optimization*

Quantum optimization provides heuristic yet efficient solutions that scale better than exhaustive classical searches for many real-world cases, often integrated into hybrid workflows where the quantum stage guides a classical solver.

Quantum machine learning

The explosion of data in modern science has created an urgent demand for models that can learn efficiently and generalize across complex datasets. QML seeks to combine the computational capabilities of quantum systems with classical learning algorithms to potentially achieve faster training, improved generalization, and compact model representations. By leveraging quantum phenomena such as superposition and entanglement, QML aims to explore high-dimensional feature spaces that may be difficult for classical models to process efficiently.

This section introduces the key aspects of QML, including its foundational concepts, representative algorithms, and integration frameworks.

- **Foundational concepts**:
  - **Quantum data encoding**: Classical data must be encoded into quantum states before quantum algorithms can process it. Techniques such as amplitude encoding and angle encoding map classical feature vectors into quantum states, enabling access to high-dimensional Hilbert spaces.
  - **Parameterized quantum circuits (PQCs)**: They are quantum circuits with tunable gate parameters optimized during training using classical techniques such as gradient-based or gradient-free optimization.
  - **Quantum kernels**: This compute similarity measures between quantum states and are used in algorithms such as **quantum support vector machines** (**QSVMs**), enabling classification in quantum feature spaces.
- **Representative algorithms**: QML includes several algorithms that combine quantum information processing with classical learning paradigms. These methods attempt to exploit quantum effects, such as superposition, entanglement, and interference to enhance pattern recognition and optimization tasks.

The following table summarizes several representative QML algorithms and their applications:

Algorithm	Core idea	Use case
QSVM	Uses quantum kernel estimation to classify data in higher-dimensional spaces.	Image and text classification.
Variational quantum classifier (VQC)	Employs a parameterized circuit to learn decision boundaries.	Binary classification and pattern recognition.
Quantum principal component analysis (QPCA)	Extracts eigenvectors of density matrices efficiently.	Dimensionality reduction and feature extraction.
Quantum Boltzmann Machines (QBM)	Uses quantum tunneling to escape local minima in optimization.	Generative modeling and energy-based learning.

***Table 1.7**: Representative algorithms in QML*

- **QML frameworks and integration**:

  Python libraries such as Qiskit ML, **TensorFlow Quantum** (**TFQ**), and PennyLane provide practical environments for developing QML models. These frameworks integrate quantum circuits with classical deep learning ecosystems, enabling hybrid workflows in which quantum circuits can function as trainable layers within neural networks. Among these platforms, PennyLane has emerged as one of the most actively developed frameworks, offering strong integration with ML libraries such as PyTorch and TensorFlow, while TFQ continues to serve primarily as an experimental platform for research and prototyping.

Training parameterized quantum circuits, however, presents several challenges. One widely discussed limitation is the barren plateau problem, where gradients become exponentially small as circuit depth or qubit count increases. In such situations, optimization landscapes become nearly flat, making it difficult for classical optimizers to update parameters effectively. Researchers are exploring strategies such as problem-inspired circuit architectures, layer-wise training methods, and improved parameter initialization to mitigate this issue.

Despite growing interest, clear quantum advantage in ML has not yet been conclusively demonstrated. Most current QML experiments rely on small datasets and NISQ devices or simulators. In many practical scenarios, classical ML models still outperform current quantum approaches in scalability and reliability.

Nevertheless, QML remains a rapidly evolving field. Early demonstrations suggest potential for applications such as pattern recognition, anomaly detection, and feature mapping as quantum hardware and hybrid algorithms continue to mature.

Quantum simulation for chemistry and material science

Quantum simulation stands at the forefront of scientific discovery, offering a way to model molecular and material systems by directly leveraging the principles of quantum mechanics. Unlike classical methods that rely on approximations, quantum algorithms can represent complex quantum states more naturally, enabling breakthroughs in chemistry, physics, and materials science.

This section introduces the main aspects of quantum simulation including its challenges in chemistry, key algorithms such as the VQE and **quantum phase estimation** (**QPE**), and their emerging industrial applications.

- **The quantum challenge in chemistry**: Accurately modeling molecular systems is one of the most computationally demanding tasks in science. Classical computers must approximate solutions to the *Schrödinger Equation*, whose complexity scales exponentially with the number of electrons. This limitation hinders accurate simulations even for modest-sized molecules such as caffeine.

- **VQE**: The VQE (algorithm offers a practical path to leveraging NISQ devices for molecular simulation. It works by expressing the molecular Hamiltonian as a set of qubit operations (using Jordan–Wigner or Bravyi–Kitaev transformations) and iteratively adjusting circuit parameters to minimize the system's expected energy.

  Steps in VQE:

  1. Encode the molecule's Hamiltonian H into a quantum circuit.
  2. Prepare an ansatz (trial state) with tunable parameters.
  3. Measure the expectation value $\langle\psi|H|\psi\rangle$ on the quantum device.
  4. Use a classical optimizer to minimize the energy until convergence.

  Figure 1.6 illustrates the parameterized ansatz circuit and measurement stage used in the VQE algorithm.

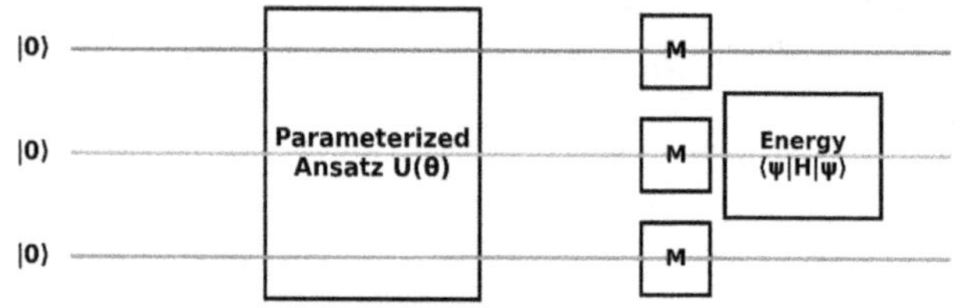

Figure 1.6: *Parameterized ansatz and measurement stage in the VQE algorithm*

  When implemented using frameworks such as Qiskit Nature, VQE has demonstrated chemical accuracy (~1.6 mHa) for small molecular systems including H_2, LiH, and BeH_2, as reported in early quantum chemistry demonstrations of the algorithm (Peruzzo et al., 2014).

- **QPE**: For fault-tolerant devices, QPE remains the most precise algorithm for computing eigenvalues of Hamiltonians, offering exponential speed-ups over classical diagonalization methods. QPE underpins simulations in materials design, drug discovery, and catalyst optimization, forming a cornerstone of quantum computational chemistry.

- **Industrial applications**: The practical potential of quantum simulation extends across multiple sectors that depend on accurate molecular modeling and materials discovery. By directly emulating the quantum nature of matter, quantum algorithms, notably the VQE and QPE can achieve levels of precision unattainable with classical approximation methods.

These capabilities are expected to revolutionize industries from pharmaceutical design to renewable energy and nanotechnology, as summarized in the following table:

Sector	Quantum benefit	Example use case
Pharmaceuticals	Predict drug–target binding energies	Design of antiviral molecules and enzymes
Energy and materials	Model catalytic reactions and battery materials	Hydrogen storage and fuel cell research
Nanotechnology	Simulate quantum dots and superconductors	Quantum sensors and photonic materials

Table 1.8: *Industrial applications of quantum simulation*

Quantum simulation thus bridges quantum physics and industrial chemistry, enabling discoveries through computational exploration rather than trial-and-error experimentation.

Cross-domain synergies and future prospects

The true potential of quantum computing emerges through its integration with other fields, where quantum methods enhance applications in chemistry, finance, and cybersecurity. As hardware advances, such cross-domain synergies will shape a future driven by quantum-assisted computing.

The real power of quantum computing emerges when these domains intersect:

- **QML for chemistry**: Using QML to predict molecular energies or reaction rates from quantum data.
- **Quantum optimization in finance**: Embedding QAOA models in risk minimization and portfolio balancing.
- **Quantum-enhanced cybersecurity**: Combining QKD with ML-based intrusion detection.

As quantum hardware matures toward error-corrected systems, these cross-domain applications will redefine fields ranging from drug discovery to AI ethics and financial forecasting. The future of computation will likely be quantum-assisted rather than quantum-exclusive, blending classical control with quantum acceleration.

Role of Python in quantum programming

Python has become the language of choice for quantum computing due to its simplicity, readability, and powerful scientific ecosystem. It provides an accessible bridge between the abstract mathematics of quantum mechanics and the practical implementation of quantum algorithms. Through Python-based frameworks such as Qiskit, Cirq, AWS Braket, and PennyLane, researchers and students can design, simulate, and execute quantum circuits across diverse hardware platforms.

By seamlessly integrating with libraries such as NumPy, SciPy, and Matplotlib, Python enables efficient numerical computation, visualization, and hybrid quantum–classical workflows. Its open-source nature and cross-platform compatibility have made it the foundation for modern quantum education, research, and cloud-based experimentation.

Python dominates the quantum ecosystem

Among all modern programming languages, Python has emerged as the de facto standard for quantum computing. Its simplicity, readability, and extensive scientific ecosystem make it ideal for bridging complex quantum mechanics with accessible computational tools.

The rise of Python-based quantum SDKs, such as *IBM Qiskit*, *Google Cirq*, *AWS Braket*, and *Xanadu PennyLane* has democratized access to quantum hardware and simulators. Researchers, educators, and developers can now write, visualize, and execute quantum algorithms without needing deep hardware-level expertise.

The following table summarizes the core features that make Python uniquely suited for the emerging quantum computing ecosystem:

Feature	Relevance in quantum computing
Readable syntax	Enables physicists and computer scientists to collaborate without steep learning curves.
Extensive libraries	Integrates seamlessly with NumPy, SciPy, Matplotlib, and Pandas for mathematical modeling and visualization.
Hybrid workflows	Supports smooth interaction between classical and quantum modules through APIs.
Community and open-source	A vast global developer base contributes to the fast evolution of quantum frameworks.
Cross-platform integration	Operates uniformly across local environments, cloud notebooks, and supercomputing clusters.

***Table 1.9**: Strategic advantages of Python in quantum computing*

Python thus functions not merely as a coding tool, but as a universal interface between theoretical quantum models and practical experimentation.

Python as the glue between classical and quantum worlds

Quantum algorithms rarely run in isolation. They depend on classical control logic for circuit construction, parameter optimization, and post-processing of results. Python's design philosophy—interpreted, modular, and dynamically typed—makes it an excellent medium for orchestrating this hybrid quantum–classical workflow.

Example:

- In the VQE or QAOA, Python executes the classical optimization loop, while a quantum backend evaluates the circuit energies.
- Python scripts handle data encoding, parameter sweeps, and noise analysis, integrating outputs into scientific notebooks for further visualization.
- Libraries such as Matplotlib and Plotly allow direct rendering of quantum histograms, Bloch sphere plots, and state vector distributions.

This flexibility allows quantum research to evolve rapidly from concept to code to experiment, often within a single Jupyter Notebook.

Key Python-based quantum frameworks

Several open-source frameworks define today's practical landscape of quantum programming. Each reflects a unique design philosophy while adhering to Python's high-level syntax.

Let us explore four key Python-based frameworks that drive the development and application of quantum computing, including IBM Qiskit, Google Cirq, Amazon Braket, and Xanadu PennyLane.

- **IBM Qiskit**: Developed by *IBM Quantum*, Qiskit provides an end-to-end Python framework for building, simulating, and executing quantum circuits on both simulators and real quantum hardware. In Qiskit 1.0 and later, the framework is distributed as a unified package, with core functionality for circuit construction, transpilation, and execution provided through Qiskit, while specialized application libraries such as *Qiskit Nature*, *Qiskit Machine Learning*, *Qiskit Finance*, and *Qiskit Optimization* support domain-specific workflows. Qiskit also enables access to IBM Quantum cloud services, including *IBM Quantum Runtime*, for scalable execution and workflow integration.
- Its modular architecture—Terra, Aer, Ignis, and Aqua (now merged into Qiskit Machine Learning and Nature)—offers:

  - Circuit construction and visualization tools.
  - Simulators for noiseless and noise-aware execution.
  - Libraries for chemistry, optimization, and ML.
  - Direct hardware access via the IBM Quantum Runtime cloud.

  Qiskit's syntax aligns with Python conventions, allowing beginners to transition smoothly from classical coding to quantum experimentation.

- **Creating and simulating a Bell state using Qiskit**: The following Python example demonstrates how easily a simple Bell state—the fundamental two qubit entangled state can be created and simulated using Qiskit. The following snippet illustrates Python's elegance and readability in the construction, execution, and interpretation of quantum circuits:

```
from qiskit import QuantumCircuit
from qiskit_aer import AerSimulator
qc = QuantumCircuit(2)
qc.h(0)
qc.cx(0, 1)
qc.measure_all()
simulator = AerSimulator()
job = simulator.run(qc, shots=1024)
result = job.result()
print(result.get_counts())
```

Figure 1.7 shows the circuit used to generate and measure a Bell state in Qiskit:

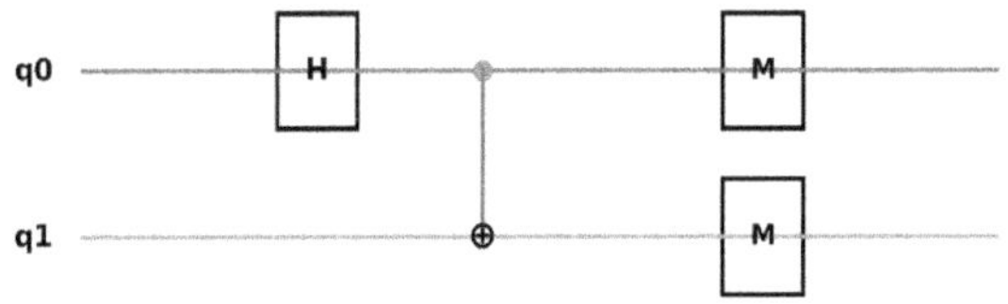

***Figure 1.7**: Bell state quantum circuit*

- **Google Cirq**: Cirq, developed by *Google Quantum AI*, targets researchers seeking fine-grained control over qubits and noise models. Its low-level access to gates, moments, and device connectivity makes it ideal for experimental work and custom circuit design. Cirq serves as the Python gateway to *Sycamore* and other Google processors through the Quantum Engine API. It integrates tightly with TFQ for quantum ML workflows. The following example demonstrates how a simple two qubit entangled state can be created and simulated using the Cirq framework:

```
import cirq
# Create two qubits
q0, q1 = cirq.LineQubit.range(2)
# Build the circuit
circuit = cirq.Circuit(
    cirq.H(q0),
    cirq.CNOT(q0, q1),
    cirq.measure(q0, q1, key='result')
)
# Simulate the circuit
simulator = cirq.Simulator()
result = simulator.run(circuit, repetitions=1024)
print(result)
```

- **Amazon Bracket**: It provides a unified Python interface for multiple quantum hardware providers (IonQ, Rigetti, QuEra, etc.). Its SDK allows users to define circuits locally, simulate them, and then execute them on cloud-based quantum processors. Braket's Python API supports hybrid jobs, enabling tight coupling between classical AWS EC2 compute and quantum tasks—a natural extension of Python's multi-platform reach. The following Python example demonstrates how a simple Bell state can be created and simulated using the AWS Braket SDK:

```
from braket.circuits import Circuit
from braket.devices import LocalSimulator
# Create the Bell state circuit
circuit = Circuit().h(0).cnot(0, 1)
# Run the circuit on a local simulator
device = LocalSimulator()
result = device.run(circuit, shots=1000).result()
print(result.measurement_counts)
```

- **Xanadu PennyLane**: PennyLane specializes in differentiable programming for QML. It unifies quantum simulators and hardware backends under a single Pythonic layer, compatible with PyTorch and TensorFlow. By treating quantum circuits as trainable computational graphs, PennyLane allows gradient-based optimization through automatic differentiation—a paradigm central to quantum deep learning research. The following example illustrates how a basic parameterized quantum circuit can be defined in PennyLane:

```
import pennylane as qml
from pennylane import numpy as np
# Define a quantum device
dev = qml.device("default.qubit", wires=2)
# Define a quantum node
@qml.qnode(dev)
def circuit(theta):
    qml.Hadamard(wires=0)
    qml.CNOT(wires=[0,1])
    qml.RY(theta, wires=0)
    return qml.expval(qml.PauliZ(0))
# Execute the circuit
theta = np.array(0.5)
result = circuit(theta)
print(result)
```

Python libraries supporting quantum research

Beyond the core quantum SDKs such as Qiskit, Cirq, and PennyLane, Python's extensive scientific computing ecosystem plays a crucial role in supporting every stage of quantum experimentation. These libraries provide the mathematical, analytical, and visualization capabilities needed to model quantum states, design experiments, and interpret results.

The following table summarizes key Python libraries and their specific contributions to the quantum research workflow:

Library	Quantum relevant use
NumPy/SciPy	Linear algebra, matrix operations, and complex-number manipulation for quantum states.
SymPy	Symbolic mathematics for deriving gate operations and parameterized circuits.
Matplotlib/Plotly	Visualization of qubit states, histograms, and interference patterns.

NetworkX	Graph-based modeling of qubit connectivity and optimization problems.
Pandas	Data analysis and results logging for hybrid experiments.
Scikit-learn	Integration with QML kernels and hybrid ML workflows.

***Table 1.10**: Python libraries supporting quantum research and experimentation*

Together, these libraries transform Python into a scientific operating system for quantum computing, supporting tasks from theoretical derivations to cloud-scale execution.

Education, community, and open research

Python's openness has made it the cornerstone of quantum education. Most online quantum learning resources, including *IBM Quantum Lab*, *Qiskit Textbook*, and *Google Cirq Colab Demos*, are built entirely in Python notebooks.

Universities worldwide now teach quantum computing with Python as part of computer science and physics curricula, often using Jupyter environments to integrate theory, simulation, and live execution. Students can visualize entanglement, run code on real quantum devices, and share results instantly—nurturing a global, collaborative learning culture.

The open-source philosophy embedded in Python also accelerates the dissemination of research. Preprints, GitHub repositories, and reproducible notebooks ensure that quantum experiments are transparent and verifiable—an essential factor in building scientific trust during the field's early, experimental phase.

Conclusion

This chapter establishes the conceptual foundation of quantum computing, tracing its evolution from the limits of classical systems to the emerging paradigm of superposition, entanglement, and interference. We examined how quantum principles redefine computation and how nations, industries, and researchers are collaborating to build a global quantum ecosystem that blends scientific discovery with technological innovation. Through real-world applications in cryptography, optimization, ML, and chemistry, we saw how quantum algorithms can achieve remarkable efficiency gains for problems beyond the reach of classical algorithms. The chapter also underscored the unifying role of Python as the primary interface for developing and simulating quantum programs, enabling a smooth bridge between theory and experimentation. Together, these discussions prepare readers to move from understanding the conceptual foundations of quantum computing to exploring its practical implementation, a journey continued in the chapters that follow.

Questions

1. **What distinguishes classical computing from quantum computing?**

   Answer: Classical computing processes definite binary states (0 or 1) through deterministic logic. Quantum computing, however, uses qubits that exist in superposition, allowing many computations to occur simultaneously, thus enabling exponential speed-ups for specific problem types.

2. **What is a qubit, and why is it central to quantum computing?**

   Answer: A qubit is the quantum analogue of a bit. It can exist in a combination of $|0\rangle$ and $|1\rangle$ states at once, making it capable of parallel information processing—something impossible in classical computation.

3. **Why is entanglement considered a powerful feature of quantum systems?**

   Answer: Entanglement links qubits in such a way that the state of one instantly influences the other, regardless of distance. This correlation enables collective computation, forming the foundation for quantum teleportation, secure communication, and advanced algorithms.

4. **What are some key advantages of quantum computing?**

   Answer: Quantum computers excel at problems involving massive parallelism, such as cryptography, optimization, ML, and molecular simulation, where classical systems face exponential scaling limits.

5. **What is meant by the NISQ era?**

   Answer: The NISQ era refers to the current stage of development featuring devices with 10s to 100s of qubits that are not yet error-corrected but can perform meaningful hybrid computations.

6. **How are global quantum missions shaping progress?**

   Answer: Nations worldwide have launched strategic programs, such as the U.S. NQI, EU Quantum Flagship, China's Quantum Lab, and India's NQM to drive innovation, develop talent, and secure leadership in quantum technologies.

7. **Where is quantum computing already showing real-world impact?**

   Answer: Early progress is evident in quantum cryptography (secure key exchange), optimization (route planning, finance), ML (pattern recognition), and chemistry (molecular energy estimation).

8. **Why has Python become the preferred language for quantum programming?**

   Answer: Python's simplicity, open-source frameworks, and integration with scientific libraries make it ideal for quantum programming. Frameworks such as Qiskit, Cirq, and PennyLane enable users to design, simulate, and execute circuits easily.

9. **What role do hybrid quantum–classical systems play?**

   Answer: Hybrid systems combine the strengths of both worlds—quantum processors handle complex parallel operations, while classical processors manage control logic and optimization—enabling near-term quantum applications in the NISQ era.

10. **What does the future hold for quantum computing?**

    Answer: The coming decade will see the rise of error-corrected processors, quantum internet networks, and AI–quantum integration, making quantum computing a practical and transformative part of the global digital ecosystem.

Exercises

1. Differentiate between classical and quantum computation by creating a comparative chart that summarizes their principles, key components, and limitations. Include examples of tasks that are classically hard but quantum-efficient.
2. Simulate a simple two qubit system using Python (NumPy or Qiskit) to demonstrate superposition and entanglement. Visualize the resulting state vector or measurement outcomes using Matplotlib.
3. Research and summarize one NQM (e.g., India's NQM, U.S. NQI, or EU Quantum Flagship). Highlight its objectives, focus areas, and strategic goals in advancing global quantum leadership.
4. Explore a real-world application of quantum computing in one domain, such as cryptography, optimization, ML, or chemistry and describe how quantum algorithms outperform their classical counterparts.
5. Write a short Python script to create a basic quantum circuit (e.g., generating a Bell state) using the Qiskit framework. Execute the circuit on a simulator backend and analyze the measurement results to explain the quantum correlation (entanglement) between the two qubits. Use the AerSimulator provided in the Qiskit ecosystem to run the circuit.
6. Analyze the hybrid nature of modern workflows by outlining how classical and quantum processors

collaborate in algorithms like VQE or QAOA. Discuss why this synergy is crucial in the NISQ era.

7. Prepare a table comparing the major industry platforms: IBM Quantum, Google Cirq, AWS Braket, and Xanadu PennyLane. List their core features, hardware types, and programming advantages.
8. Investigate one emerging quantum startup (e.g., IonQ, Rigetti, or Xanadu) and write a brief report of 300–400 words describing the company's role in the quantum ecosystem. Your report should include the company background, technological approach, hardware platform or architecture, and its key innovations or differentiating contributions to quantum computing.
9. Use Python libraries such as NumPy, SciPy, and Matplotlib to model a simple quantum probability distribution. Show how these tools form the mathematical foundation of quantum programming.
10. Write a reflective essay (300–400 words) on how Python has democratized access to quantum computing. Discuss its role in education, research, and industry, and how it unites global efforts to advance the quantum era.

References

Peruzzo A., McClean J., Shadbolt P., et al., A Variational Eigenvalue Solver on a Photonic Quantum Processor, Nature Communications, vol. 5, 2014.

CHAPTER 2
Qubits and Quantum States

Introduction

At the core of quantum computing lies the qubit, a remarkable construct that extends the binary logic of classical bits into the quantum realm. Unlike a bit, which must be either 0 or 1, a qubit can exist in a superposition of both states simultaneously. This unique property, governed by the laws of quantum mechanics, enables quantum computers to process vast combinations of information in parallel rather than sequentially.

This chapter explores the foundations of quantum information, beginning with the contrast between bits and qubits and examining how principles such as superposition, entanglement, and interference enable quantum systems to outperform their classical counterparts on specific computational tasks. Readers will learn how qubits are represented mathematically using *Dirac's braket notation* and how these abstract states can be visualized geometrically on the *Bloch sphere*, thereby revealing the continuous, phase-dependent nature of quantum states.

Beyond single-qubit behavior, the chapter introduces multi-qubit systems and the concept of measurement, illustrating how quantum information transforms into classical outcomes. Through step-by-step explanations and Python-based simulations using Qiskit and NumPy, readers will gain both conceptual understanding and practical experience in representing and analyzing quantum states.

By the end of this chapter, the reader will grasp how quantum information is structured, manipulated, and observed, forming the essential groundwork for studying quantum gates, circuits, and algorithms in the chapters that follow.

Structure

The chapter covers the following topics:

- Bits vs. qubits
- Braket notation and state vectors
- Multi-qubit systems and measurement
- Superposition, entanglement, and interference
- Bloch sphere representation

Objectives

This chapter introduces the fundamental nature of quantum information through the study of qubits and quantum states. Readers will understand how qubits extend classical bits by existing in superposition, allowing simultaneous representation of multiple possibilities. The chapter explores superposition, entanglement, and interference as key quantum phenomena that enable non-classical computation. It also presents the mathematical formalism of Dirac's braket notation, offering a compact way to express and manipulate quantum states. Using the Bloch sphere, readers will visualize how qubit orientations encode both amplitude and phase information. Through Python-based demonstrations with Qiskit and NumPy, the chapter bridges theory and experimentation, showing how single and multi-qubit systems can be modeled and measured. By the end, readers will gain a clear understanding of how qubits represent, evolve, and collapse laying the essential groundwork for quantum gates, circuits, and algorithmic operations discussed in later chapters.

Bits vs. qubits

The shift from classical to quantum computation begins with understanding how information itself is represented. In classical computing, every piece of data, text, image, or algorithm is ultimately encoded as combinations of bits, each taking a definite value of 0 or 1. In quantum computing, however, information is stored in qubits that follow the laws of quantum mechanics, allowing them to exist in a blend of 0 and 1 simultaneously. This transition from certainty to probability marks the true beginning of the quantum era.

Classical bits as the foundation of digital logic

A bit is the smallest and most fundamental unit of classical information. Every operation performed by digital systems, whether sorting data, processing images, or simulating complex models, ultimately reduces to a sequence of deterministic manipulations on bits.

A bit can exist in only one of two discrete states, conventionally labeled 0 or 1, corresponding physically to off/on conditions, low/high voltage levels, or false/true logical values. This binary structure makes classical computation predictable and repeatable: identical inputs will always produce identical outputs.

Mathematically, the two fundamental bit states can be represented as **basis vectors**:

$$|0\rangle = \begin{bmatrix}1\\0\end{bmatrix}, |1\rangle = \begin{bmatrix}0\\1\end{bmatrix}$$

These two vectors form the computational basis for all classical information. A register containing n bits can represent one of 2^n possible configurations, but *only* one at any given moment.

For example, a 3 bit register can represent eight distinct binary strings (from 000 to 111), yet at any instant, it occupies exactly one of those configurations. This single-state limitation defines the essence of classical computation: precise, unambiguous, and sequential.

Quantum bits and information in superposition

A qubit extends the concept of a classical bit into the quantum domain. Unlike a bit, which must be either 0 or 1, a qubit can exist in a superposition of both states simultaneously, embodying the core principle of quantum mechanics.

Mathematically, a qubit's state is represented as:

$$|\psi\rangle = \alpha|0\rangle + \beta|1\rangle$$

Here:

α and β are complex probability amplitudes, and

They satisfy the normalization condition $|\alpha|^2 + |\beta|^2 = 1$.

When a measurement is performed, the qubit collapses into one of the two classical basis states:

- $|0\rangle$ with probability $|\alpha|^2$
- $|1\rangle$ with probability $|\beta|^2$

Until that measurement occurs, the qubit exists in both possibilities at once—not as a mixture of 0 and 1, but as a coherent combination where amplitudes can interfere with each other. This property, known as superposition, allows quantum systems to process multiple potential outcomes simultaneously.

Consequently, a register of n qubits can represent 2^n classical states at the same time, forming the mathematical foundation of quantum parallelism, the phenomenon that gives quantum computers their exponential representational power.

Comparing classical and quantum information

To fully appreciate the distinction between classical and quantum computation, it is essential to compare how each represents and manipulates information at the most fundamental level. While classical bits operate within a binary, deterministic framework, qubits function within the realm of probabilities, phases, and superpositions—enabling an entirely new model of computation.

The following table summarizes the key conceptual and mathematical differences between classical bits and quantum bits (qubits), highlighting how quantum mechanics extends the boundaries of conventional information theory:

Feature	Classical bit	Qubit
State	**Definite**: 0 or 1	**Superposed**: (\alpha)
Nature of information	Deterministic	Probabilistic
Mathematical form	Binary digit (0/1)	Complex vector in $\mathbb{C}^2$
Operation type	Irreversible Boolean logic	Reversible unitary transformations
Measurement	Reveals a fixed value	Collapses a probabilistic state
Parallelism	One state at a time	Multiple states simultaneously

***Table 2.1**: Comparison between classical and quantum information representations*

In short, store certainty, while qubits encode potential. Where classical computation follows a single path, quantum computation explores many paths at once.

Representing a qubit in Python

We can model a single-qubit state directly with NumPy, treating basis states as vectors and superpositions as linear combinations of them. The example below builds the equal superposition $|\psi\rangle = \frac{1}{\sqrt{2}}|0\rangle + \frac{1}{\sqrt{2}}|1\rangle$.

Python demo: Representing a qubit with NumPy:

```
import numpy as np
# Define basis states |0> and |1>
zero = np.array([[1], [0]])
one  = np.array([[0], [1]])
# Define amplitudes for equal superposition
alpha, beta = 1/np.sqrt(2), 1/np.sqrt(2)
# Construct the qubit state |ψ⟩ = α|0⟩ + β|1⟩
psi = alpha * zero + beta * one
print("Qubit state |ψ⟩:\n", psi)
print("Normalization:", np.linalg.norm(psi)**2)
```

Expected output:

```
Qubit state |ψ⟩:
[[0.70710678]
 [0.70710678]]
Normalization: 1.0
```

This result shows that the qubit is in an equal superposition of $|0\rangle$ and $|1\rangle$.

If we measure it repeatedly, approximately half the outcomes will be 0 and half 1—yet until measurement, it genuinely exists in both states at once.

Geometric intuition of the Bloch sphere

A powerful way to visualize a qubit is through the Bloch sphere, a geometric model in which every possible qubit state lies on its surface. The north and south poles correspond to the classical states $|0\rangle$ and $|1\rangle$, while all other points represent quantum superpositions defined by two angles θ and φ:

$$|\psi\rangle = \cos\frac{\theta}{2}|0\rangle + e^{i\phi}\sin\frac{\theta}{2}|1\rangle$$

Here, θ controls the balance between $|0\rangle$ and $|1\rangle$, and φ determines the relative phase.

This continuous representation reveals why qubits can encode an infinite number of possible states, unlike bits, which are confined to just two.

Later in this chapter, we will visualize such states using *Qiskit* and *Matplotlib*.

Thinking of qubits as waves

Just as light or sound waves interfere and combine, quantum states behave like *waves of probability*. Their amplitudes can reinforce or cancel each other depending on their phase. This phenomenon, known as **quantum interference**, lies at the core of powerful algorithms such as Grover's and Shor's, where wave-like effects are exploited to amplify correct answers and suppress incorrect ones.

Significance of this transition

The transition from bits to qubits represents far more than a technological change—it signifies a conceptual revolution. A classical bit conveys a single outcome; a qubit represents a continuum of possibilities, governed by the principles of superposition and phase. To harness this new paradigm, we must think not in terms of logic gates and truth tables, but in terms of vectors, amplitudes, and transformations.

Superposition, entanglement, and interference

Quantum computing derives its power from three extraordinary phenomena that have no classical counterparts: superposition, entanglement, and interference. Together, these principles enable quantum computers to represent, connect, and manipulate information in ways that far exceed those of conventional systems. This section unpacks each of these phenomena—conceptually, mathematically, and through Python-based simulation—to help readers see how they collectively enable quantum advantage.

Superposition as the basis of quantum parallelism

In classical systems, a bit can only be in one of two states: 0 or 1. In contrast, a qubit can exist in both states simultaneously through a phenomenon known as superposition.

Mathematically, a superposed state is represented as:

$$|\psi\rangle=\alpha|0\rangle+\beta|1\rangle,$$

Where $|\alpha|^2+|\beta|^2=1$.

This means the qubit does not hold just one value—it represents a probability distribution over multiple outcomes. When measured, the qubit collapses into either $|0\rangle$ or $|1\rangle$, but until then, it behaves as though it were both.

This unique feature allows quantum computers to evaluate many possibilities at once—often called quantum parallelism.

Creating superposition with the Hadamard gate

A **Hadamard gate** (H) transforms a classical basis state into an equal superposition:

$$H \mid 0\rangle = \frac{\mid 0\rangle + \mid 1\rangle}{\sqrt{2}}, H \mid 1\rangle = \frac{\mid 0\rangle - \mid 1\rangle}{\sqrt{2}}$$

Example: Simulating superposition in Qiskit:

```
from qiskit import QuantumCircuit, Aer, execute
from qiskit.visualization import plot_histogram
# Create a single-qubit circuit
qc = QuantumCircuit(1)
qc.h(0)             # Apply Hadamard gate to create superposition
qc.measure_all()  # Measure the qubit
# Execute on simulator
sim = Aer.get_backend('qasm_simulator')
result = execute(qc, sim, shots=1024).result()
counts = result.get_counts()
print(counts)
plot_histogram(counts)
```

Expected outcome: A nearly 50–50 split between outcomes 0 and 1, confirming an equal superposition.

Insight: Superposition is not randomness—it has controlled probability. The amplitudes α and β define precise likelihoods that can be manipulated through quantum gates.

Entanglement and its role in linking qubits

Entanglement is a uniquely quantum phenomenon where two or more qubits become correlated in such a way that the state of one instantly determines the state of the other, no matter the distance between them. Einstein famously described it as spooky action at a distance, yet it forms the backbone of quantum computation and communication.

An entangled state cannot be described as the product of individual qubit states.

The most well-known example is the Bell state, written as:

$$\mid \Phi^{+} \rangle = \frac{\mid 00\rangle + \mid 11\rangle}{\sqrt{2}}$$

If one qubit is measured as 0, the other must also be 0. If the first is 1, the second will be 1 as well—an inseparable link formed by quantum mechanics.

Example: Generating entanglement in Qiskit:

```
from qiskit import QuantumCircuit
from qiskit.visualization import plot_histogram
qc = QuantumCircuit(2)
qc.h(0)        # Step 1: Create superposition on first qubit
qc.cx(0, 1)    # Step 2: Entangle both qubits
qc.measure_all()
qc.draw('mpl')
```

This circuit produces the Bell state $\mid \Phi^{+} \rangle$. When simulated, it yields only two possible outcomes: 00 and 11, each with nearly equal probability.

Observation: Entanglement allows quantum systems to act as a single entity, even when composed of separate particles. This collective behavior underlies quantum teleportation, superdense coding, and the parallelism of multi-qubit algorithms.

Interference and its role in quantum probabilities

Interference is the process by which quantum probability amplitudes combine—sometimes amplifying specific outcomes (constructive interference) and sometimes canceling others (destructive interference). Just as ripples on water can add or cancel each other depending on their phase, so too can quantum amplitudes reinforce or suppress measurement results.

This mechanism enables quantum algorithms to amplify the probability of correct answers while minimizing incorrect ones—effectively *tuning* the outcome space through interference.

Example: Demonstrating interference in a single-qubit:

```
from qiskit import QuantumCircuit, Aer, execute
from qiskit.visualization import plot_histogram
qc = QuantumCircuit(1)
qc.h(0)        # Create superposition
qc.z(0)        # Apply phase shift (introduces interference)
qc.h(0)        # Second Hadamard recombines amplitudes
qc.measure_all()
sim = Aer.get_backend('qasm_simulator')
result = execute(qc, sim, shots=1024).result()
counts = result.get_counts()
plot_histogram(counts)
```

Expected outcome:

After the second Hadamard gate, interference causes the qubit to collapse into state 1 predominantly. This shows how phase manipulation can direct probability amplitudes to desired outcomes.

Mathematical summary of the three principles

The three core principles: superposition, entanglement, and interference, define the mathematical and physical behavior of qubits. Each can be described through simple yet powerful equations that capture how quantum systems encode, connect, and manipulate information. The following table summarizes key quantum phenomena, their mathematical representations, and the core ideas that distinguish them from classical concepts:

Phenomenon	Mathematical form	Core idea
Superposition	(	`\psi\rangle = \alpha`
Entanglement	(	`\Phi^+\rangle = \frac{`
Interference	`( \text{Probabilities} \propto`	`\text{sum of amplitudes}`

***Table 2.2:** Mathematical representation of quantum phenomena*

Each principle contributes uniquely, superposition expands the state space, entanglement links states across qubits, and interference guides computation to the right answer.

Visualizing the concepts

While mathematics explains the mechanics of quantum behavior, visualization reveals its intuition.

The following table provides a conceptual overview of how superposition, entanglement, and interference manifest in simple quantum circuits. Each phenomenon represents a distinct way in which quantum systems encode, connect, and manipulate information—often in ways that defy classical expectations. The following table illustrates fundamental quantum concepts along with their descriptions, representative circuits, and observable outcomes:

Concept	Description	Example circuit	Outcome
Superposition	A qubit exists in both	0⟩ and	1⟩ simultaneously
Entanglement	Two qubits share correlated states	H + CNOT	Outcomes 00 or 11 only
Interference	Amplitudes reinforce or cancel	H–Z–H	State 1 favored over 0

Table 2.3: *Conceptual visualization of core quantum effects*

These effects do not operate in isolation; most quantum algorithms rely on all three working together in a delicate balance.

Understanding the wave nature of computation

Think of each qubit as a probability wave rather than a simple data unit. Quantum computation is essentially the engineering of wave patterns:

- Superposition creates the waves.
- Entanglement connects them.
- Interference shapes them toward beneficial results.

This intuition helps in understanding complex algorithms, such as *Grover's search*, which finds target items by amplifying specific probability amplitudes through controlled interference.

Significance of these principles

Superposition allows a quantum system to explore many possibilities simultaneously. Entanglement lets those possibilities interact coherently across multiple qubits. Interference then prunes the exploration space, amplifying correct results and suppressing wrong ones.

Together, these three effects transform quantum computation from theoretical elegance into practical power. They are the engine room of every quantum algorithm, from simple Bell state preparation to large-scale optimization using QAOA and VQE.

Braket notation and state vectors

Quantum computing builds upon a mathematical language elegant enough to describe both uncertainty and structure: Dirac's braket notation. Proposed by physicist *Paul Dirac*, this notation simplifies complex linear-algebraic relationships, providing a concise and intuitive way to represent quantum states, their transformations, and measurements. Understanding this framework is essential for effectively reading, analyzing, and programming quantum systems.

Need for a new notation

In classical computation, states such as 0 and 1 are sufficient descriptors. However, a qubit's state—comprising complex amplitudes, probabilities, and phases—requires a more sophisticated formalism.

We need a way to represent:

- Multiple possible configurations at once.
- Operations acting on those configurations.
- Measurable probabilities derived from them.

The braket notation provides precisely this: a compact language built on the foundations of linear algebra and vector spaces.

Understanding kets as representations of quantum states

In Dirac's notation, a ket, written as $|\psi\rangle$, denotes a column vector representing the quantum state of a system.

For a single-qubit, the two basic or computational basis states are:

$$|0\rangle = \begin{bmatrix}1\\0\end{bmatrix}, |1\rangle = \begin{bmatrix}0\\1\end{bmatrix}$$

A general qubit state is a linear combination of these basis vectors:

$$|\psi\rangle=\alpha|0\rangle+\beta|1\rangle, \text{where } \alpha,\beta\in C, |\alpha|^2+|\beta|^2=1$$

Here, α and β are complex amplitudes, encapsulating both magnitude (probability) and phase (direction).

Understanding bras as the dual of quantum states

Every ket $|\psi\rangle$ has a corresponding bra, denoted $|\psi\rangle$, which is the *conjugate transpose* of the ket:

$$\langle\psi|=[\alpha^* \ \ \beta^*]$$

Together, bras and kets form the braket pair, a structure that enables two critical operations:

- **Inner product** $\langle\psi|\phi\rangle$: measures the similarity between two states.
- **Outer product** $|\psi\rangle\langle\phi|$: used to build operators and density matrices.

For example, the inner product of a state with itself always equals *1*:

$$\langle\psi|\psi\rangle=|\alpha|^2+|\beta|^2=1$$

This confirms that the state is normalized, a requirement for all valid quantum states.

Computing with kets and bras in Python

We can implement braket operations directly in NumPy, using column vectors for kets and conjugate-transposed row vectors for bras. The example below constructs a normalized qubit and verifies $\langle\psi|\psi\rangle=1$.

NumPy demo: Inner product of a qubit state:

```
import numpy as np
# Define amplitudes
alpha, beta = 1/np.sqrt(3), np.sqrt(2)/np.sqrt(3)
# Define ket (column vector)
ket = np.array([[alpha], [beta]])
# Define bra (row vector, complex conjugate transpose)
bra = np.conjugate(ket.T)
# Compute inner product <ψ|ψ>
inner_product = bra @ ket
print("Ket |ψ⟩:\n", ket)
print("Bra ⟨ψ|:\n", bra)
print("Inner product ⟨ψ|ψ⟩ =", inner_product[0,0])
```

Expected output:

```
Ket |ψ⟩:
[[0.57735027]
 [0.81649658]]
Bra ⟨ψ|:
[[0.57735027 0.81649658]]
Inner product ⟨ψ|ψ⟩ = 1.0
```

This confirms that $|\psi\rangle$ is a properly normalized quantum state.

Inner and outer products in quantum mechanics

In quantum mechanics, inner and outer products serve as the fundamental operations for analyzing and constructing quantum states. They form the mathematical backbone for computing probabilities, measuring state similarity, and defining projection operators used in measurements and density matrices. The following points highlight the essential interpretations of the inner product between two states:

- **Inner product ($\langle\psi|\phi\rangle$)**: The inner product between two quantum states $|\psi\rangle$ and $|\phi\rangle$ yields a **scalar** that represents how similar or aligned the two states are within Hilbert space:

$$\langle \psi \mid \phi \rangle = \alpha_\psi^* \alpha_\phi + \beta_\psi^* \beta_\phi$$

- **Key interpretations**:
  - If $\langle\psi|\phi\rangle=0$, the states are orthogonal, completely distinct and non-overlapping.
  - If $|\langle\psi|\phi\rangle|^2=1$, they are identical (up to a global phase).
  - The magnitude squared of the inner product, $|\langle\psi|\phi\rangle|^2$, represents the probability that a system is in state $|\psi\rangle$ will be found in state $|\phi\rangle$ after measurement.

This operation allows quantum computers to compare states and determine their degree of overlap—a key step in evaluating transitions and fidelities between quantum configurations.

- **Outer product ($|\psi\rangle\langle\phi|$)**: The *outer* product produces a matrix (operator) that acts on quantum states. While the inner product compresses information into a scalar, the outer product expands it into an operator that can project or transform states:

$$|\psi\rangle\langle\phi| = \begin{bmatrix}\alpha_\psi \\ \beta_\psi\end{bmatrix} \begin{bmatrix}\alpha_\phi^* & \beta_\phi^*\end{bmatrix} = \begin{bmatrix}\alpha_\psi\alpha_\phi^* & \alpha_\psi\beta_\phi^* \\ \beta_\psi\alpha_\phi^* & \beta_\psi\beta_\phi^*\end{bmatrix}$$

One of the most common applications of outer products is the construction of projection operators, which extract specific components of a state during measurement or form part of a density matrix representation.

- **Example**: Projection operator onto the state $|0\rangle$

  The projection operator for the basis state $|0\rangle$ is obtained by the outer product $|0\rangle\langle 0|$:

$$|0\rangle\langle 0| = \begin{bmatrix}1 & 0 \\ 0 & 0\end{bmatrix}$$

  This operator, when applied to any quantum state, filters out the $|1\rangle$ component, leaving only the amplitude corresponding to $|0\rangle$. Such projectors are central to measurement theory, where each possible outcome corresponds to a projection onto a particular basis vector.

- **Quick implementation in Python**:

```
import numpy as np
# Define |0> basis vector
ket_0 = np.array([[1], [0]], dtype=complex)
# Compute projection operator |0><0|
proj_0 = ket_0 @ np.conjugate(ket_0.T)
print("Projection operator |0><0|:\n", proj_0)
```

- **Output**:

```
Projection operator |0><0|:
[[1.+0.j 0.+0.j]
 [0.+0.j 0.+0.j]]
```

Orthogonality and normalization of basis states

The basis states $|0\rangle$ and $|1\rangle$ are orthonormal, meaning they are both orthogonal and normalized:

$$\langle 0|0\rangle=1,\langle 1|1\rangle=1,\langle 0|1\rangle=\langle 1|0\rangle=0$$

This property allows any qubit state to be expressed as a combination of these two basis vectors. It also ensures that measurements collapse states cleanly into either $|0\rangle$ or $|1\rangle$ without ambiguity.

Example: Verifying orthonormality in Python:

```
zero = np.array([[1], [0]])
one  = np.array([[0], [1]])
# Compute inner products
print("⟨0|0⟩ =", np.conjugate(zero.T) @ zero)
print("⟨1|1⟩ =", np.conjugate(one.T) @ one)
print("⟨0|1⟩ =", np.conjugate(zero.T) @ one)
```

Output:

```
⟨0|0⟩ = [[1]]
⟨1|1⟩ = [[1]]
⟨0|1⟩ = [[0]]
```

These results confirm that $|0\rangle$ and $|1\rangle$ form an orthonormal basis.

Importance of braket notation

Braket notation serves as the grammar of quantum mechanics. It lets us describe operations (such as gates and measurements) with elegance and precision while keeping the underlying mathematics consistent and compact. In quantum computing, we use it to:

- Define states and operators mathematically.
- Represent multi-qubit systems using tensor products.
- Compute probabilities and expectation values efficiently.

This notation serves as a bridge between theoretical physics and practical computation, enabling software frameworks such as Qiskit and Cirq to express abstract quantum concepts as concrete matrices and vectors.

Bloch sphere representation

One of the most intuitive ways to visualize a qubit is through the Bloch sphere, a three-dimensional geometric model that elegantly represents all possible states of a single-qubit. While the mathematical form of a qubit describes probabilities and phases, the Bloch sphere visualizes those equations, allowing them to be rotated, measured, and understood visually. This section explores how the Bloch sphere captures both the structure and dynamics of quantum states, supported by practical demonstrations using *Qiskit* and *Matplotlib*.

Geometry of a qubit

A single-qubit can be described both algebraically and geometrically. Algebraically, its state is expressed as a linear combination of the two computational basis states:

$$|\psi\rangle=\alpha|0\rangle+\beta|1\rangle$$

where α and β are complex probability amplitudes satisfying the normalization condition:

$$|\alpha|^2+|\beta|^2=1$$

While this form captures the probabilistic essence of a qubit, it does not immediately convey its geometric structure. To visualize it, we can rewrite the same state using two real parameters, an angle θ and a phase ϕ, which correspond to coordinates on a sphere:

$$|\psi\rangle = \cos\frac{\theta}{2}|0\rangle + e^{i\phi}\sin\frac{\theta}{2}|1\rangle$$

Here:

- θ *(theta)* determines the latitude, showing how much the state leans toward $|0\rangle$ or $|1\rangle$.
- ϕ *(phi)* determines the longitude, representing the relative phase between the two amplitudes.

This parameterization places every possible qubit state on the surface of a unit sphere, known as the Bloch sphere.

- The north pole ($\theta=0$) represents the pure state $|0\rangle$.
- The south pole ($\theta=\pi$) represents the pure state $|1\rangle$.
- Points along the equator correspond to equal superpositions of $|0\rangle$ and $|1\rangle$ that differ only by phase.
- Any point between these extremes represents a unique superposition, determined by the amplitudes and their relative phase.

This sphere, called the Bloch sphere after Swiss physicist *Felix Bloch*, provides an elegant geometric visualization of the qubit's state space. Each point on its surface corresponds to a valid quantum state, while rotations around the sphere correspond to quantum gates, the operations that drive computation in quantum circuits.

Interpreting coordinates on the Bloch sphere

Every point on the Bloch sphere represents a distinct qubit state, defined by a specific combination of amplitudes and phases. The sphere provides a compact and intuitive visualization of how these parameters interact to determine a qubit's behavior during computation.

The state of a qubit can be expressed as:

$$|\psi\rangle = \cos\frac{\theta}{2}|0\rangle + e^{i\phi}\sin\frac{\theta}{2}|1\rangle$$

From this expression, we can interpret the two defining angles:

- **Polar angle (θ)**: Determines the probability balance between $|0\rangle$ and $|1\rangle$. Smaller values of ϑ indicate a higher probability of measuring $|0\rangle$, while larger values (approaching π) indicate dominance of $|1\rangle$.
- **Azimuthal angle (ϕ)**: Defines the relative phase between the two components. It influences how the qubit interferes with other states during computation—an essential factor in algorithms like Grover's and Shor's.
- The geometric position of a qubit on the Bloch sphere can thus be captured by its Bloch vector:

$$\mathbf{r} = \begin{bmatrix} x \\ y \\ z \end{bmatrix} = \begin{bmatrix} \sin\theta\cos\phi \\ \sin\theta\sin\phi \\ \cos\theta \end{bmatrix}$$

Here:

- x, y, and z represent the coordinates of the qubit in three-dimensional space, and
- the vector r points from the center of the sphere to its surface, uniquely identifying the qubit's state.

This geometric representation allows us to visualize complex quantum phenomena—such as phase shifts and rotations—as simple spatial transformations. In later sections, we will see how quantum gates correspond to rotations of this Bloch vector, providing an elegant bridge between linear algebra and geometric intuition.

Visualizing a qubit state using Qiskit

We can visualize any single-qubit state as a point on the Bloch sphere. The snippet here constructs a state parameterized by the angles θ (latitude) and ϕ (longitude) and plots its Bloch vector.

Tip: **Ensure Qiskit [visualization] and Matplotlib are installed.**

Plotting a Bloch vector with Qiskit:

```
from qiskit.visualization import plot_bloch_vector
import numpy as np
# Define theta and phi angles
theta = np.pi / 3     # 60 degrees
phi = np.pi / 4       # 45 degrees
# Compute Bloch vector components
x = np.sin(theta) * np.cos(phi)
y = np.sin(theta) * np.sin(phi)
z = np.cos(theta)
bloch_vector = [x, y, z]
# Plot the vector on the Bloch sphere
plot_bloch_vector(bloch_vector, title="Qubit on the Bloch Sphere")
```

Interpretation: The resulting Bloch vector can be interpreted geometrically to understand how the qubit's orientation reflects its probabilistic and phase characteristics:

- The qubit lies 60° down from the north pole (closer to |0⟩ than |1⟩).
- It has a phase angle of 45°, indicating a complex phase relationship between the amplitudes.

This visualization transforms abstract equations into an interactive geometric picture—ideal for understanding how quantum gates affect qubits.

Common qubit states on the Bloch sphere

Certain single-qubit states appear so frequently in quantum computation that they serve as reference points on the Bloch sphere. These states— |0⟩,|1⟩,|+⟩,|-⟩ and |i⟩—represent key orientations corresponding to pure, superposed, and phase-shifted configurations. Understanding their geometric positions helps visualize how quantum gates rotate and transform qubits during computation. Refer to the following table:

Qubit state	Mathematical expression	Bloch sphere coordinates (θ, φ)	Position
	0⟩	(\cos\frac{0}{2}	0⟩ + e^{i0}\sin\frac{0}{2}
	1⟩	(\cos\frac{\pi}{2}	0⟩ + e^{i0}\sin\frac{\pi}{2}
(	+\rangle)	(\frac{	0⟩ +
(	-\rangle)	(\frac{	0⟩ -
(	i\rangle)	(\frac{	0⟩ + i

***Table 2.6**: Representative qubit states and their Bloch sphere coordinate*

These special states form the cardinal points on the Bloch sphere and serve as reference orientations for most quantum gates.

Exploring quantum rotations

Quantum gates can be visualized not merely as abstract linear transformations, but as rotations of the qubit state vector on the Bloch sphere. Each gate corresponds to a specific axis of rotation (x, y, or z) and a rotation angle, determining how the qubit's position changes in space. This geometric interpretation provides an intuitive grasp of how unitary operations manipulate amplitude and phase without violating normalization. The following table summarizes key single-qubit quantum gates, indicating their rotation axes, rotation angles, and corresponding effects on the qubit state:

Gate	Rotation axis	Rotation angle	Effect
Pauli-X	X-axis	π	Flips
Pauli-Y	Y-axis	π	Rotates 180° about y-axis
Pauli-Z	Z-axis	π	Changes relative phase
Hadamard	X–z diagonal	π	Moves poles to the equator

***Table 2.7**: Geometric interpretation of common single-qubit gates*

These operations correspond to unitary transformations that rotate the qubit's Bloch vector while preserving its length (i.e., normalization).

Example: Visualizing rotations with Qiskit:

```
from qiskit import QuantumCircuit
from qiskit.visualization import plot_bloch_multivector
from qiskit.quantum_info import Statevector
# Apply Hadamard to |0>
qc = QuantumCircuit(1)
qc.h(0)
# Extract the final state and plot
state = Statevector.from_instruction(qc)
plot_bloch_multivector(state, title="Bloch Sphere after Hadamard Gate")
```

This code shows the $|0\rangle$ state moving from the north pole to the equator, creating an equal superposition of $|0\rangle$ and $|1\rangle$.

Bloch sphere as a learning tool

The Bloch sphere is more than a visual aid; it is a conceptual bridge between physics and computation. It allows us to:

- Understand superposition as a spatial blend between poles.
- Visualize the phase as a rotation around the vertical (z) axis.
- Interpret quantum gates as geometric transformations.

By tracking how states move across the sphere, we can gain intuition for complex algorithms and error behaviors that would otherwise seem abstract.

Insight: In the Bloch representation, every valid single-qubit gate corresponds to a rotation of the vector around some axis. This makes quantum logic a form of vector choreography, precise, reversible, and geometrically interpretable.

Significance of Bloch visualization

The Bloch sphere condenses an infinite mathematical space into a single, comprehensible picture. It helps learners see how unitary operations manipulate amplitude and phase while preserving overall probability.

For experimentalists and developers, it serves as a diagnostic tool to:

- Visualize decoherence (as shrinking toward the center).
- Verify qubit calibration.
- Understand gate performance.

Ultimately, it reinforces the intuition that quantum computation is geometric at its core, a dance of vectors, phases, and rotations in complex space.

Multi-qubit systems and measurement

Up to this point, we have studied individual qubits, their mathematical form, geometric representation, and transformation under quantum gates. However, real quantum computation rarely involves single-qubits acting alone. Powerful quantum behavior emerges when multiple qubits interact, forming composite systems capable of representing exponentially many states. Equally important is understanding measurement, the process that extracts information from such systems and converts it into classical data. This section explores both aspects: how multi-qubit states are formed and how measurement collapses their quantum potential into concrete results.

Constructing multi-qubit systems

A multi-qubit system is formed by combining individual qubits using the tensor product, symbolized by $\otimes$.

If qubit A has the state:

$$|\psi_1\rangle=\alpha_1|0\rangle+\beta_1|1\rangle$$

And qubit B has the state:

$$|\psi_2\rangle=\alpha_2|0\rangle+\beta_2|1\rangle,$$

Then the joint two-qubit system is expressed as:

$$|\Psi\rangle=|\psi_1\rangle\otimes|\psi_2\rangle=\alpha_1\,\alpha_2|00\rangle+\alpha_1\,\beta_2|01\rangle+\beta_1\,\alpha_2|10\rangle+\beta_1\,\beta_2|11\rangle$$

Each added qubit doubles the dimension of the system's state space.

For n qubits, the total space contains 2^n basis states, meaning even modest systems represent enormous complexity.

Example: Two-qubit tensor product in Python:

```
import numpy as np
# |ψ1> = |0>, |ψ2> = (|0> + |1>)/√2
psi1 = np.array([[1], [0]])
psi2 = (1/np.sqrt(2)) * np.array([[1], [1]])
# Tensor (Kronecker) product
psi_total = np.kron(psi1, psi2)
print("Two-qubit state |Ψ⟩:\n", psi_total)
```

```
Output: Two-qubit state |Ψ⟩:
[[0.70710678]
 [0.70710678]
 [0.        ]
 [0.        ]]
```

This result represents the state $|\Psi\rangle=(|00\rangle+|01\rangle)/\sqrt{2}$, a simple two-qubit superposition.

Separable and entangled states

Multi-qubit states can be either separable or entangled.

- Separable state can be expressed as the tensor product of individual qubit states.

  Example: $|\psi\rangle=|0\rangle\otimes|1\rangle=|01\rangle$

- Entangled state cannot be decomposed into separate qubit states.

  Example: The Bell state:

$$|\Phi^+\rangle=\frac{|00\rangle+|11\rangle}{\sqrt{2}}$$

Cannot be written as $|\psi_1\rangle \otimes |\psi_2\rangle$

Entangled states are crucial because they enable quantum correlations used in teleportation, quantum cryptography, and parallel algorithms.

Example: Creating entanglement in Qiskit:

```
from qiskit import QuantumCircuit, Aer, execute
from qiskit.visualization import plot_histogram
qc = QuantumCircuit(1)
qc.h(0)            # Superposition
qc.measure_all()
sim = Aer.get_backend('qasm_simulator')
result = execute(qc, sim, shots=1024).result()
plot_histogram(result.get_counts())
```

This histogram displays roughly equal counts of 0 and 1, illustrating probabilistic collapse.

Probabilistic nature of measurement

If a qubit is in state $|\psi\rangle = \alpha|0\rangle + \beta|1\rangle$, then measurement yields:

$$P(0) = |\alpha|^2, P(1) = |\beta|^2$$

For multi-qubit systems, the probability of measuring a specific bitstring (e.g., 101) is the squared magnitude of its corresponding amplitude in the overall state vector.

Measurement thus converts amplitudes into frequencies; it is how quantum systems reveal information about computation results.

Collapsing and post-measurement states

Once the measurement is performed, the system collapses to the observed basis state. For example, measuring $|\Psi\rangle = (|00\rangle + |11\rangle)/\sqrt{2}$

Subsequent measurements will always yield $|11\rangle$ until the system is re-initialized. This collapse ensures that quantum probabilities translate into classical certainties.

Insight: Quantum algorithms are designed so that, after interference and entanglement, the desired output state has a high probability amplitude, increasing the likelihood of appearing when measured.

The significance of multi-qubit systems and measurement is that they embody the true computational potential of quantum computing. They enable exponentially large state spaces, complex correlations, and interference patterns that classical computers cannot replicate. Measurement, meanwhile, serves as the gateway back to reality, allowing us to extract useful classical information from this probabilistic landscape.

Together, they define the complete computational cycle:

- **Preparation**: Initialize qubits.
- **Transformation**: Apply gates to create superposition and entanglement.
- **Measurement**: Collapse the system to reveal a classical answer.

This triad forms the heartbeat of every quantum algorithm.

Conclusion

This chapter deepened our understanding of the qubit as the fundamental building block of quantum information, distinguishing it from the deterministic behavior of classical bits. We explored how superposition, entanglement, and interference transform the way information is represented and processed, enabling qubits to encode multiple possibilities simultaneously. These quantum phenomena underpin computational parallelism and the extraordinary potential of quantum systems. By introducing Dirac's braket notation, we established a concise mathematical language for describing quantum states, while the Bloch sphere provided an intuitive geometric view of how amplitude and phase define a qubit's orientation. Through Python-based simulations using Qiskit and NumPy, theory was connected to practice, demonstrating how qubits can be constructed, visualized, and measured. Together, these concepts form the essential groundwork for understanding quantum logic operations.

The next chapter builds upon this foundation by exploring quantum gates and circuits, where the true power of quantum computation emerges through the controlled manipulation of qubit states.

Questions

1. **What is a qubit, and how does it differ from a classical bit?**

   Answer: A qubit is the quantum analog of a classical bit. While a bit can exist only as 0 or 1, a qubit can exist in a superposition of both states simultaneously. This allows quantum computers to represent and process many possibilities simultaneously, enabling computations not possible with classical logic.

2. **What is meant by superposition in quantum computing?**

   Answer: Superposition refers to the ability of a qubit to exist in a combination of states $|0\rangle$ and $|1\rangle$ at the same time. The probabilities of observing each outcome are determined by the squared magnitudes of their complex amplitudes $|\alpha|^2$ and $|\beta|^2$, which always sum to one.

3. **Why is entanglement important in quantum systems?**

   Answer: Entanglement occurs when two or more qubits share a correlated quantum state, such that the state of one qubit instantly affects the others, regardless of distance. This phenomenon enables coordinated behavior across qubits and is crucial for quantum teleportation, error correction, and multi-qubit algorithms.

4. **What role does interference play in quantum computation?**

   Answer: Interference allows probability amplitudes to reinforce or cancel each other. Quantum algorithms use constructive and destructive interference to amplify correct outcomes and suppress incorrect ones—one of the key mechanisms behind quantum advantage.

5. **What is the significance of the Bloch sphere representation?**

   Answer: The Bloch sphere provides a geometric visualization of a qubit's state, where each point on the sphere represents a unique combination of amplitude and phase. It helps illustrate how quantum gates rotate qubit states in three-dimensional space.

6. **How are qubit states represented mathematically?**

   Answer: Qubit states are expressed using Dirac's braket notation, such as $|\psi\rangle=\alpha|0\rangle+\beta|1\rangle$. This compact notation allows for elegant manipulation of state vectors and operators in complex Hilbert spaces.

7. **Why do quantum measurements cause state collapse?**

   Answer: Measurement forces a qubit's superposed state to collapse into one of its basis states—$|0\rangle$ or $|1\rangle$—with probabilities determined by its amplitudes. After measurement, the qubit loses its superposition and behaves classically.

8. **How do multi-qubit systems scale computationally?**

   Answer: A system of n qubits can represent 2^n possible states simultaneously. This exponential growth gives quantum computers their immense representational power, but it also makes the classical simulation of large quantum systems extremely resource-intensive.

9. **How does Python help in understanding qubit behavior?**

   Answer: Python, combined with libraries such as Qiskit and NumPy, enables users to create, visualize, and manipulate qubit states easily. It bridges theory and practice by allowing learners to simulate real quantum circuits and observe results.

10. **What is the key takeaway from understanding qubits and quantum states?**

    Answer: Grasping the nature of qubits, superposition, entanglement, and measurement forms the foundation of quantum computing. These principles explain how quantum systems encode and evolve information—knowledge that underpins all quantum algorithms and technologies explored in later chapters.

Exercises

1. Create a comparative table illustrating the differences between classical bits and qubits in terms of information representation, computation, and measurement. Include physical realizations and examples where qubits demonstrate clear advantages.
2. Write a Python (NumPy) program to construct a single-qubit superposition state $|\psi\rangle = \frac{|0\rangle+|1\rangle}{\sqrt{2}}$. Verify its normalization and plot the probability distribution of measurement outcomes.
3. Using Qiskit, build a simple two-qubit circuit that produces an entangled Bell state. Visualize the circuit, simulate it on the statevector_simulator, and interpret the measurement histogram.
4. Illustrate how superposition and interference combine to influence quantum outcomes. Provide a Python example (using NumPy or Qiskit) that demonstrates how changing the relative phase affects measurement probabilities.
5. Draw or simulate the Bloch sphere representation of three distinct qubit states: $|0\rangle$, $|1\rangle$, and $|+\rangle$. Explain what the coordinates (θ,φ) reveal about each state's orientation.
6. Develop a Python function that generates a random qubit state by sampling valid amplitudes α and β. Verify that $|\alpha|^2+|\beta|^2=1$ and visualize the corresponding Bloch vector.
7. Experiment with Pauli gates (X, Y, Z) in Qiskit. Apply them sequentially to a qubit initialized in $|0\rangle$ and observe how the Bloch vector rotates along different axes. Document your observations.
8. Using mathematical derivation, explain why an *n*-qubit system spans a Hilbert space of dimension 2^n. Provide examples for *n=2,3,* and *4* to illustrate how state-space growth leads to quantum parallelism.
9. Perform a short research summary (200–300 words) on how quantum measurement collapses a superposed state into a definite classical outcome. Discuss its philosophical and computational implications.
10. Write a reflective essay (300–400 words) on how learning about qubits, superposition, and measurement has changed your perception of information and computation. Describe how visualization tools like the Bloch sphere aid intuition in quantum learning.

CHAPTER 3
Quantum Gates and Circuits

Introduction

Quantum gates are the operational foundation of quantum computing, providing the precise mechanisms through which abstract quantum principles are translated into controlled actions on qubits. Much like logic gates in classical computing manipulate bits, quantum gates manipulate qubits through rotations, phase shifts, and conditional interactions, enabling computational behaviors that have no direct classical equivalent.

This chapter introduces the fundamental quantum gates that form the basis of all quantum circuits and algorithms. It begins with single-qubit gates, including the Pauli (X, Y, Z) gates, the Hadamard (H) gate, and the phase gates (S and T). These operations demonstrate how individual qubits can be flipped, placed into superposition, and subjected to controlled phase adjustments. The Bloch sphere representation is used to provide geometric intuition for how these gates transform quantum states.

The discussion then progresses to multi-qubit gates such as the Controlled-NOT (CNOT), the Toffoli gate, also known as the Controlled-Controlled-NOT (CCNOT) gate, and the SWAP gate (state exchange gate), which introduce conditional logic, entanglement, and state exchange between qubits. These gates are essential for constructing meaningful quantum circuits and implementing complex quantum algorithms.

Beyond individual gate operations, the chapter explores the concept of universal gate sets, explaining how a small collection of primitive gates can approximate any quantum computation to arbitrary accuracy. Key ideas such as gate decomposition and approximation techniques illustrate how ideal mathematical operations are adapted to hardware-supported gate sets. Throughout the chapter, concepts are reinforced through practical examples using Qiskit and Cirq, enabling readers to connect theoretical principles with executable quantum circuits.

Structure

The chapter covers the following topics:

- Single-qubit gates
- Multi-qubit gates
- Universal gate sets
- Building circuits with Qiskit and Cirq
- Simulation using Qiskit Aer and Cirq simulators

Objectives

This chapter aims to provide a clear and structured understanding of quantum gates as the core mechanisms for manipulating qubits and implementing quantum computation. Readers will learn how fundamental single-qubit gates, including Pauli (X, Y, Z), Hadamard (H), and phase gates (S, T), enable state rotations, superposition, and phase control on the Bloch sphere. The chapter also introduces essential multi-qubit gates such as CNOT, Toffoli, and SWAP, highlighting their roles in entanglement, conditional operations, and quantum information exchange. In addition, the concept of universal gate sets, particularly the Clifford + T framework, is explored to demonstrate how complex quantum operations can be constructed from a small set of primitives. Through mathematical formulations, geometric intuition, and practical implementations using Qiskit and Cirq, the chapter equips readers with both conceptual clarity and practical insight into building and simulating quantum circuits.

Single-qubit gates

Single-qubit gates form the foundation of quantum computation. They define how individual qubits evolve through rotations and phase shifts on the Bloch sphere, enabling the creation of superposition, interference, and controlled phase relations. These fundamental operations, such as Pauli (X, Y, Z), Hadamard (H), and Phase (S, T), serve as the essential building blocks for all quantum algorithms and multi-qubit interactions.

Pauli gates

The Pauli gates are fundamental quantum operations that perform 180° rotations of a qubit about the X, Y, and Z axes of the Bloch sphere. Being unitary and Hermitian, they are reversible and probability-preserving, forming the basis of all single-qubit transformations.

$$X = \begin{bmatrix} 0 & 1 \\ 1 & 0 \end{bmatrix}, Y = \begin{bmatrix} 0 & -1 \\ i & 0 \end{bmatrix}, Z = \begin{bmatrix} 1 & 0 \\ 0 & -1 \end{bmatrix}$$

Some implementation examples are as follows:

- **Qiskit**:
```
from qiskit import QuantumCircuit
qc = QuantumCircuit(1)
qc.x(0); qc.y(0); qc.z(0)
qc.draw('mpl')
```
- **Cirq**:
```
import cirq
q = cirq.LineQubit(0)
circuit = cirq.Circuit(cirq.X(q), cirq.Y(q), cirq.Z(q))
print(circuit)
```

We get the following output:

```
0: ───X───Y───Z───
```

Hadamard gate

The Hadamard gate is one of the most important single-qubit operations in quantum computing. It transforms a classical bit state into a quantum superposition, creating an equal probability of measuring 0 or 1. In effect, it allows a qubit to explore both states simultaneously, a principle that gives rise to quantum parallelism.

Mathematical definition

The Hadamard matrix is expressed as:

$$H = \frac{1}{\sqrt{2}} \begin{bmatrix} 1 & 1 \\ 1 & -1 \end{bmatrix}$$

Its action on a computational basis states:

$$H \mid 0\rangle = \frac{\mid 0\rangle + \mid 1\rangle}{\sqrt{2}}, H \mid 1\rangle = \frac{\mid 0\rangle - \mid 1\rangle}{\sqrt{2}}.$$

Thus, when $|0\rangle$ passes through H, the result is an equal-amplitude mixture of $|0\rangle$ and $|1\rangle$.

Geometric interpretation

On the Bloch sphere, H rotates the qubit 180° about the axis halfway between X and Z. This rotation is what introduces superposition and enables interference among computational paths.

Some implementation examples are as follows:

- **Qiskit**:

```
from qiskit import QuantumCircuit
qc = QuantumCircuit(1)
qc.h(0)
qc.measure_all()
qc.draw('mpl')
```

- **Cirq**:

```
import cirq
q = cirq.LineQubit(0)
circuit = cirq.Circuit(cirq.H(q), cirq.measure(q))
print(circuit)
```

The output is:

```
0: ───H───M───
```

Phase gates

While Pauli and Hadamard gates change the orientation of a qubit on the Bloch sphere, phase gates alter its relative phase, the invisible component that drives quantum interference. These gates do not affect measurement probabilities directly, yet they play a crucial role in how qubits interact and interfere within a circuit.

Mathematical definition

The two most common phase gates are S (also called the **phase gate**) and T (often called the **π/8 gate**).

Both are rotations about the z-axis of the Bloch sphere, as shown:

$$S = \begin{bmatrix} 1 & 0 \\ 0 & i \end{bmatrix}, T = \begin{bmatrix} 1 & 0 \\ 0 & e^{i\pi/4} \end{bmatrix}$$

Here, S performs a 90° ($\pi/2$) rotation, while T applies a 45° ($\pi/4$) rotation around the z-axis.

Its effect on basis states is:

$$S|0\rangle=|0\rangle, S|1\rangle=i|1\rangle,$$
$$T|0\rangle=|0\rangle, T|1\rangle=e^{i\pi/4}|1\rangle.$$

Some implementation examples are as follows:

- **Qiskit**:

```
from qiskit import QuantumCircuit
qc = QuantumCircuit(1)
qc.s(0)
qc.t(0)
qc.draw('mpl')
```

- **Cirq**:

```
import cirq
q = cirq.LineQubit(0)
circuit = cirq.Circuit(cirq.S(q), cirq.T(q))
print(circuit)
```

The following is the output:

```
0: ──S──T──
```

Bloch sphere perspective

To truly understand how single-qubit gates operate, one must visualize their effect on the Bloch sphere, a geometric model where every pure qubit state corresponds to a point on the surface of a unit sphere. The north pole represents $|0\rangle$, the south pole represents $|1\rangle$, and any superposition lies somewhere in between. Each quantum gate acts as a rotation of this state-vector about one of the coordinate axes.

Mathematical representation

A general single-qubit rotation is expressed as:

$$R_n(\theta) = e^{-i\left(\frac{\theta}{2}\right) n\cdot\sigma},$$

where $n=(n_x,n_y,n_z)$ defines the rotation axis and $\sigma=(X,Y,Z)$ are the Pauli matrices. By choosing different axes n and angles θ, we can reproduce all standard single-qubit gates.

The following table summarizes the rotational behavior of key single-qubit gates, showing their rotation axes, angles, and corresponding effects on the Bloch sphere representation:

Gate	Rotation axis	Angle (θ)	Effect on Bloch vector
X	x-axis	π	Flips the state between $|0\rangle$ and $|1\rangle$
Y	y-axis	π	Bit + phase flip
Z	z-axis	π	Adds π phase to (
H	$(X+Z)/\sqrt{2}$	π	Creates superposition
S	z-axis	$\pi/2$	Quarter-turn phase shift
T	z-axis	$\pi/4$	Eighth-turn phase shift

***Table 3.1**: Bloch sphere representation of single-qubit gates*

Some visualization examples are as follows:

- **Qiskit**:

```
from qiskit import QuantumCircuit
from qiskit.quantum_info import Statevector
from qiskit.visualization import plot_bloch_multivector
qc = QuantumCircuit(1)
qc.h(0)
state = Statevector.from_instruction(qc)
plot_bloch_multivector(state)
```

Multi-qubit gates

Multi-qubit gates enable interactions between qubits, forming the foundation of entanglement, conditional logic, and quantum communication. Unlike single-qubit operations that manipulate individual states, these gates coordinate multiple qubits to perform controlled operations, essential for realizing complex quantum algorithms. The CNOT, Toffoli, and SWAP gates represent the most fundamental multi-qubit operations, collectively enabling universal quantum computation and circuit optimization across diverse architectures.

Controlled-NOT gate

The CNOT gate is the simplest and most widely used two-qubit operation. It flips the state of one qubit (the target) only when another qubit (the control) is in the state $|1\rangle$.

The matrix representation is as follows:

$$\text{CNOT} = \begin{bmatrix} 1 & 0 & 0 & 0 \\ 0 & 1 & 0 & 0 \\ 0 & 0 & 0 & 1 \\ 0 & 0 & 1 & 0 \end{bmatrix}$$

Entanglement example

Applying a Hadamard on the control qubit followed by a CNOT produces the famous Bell state, an equal superposition of $|00\rangle$ and $|11\rangle$:

$$|\psi\rangle = \frac{1}{\sqrt{2}}(|00\rangle + |11\rangle)$$

Some examples include:

- **Qiskit**:

```
from qiskit import QuantumCircuit
qc = QuantumCircuit(2)
qc.h(0)
qc.cx(0, 1)
qc.draw('mpl')
```

- **Cirq**:

```
import cirq
q0, q1 = cirq.LineQubit.range(2)
circuit = cirq.Circuit(cirq.H(q0), cirq.CNOT(q0, q1))
print(circuit)
```

We get the following output:

```
0: ───H───@───
          │
1: ───────X───
```

Toffoli gate

The Toffoli gate, also known as the **CCNOT gate**, is a three-qubit operation that extends the logic of the CNOT gate. It flips the target qubit only when both control qubits are in the state $|1\rangle$. This behavior makes it the quantum equivalent of the classical AND-controlled XOR function, yet unlike its classical counterpart, it remains fully reversible, preserving information.

The matrix representation is as shown:

$$\text{Toffoli} = \begin{bmatrix} 1 & 0 & 0 & 0 & 0 & 0 & 0 & 0 \\ 0 & 1 & 0 & 0 & 0 & 0 & 0 & 0 \\ 0 & 0 & 1 & 0 & 0 & 0 & 0 & 0 \\ 0 & 0 & 0 & 1 & 0 & 0 & 0 & 0 \\ 0 & 0 & 0 & 0 & 1 & 0 & 0 & 0 \\ 0 & 0 & 0 & 0 & 0 & 1 & 0 & 0 \\ 0 & 0 & 0 & 0 & 0 & 0 & 0 & 1 \\ 0 & 0 & 0 & 0 & 0 & 0 & 1 & 0 \end{bmatrix}$$

In simple terms, the Toffoli gate performs the transformation:

$$|a,b,c\rangle \rightarrow |a,b,c\oplus(a\wedge b)\rangle$$

Some implementation examples are as follows:

- **Qiskit**:

```
from qiskit import QuantumCircuit
qc = QuantumCircuit(3)
qc.ccx(0, 1, 2)
qc.draw('mpl')
```

- **Cirq**:

```
import cirq
a, b, c = cirq.LineQubit.range(3)
circuit = cirq.Circuit(cirq.TOFFOLI(a, b, c))
print(circuit)
```

We will get the following output:

```
0: ───@───
      │
1: ───@───
      │
2: ───X───
```

SWAP gate

The SWAP gate is a simple yet essential two-qubit operation that exchanges the quantum states of its input qubits. If the first qubit holds the state and the second holds, applying the SWAP gate results in their states being interchanged.

The matrix representation is as shown:

$$\text{SWAP} = \begin{bmatrix} 1 & 0 & 0 & 0 \\ 0 & 0 & 1 & 0 \\ 0 & 1 & 0 & 0 \\ 0 & 0 & 0 & 1 \end{bmatrix}$$

In a circuit diagram, the *SWAP* gate is drawn as two crossing lines with × symbols on each qubit wire.

The following examples illustrate how the SWAP gate can be implemented using popular quantum computing frameworks:

- **Qiskit**:

```
from qiskit import QuantumCircuit
qc = QuantumCircuit(2)
qc.swap(0, 1)
qc.draw('mpl')
```

- **Cirq**:

```
import cirq
q0, q1 = cirq.LineQubit.range(2)
circuit = cirq.Circuit(cirq.SWAP(q0, q1))
print(circuit)
```

We will get the following output:

```
0: ───×───
      │
1: ───×───
```

The SWAP gate can be decomposed into three CNOT gates, allowing implementation on hardware that only supports two-qubit interactions:

$$SWAP(q_0, q_1)=CNOT(q_0, q_1)\ CNOT\ (q_1, q_0)\ CNOT\ (q_0, q_1)$$

This decomposition preserves the same behavior but aligns with the connectivity restrictions of most superconducting and trapped-ion quantum devices.

Universal gate sets

Universal gate sets form the cornerstone of quantum computation, defining the minimal collections of gates capable of constructing any quantum algorithm. Just as classical computing achieves universality through gates like **NOT–AND** (**NAND**) or **NOT–OR** (**NOR**), quantum computing attains it through specific combinations of single and multi-qubit operations that can approximate any unitary transformation. Understanding universality is essential for both hardware and software design, as it ensures that complex quantum processes can be built efficiently from a small set of high-fidelity primitive gates.

Concept of universality

In classical computing, any logical operation can be implemented using a small set of universal gates, such as NAND or NOR. Quantum computing follows the same philosophy; a finite group of quantum gates can generate any unitary transformation to arbitrary precision. This property is known as **quantum universality**.

Mathematical foundation

A gate set G is said to be universal if any n-qubit unitary operator U can be approximated as a finite product of gates from G, as follows:

$$U \approx G_1\ G_2\ G_3 \dots G_m,\ G_i \in G.$$

The following table lists representative examples of universal quantum gate sets, outlining their key components and noting their relevance across different computational and hardware contexts:

Universal gate set	Components	Remarks
{H, T, CNOT}	Hadamard, $\pi/8$, CNOT	Widely used; forms the Clifford + T group
{RX, RZ, CNOT}	Arbitrary rotations + entanglement	Hardware-friendly for many platforms
{H, S, T, CNOT}	Adds a phase gate for error correction compatibility	Common in fault-tolerant designs

***Table 3.2**: Examples of universal quantum gate sets*

Clifford + T gate set

Among the many universal gate families, the Clifford + T set has become the de facto standard for both theoretical study and hardware implementation. It balances mathematical completeness, fault-tolerance, and physical realizability, making it the preferred choice for modern quantum architectures.

Clifford group

The Clifford group consists of gates that map Pauli operators (X, Y, Z) onto other Pauli operators through conjugation.

Common members include:

- Hadamard (H) creates superposition.
- CNOT entangles control and target qubits.
- Phase (S) introduces $\pi/2$ phase rotation.

Collectively, these gates form the non-universal Clifford group, powerful but limited because they cannot generate arbitrary rotations.

Extending with the T gate

To achieve universality, we add the *T* gate ($\pi/8$ gate) as follows:

$$T = \begin{bmatrix} 1 & 0 \\ 0 & e^{i\pi/4} \end{bmatrix}$$

This gate introduces a non-Clifford rotation, enriching the gate set's expressive power. When combined with Clifford gates, it enables the synthesis of any single-qubit unitary operation with arbitrary precision.

Some implementation examples include:

- **Qiskit**:

```
from qiskit import QuantumCircuit
qc = QuantumCircuit(1)
qc.h(0)
qc.t(0)
qc.s(0)
qc.draw('mpl')
```

- **Cirq**:

```
import cirq
q = cirq.LineQubit(0)
circuit = cirq.Circuit(cirq.H(q), cirq.T(q), cirq.S(q))
print(circuit)
```

Approximation and decomposition

A universal gate set, such as Clifford + T, allows any quantum operation to be constructed through a sequence of simpler gates. However, most real quantum algorithms rely on arbitrary rotation angles that cannot be implemented exactly with a finite number of discrete gates. To bridge this gap, we use approximation and gate decomposition techniques that express complex unitaries as near-equivalent combinations of basic gates.

Need for approximation

Unlike classical logic, where Boolean functions are exact, quantum operations involve continuous rotations on the Bloch sphere. A universal gate set provides only a finite alphabet of rotations, so arbitrary unitaries must be approximated by repeating and composing those basic rotations until the desired accuracy is achieved.

Mathematically, for a target unitary U, we find a circuit $\tilde{U}$, such that:

$$\| U - \tilde{U} \| < \epsilon,$$

where ϵ represents the acceptable approximation error.

Solovay-Kitaev theorem

The Solovay-Kitaev theorem provides the theoretical guarantee that any unitary can be efficiently approximated using a finite universal gate set.

It states that:

Given any universal set G, there exists an algorithm that approximates any unitary U to within ε using $O(\log^c(1/\varepsilon))$ gates, where $c \approx 3.97$.

The following is the gate decomposition example. Consider the arbitrary rotation about the y-axis as:

$$R_y(\theta) = \begin{bmatrix} \cos\left(\frac{\theta}{2}\right) & -\sin\left(\frac{\theta}{2}\right) \\ \sin\left(\frac{\theta}{2}\right) & \cos\left(\frac{\theta}{2}\right) \end{bmatrix}$$

In most hardware, such a rotation is approximated using combinations of *H*, *S*, and *T* gates:

$$R_y(\theta) \approx H\ R_z(\theta)\ H, \text{ and } R_z(\theta) \text{ is approximated via } \{S,\ T\}.$$

An example of approximation in code includes:

- **Qiskit**:

```
from qiskit.circuit.library import RYGate
from qiskit.transpiler import PassManager
from qiskit.transpiler.passes import Unroller
from qiskit import QuantumCircuit
qc = QuantumCircuit(1)
qc.append(RYGate(1.234), [0])
pm = PassManager([Unroller([‚u3‘, ‚cx‘])])
decomposed = pm.run(qc)
print(decomposed)
```

This example decomposes an arbitrary rotation into a sequence of basis gates (**u3** and **cx**), demonstrating automatic approximation during transpilation.

Hardware perspective

Each physical quantum processor supports only a native gate set, for instance:

- **IBM Quantum devices**: {u3, cx}
- **Google Cirq**: { √X, CZ}
- **IonQ systems**: {Rz, Rx, MS}

Gate decomposition ensures that high-level algorithms can run on any platform by translating abstract gates into device-specific equivalents while maintaining functionality.

Building circuits with Qiskit and Cirq

The concept of quantum circuits provides the structural foundation for implementing quantum algorithms. A quantum circuit models computation as a sequence of operations, initialization, unitary evolution, and measurement, acting on qubits. Unlike classical circuits, which follow deterministic logic, quantum circuits harness superposition, entanglement, and interference to process information probabilistically yet reversibly. This framework enables both theoretical analysis and practical implementation of quantum computations across different hardware and software platforms.

Concept of quantum circuits

A quantum circuit is the fundamental model for describing and executing quantum algorithms. It represents computation as a sequence of quantum gates acting on one or more qubits, similar to how classical circuits use logic gates on bits.

Structure of a quantum circuit

A typical circuit consists of three conceptual layers:

- **Initialization**: Each qubit begins in the ground state $|0\rangle$ unless explicitly prepared otherwise.
- **Unitary operations**: A sequence of quantum gates (single and multi-qubit) evolves the state-vector through reversible transformations.

- **Measurement**: Qubits are projected onto the classical basis |0⟩ or |1⟩, producing classical output bits that can be statistically analyzed.

Circuit representation

Mathematically, a circuit corresponds to the cumulative unitary operation:

$$U = U_n U_{n-1} \dots U_1,$$

The overall transformation of an initial state is then:

$$|\psi_{out}\rangle = U|\psi_0\rangle.$$

The following table summarizes the key properties that define quantum circuits, outlining how their unique features distinguish quantum computation from classical logic systems:

Property	Description
Reversibility	All gates (except measurement) are unitary, hence reversible.
Parallelism	Qubits in superposition represent many classical states simultaneously.
Entanglement	Multi-qubit gates link states, enabling quantum correlations.
Measurement collapse	Converts quantum probabilities into definite classical outcomes.

Table 3.3: Core characteristics of quantum circuits

Building circuits in Qiskit

Qiskit, developed by *IBM Quantum*, is one of the most widely used frameworks for designing, simulating, and executing quantum circuits. It provides a pythonic interface that closely follows the mathematical structure of quantum mechanics, allowing researchers and learners to construct circuits from basic building blocks and execute them either on local simulators or real IBM Quantum hardware.

Creating a quantum circuit

Every Qiskit program begins by creating a **`QuantumCircuit`** object, which defines the number of qubits and classical bits required:

```
from qiskit import QuantumCircuit
# Create a 2-qubit, 2-classical-bit circuit
qc = QuantumCircuit(2, 2)
```

Adding gates

Once initialized, quantum gates are added using intuitive method calls that mirror their symbolic names as follows:

```
qc.h(0)       # Apply Hadamard to qubit 0
qc.cx(0, 1)  # Apply CNOT with qubit 0 as control and 1 as target
qc.measure([0, 1], [0, 1])  # Measure both qubits
```

Circuit visualization

Qiskit provides built-in tools to visualize circuits graphically or as text diagrams.

The output is as follows:

```
     ┌───┐     ┌─┐
q_0: ┤ H ├──■──┤M├──
     └───┘┌─┴─┐└╥┘
q_1: ─────┤ X ├─╫───
          └───┘ ║
```

```
c: 2/══════════╩══╩═
               0  1
```

Running the circuit on a simulator

For local testing, Qiskit Aer offers the **AerSimulator**, which executes circuits and returns measurement outcomes, as shown:

```
from qiskit import QuantumCircuit, transpile
from qiskit_aer import AerSimulator
# qc = QuantumCircuit(...)
sim = AerSimulator()
qc_t = transpile(qc, sim)
result = sim.run(qc_t, shots=1024).result()
counts = result.get_counts()
print(counts)
```

Building circuits in Cirq

Cirq, developed by *Google Quantum AI*, is a Python framework designed for building, simulating, and executing quantum circuits, particularly on *Google's Sycamore* and other experimental processors. Where Qiskit focuses on simplicity and abstraction, Cirq emphasizes hardware realism and explicit control over gate timing, qubit connectivity, and noise modeling. It is widely used in research environments where fine-grained simulation of physical devices is required.

Creating qubits and circuits

Cirq represents qubits as explicit objects. The most common type is **LineQubit**, which arranges qubits along a one-dimensional line for convenience. The following example demonstrates how qubits are created and how an empty circuit is initialized in Cirq using **LineQubit** objects:

```
import cirq
# Define two-qubits
q0, q1 = cirq.LineQubit.range(2)
# Create a circuit
circuit = cirq.Circuit()
```

Adding gates

Gates are added sequentially using Cirq's built-in gate classes, such as **H**, **X**, **Y**, **Z**, and multi-qubit operations like **CNOT** and **CZ**, as shown through the following command:

```
circuit.append([
    cirq.H(q0),
    cirq.CNOT(q0, q1),
    cirq.measure(q0, q1)
])
print(circuit)
```

We get the following output:

```
0: ───H───@───M───
          │   │
1: ───────X───M───
```

This example applies a Hadamard to the first qubit, entangles it with the second using a CNOT, and then measures both.

Circuit execution and simulation

Cirq includes efficient simulators for testing circuits locally. The following example illustrates how a quantum circuit can be executed using Cirq's built-in **Simulator** to obtain measurement results through repeated runs:

```
sim = cirq.Simulator()
result = sim.run(circuit, repetitions=1000)
print(result.histogram(key='0,1'))
```

The simulator executes the circuit many times (repetitions) and returns a histogram of measurement outcomes, similar to Qiskit's **execute()** method.

The following table highlights the main features of Cirq, emphasizing its focus on explicit hardware control, realistic device mapping, noise modeling, and parameterized experimentation:

Feature	Description
Explicit control	Users specify qubits, timing, and moment ordering manually.
Hardware mapping	Provides realistic device constraints (connectivity, calibration).
Noise modeling	Allows user-defined error insertion for testing fidelity.
Parameter sweeps	Built-in tools for variable-angle gates and hybrid algorithms.

Table 3.4: *Key features of Cirq's design philosophy*

Circuit execution workflow

Designing a quantum circuit is only half of the process. The next phase, execution, translates that logical design into measurable results. In practice, every quantum experiment follows the same structured workflow as follows:

Build | Transpile | Execute | Analyze

This pipeline ensures that circuits are both optimized for the target device and interpreted correctly after measurement:

1. **Build phase**: In the build stage, the programmer defines qubits, applies gates, and adds measurement operations to form a **QuantumCircuit** object (Qiskit) or a Cirq circuit. At this point, the circuit is purely mathematical, a list of operations with no physical mapping, as shown in the following command:

   ```
   from qiskit import QuantumCircuit
   qc = QuantumCircuit(2, 2)
   qc.h(0)
   qc.cx(0, 1)
   qc.measure([0, 1], [0, 1])
   ```

2. **Transpile phase**: Before execution, circuits must be transpiled (Qiskit) or optimized (Cirq) to match the native gate set and connectivity of the target backend:

   ```
   from qiskit import transpile
   from qiskit_aer import AerSimulator
   sim = AerSimulator()
   qc_opt = transpile(qc, sim, optimization_level=2)
   ```

   Transpilation may re-order, merge, or decompose gates, but it preserves logical behavior while improving efficiency. This step is analogous to compiler optimization in classical computing.

3. **Execution phase**: Once optimized, the circuit is submitted to a simulator or physical device for execution. Each execution involves multiple shots to obtain statistically reliable results, as follows:

   a. **Qiskit example**:

      ```
      from qiskit import transpile
      from qiskit_aer import AerSimulator
      ```

```
sim = AerSimulator()
qc_t = transpile(qc_opt, sim)
result = sim.run(qc_t, shots=1024).result()
print(result.get_counts())
```

b. **Cirq example**:

```
import cirq
sim = cirq.Simulator()
result = sim.run(circuit, repetitions=1000)
print(result.histogram(key='0,1'))
```

Both frameworks return frequency distributions of measurement outcomes, representing the probabilistic nature of quantum systems.

4. **Analysis phase**: After execution, results are analyzed to interpret quantum behavior or to verify theoretical predictions. Qiskit and Cirq include built-in visualization tools for histogram plots, Bloch vectors, and expectation values, as follows:

```
from qiskit.visualization import plot_histogram
plot_histogram(result.get_counts())
```

The following table summarizes the standard workflow for executing quantum circuits, outlining each stage, its purpose, and the corresponding tools or methods used:

Stage	Purpose	Tools/methods
Build	Construct a logical circuit	`QuantumCircuit, Circuit()`
Transpile	Optimize for hardware	`transpile(), optimize_circuit()`
Execute	Run on the simulator or device	`execute(), Simulator.run()`
Analyze	Interpret measurement data	`get_counts(), histograms, Bloch plots`

***Table 3.5**: Standard quantum circuit execution workflow*

Simulation using Qiskit Aer and Cirq simulators

Quantum simulators such as Qiskit Aer and Cirq provide a vital testing ground for quantum algorithms, allowing developers to explore and validate circuit behavior before deployment on physical hardware. They replicate the mathematical evolution of qubits and gates within a classical environment, supporting both ideal and noise-aware execution modes. By offering flexibility, precision, and accessibility, these simulators serve as indispensable tools for education, research, and performance optimization across diverse quantum computing platforms.

Purpose of quantum simulation

Before executing quantum programs on real hardware, developers almost always test them on quantum simulators. These simulators emulate the mathematical behavior of qubits and gates on classical computers, providing a safe, noise-free environment to debug, optimize, and verify algorithms.

Importance of quantum simulation

The following points outline the key reasons quantum simulation is essential for testing, learning, noise control, and performance evaluation:

- **Algorithm validation**: Ensures that circuits behave as intended before committing them to costly or queue-limited hardware runs.
- **Educational clarity**: Allows learners to explore concepts like superposition, entanglement, and interference visually and interactively.

- **Noise control**: Provides the ability to toggle between ideal (noise-free) and realistic (noisy) models to study hardware imperfections.
- **Performance benchmarking**: Helps researchers test algorithmic scalability and resource requirements using state-vector or density matrix methods.

Types of simulation models

The following table summarizes the main types of quantum simulation models, describing their characteristics and typical use cases in algorithm testing and analysis:

Simulator type	Description	Use case
State-vector	Tracks the full complex-amplitude vector of the system.	Ideal for small systems (< 25 qubits).
Density matrix	Includes decoherence and noise effects.	Used in noise modeling and fidelity analysis.
Stabilizer	Efficiently simulates Clifford-only circuits.	Useful for error correction codes.
Quantum assembly language (QASM)/shot-based	Sample outcomes as if measured on real hardware.	Practical for algorithm verification.

Table 3.6: *Common simulation modes*

Simulation with Qiskit Aer

Qiskit Aer is IBM's high-performance simulation framework that replicates the behavior of quantum circuits on classical computers. It allows users to test algorithms under both ideal and noisy conditions, offering several backends optimized for speed, accuracy, and realism. Aer serves as the default testing ground for Qiskit circuits before deploying them on actual IBM Quantum hardware.

Overview of Aer backends

Qiskit Aer offers different simulators to match various computational goals. The following table lists the primary Qiskit Aer backends, outlining their purposes and key features for simulating quantum circuits under various conditions:

Backend	Purpose	Key features
aer_simulator	General-purpose simulator	Supports state-vector, density matrix, and noise models
statevector_simulator	Tracks the full quantum state	Ideal for theoretical analysis and visualization
qasm_simulator	Performs shot-based sampling	Mimics real hardware measurement results
unitary_simulator	Calculates the total unitary matrix	Useful for verifying analytical expressions

Table 3.7: *Qiskit Aer simulation backends*

Basic circuit simulation

The simplest workflow involves building a circuit, running it on **aer_simulator**, and analyzing the resulting probability distribution, as shown in the following command:

```
from qiskit import QuantumCircuit, transpile
from qiskit_aer import AerSimulator
qc = QuantumCircuit(2, 2)
qc.h(0)
qc.cx(0, 1)
```

```
qc.measure([0, 1], [0, 1])
sim = AerSimulator()
qc_t = transpile(qc, sim)
result = sim.run(qc_t, shots=1024).result()
print(result.get_counts())
```

We get the following output (approximate):

```
{'00': 520, '11': 504}
```

State-vector visualization

To gain a deeper understanding of the circuit's quantum behavior, the state-vector representation can be retrieved and plotted on the Bloch sphere as follows:

```
from qiskit.quantum_info import Statevector
from qiskit.visualization import plot_bloch_multivector
state = Statevector.from_instruction(qc.remove_final_measurements(inplace=False))
plot_bloch_multivector(state)
```

This provides geometric insight into how the qubit's orientation changes under the applied gates.

Noise model simulation

Real quantum hardware suffers from gate errors, readout errors, and decoherence. Aer can inject these imperfections through noise models to test error resilience:

```
from qiskit import transpile
from qiskit_aer import AerSimulator
from qiskit_aer.noise import NoiseModel
noise = NoiseModel()
sim_noise = AerSimulator(noise_model=noise)
qc_t = transpile(qc, sim_noise)
result = sim_noise.run(qc_t, shots=1024).result()
```

This approach helps in developing error-mitigation strategies and evaluating algorithm robustness.

Simulation with Cirq and comparative analysis

While Qiskit Aer provides a robust general-purpose simulator, Cirq focuses on realistic hardware emulation, particularly for Google's superconducting qubit architectures. It allows users to model circuit execution, noise effects, and calibration constraints with exceptional control, making it an excellent tool for algorithm testing and experimental replication.

Cirq simulator basics

Cirq provides two main simulation classes. The following table lists the main Cirq simulators with their purposes and key characteristics:

Simulator	Purpose	Characteristics
`Simulator()`	Ideal (noiseless) quantum execution	Accurately emulates pure-state evolution
`DensityMatrixSimulator()`	Noisy simulation including decoherence	Models mixed states and open-system dynamics

***Table 3.8:** Primary Cirq simulation modes*

Running a basic simulation

A typical simulation involves defining a circuit, executing it with a simulator, and analyzing measurement outcomes:

```
import cirq
# Define two-qubits and a circuit
q0, q1 = cirq.LineQubit.range(2)
circuit = cirq.Circuit(cirq.H(q0), cirq.CNOT(q0, q1), cirq.measure(q0, q1))
# Run the simulation
sim = cirq.Simulator()
result = sim.run(circuit, repetitions=1000)
print(result.histogram(key='0,1'))
```

Here is the output (approximate):

```
Counter({3: 495, 0: 505})
```

Binary 11 and 00 correspond to the two Bell states, demonstrating the expected entanglement pattern.

Density matrix simulation

To include realistic imperfections, the **DensityMatrixSimulator** can be used to account for decoherence and readout errors:

```
sim_dm = cirq.DensityMatrixSimulator()
result = sim_dm.run(circuit, repetitions=1000)
```

This model is valuable for quantum error correction experiments and for studying how noise affects algorithmic fidelity.

Visualizing results

Cirq allows direct inspection of simulation data through built-in methods as follows:

```
import matplotlib.pyplot as plt
from collections import Counter
hist = result.histogram(key='0,1')
plt.bar(hist.keys(), hist.values())
plt.xlabel('Bitstring')
plt.ylabel('Counts')
plt.title('Cirq Simulation Results')
plt.show()
```

This simple visualization reveals the distribution of measurement outcomes and can be used to compare ideal vs. noisy runs.

Comparing Qiskit Aer and Cirq simulators

The following table compares Qiskit Aer and Cirq simulators in terms of design, features, and use cases:

Aspect	Qiskit Aer	Cirq simulator
Design philosophy	High-level, user-friendly, integrated with the IBM Quantum ecosystem	Hardware-realistic, low-level control of timing and noise
Supported models	State-vector, density matrix, unitary, QASM	Pure-state, density matrix, Clifford (noisy)
Noise modeling	Uses **NoiseModel** API and hardware calibration data	User-defined decoherence channels and amplitude damping
Performance optimization	GPU support and multithreading for large state spaces	Efficient stabilizer and moment-based simulation

Best use case	Educational and hardware validation on IBM platforms	Research-grade experiments on Google devices or custom hardware

***Table 3.9**: Qiskit Aer vs. Cirq simulation comparison*

Choosing between them

The following points suggest when to choose Qiskit Aer or Cirq based on simulation needs and platform compatibility:

- Use Qiskit Aer for rapid prototyping, visual teaching, and seamless execution on IBM hardware.
- Use Cirq for experimental simulation requiring precise timing, custom noise models, or hybrid algorithm development (Google Quantum AI platforms).

In many academic workflows, both are used complementarily, Qiskit for clarity and Cirq for granular hardware emulation.

Conclusion

This chapter demonstrated how quantum gates constitute the operational backbone of quantum computation, translating abstract quantum principles into controllable actions on qubits. We examined how single-qubit gates, including the Pauli (X, Y, Z), Hadamard (H), and phase gates (S, T), govern state rotations, superposition, and phase evolution on the Bloch sphere. Building on this foundation, the chapter explored multi-qubit gates such as CNOT, Toffoli, and SWAP, which enable entanglement, conditional logic, and quantum information exchange essential for complex algorithms. The discussion on universal gate sets, particularly the Clifford + T framework, highlighted how any quantum operation can be approximated using a finite set of primitive gates. Practical implementations using Qiskit and Cirq connected theory with execution, illustrating how individual gates combine to form functional quantum circuits. Together, these concepts bridge the gap between quantum theory and implementable quantum computation, laying the foundation for advanced algorithmic design and optimization. Building on the gate-level foundations established in this chapter, the next chapter advances from circuit construction to algorithmic thinking, demonstrating how quantum gates and circuits are orchestrated to solve computational problems more efficiently than their classical counterparts. This progression highlights how abstract gate operations scale into meaningful quantum algorithms with real computational advantage.

Questions

1. **What is a quantum gate, and how does it differ from a classical logic gate?**

   Answer: A quantum gate is a reversible, unitary operation that manipulates qubits by changing their amplitudes and phases. Unlike classical logic gates that operate on definite binary values (0 or 1), quantum gates act on superposition states, enabling interference and probabilistic outcomes.

2. **What are Pauli gates, and what do they represent on the Bloch sphere?**

   Answer: The Pauli gates, X, Y, and Z, correspond to 180° rotations of a qubit around the X, Y, and Z axes of the Bloch sphere. The X gate flips $|0\rangle$ and $|1\rangle$, the Y gate applies a combined bit and phase flip, and the Z gate introduces a π phase shift.

3. **Why is the Hadamard gate important in quantum computing?**

   Answer: The Hadamard (H) gate creates quantum superposition by transforming a basis state into an equal combination of $|0\rangle$ and $|1\rangle$. It is essential for quantum parallelism and forms the starting point of many quantum algorithms.

4. **What role do phase gates S and T play in quantum circuits?**

   Answer: Phase gates modify the relative phase of a qubit without changing measurement probabilities. The S gate applies a $\pi/2$ rotation, while the T gate applies a $\pi/4$ rotation, both of which are critical for controlling interference and achieving universality.

5. **How does the CNOT gate create entanglement?**

   Answer: The CNOT gate flips the target qubit when the control qubit is in the $|1\rangle$ state. When combined with a Hadamard gate on the control qubit, it generates entangled states such as Bell states.

6. **What is the significance of the Toffoli gate in quantum computation?**

   Answer: The Toffoli (CCNOT) gate flips a target qubit only when both control qubits are $|1\rangle$. It enables reversible classical logic within quantum circuits and is widely used in arithmetic operations and error correction.

7. **Why is the SWAP gate important in hardware implementations?**

   Answer: The SWAP gate exchanges the states of two-qubits, allowing logical qubits to be repositioned in hardware with limited connectivity. This is essential for efficient routing and circuit optimization.

8. **What is meant by a universal gate set?**

   Answer: A universal gate set is a small collection of gates capable of approximating any quantum operation to arbitrary accuracy. Examples include {H, T, CNOT} and {RX, RZ, CNOT}.

9. **What is the Clifford + T gate set, and why is it widely used?**

   Answer: The Clifford + T gate set combines Clifford gates (H, S, CNOT) with the non-Clifford + T gate to achieve universality while remaining compatible with fault-tolerant quantum error correction.

10. **What is the key takeaway from understanding quantum gates and circuits?**

    Answer: Understanding quantum gates is essential for building and interpreting quantum circuits. These gates translate quantum theory into executable operations, forming the foundation of all quantum algorithms and practical quantum computation.

Exercises

1. Construct a comparative table showing the differences between single-qubit and multi-qubit gates in terms of their function, mathematical representation, Bloch sphere effect, and practical applications in quantum circuits.
2. Using Qiskit, create a single-qubit circuit that applies the Hadamard (H), phase (S), and T gates sequentially. Visualize the circuit and observe how the qubit's Bloch vector changes at each step.
3. Build and simulate a two-qubit CNOT circuit in Qiskit. Initialize the control qubit in superposition using a Hadamard gate, execute the circuit on a simulator, and display the resulting entangled Bell-state measurement outcomes.
4. Demonstrate the action of Pauli gates (X, Y, Z) using Python or Qiskit. For each gate, record how the qubit's state-vector rotates along its respective axis on the Bloch sphere.
5. Implement the Toffoli gate (CCNOT) in Qiskit and verify its truth table through simulation. Discuss how it represents reversible classical logic within quantum computation.
6. Show how a SWAP gate can be decomposed into three CNOT gates. Construct both versions in Qiskit or Cirq, run simulations, and confirm that they yield identical results.
7. Illustrate the concept of a universal gate set by combining single-qubit rotations and a CNOT gate to approximate an arbitrary two-qubit unitary operation. Analyze the accuracy of the approximation.
8. Research and summarize (200–300 words) the significance of the Clifford + T gate set in fault-tolerant quantum computing. Explain why reducing T-count is vital for efficient circuit design.
9. Visualize on the Bloch sphere how different combinations of H, S, and T gates change the orientation of a qubit. Explain how these transformations relate to phase manipulation and interference control.
10. Write a reflective essay (300–400 words) on how learning about quantum gates, universality, and circuit design deepens your understanding of quantum computation. Discuss how visualization and simulation tools bridge theoretical learning with practical experimentation.

CHAPTER 4
Quantum Algorithms

Introduction

Quantum algorithms translate the core principles of quantum mechanics, superposition, interference, and entanglement, into real computational power. They demonstrate how quantum systems can process information in fundamentally different ways, achieving speedups that classical computers cannot.

The *Deutsch* and *Deutsch–Jozsa* algorithms mark the earliest demonstrations of quantum advantage, showing how a single quantum query can reveal global information about a function. Grover's search algorithm achieves a quadratic speedup in finding a target item within an unstructured database, while Shor's factoring algorithm provides an exponential improvement in factoring large integers, posing deep implications for modern cryptography. Underlying many of these breakthroughs are two powerful mathematical tools, the **quantum Fourier transform** (**QFT**) and **quantum phase estimation** (**QPE**), which uncover hidden periodicities and phase information within quantum states.

A key strength of these algorithms lies in their universality and implementation flexibility. They can be designed and executed across multiple platforms such as Qiskit and Cirq, allowing learners and researchers to experiment with algorithmic logic and observe quantum interference directly through simulation.

This chapter introduces these foundational algorithms step-by-step, explaining their theoretical principles, circuit design, and implementation in Python. By the end, you will understand how quantum algorithms harness interference to amplify correct outcomes, detect periodicity, and perform complex computations efficiently, laying the groundwork for exploring advanced applications of quantum computing.

Structure

The chapter covers the following topics:

- Deutsch algorithm
- Deutsch Jozsa algorithm
- Grover's Search algorithm
- Shor's Factoring algorithm
- Quantum Fourier transform and phase estimation

Objectives

This chapter aims to equip readers with the knowledge and skills to understand and implement the most influential quantum algorithms that demonstrate real quantum advantage. Readers will explore how fundamental principles such as superposition, interference, and entanglement enable computational speedups in problems where classical methods fall short. The chapter introduces core algorithms, Deutsch, Deutsch–Jozsa, Grover, Shor, and the QFT, along with QPE, explaining their logic, structure, and significance in quantum computation. Each algorithm is presented with clear explanations, circuit diagrams, and hands-on implementations using both Qiskit and Cirq, offering flexibility for experimentation and deeper learning. Practical examples reinforce the relationship between theory and application, showing how quantum interference can amplify, distinguish, and reveal hidden information.

By the end of this chapter, readers will have gained the confidence to design, simulate, and interpret foundational quantum algorithms across different quantum programming platforms.

Deutsch algorithm

The Deutsch algorithm holds a special place in the history of quantum computing as the first demonstration of quantum advantage. It shows that a quantum computer can outperform a classical one even for a simple logical task. By harnessing superposition and interference, the algorithm extracts global information about a function with a single evaluation, whereas a classical approach would require two. Though modest in scale, it elegantly captures the fundamental intuition behind quantum parallelism and serves as the conceptual foundation for many later algorithms.

Problem definition

Consider a hidden Boolean function:

$$f:\{0,1\}\rightarrow\{0,1\},$$

which is guaranteed to be one of the following two types:

- **Constant:** $f(0)=f(1)$
- **Balanced:** $f(0)\neq f(1)$

A classical computer must evaluate the function twice—once for each possible input—to determine whether it is constant or balanced. A quantum computer, however, can determine the same information with a single evaluation by preparing the input in a superposition of $|0\rangle$ and $|1\rangle$ and exploiting quantum interference to reveal the global property of the function.

Algorithmic principle

The algorithm employs a two-qubit oracle gate U_f defined as:

$$U_f\,|x, y\rangle = |x, y \oplus f(x)\rangle,$$

Where $\oplus$ denotes the XOR operation.

The first qubit $|x\rangle$ represents the input, and the second qubit $|y\rangle$ serves as an auxiliary register that stores the result of the oracle evaluation.

By initializing the auxiliary qubit in the state $|1\rangle$ and applying Hadamard gates to both qubits, the oracle's effect manifests as a phase flip that depends on the value of $f(x)$.

A final Hadamard operation on the first qubit produces interference between the probability amplitudes.

This interference translates the encoded phase information into a measurable distinction:

- If the function is constant, the measurement yields $|0\rangle$.
- If the function is balanced, the measurement yields $|1\rangle$.

Circuit design and operation

The overall structure of the Deutsch algorithm circuit is shown conceptually below, followed by a step-wise explanation of each stage.

Deutsch algorithm circuit: Circuit representation of the Deutsch algorithm showing the input qubit ($|x\rangle$) and the auxiliary qubit ($|y\rangle$):

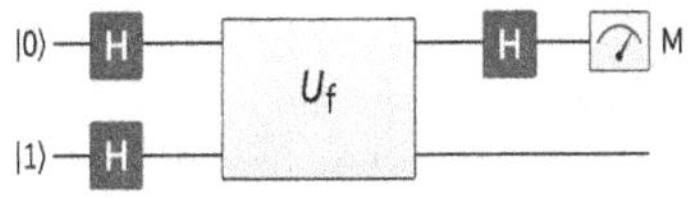

***Figure 4.1:** Algorithm circuit*

The oracle `U(f)` is implemented as a controlled operation represented by the ⊕ symbol.

The circuit's operational flow can be understood through the sequential stages summarized in the following table. Each stage corresponds to a distinct quantum transformation that collectively encodes, manipulates, and reveals information about the hidden function `f(x)`.

Stage	Operation	Purpose
1	Initialize	Set
2	Apply Hadamard to both qubits	Create a uniform superposition of input states.
3	Oracle `U(f)`	Encode `f(x)` as a phase pattern in the superposed state.
4	Hadamard on the first qubit	Interfere amplitudes to reveal global information about f.
5	Measurement	Measure the first qubit. Output 0 → constant; 1 → balanced.

***Table 4.1:** Step-by-step operations of the Deutsch algorithm circuit*

Intuitive state evolution

The evolution of the quantum state through the circuit can be described step-by-step as follows:

1. **Initialization:**

$$|\psi_0\rangle = |0\rangle|1\rangle$$

The input qubit is set to $|0\rangle$ and the auxiliary qubit to $|1\rangle$.

2. **Hadamard preparation**: Both qubits are placed into equal superposition states:

$$|\psi_1\rangle = \frac{1}{2}(|0\rangle + |1\rangle)(|0\rangle - |1\rangle)$$

3. **Oracle action**: The oracle applies a phase shift to each basis component depending on the value of $f(x)$:

$$|x\rangle \rightarrow (-1)^{f(x)}|x\rangle$$

4. **Final Hadamard and measurement**: The Hadamard gate on the first qubit converts phase information into measurable amplitude differences, producing constructive or destructive interference:

   a. **Result 0** → f is constant.
   b. **Result 1** → f is balanced.

Hence, the quantum computer determines the nature of f with a single query to the oracle—demonstrating the core principle of quantum parallelism.

Implementation in Python using Qiskit

The following implementation demonstrates the Deutsch algorithm using Qiskit's simulation framework. Two oracles are defined: one for a *constant function* $f(x)=0$ and one for a balanced function $f(x)=x$. The algorithm circuit prepares qubits, applies Hadamard gates, invokes the oracle, and measures the result to determine the type of function. Here it is shown as follows:

```
from qiskit import QuantumCircuit, Aer, execute
# --- Oracle Definitions ---
def constant_oracle():
```

```
    qc = QuantumCircuit(2)
    return qc                       # f(x) = 0 (constant)
def balanced_oracle():
    qc = QuantumCircuit(2)
    qc.cx(0, 1)                     # f(x) = x (balanced)
    return qc
# --- Deutsch Algorithm ---
def deutsch_algorithm(oracle):
    qc = QuantumCircuit(2, 1)
    qc.x(1)                         # Prepare |y> = |1>
    qc.h([0, 1])                    # Create superposition
    qc.compose(oracle, inplace=True)
    qc.h(0)                         # Interference step
    qc.measure(0, 0)
    return qc
# --- Execution ---
backend = Aer.get_backend(‚qasm_simulator')
for label, oracle in [(„Constant", constant_oracle()),
                      („Balanced", balanced_oracle())]:
    circuit = deutsch_algorithm(oracle)
    result = execute(circuit, backend, shots=1024).result()
    print(f"{label} Oracle Output:", result.get_counts())
```

Interpretation:

- Output {'0': 1024} → The function is constant.
- Output {'1': 1024} → The function is balanced.

The algorithm evaluates both possible inputs simultaneously and uses quantum interference to reveal the global property of the hidden function in a single oracle query.

Implementation in Python using Cirq

The following implementation recreates the Deutsch algorithm using Cirq, Google's quantum computing framework. The logic mirrors the Qiskit version: an oracle is defined for the balanced case, and the circuit prepares, executes, and measures the qubits to determine the function type:

```
import cirq
# --- Qubit Allocation ---
q0, q1 = cirq.LineQubit.range(2)
# --- Oracle Definition ---
def balanced_oracle():
    return [cirq.CNOT(q0, q1)]     # f(x) = x  (balanced function)
# --- Deutsch Algorithm Circuit ---
def deutsch_circuit(oracle):
    circuit = cirq.Circuit()
    circuit.append([cirq.X(q1), cirq.H(q0), cirq.H(q1)])     # Initialization & superposition
    circuit.append(oracle)                                    # Oracle action
    circuit.append([cirq.H(q0), cirq.measure(q0, key='result')]) # Interference & measurement
    return circuit
# --- Simulation and Results ---
sim = cirq.Simulator()
for label, oracle in [(„Constant", []), („Balanced", balanced_oracle())]:
    circuit = deutsch_circuit(oracle)
    print(f"\n{label} Oracle Circuit:\n{circuit}")
```

```
result = sim.run(circuit, repetitions=10)
print(„Results:", result)
```

Interpretation: Both Qiskit and Cirq implementations follow the same logical structure—differing only in syntax and circuit construction style. Each performs a single oracle call, allowing quantum interference to classify the hidden function as constant or balanced.

The consistency across platforms reinforces the universality of quantum-algorithm design principles.

Deutsch–Jozsa algorithm

The Deutsch–Jozsa algorithm extends the elegant logic of the Deutsch algorithm to the multi-qubit domain and provides the first theoretical demonstration of an exponential quantum speedup.

Where the original algorithm distinguishes between a constant and a balanced one-bit function, this generalization solves the same problem for an n-bit function with a single oracle query, while any classical algorithm would require up to $2^{n-1}+1$ evaluations.

Thus, the Deutsch–Jozsa algorithm provides the first convincing proof that quantum computation can be exponentially faster than any classical approach, laying the foundation for future breakthroughs in quantum algorithm design.

Problem definition

Consider a Boolean function:

$$f:\{0,1\}^n \rightarrow \{0,1\}.$$

The function is guaranteed to be one of two types:

- **Constant**: $f(x)=0$ for all inputs x, or $f(x)=1$ for all inputs x.
- **Balanced**: $f(x)=0$ for exactly half of the possible inputs and $f(x)=1$ for the remaining half.

The objective is to determine whether f is constant or balanced.

A classical computer, even under the best circumstances, may need to evaluate more than half of all possible inputs—requiring exponentially many queries for large n.

A quantum computer, however, can determine the correct classification with a single query to the oracle U_f, by exploiting superposition and quantum interference to process all inputs simultaneously.

Algorithmic principle

The oracle acts on an $(n+1)$-qubit system according to:

$$U_f\,|x, y\rangle = |x, y \oplus f(x)\rangle,$$

Where $\oplus$ denotes the XOR operation.

As in the Deutsch algorithm, the auxiliary qubit $|y\rangle$ is initialized in the state $|1\rangle$ so that the oracle introduces a phase factor $(-1)^{f(x)}$ on each computational basis state $|x\rangle$..

When the input register is placed in a uniform superposition of all 2^n possible inputs, the oracle effectively evaluates $f(x)$ for every input simultaneously.

A final layer of Hadamard transformations on the input register converts these encoded phases into measurable amplitude patterns, allowing the quantum system to reveal—after a single oracle call—whether the hidden function is constant or balanced.

Circuit design

The Deutsch–Jozsa algorithm circuit generalizes the logic of the Deutsch algorithm to n input qubits and one auxiliary qubit. The circuit's structure enables the quantum system to evaluate the hidden function for all possible inputs simultaneously, encoding the global property of the function in the amplitude pattern of the final state.

Deutsch–Jozsa algorithm circuit: Generalized circuit for the Deutsch–Jozsa algorithm:

```
|0> —H————————■————————————H—┐
              |              |
|0> —H————————■————————————H—┤
 ⋮            |              |
|0> —H————————■————————————H—┤  (n input qubits)
|1> —H————————⊕——————————————M
```

The upper n lines form the input register, and the bottom line represents the auxiliary qubit. The oracle U_f encodes the function $f(x)$ using controlled operations that imprint phase information on the input register.

The circuit's operational flow is summarized in the following table. Each stage corresponds to a distinct quantum operation that transforms the system from initialization to measurement:

Stage	Operation	Purpose
1	Initialize	Set n input qubits to
2	Hadamard Transform	Create a uniform superposition over all input states.
3	Oracle Call U_f	Imprint phase $(-1)^{f(x)}$ onto each input state.
4	Hadamard on Input Register	Interfere amplitudes so that constant and balanced cases separate.
5	Measurement	Observe the input register: All 0s → constant; any 1 → balanced.

***Table 4.2**: Step-by-step operations of the Deutsch–Jozsa algorithm circuit*

Conceptual flow of the algorithm

The step-by-step operation of the Deutsch–Jozsa algorithm can be understood intuitively as follows:

1. **Initialization**: All n input qubits are initialized in the state $|0\rangle$, and one auxiliary qubit is prepared in $|1\rangle$.
2. **First Hadamard layer**: Applying Hadamard gates to all qubits creates an equal superposition of all 2^n possible input states, enabling the oracle to evaluate $f(x)$ for every input x in parallel.
3. **Oracle action**: The oracle applies a phase inversion to each state $|x\rangle$, depending on $f(x)$. This step encodes the entire truth table of the function into the phase structure of the superposed state.
4. **Second Hadamard layer**: When Hadamard gates are applied again to the input register, interference between amplitudes determines the final measurement outcome:
    a. For a constant function, all amplitudes add constructively, yielding the state $|00\ldots0\rangle$.
    b. For a balanced function, half of the amplitudes cancel out, producing any non-zero bitstring.
5. **Measurement**:
    a. Output 000…0 → f is constant.
    b. Any other output → f is balanced.

This sequence captures the entire logical flow of the algorithm without delving into heavy algebra, while still reflecting the true quantum-mechanical behavior of superposition and interference.

Implementation in Python using Qiskit

The implementation demonstrates the Deutsch–Jozsa algorithm using Qiskit. Two oracle types are defined: one that represents a constant function ($f(x)=0$ for all x) and another that represents a balanced function *(f(x)=parity(x))*. The circuit prepares an equal superposition of all inputs, invokes the oracle once, and then applies Hadamard gates to extract the global property of the hidden function.

```
from qiskit import QuantumCircuit, Aer, execute
from qiskit.visualization import plot_histogram
# --- Oracle Definitions ---
def constant_oracle(n):
    qc = QuantumCircuit(n + 1)
    # f(x) = 0 for all x  → no operation applied
    return qc
def balanced_oracle(n):
    qc = QuantumCircuit(n + 1)
    for qubit in range(n):
        qc.cx(qubit, n)            # f(x) = parity(x)
    return qc
# --- Deutsch-Jozsa Algorithm ---
def deutsch_jozsa(n, oracle):
    qc = QuantumCircuit(n + 1, n)
    qc.x(n)                        # Prepare |y> - |1>
    qc.h(range(n + 1))             # First Hadamard Layer
    qc.compose(oracle, inplace=True)
    qc.h(range(n))                 # Second Hadamard Layer (interference)
    qc.measure(range(n), range(n))
    return qc
# --- Simulation and Output ---
backend = Aer.get_backend('qasm_simulator')
for label, oracle in [("Constant", constant_oracle(2)),
                      ("Balanced", balanced_oracle(2))]:
    qc = deutsch_jozsa(2, oracle)
    result = execute(qc, backend, shots=1024).result()
    counts = result.get_counts()
    print(f"{label} Oracle Output:", counts)
```

Interpretation:

- Output {'00': 1024} → The function is constant.
- Any other bitstring → The function is balanced.

Through quantum parallelism, the Deutsch–Jozsa algorithm determines the global nature of the function with a single oracle query, achieving exponential efficiency over the classical approach.

Implementation in Python using Cirq

The following implementation presents the Deutsch–Jozsa algorithm using Cirq, Google's open-source quantum framework. The structure mirrors the Qiskit version: one oracle represents a constant function, and the other represents a balanced function.

After a single oracle call, the algorithm reveals whether the hidden function is constant or balanced.

The following code constructs the Deutsch–Jozsa circuit in Cirq, defines constant and balanced oracles, and runs the circuit on Cirq's simulator to observe the measurement outcomes for both cases:

```
import cirq
# --- Deutsch-Jozsa Circuit Construction ---
def deutsch_jozsa_circuit(n, oracle):
    qubits = cirq.LineQubit.range(n + 1)
    circuit = cirq.Circuit()
```

```
    circuit.append(cirq.X(qubits[n]))                 # Prepare |y> = |1>
    circuit.append(cirq.H.on_each(*qubits))           # First Hadamard Layer
    circuit.append(oracle)                            # Oracle action
    circuit.append(cirq.H.on_each(*qubits[:-1]))      # Second Hadamard Layer (interference)
    circuit.append(cirq.measure(*qubits[:-1], key='result'))
    return circuit
# --- Oracle Definitions ---
def constant_oracle_cirq(n, qubits):
    # f(x) = 0 for all x → No operation
    return []
def balanced_oracle_cirq(n, qubits):
    # f(x) = parity(x)
    return [cirq.CNOT(qubits[i], qubits[n]) for i in range(n)]
# --- Simulation and Output ---
sim = cirq.Simulator()
for label, oracle_func in [("Constant", constant_oracle_cirq),
                           ("Balanced", balanced_oracle_cirq)]:
    qubits = cirq.LineQubit.range(3)
    oracle = oracle_func(2, qubits)
    circuit = deutsch_jozsa_circuit(2, oracle)
    print(f"\n{label} Oracle Circuit:\n{circuit}")
    result = sim.run(circuit, repetitions=10)
    print("Results:", result)
```

Interpretation: Both Qiskit and Cirq implementations confirm the same outcome: the quantum circuit distinguishes whether the hidden Boolean function is constant or balanced with a single oracle query. This demonstrates the exponential efficiency of the Deutsch–Jozsa algorithm—its ability to evaluate global properties of functions that would require exponentially many classical evaluations.

Grover's search algorithm

The Grover algorithm is one of the cornerstones of quantum computing, renowned for providing a quadratic speedup in search problems. In a classical setting, searching an unstructured database of N elements requires, on average, $N/2$ queries to locate a desired item. Grover's algorithm, however, can identify the correct element using only $O(\sqrt{N})$ oracle queries, an extraordinary improvement achieved through a uniquely quantum phenomenon called **amplitude amplification**.

While formulated initially for database search, Grover's principle extends far beyond that domain. Its underlying mechanism can be applied to optimization, pattern matching, and even search-space acceleration in machine learning, making it a fundamental algorithmic paradigm in modern quantum computation.

Problem statement

Suppose we have an unstructured database of $N = 2^n$ items, represented by computational basis states $|x\rangle$, where $x \in \{0, 1, \ldots, N-1\}$. Among these, one state $|x_0\rangle$ satisfies a particular condition $f(x_0) = 1$, while all others yield $f(x) = 0$. The task is to identify this *marked state* using as few oracle calls as possible. The contrast between classical and quantum search strategies can be summarized as follows:

- **Classical approach**: Examine, on average, $N / 2$ entries.
- **Quantum approach (Grover)**: Use interference to amplify the probability of the marked state, requiring only $\approx \sqrt{N}$ oracle queries.

Grover's algorithm thus achieves a quadratic speedup over the best possible classical search strategy, marking a pivotal step toward practical quantum advantage.

Algorithmic principle

Grover's algorithm operates through a sequence of iterative transformations that systematically amplify the probability amplitude of the marked state.

The process can be understood in four conceptual steps:

1. **Initialization**: Prepare an equal superposition of all basis states using Hadamard gates. This ensures that every state $|x\rangle$ begins with equal amplitude $\frac{1}{\sqrt{N}}$
2. **Oracle query**: Apply the oracle operator, which identifies the marked state $|x_0\rangle$ by inverting its phase:

$$|x_0\rangle \longrightarrow -|x_0\rangle.$$

   This operation multiplies the amplitude of the desired state by *-1*, leaving all others unchanged.
3. **Diffusion operator (amplitude amplification)**: Apply the diffusion operator, also called the inversion-about-the-mean transformation. It reflects all amplitudes relative to their average, thereby amplifying the marked state's probability amplitude.
4. **Iteration**: Repeat the oracle + diffusion steps approximately $\sqrt{N}$ times. Each iteration increases the marked state's amplitude, rotating the system's overall state closer to $|x_0\rangle$. When the amplitudes reach their maximum separation, a measurement will reveal the marked item with high probability.

Mathematically, these two reflections, one about the marked state and one about the mean amplitude, combine to form a rotation within a two-dimensional subspace spanned by the marked state and the uniform superposition.

This elegant geometric interpretation lies at the heart of Grover's quadratic speedup.

Circuit design

The Grover circuit combines two central quantum operations, the oracle and the diffusion operator, which together drive amplitude amplification. The oracle identifies the marked state by introducing a phase inversion, while the diffusion operator reflects all amplitudes about their mean, reinforcing the probability of the desired solution with each iteration.

Grover's search algorithm circuit: Circuit representation of Grover's Search Algorithm:

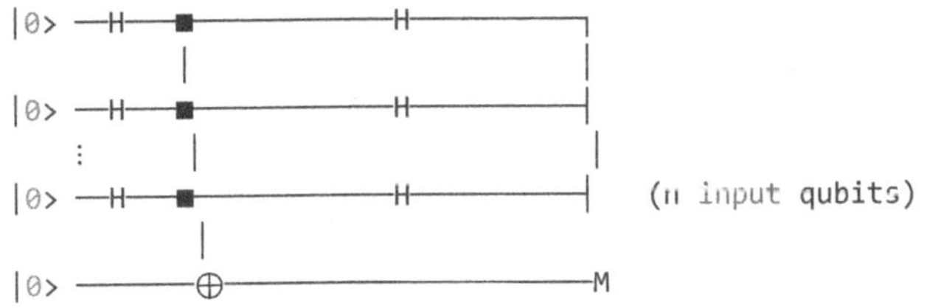

The oracle flips the phase of the target state, while the diffusion operator amplifies its probability through inversion-about-the-mean.

The operational flow of Grover's algorithm is summarized in the following table, where each stage corresponds to a key transformation step within one Grover iteration:

Stage	Operation	Purpose
1	Initialization	Apply Hadamard gates to all n qubits to create a uniform superposition.
2	Oracle O_f	Flip the phase of the marked state $|x\rangle$ to distinguish it from other states.
3	Diffusion operator D	Reflect all amplitudes about their average to amplify the marked state.
4	Repeat $k \approx \sqrt{N}$ times	Gradually increase the marked state's probability amplitude.

5	Measurement	Observe the register to read the index of the marked item with high probability.

Table 4.3: Step-by-step operations of Grover's algorithm circuit

Conceptual flow of operation

The execution of Grover's algorithm can be visualized as a sequence of transformations that gradually amplify the marked state's probability amplitude:

1. **Initialization**: The system begins in a uniform superposition of all N basis states, each with amplitude $1/\sqrt{N}$
2. **Oracle phase flip**: The oracle inverts the phase of the marked state, multiplying its amplitude by -1 and introducing a subtle imbalance among the amplitudes.
3. **Diffusion step**: The diffusion (or inversion-about-the-mean) operator reflects every amplitude about its mean value. This reflection amplifies the probability of the marked state while slightly diminishing the others.
4. **Iteration**: Repeating the oracle and diffusion steps $r \approx \frac{\pi}{4}\sqrt{N}$
5. **Measurement**: When measured, the quantum state collapses to the correct basis state |x_0⟩ with high probability.

Through this iterative interference process, Grover's algorithm transforms uniform uncertainty into near-certainty—demonstrating how constructive and destructive interference can yield a measurable computational advantage.

Implementation in Python using Qiskit

The following is a two-qubit implementation of Grover's algorithm using Qiskit, where the oracle marks the target state |11⟩. This example demonstrates how the algorithm amplifies the probability amplitude of the marked state through the combined action of the oracle and diffusion operators.

```
from qiskit import QuantumCircuit, Aer, execute
from qiskit.visualization import plot_histogram
# --- Oracle Definition ---
def grover_oracle(n):
    qc = QuantumCircuit(n)
    qc.cz(0, 1)                     # Phase flip on |11>
    return qc
# --- Diffusion Operator ---
def diffusion_operator(n):
    qc = QuantumCircuit(n)
    qc.h(range(n))
    qc.x(range(n))
    qc.h(n - 1)
    qc.mcx(list(range(n - 1)), n - 1)  # Multi-controlled Z gate
    qc.h(n - 1)
    qc.x(range(n))
    qc.h(range(n))
    return qc
# --- Grover's Algorithm Circuit ---
def grover_algorithm(n, iterations=1):
    qc = QuantumCircuit(n, n)
    qc.h(range(n))                  # Step 1: Initialization
    oracle = grover_oracle(n)
```

```
    diffusion = diffusion_operator(n)
    for _ in range(iterations):
        qc.compose(oracle, inplace=True)
        qc.compose(diffusion, inplace=True)
    qc.measure(range(n), range(n))
    return qc
# --- Execution ---
backend = Aer.get_backend('qasm_simulator')
qc = grover_algorithm(2, iterations=1)
result = execute(qc, backend, shots=1024).result()
print(result.get_counts())
```

Expected output: A sharp probability peak appears at **11**, confirming that Grover's algorithm amplifies the amplitude of the marked state, allowing it to be found with high probability after just one iteration.

Implementation in Python using Cirq

The following implementation demonstrates Grover's search algorithm using Cirq, following the same amplitude amplification principle as in Qiskit. Here, the oracle flips the phase of the target state |11⟩, and the diffusion operator amplifies its amplitude to make it the most probable outcome upon measurement:

```
import cirq
# --- Oracle Definition ---
def grover_oracle_cirq(q0, q1):
    return [cirq.CZ(q0, q1)]          # Phase flip on |11>
# --- Diffusion Operator ---
def diffusion_operator_cirq(qubits):
    circuit = cirq.Circuit()
    circuit.append([cirq.H.on_each(*qubits), cirq.X.on_each(*qubits)])
    circuit.append(cirq.H(qubits[-1]))
    circuit.append(cirq.CZ(qubits[0], qubits[1]))
    circuit.append(cirq.H(qubits[-1]))
    circuit.append([cirq.X.on_each(*qubits), cirq.H.on_each(*qubits)])
    return circuit
# --- Grover's Algorithm Circuit ---
def grover_circuit():
    q0, q1 = cirq.LineQubit.range(2)
    circuit = cirq.Circuit()
    circuit.append(cirq.H.on_each(q0, q1))                # Step 1: Initialization
    circuit.append(grover_oracle_cirq(q0, q1))            # Step 2: Oracle phase inversion
    circuit += diffusion_operator_cirq([q0, q1])          # Step 3: Diffusion step
    circuit.append(cirq.measure(q0, q1, key='result'))    # Step 4: Measurement
    return circuit
# --- Simulation and Output ---
sim = cirq.Simulator()
circuit = grover_circuit()
print(circuit)
result = sim.run(circuit, repetitions=20)
print("Results:", result)
```

Interpretation: Both Qiskit and Cirq implementations demonstrate the same underlying phenomenon: the measurement histogram shows a pronounced peak for the marked state |11⟩. This confirms that Grover's algorithm successfully amplifies the probability amplitude of the correct result through iterative interference, achieving the expected quadratic speedup.

Shor's factoring algorithm

Among all quantum algorithms developed to date, Shor's algorithm remains the most transformative and consequential. Proposed by *Peter Shor* in 1994, it offers an exponential speedup over the best classical algorithms for integer factorization, a problem that underpins modern cryptographic systems such as **Rivest-Shamir-Adleman** (**RSA**). Classical factoring algorithms operate in sub-exponential time, which makes large cryptographic key sizes (e.g., 2048-bit RSA keys) practically secure against brute-force attacks.

In contrast, Shor's quantum algorithm can find the prime factors of an n-bit integer in polynomial time, drastically lowering the computational barrier that ensures cryptographic safety today. The significance of Shor's algorithm extends far beyond cryptography: it provided the first definitive proof that quantum computation can outperform all known classical methods on a problem of genuine real-world importance, thereby igniting global interest in the development of large-scale quantum computers.

Problem statement

Given a positive integer N, the goal is to determine its non-trivial prime factors.

Classically, this requires trial division or advanced number-theoretic techniques such as the **general number field sieve** (**GNFS**), both of which demand super-polynomial time as N grows larger.

The challenge can be stated as:

$$\text{Find } p,q \text{ such that } N=p\times q, 1<p, q<N.$$

While classical methods become infeasible for large values of N, Shor's algorithm revolutionizes the approach by transforming the factoring problem into one of period-finding—a task that can be solved exponentially faster on a quantum computer using the QFT.

Algorithmic principle

The power of Shor's algorithm arises from a profound property of modular arithmetic—its inherent periodicity, which quantum computation can exploit efficiently.

1. **Random selection**: Choose a random integer $a<N$ such that $\gcd(a,N)=1$.

   This ensures that a and N are coprime, forming the basis for the periodic structure leveraged by the algorithm.

2. **Period-finding**: Define the modular function:

   $$f(x)=a^x \bmod N.$$

   The function f(x) is periodic with period r, satisfying:

   $$f(x)=f(x+r).$$

   The task is to determine this unknown period r.

3. **Quantum step**: Construct a quantum circuit that computes $f(x)$ in superposition. By applying the QFT to the quantum register, the periodicity r is efficiently extracted from interference patterns in the amplitude distribution.

4. **Classical step**: Once the period r is known, compute the following to obtain non-trivial factors of N:

   $$p=\gcd(a^{r/2}-1,N), q=\gcd(a^{r/2}+1,N).$$

These typically yield the prime factors p and q.

The quantum subroutine, the period-finding stage, is what provides Shor's exponential advantage. While the classical components (random selection and **greatest common divisor** (**GCD**) computation) remain efficient but traditional, the quantum discovery of the period r transforms the factoring challenge from a super-polynomial to a polynomial time problem.

High-level flow of the algorithm

The high-level structure of Shor's algorithm integrates classical number theory with quantum period-finding. Each stage of the process converts the arithmetic problem of integer factorization into a period-detection problem, which the quantum subroutine solves exponentially faster:

Stage	Operation	Purpose
1	Randomly choose $a<N$	Initialize a coprime base a by ensuring gcd(a,N)=1.
2	Prepare superposition of inputs	Enable quantum parallel evaluation of $f(x)$.
3	Compute a^x mod N using controlled modular exponentiation	Encode the periodic structure of $f(x)$ into quantum states.
4	Apply QFT	Extract the frequency component corresponding to the period r.
5	Measure and estimate r	Convert the quantum interference pattern into measurable classical data.
6	Compute gcd($a^{r/2}\pm1$,N)	Obtain the non-trivial factors of N.

***Table 4.4**: Step-by-step high-level operations of Shor's factoring algorithm*

Circuit design

The quantum circuit for Shor's algorithm implements the crucial period-finding subroutine that underpins the factoring process. It consists of two main quantum registers: a control register for encoding the input powers of two, and a work register for computing modular exponentiation. After the modular arithmetic operation, a QFT is applied to the control register to extract the period from the phase information.

Conceptual circuit of Shor's algorithm: Conceptual layout of Shor's algorithm circuit:

```
|0> —H———————•——————————┐
             |          |
|0> —H———————•——————————┤
  ⋮          |          |  (n control qubits)
|0> —H———————•——————————┤
|1> ————————U^(2^k)—————┤  (modular exponentiation register)
              |
|0> ——————————┴—————————M
```

The control register encodes powers of two, while controlled modular-exponentiation gates apply $a^{2^k} mod N$ to the work register. A QFT on the control register reveals the period r of the modular function.

The primary components and their roles are summarized in the following table:

Component	Quantum operation	Role
Control register	Hadamard gates + QFT	Encodes phase information to reveal the period.
Work register	Controlled modular exponentiation	Implements a^xmodN for all x in superposition.

Measurement	State collapse + classical post-processing	Extracts the period r, enabling computation of the factors of N.

Table 4.5: Major components and their roles in Shor's algorithm circuit

Conceptual intuition

The operational sequence of Shor's algorithm can be intuitively understood as follows:

1. **Superposition preparation**: The first n qubits form a uniform superposition over all possible input values x, creating the basis for parallel quantum evaluation.
2. **Controlled modular exponentiation:** Each state $|x\rangle$ in the control register is entangled with the corresponding $|f(x)\rangle=|a^x \bmod N\rangle$** in the work register**, encoding the periodic function into the quantum system.
3. **QFT**: Applying the QFT to the control register converts the hidden periodicity of $f(x)$ into frequency domain information—visible as sharp peaks in the measurement distribution.
4. **Measurement and classical post-processing**: The measured value from the control register, when analysed classically using the continued-fraction expansion, yields an estimate of the period r.
5. **Factor extraction**: The period r is then used in classical computation to evaluate:

$$p=\gcd(a^{r/2}-1,N),q=\gcd(a^{r/2}+1,N),$$

Thereby revealing the prime factors of N.

The quantum magic occurs during the QFT step, where the system transforms hidden periodicity into observable interference patterns, allowing the period to emerge naturally from quantum superposition and measurement.

Implementation in Python using Qiskit

Qiskit provides a ready-to-use implementation of Shor's algorithm in its `algorithm's` module, allowing users to experiment with small composite numbers and study the complete factoring workflow. The following is a simplified demonstration of the factors N=15, revealing its prime factors:

```
from qiskit import Aer
from qiskit.algorithms import Shor
from qiskit.utils import QuantumInstance
# --- Backend and Quantum Instance Setup ---
backend = Aer.get_backend('aer_simulator')
qi = QuantumInstance(backend)
# --- Run Shor's Algorithm ---
shor = Shor()
result = shor.factorize(15)
# --- Display Results ---
print("Factors of 15:", result.factors)
```

Expected output:

```
Factors of 15: [[3, 5]]
```

This small-scale simulation captures the essential workflow of Shor's algorithm, from initializing the quantum instance and running the period-finding subroutine to extracting the classical factors. While this example uses $N=15$ for illustration, factoring large numbers (such as RSA-2048) would require thousands of high-fidelity qubits and extremely low error rates, well beyond the reach of today's quantum hardware.

Implementation in Python using Cirq

Unlike Qiskit, Cirq does not include a built-in implementation of Shor's algorithm.

However, its flexible circuit framework allows developers to construct modular components, such as controlled modular exponentiation and the QFT, manually. The following minimal demonstration outlines the basic structure of a Shor-like circuit in Cirq:

```
import cirq
import numpy as np
# --- Placeholder for Modular Exponentiation ---
def modular_exp(a, N, exponent):
    # Classical computation for demonstration purposes
    return pow(a, exponent, N)
# --- Simplified Shor Demonstration ---
def shor_demo(N=15, a=7):
    q0, q1, q2 = cirq.LineQubit.range(3)
    circuit = cirq.Circuit()

    # Step 1: Initialize and create superposition
    circuit.append([cirq.H.on_each(q0, q1)])

    # Step 2: Placeholder for modular exponentiation and QFT
    # (To be replaced with controlled-U and QFT blocks in a full implementation)

    # Step 3: Measurement
    circuit.append(cirq.measure(q0, q1, key='result'))

    print("\nSimplified Cirq demonstration:\n", circuit)
# --- Execute Demonstration ---
shor_demo()
```

Interpretation: This simplified structure highlights the core architecture of Shor's algorithm: a superposition preparation, a modular arithmetic operation, and Fourier analysis. In practical implementations, Cirq users typically integrate custom QFT and controlled modular exponentiation routines to simulate the full Shor's algorithm. Although this example omits the full modular arithmetic and phase estimation steps, it captures the conceptual layout of Shor's quantum period-finding workflow.

Quantum Fourier transform and phase estimation

The QFT stands as one of the most fundamental and elegant constructs in quantum computation. It serves as the quantum analogue of the classical **discrete Fourier transform** (**DFT**), but is implemented as a unitary transformation acting on the amplitudes of quantum states.

The QFT forms the mathematical backbone for many advanced quantum algorithms, most notably Shor's factoring algorithm, phase estimation, and quantum signal processing. While the classical Fourier transform operates on vectors of numerical values, the QFT acts directly on superpositions of quantum basis states, transforming periodicity in amplitudes into phase information that can be revealed through measurement.

Mathematical foundation

For an n-qubit register, the QFT is defined as:

$$\text{QFT}: |x\rangle \longrightarrow \frac{1}{\sqrt{2^n}} \sum_{y=0}^{2^n-1} e^{2\pi i xy/2^n} |y\rangle.$$

This transformation maps each computational basis state $|x\rangle$ to a superposition of all possible basis states $|y\rangle$, each weighted by a complex phase factor $e^{2\pi ixy/2^n}$.

Conceptually, the QFT converts periodic patterns in amplitude space into phase information, the same mathematical relationship that the classical Fourier transform exploits in signal analysis.

In practice, the QFT can be implemented efficiently on a quantum computer using a cascade of Hadamard gates and controlled-phase rotation gates, achieving a circuit complexity of $O(n^2)$—an exponential improvement over the classical DFT's $O(N^2)$ runtime, where $N=2^n$.

Circuit structure

The QFT can be implemented using a compact, elegant circuit composed of Hadamard and controlled-phase rotation gates. Each rotation gate R_k applies a phase shift of $2\pi/2^k$ radians, and the circuit concludes with a SWAP network to reverse the qubit order, aligning the output with binary significance.

QFT circuit: Conceptual layout of the QFT circuit:

```
|x0> —H———R2———R3——————————————┐
          |     |              |
|x1> —————+—————H————R2————————┤
                |    |         |
|x2> ———————————+————H—————————┘
                             SWAP
```

Each R_k is a controlled-phase rotation gate with angle $2\pi/2^k$. The final SWAP layer reverses the bit order to match the binary output alignment.

The primary operations of the QFT are summarized in the following table:

Step	Operation	Purpose
1	Apply Hadamard on the most significant qubit	Creates an equal superposition of basis states.
2	Apply controlled-phase rotations $R_2, R_3, \ldots$	Introduces progressive phase shifts between qubits.
3	Repeat on the remaining qubits	Accumulates interference patterns representing Fourier phases.
4	Apply the SWAP network	Reverses qubit order to produce correctly aligned output.

***Table 4.6:** Sequential operations in the QFT circuit*

This recursive pattern allows the QFT to scale efficiently with only $O(n^2)$ gate complexity, enabling large-register transforms to be executed in polynomial time—a crucial advantage in algorithms such as Shor's factoring and QPE.

Phase estimation concept and connection

The QPE algorithm is one of the most profound and versatile applications of the QFT. It provides a powerful method to estimate the phase ϕ in the eigenvalue equation of a unitary operator U:

$$U|\psi\rangle = e^{2\pi i\phi}|\psi\rangle.$$

Here, $|\psi\rangle$ is an *eigenstate* of the unitary operator U, and the goal of the algorithm is to determine the corresponding eigenphase ϕ with high precision.

The QPE circuit utilizes an ancillary (control) register and a target register. The control register is prepared in a superposition of all possible computational basis states, enabling parallel phase sampling, while the target register stores the eigenstate $|\psi\rangle$. By applying a sequence of controlled powers of U (namely U^{2^k}) to the target register, the phase information becomes encoded as relative phase shifts across the control qubits. Finally, an inverse QFT^{-1} is applied to the control register, transforming the accumulated phase information into a binary-encoded approximation of ϕ, which is then measured.

The sequence of operations in QPE follows a structured interplay between superposition, controlled unitary evolution, and the inverse QFT. Each stage systematically transforms hidden phase information into a measurable binary output, as summarized in the following table:

Stage	Operation	Purpose
1	Initialize the control register in superposition	Encodes all possible phase samples simultaneously.
2	Apply controlled-U^{2^k} operations	Accumulates phase rotations proportional to $2^k \phi$.
3	Perform inverse QFT on the control register	Converts phase information into measurable bitstring form.
4	Measure the control register	Produces a binary approximation of the phase ϕ.

***Table 4.7**: Stepwise operations of the QPE algorithm*

The QPE technique lies at the heart of many advanced quantum algorithms. It enables the determination of eigenvalues, periodicities, and amplitudes, making it indispensable in fields such as quantum simulation, quantum chemistry, and amplitude estimation. Through its intrinsic connection with the QFT, the QPE effectively transforms hidden phase rotations into observable interference patterns, allowing the elusive phase ϕ to emerge clearly through measurement.

Implementation in Python using Qiskit

The following program manually constructs a three-qubit QFT using Hadamard and controlled-phase rotations, then simulates the resulting state-vector.

This mirrors the structure of Qiskit's built-in `QFT` circuit, helping readers understand the gate-level composition:

```
from qiskit import QuantumCircuit, Aer, execute
from qiskit.circuit.library import QFT
import numpy as np
# --- Manual 3-Qubit QFT Construction ---
qc = QuantumCircuit(3)
# Qubit 0 (MSB in this diagram)
qc.h(0)
qc.cp(np.pi/2, 1, 0)   # R2 on (control=1, target=0)
qc.cp(np.pi/4, 2, 0)   # R3 on (control=2, target=0)
# Qubit 1
qc.h(1)
qc.cp(np.pi/2, 2, 1)   # R2 on (control=2, target=1)
# Qubit 2
qc.h(2)
# Bit reversal to match canonical QFT output order
qc.swap(0, 2)
print(qc.draw())
```

```
# --- Simulation ---
backend = Aer.get_backend('statevector_simulator')
result = execute(qc, backend).result()
state = result.get_statevector()
print("Statevector after QFT:\n", state)
# --- (Optional) Compare with the built-in QFT circuit ---
qft_builtin = QFT(num_qubits=3, do_swaps=True, approximation_degree=0)
print("\nBuilt-in QFT(3) circuit:\n", qft_builtin)
```

Interpretation:

- The sequence H + controlled-Rk gates realizes the exact QFT pattern; the final SWAP performs bit reversal so the output aligns with binary significance.
- The printed state-vector shows the Fourier-transformed amplitudes of the initial computational basis state ($|000\rangle$ here).
- The built-in `QFT` (`3`) (shown at the end) implements the same unitary more compactly and can be inverted with `inverse()` when needed.

Note: **In practical algorithms (e.g., phase estimation), you will use inverse QFT (`QFT(...).inverse()`) on the control register to decode accumulated phases into a binary approximation of ϕ .**

Implementation in Python using Cirq

Just like in Qiskit, the QFT can be implemented in Cirq using Hadamard and controlled-phase operations. Although Cirq does not include a built-in QFT class, it provides the flexibility to build the transformation gate-by-gate. The following example demonstrates a three-qubit QFT circuit constructed using controlled-Z rotations and SWAP gates for bit reversal:

```
import cirq
import numpy as np
# --- Define the QFT circuit ---
def qft_circuit(qubits):
    circuit = cirq.Circuit()
    n = len(qubits)
    for i in range(n):
        circuit.append(cirq.H(qubits[i]))
        for j in range(i + 1, n):
            angle = np.pi / (2 ** (j - i))
            circuit.append(cirq.CZPowGate(exponent=angle / np.pi)(qubits[j], qubits[i]))
    # Final SWAP operations for bit reversal
    circuit.append([cirq.SWAP(qubits[i], qubits[n - i - 1]) for i in range(n // 2)])
    return circuit
# --- Construct and display the circuit ---
qbs = cirq.LineQubit.range(3)
circuit = qft_circuit(qbs)
print(circuit)
```

Interpretation:

- Each Hadamard gate creates a superposition on the corresponding qubit.
- The controlled-*Z* rotations apply phase shifts of $\pi/2^k$, introducing the Fourier interference structure.
- The final SWAP network reverses qubit ordering to match binary output alignment.

This Cirq implementation follows the same logical pattern as Qiskit's version, reinforcing that the QFT is a platform-independent concept grounded in the same mathematical principles. Developers can extend this foundation to build higher-order QFTs or integrate them into algorithms such as QPE and Shor's factoring algorithm.

Conclusion

This chapter explored the foundational quantum algorithms that showcase the true potential of quantum computation. Beginning with the Deutsch and Deutsch–Jozsa algorithms, we observed how quantum systems can identify global properties of functions using only a single oracle query. The Grover algorithm demonstrated amplitude amplification as a powerful tool for accelerating unstructured searches, while Shor's algorithm revealed how quantum period-finding can revolutionize integer factorization and challenge classical cryptography. The QFT and QPE were introduced as core mathematical frameworks enabling many advanced quantum algorithms. Through detailed explanations and hands-on implementations in Qiskit and Cirq, readers connected theory to practical simulation. Together, these algorithms form the cornerstone of quantum computing, illustrating how quantum mechanics transforms computational limits and laying a strong foundation for future exploration into quantum optimization, cryptography, and simulation. Building on the algorithmic foundations developed in this chapter, *Chapter 5, Quantum Hardware and Noise,* shifts the focus from abstract algorithms to real quantum hardware, examining how physical constraints, noise, and imperfections influence the execution of quantum algorithms on practical devices.

Questions

1. **What are quantum algorithms, and why are they significant?**

   Answer: Quantum algorithms are computational procedures that leverage principles like superposition, entanglement, and interference to solve problems faster than classical methods. Their significance lies in demonstrating quantum advantage, where specific tasks—such as database search or factorization—can be performed exponentially or quadratically faster, redefining computational possibilities.

2. **What does the Deutsch algorithm demonstrate?**

   Answer: The Deutsch algorithm is the first to show that a quantum computer can outperform a classical one, determining whether a function is constant or balanced using a single oracle query. It illustrates quantum parallelism, in which a function can be evaluated for multiple inputs simultaneously via superposition.

3. **How does the Deutsch–Jozsa algorithm extend the Deutsch algorithm?**

   Answer: The Deutsch–Jozsa algorithm generalizes the concept to an n-bit function, identifying whether it is constant or balanced with just one quantum query, while classical methods may require exponentially many. It marks the first theoretical proof of exponential quantum speedup.

4. **What makes Grover's search algorithm important?**

   Answer: Grover's algorithm provides a quadratic speedup for searching an unsorted database of N items, reducing the search time from $O(N)$ to $O(\sqrt{N})$. Its core mechanism, amplitude amplification, has broader applications in optimization, pattern recognition, and **quantum machine learning** (**QML**).

5. **Why is Shor's algorithm considered revolutionary?**

   Answer: Shor's algorithm can factor large integers in polynomial time, a task that classical algorithms handle only in super-polynomial time. This threatens modern cryptographic systems such as RSA, providing a compelling case for the real-world impact of quantum computation.

6. **What is the QFT, and why is it essential?**

   Answer: The QFT is the quantum analogue of the DFT. It efficiently transforms quantum states from the time domain to the frequency domain, uncovering hidden periodicities. It is the mathematical foundation for many algorithms, including Shor's and phase estimation.

7. **How does QPE relate to the QFT?**

   Answer: The QPE algorithm uses the inverse QFT to extract phase information from a unitary operator's eigenstate. It allows for precise eigenvalue estimation, forming the basis for advanced applications in quantum chemistry, simulation, and amplitude estimation.

8. **How are these algorithms implemented using Qiskit and Cirq?**

   Answer: Both Qiskit (IBM) and Cirq (Google) provide Python-based frameworks for constructing and simulating quantum circuits. While Qiskit offers built-in algorithms like Shor and Grover, Cirq emphasizes flexible, low-level circuit design—enabling users to implement the same logic across platforms.

9. **What practical insights do these implementations provide?**

   Answer: Hands-on implementations help readers visualize circuit behavior, simulate measurement outcomes, and observe how interference patterns produce computational advantages. They bridge the gap between mathematical theory and executable quantum programs.

10. **What foundational skills does this chapter develop for learners?**

    Answer: This chapter equips readers to understand, construct, and simulate key quantum algorithms; interpret their measurement results; and recognize how these algorithms form the core of modern quantum applications, from cryptography to optimization and quantum simulation.

Exercises

1. Implement the Deutsch algorithm in Qiskit using a two-qubit circuit. Create both a constant oracle (f(x)=0) and a balanced oracle (f(x)=x). Run the circuit on the QASM simulator and verify that the output is '0' for the constant case and '1' for the balanced case.
2. Extend the Deutsch–Jozsa algorithm to three input qubits in Qiskit. Implement both constant and balanced oracles, execute the program, and confirm that the circuit correctly distinguishes the two types of functions with a single oracle query.
3. Construct Grover's search algorithm in Qiskit for a two-qubit database where the marked state is $|11\rangle$. Run the circuit on the simulator, plot the histogram, and explain how amplitude amplification produces a sharp peak for the target state.
4. Recreate the same Grover algorithm using Cirq. Compare the circuit diagram, syntax, and simulation results with the Qiskit version, highlighting how both frameworks achieve identical logical behavior.
5. Run Shor's factoring algorithm in Qiskit using the built-in Shor() function to factor N = 15. Verify that the output yields the prime factors [3, 5] and explain the role of the period-finding subroutine in the process.
6. Manually construct a three-qubit QFT circuit in Qiskit using Hadamard and controlled-phase gates. Print the ASCII diagram and describe how each rotation introduces the Fourier interference pattern.
7. Implement the same three-qubit QFT circuit in Cirq using controlled-Z rotation gates and a final SWAP network. Compare the structure and verify that both implementations yield equivalent transformations.
8. Design and simulate a simplified QPE circuit in Qiskit for a known unitary operator (for example, a phase rotation). Observe how the inverse QFT converts phase information into a measurable bitstring.
9. Compare the number of oracle calls required in classical vs. quantum versions of the Deutsch–Jozsa and Grover algorithms. Discuss how superposition and interference contribute to computational speedup.
10. Write a short reflection explaining how the algorithms studied in this chapter, Deutsch, Deutsch–Jozsa, Grover, Shor, QFT, and QPE, illustrate the fundamental principles of quantum advantage and form the basis for advanced quantum applications.

CHAPTER 5
Quantum Hardware and Noise

Introduction

Quantum computing has evolved from a theoretical curiosity into a rapidly advancing experimental science, one that now operates on real, physical hardware. As researchers push the boundaries of what qubits can do, the focus of learning and development has shifted from pure mathematics to tangible systems that can be programmed, measured, and optimized. However, these devices are not perfect. Every real qubit exists within the constraints of nature, susceptible to noise, environmental disturbance, and loss of coherence.

This chapter explores the hardware reality behind quantum computing. It examines how qubits are physically implemented using superconducting circuits, trapped ions, and photons, each approach reflecting a different balance between speed, stability, and scalability. From there, the discussion moves to the sources of decoherence and noise, the central challenges that limit quantum performance.

To bridge theory and practice, readers will learn to simulate noise models and apply error mitigation techniques using frameworks such as Qiskit and Cirq, gaining insight into how quantum systems behave under realistic conditions. The chapter concludes with an introduction to **quantum error correction** (**QEC**) and **noisy intermediate-scale quantum** (**NISQ**) devices, highlighting how researchers extract reliable computation from imperfect machines.

By the end of this chapter, you will understand not only how quantum hardware functions, but also why it struggles, and how engineers and scientists are overcoming these limitations through noise modeling, mitigation, and emerging fault-tolerant architectures.

Structure

The chapter covers the following topics:

- Physical implementations of superconducting qubits, ion traps, and photonics
- Sources of decoherence and noise
- Error mitigation basics
- Quantum error correction concepts
- Simulating noise models with Qiskit and Cirq
- Working with NISQ devices

Objectives

This chapter aims to equip readers with a practical, hardware-aware understanding of how real quantum computers operate, and why they exhibit errors. Learners will explore the major physical implementations of qubits (superconducting circuits, trapped ions, and photonics) and relate their distinct control methods to measurable noise and decoherence processes. They will learn to quantify device performance using fidelity, error rates, and coherence times (T_1, T_2), and to simulate realistic noise models in both Qiskit and Cirq (e.g., depolarizing, amplitude/phase damping, and readout noise). Through guided exercises, readers will apply error mitigation techniques such as readout calibration, **zero-noise extrapolation** (ZNE), dynamical decoupling, and gain a conceptual grasp of QEC (bit-flip/phase-flip codes, Shor's code, and the intuition behind surface codes and fault-tolerance). They will also practice working with NISQ devices: inspecting backend calibration data, mapping circuits to coupling graphs, optimizing depth via transpilation, and interpreting noisy hardware results against ideal simulations. By the end of the chapter, readers will be able to design experiments under realistic constraints, model and mitigate noise, and reason about the pathway from today's NISQ processors to tomorrow's fault-tolerant architectures.

Physical implementations of superconducting qubits, ion traps, and photonics

The transition from abstract qubits on paper to real qubits in hardware is one of the most remarkable achievements of modern physics and engineering. A physical implementation is the medium through which quantum states are created, manipulated, and measured. The challenge is immense; qubits must be sufficiently isolated to preserve quantum behavior while still being accessible for control and readout.

Over the past two decades, several approaches have emerged, each based on a different physical system capable of exhibiting quantum coherence. Among them, superconducting qubits, ion traps, and photonic qubits have evolved into the dominant hardware platforms. Though they share the same theoretical foundation, their practical realization, control mechanisms, and performance characteristics differ significantly.

Superconducting qubits

Superconducting qubits are artificial atoms fabricated on silicon chips using superconducting materials such as niobium or aluminum. The key component in these devices is the **Josephson junction**, a nonlinear circuit element that creates discrete quantum energy levels. The two lowest levels represent the computational basis states $|0\rangle$ and $|1\rangle$.

To better understand their practical relevance, superconducting qubits can be examined in terms of their operating principle, advantages, challenges, and real-world implementations, as outlined:

- **Operating principle**: Quantum operations are performed using microwave pulses that drive transitions between these energy levels. By precisely tuning the pulse amplitude, frequency, and phase, one can implement arbitrary single-qubit rotations and multi-qubit entangling gates. Measurement is achieved through coupled resonators that detect subtle changes in the circuit's electromagnetic response.
- **Advantages**: Superconducting qubits are fast, typically executing gates within 10s of nanoseconds, and benefit from scalable microfabrication techniques compatible with modern semiconductor processes. They form the foundation of today's most accessible quantum processors.
- **Challenges**: Extreme cooling requirements are a major limitation. These circuits operate at temperatures near 15 millikelvin to maintain superconductivity and minimize thermal noise. Coherence times, while improving, remain in the microsecond range, limiting the depth of executable circuits.
- **Examples and industry use**: *IBM* Eagle and Condor *chips*, *Google* Sycamore processor, and *Rigetti* Aspen family are prominent examples. These systems have enabled demonstrations of quantum advantage and serve as platforms for algorithm development and noise characterization.

Ion trap qubits

Ion trap quantum computers take a fundamentally different approach. Instead of artificial atoms, they use naturally occurring ions, atoms that have lost one or more electrons, as qubits. Each ion is confined in free space by oscillating electric fields within an ultra-high vacuum chamber. The ion's internal electronic states form the qubit basis states.

To provide a clear and systematic understanding, ion trap qubits can be analyzed in terms of their operating principle, advantages, challenges, and representative industry implementations, as summarized:

- **Operating principle**: Precise laser pulses manipulate these ions, driving transitions between internal states to perform single-qubit gates. Coupling ions realize two-qubit gates through their shared vibrational modes; the quantum mechanical motion of the ions within the trap acts as a communication channel. Measurement is performed optically by detecting the ion's fluorescence.
- **Advantages**: Ion traps offer exceptionally long coherence times, often measured in seconds, and gate fidelities exceeding 99% because all ions of a given species are identical, the system exhibits uniform behavior across qubits, simplifying calibration.
- **Challenges**: The system's complexity increases rapidly with scale. Maintaining precise laser alignment and synchronization across many ions is difficult, and gate operations are slower, typically in the microsecond-to-millisecond range, than in superconducting systems.
- **Examples and industry use**: Organizations such as *IonQ* and *Quantinuum* have developed commercial trapped ion systems that deliver state-of-the-art accuracy. Their devices are frequently used in high-fidelity demonstrations of quantum algorithms and error mitigation techniques.

Photonic qubits

Photonic qubits use light as the medium for quantum information. In these systems, qubits are encoded in the polarization, phase, or path of single photons because photons interact very weakly with their surroundings, they exhibit extremely low decoherence, making them ideal for quantum communication and distributed processing.

For a structured comparison with other hardware platforms, photonic qubits can be discussed in terms of their operating principle, advantages, challenges, and representative industrial implementations, as outlined:

- **Operating principle**: Single photon sources generate qubits that are routed through beam splitters, interferometers, and phase shifters to perform quantum operations. Measurement is performed using photon detectors that record whether a photon arrives in a specific mode. Unlike other platforms, photonic qubits can be generated, manipulated, and transmitted at room temperature.
- **Advantages**: Photonic systems offer unmatched resilience to environmental noise and can be seamlessly integrated with optical fiber networks, paving the way for quantum internet infrastructure. They are particularly well-suited for measurement-based or cluster-state quantum computing architectures.
- **Challenges**: The weak interaction between photons makes implementing deterministic two-qubit gates difficult. Optical losses, imperfect detectors, and probabilistic entanglement generation remain major barriers to large-scale computation.
- **Examples and industry use**: Companies like *Xanadu* and *PsiQuantum* are at the forefront of photonic quantum computing. Xanadu's *Borealis* platform utilizes continuous variable photonic states to perform Gaussian boson sampling, a key step toward scalable optical quantum processors.

Comparative overview

Each major hardware platform embodies a different balance of speed, coherence, and scalability. While superconducting qubits dominate short-term commercial deployments, ion traps excel in precision, and photonics promises global connectivity. Their coexistence reflects the richness of the quantum hardware landscape.

The following table summarizes the strengths and limitations of the three leading qubit implementations, namely, superconducting, ion trap, and photonic, that currently shape the trajectory of quantum hardware development:

Platform	Physical medium	Typical coherence time	Gate speed	Primary strengths	Key limitations	Representative systems
Superconducting qubits	Electrical circuits at millikelvin temperatures	10-100 μs	~10 ns	Fast gates, scalable fabrication	Requires cryogenic cooling, short coherence	IBM, Google, Rigetti
Trapped ions	Atomic ions in electromagnetic traps	1–10 s	μs-ms	Long coherence, high fidelity	Slow gates, complex optics	IonQ, Quantinuum
Photonic qubits	Single photons in optical circuits	Practically unlimited	ps–ns	Room-temperature operation, minimal decoherence	Probabilistic gates, photon loss	Xanadu, PsiQuantum

***Table 5.1**: Comparative overview of leading quantum hardware platforms*

The diversity of quantum hardware reflects the multiplicity of paths toward the same destination, scalable quantum computation. No single technology currently satisfies all desired properties, and future systems will likely adopt hybrid architectures that combine the fast logic of superconducting qubits, the precision of trapped ions, and the communication advantages of photons.

Sources of decoherence and noise

Quantum computers rely on the fragile coherence of qubits, the property that allows them to exist in superposition and entanglement. However, in the real-world, every qubit interacts, however slightly, with its surrounding environment. These interactions cause decoherence, the gradual loss of quantum information, and introduce noise, which manifests as random fluctuations or errors during operations. Understanding these effects is essential for anyone who wishes to design or simulate realistic quantum systems.

In practice, noise limits both the lifetime of quantum states and the fidelity of quantum gates. Even with advanced shielding and cooling, no qubit can remain perfectly isolated. The study of decoherence and noise, therefore, defines the boundary between theoretical perfection and experimental reality in quantum computing.

Decoherence and the loss of quantum information

Decoherence refers to the process by which a quantum system gradually loses its ability to maintain superposition due to unwanted interactions with its environment. When this occurs, the system begins to behave more classically, erasing the quantum advantage.

Key mechanisms

The two most critical processes governing this decay are outlined as follows:

- **Energy relaxation (T_1)**: The qubit spontaneously releases energy, transitioning from the excited state $|1\rangle$ to the ground state $|0\rangle$. This process defines the relaxation time T_1, after which the qubit's energy state effectively resets.
- **Dephasing (T_2)**: Even if the energy levels remain stable, random fluctuations in the qubit's phase destroy the delicate interference patterns essential for computation. The dephasing time T_2 is typically shorter than T_1, thereby setting an upper limit on the duration of coherent operations.

Illustrative example

A superconducting qubit initially prepared in an equal superposition gradually drifts toward the ground state as its phase information disperses. After a few microseconds, the system no longer exhibits quantum interference, and measurement outcomes become purely random.

Operational noise

Even in the absence of environmental interference, imperfections in control and measurement introduce additional errors. These operational errors arise during the manipulation or observation of qubits.

Common sources

The principal sources of such operational errors are outlined as follows:

- **Gate errors**: Microwave or laser pulses may slightly deviate in timing or amplitude, producing imperfect rotations on the Bloch sphere.
- **Crosstalk**: Operations targeting one qubit inadvertently affect neighboring qubits, especially in dense arrays.
- **Measurement errors**: Readout mechanisms can misidentify a qubit's state, for example, recording $|1\rangle$ when the actual state was $|0\rangle$.
- **Leakage**: The qubit unintentionally transitions to higher-energy levels outside the computational subspace, invalidating the circuit's logic.

Operational noise accumulates as circuits grow deeper, limiting the complexity of algorithms that can be executed reliably on today's NISQ devices.

Environmental disturbances

Even with precise engineering, the external environment imposes subtle yet persistent disturbances. These external noise sources are often stochastic and difficult to eliminate completely.

Major contributors

The most significant environmental factors affecting quantum stability are summarized as follows:

- **Thermal fluctuations**: Residual heat introduces random energy exchanges that disturb qubit states.
- **Magnetic and electric field variations**: Stray fields shift energy levels and cause unwanted phase rotations.
- **Vibrational and acoustic noise**: Mechanical vibrations, especially in ion traps, alter trapping potential and detune resonances.
- **Cosmic rays and radiation**: High-energy particles can induce transient voltage spikes or flip qubit states, particularly in superconducting systems.

To counter these effects, laboratories employ cryogenic environments, electromagnetic shielding, and vibration isolation systems, yet absolute isolation remains physically impossible.

Quantifying noise in practice

To evaluate and compare the performance of quantum devices, researchers rely on quantitative metrics that describe how accurately qubits maintain and process information. These measures provide insight into the quality of gates, the stability of quantum states, and the overall computational reliability of a system. The key parameters used for practical noise characterization are outlined as follows:

- **Fidelity**: Probability that a gate or measurement produces the intended result.

- **Error rate**: Complement of fidelity, representing the likelihood of an incorrect operation.
- **Coherence times (T_1, T_2)**: Determine how long a qubit can reliably store information.
- **Quantum volume (QV)**: A composite metric that considers qubit count, connectivity, and error rates to gauge practical computational capacity.

Qiskit and Cirq both provide tools for noise characterization, allowing researchers to visualize these parameters before running experiments.

Decoherence and noise together form the central obstacle to reliable quantum computation. They represent the tension between the ideal mathematical abstraction of qubits and their physical implementation in the real-world. The better we understand their causes and dynamics, the more effectively we can design systems that resist or compensate for them.

Error mitigation basics

Even though noise and decoherence are unavoidable in current quantum hardware, their detrimental effects can often be reduced or compensated for. This process is known as **error mitigation**. Unlike full QEC, which redundantly encodes information across multiple qubits, mitigation strategies focus on estimating and removing the effects of noise from the output of a computation.

Error mitigation plays a crucial role in the NISQ era, where device imperfections limit circuit depth and accuracy. Through clever statistical and calibration-based techniques, it allows researchers to extract meaningful results from imperfect hardware without the overhead of additional qubits.

Error mitigation does not eliminate errors; it models, measures, and counterbalances them to approximate the results of an ideal noise-free computation.

Rationale for error mitigation

Every quantum gate, measurement, and idle period introduces small inaccuracies that compound as circuits become more complex. In the NISQ regime, full fault-tolerant error correction is beyond reach because it demands thousands of physical qubits for each logical qubit. Error mitigation, therefore, serves as a practical compromise, a way to stretch the reliability of limited quantum resources.

The goal is to estimate how noise affects the final result, then adjust or post-process the output data to reflect the ideal quantum state better.

Common error mitigation techniques

Once the sources and effects of noise are understood, the next step is to minimize its impact on computation. While complete elimination of noise is not possible with current hardware, several error mitigation techniques have been developed to reduce its impact on quantum results. These strategies rely on calibration, statistical inference, and pulse-level control to approximate the outcomes of an ideal, noiseless circuit. The following are the most widely adopted approaches:

- **Readout error calibration**: Measurement errors occur when detectors misclassify the qubit's final state. By preparing known basis states ($|0\rangle$ and $|1\rangle$), measuring repeatedly, and recording how often each is misidentified, a confusion matrix can be constructed. This matrix is then inverted and applied to future measurement outcomes to statistically correct misreadings.
    - **Example**: If a qubit prepared in $|0\rangle$ is measured as $|1\rangle$ 3% of the time, the correction model can adjust all results accordingly to compensate for this bias.
- **ZNE**: This technique artificially increases the level of noise by stretching circuit operations (e.g., repeating gates multiple times) and observing how results degrade. By fitting these data points to a mathematical model and extrapolating backward to zero noise, one can estimate the ideal, noiseless expectation value.

- **Analogy**: Like measuring the trajectory of a falling object in different wind conditions, ZNE predicts where it would land if there were no wind at all.

- **Probabilistic error cancellation (PEC)**: It constructs an explicit noise model of the hardware and then reweighs circuit outcomes using inverse probabilities to cancel errors statistically.

  This method can theoretically recover perfect results, but at the cost of increased sampling effort and computational overhead.

- **Dynamical decoupling**: In idle periods, qubits accumulate phase errors due to slow environmental fluctuations. By applying carefully timed sequences of π-pulses, the system averages out these fluctuations, preserving coherence for longer durations.
  - **Example**: IBM Quantum's hardware automatically inserts such echo sequences to extend T_2 times between operations.

Implementing mitigation in Qiskit and Cirq

Modern quantum development frameworks simplify the study and mitigation of noise by providing built-in tools for mitigation and calibration. Both Qiskit and Cirq enable researchers to model noisy behavior, apply correction routines, and verify the improvement in output accuracy, all within a few lines of Python code.

The following examples demonstrate how these platforms implement measurement calibration and simple depolarizing noise models to evaluate the effectiveness of mitigation strategies:

- **Example in Qiskit**:

```
from qiskit import QuantumCircuit, Aer, execute
from qiskit.providers.aer.noise import NoiseModel, depolarizing_error
from qiskit.utils import algorithm_globals
from qiskit.ignis.mitigation.measurement import complete_meas_cal, CompleteMeasFitter
# Simple 1-qubit circuit
qc = QuantumCircuit(1, 1)
qc.h(0)
qc.measure(0, 0)
# Add depolarizing noise
noise_model = NoiseModel()
noise_model.add_all_qubit_quantum_error(depolarizing_error(0.02, 1), ['h'])
# Generate calibration circuits
cal_circuits, state_labels = complete_meas_cal(qr=qc.qregs[0])
backend = Aer.get_backend('qasm_simulator')
cal_results = execute(cal_circuits, backend, shots=1000).result()
meas_fitter = CompleteMeasFitter(cal_results, state_labels)
# Apply error mitigation
job = execute(qc, backend, noise_model=noise_model, shots=1000)
raw_result = job.result()
mitigated_counts = meas_fitter.filter.apply(raw_result.get_counts(qc))
print(mitigated_counts)
```

- **Example in Cirq**:

```
import cirq
q = cirq.LineQubit(0)
circuit = cirq.Circuit(cirq.H(q), cirq.measure(q))
# Add depolarize noise
noisy_circuit = circuit.with_noise(cirq.depolarize(p=0.02))
simulator = cirq.DensityMatrixSimulator()
```

```
result = simulator.run(noisy_circuit, repetitions=1000)
print(result.histogram(key='0'))
```

These examples demonstrate how measurement calibration or simple depolarizing noise models can be introduced to test the effectiveness of mitigation techniques.

Advantages and limitations

Like any practical approach, error mitigation offers clear benefits but also comes with inherent trade-offs. It serves as an effective bridge between noisy hardware and reliable computation, yet its scope remains limited by the very imperfections it seeks to correct. The key advantages and limitations of current error mitigation strategies are summarized.

Let us look at the advantages:

- Enables practical quantum computation on NISQ devices.
- Requires no additional physical qubits.
- Can be implemented at the software or post-processing level.
- Improves the accuracy of expectation values and algorithm outputs.

Let us look at the limitations:

- Not suitable for arbitrarily deep circuits; noise still accumulates.
- Statistical methods may increase computational cost.
- Effectiveness depends heavily on accurate hardware calibration.
- Cannot fully replace true error correction for scalable systems.

Error mitigation marks a pragmatic middle ground between noisy experimentation and theoretical perfection. It empowers researchers to work productively within current technological constraints while building intuition for how real devices behave. As hardware improves, these techniques will remain essential tools for calibration, validation, and benchmarking of quantum systems.

Quantum error correction concepts

While error mitigation helps reduce the impact of noise, it does not truly prevent errors from occurring. To achieve large-scale, reliable quantum computation, we must move beyond passive correction and design mechanisms that can actively detect and repair quantum errors. This is the central goal of QEC.

Unlike classical systems, where one can simply copy bits to preserve information, quantum states cannot be cloned due to the no-cloning theorem. QEC, therefore, works by encoding one logical qubit into multiple physical qubits, distributing its information redundantly so that individual errors can be identified and corrected without measuring the logical state directly.

QEC safeguards fragile quantum states by spreading their information across several physical qubits and detecting errors indirectly through carefully designed measurements.

Types of quantum errors

In classical computers, errors are typically limited to bit-flips (0 to 1 or 1 to 0). Quantum systems, however, can experience a richer set of errors because qubits exist in superposition. The three principal types are:

- **Bit-flip error (X error)**: The qubit's state flips from $|0\rangle$ to $|1\rangle$ or vice versa, analogous to a classical bit error.
- **Phase-flip error (Z error)**: The relative phase between $|0\rangle$ and $|1\rangle$ changes sign ($|+\rangle$ becomes $|-\rangle$). This has no classical counterpart and is unique to quantum systems.
- **Combined errors (Y error)**: A combination of both bit-flip and phase-flip errors, representing the most general single-qubit error.

Quantum error-correcting codes are designed to detect and correct these without collapsing the superposition state.

Three-qubit bit-flip code

The simplest example of QEC is the bit-flip code, which protects against X-type errors.

Encoding scheme

A single logical qubit $|\psi\rangle = \alpha|0\rangle + \beta|1\rangle$ is encoded as:

$$|\psi\_L\rangle=\alpha|000\rangle+\beta|111\rangle$$

Suppose one of the three-qubits flips (say, the second qubit becomes $|010\rangle$), parity measurements between qubits can identify which one was affected, without revealing α or β. The system then applies a corrective X gate to restore the original encoded state.

Conceptual summary

The three-qubit bit-flip code detects and corrects single-qubit errors by measuring parity relationships among the encoded qubits. These parity checks identify which qubit, if any, has flipped, allowing the system to apply the appropriate correction without directly observing the encoded quantum information. The following table summarizes this logic:

Error pattern	Parity check result	Correction applied
No error	(0,0)	None
Qubit 1 flipped	(1,1)	Flip qubit 1
Qubit 2 flipped	(1,0)	Flip qubit 2
Qubit 3 flipped	(0,1)	Flip qubit 3

***Table 5.2**: Error detection and correction logic*

Phase-flip and Shor's code

Phase-flip errors require a different strategy because they change the relative sign rather than the bit value. The phase-flip code mirrors the bit-flip scheme but operates in the Hadamard-transformed basis ($|+\rangle$ and $|-\rangle$ states).

To correct both bit-flip and phase-flip errors simultaneously, Shor's code combines both methods. It encodes one logical qubit into nine physical qubits, achieving protection from arbitrary single-qubit errors. Shor's approach was the first full demonstration that quantum information can be made resilient against both types of noise.

Surface codes and fault-tolerance

While small codes like Shor's are useful conceptually, scalable quantum computing requires an architecture that can be implemented physically on large arrays of qubits. The leading candidate today is the surface code.

Key principles of surface codes

The key operational principles of surface codes are outlined as follows:

- Qubits are arranged on a two-dimensional lattice.
- Each logical qubit is represented by a patch of many physical qubits.
- Stabilizer measurements detect local error syndromes using only nearest-neighbor interactions.
- Logical operations are performed by braiding or merging regions of encoded qubits.

Surface codes are attractive because they can tolerate relatively high error rates (around 1%) while remaining compatible with planar chip layouts such as superconducting qubit arrays.

Fault-tolerance

A fault-tolerant quantum computer ensures that even if errors occur during the correction process itself, they do not cascade uncontrollably. This requires designing gates, measurements, and encodings that limit error propagation.

Overheads and future directions

QEC comes at a cost. Implementing a single logical qubit may require hundreds or thousands of physical qubits, depending on the target fidelity. Researchers are therefore working on hardware-efficient codes and error-resilient algorithms that reduce this overhead.

Emerging approaches, such as bosonic codes and cat-state encodings, exploit continuous variables or special states of light to protect quantum information more compactly. Meanwhile, AI-driven optimization is being explored to adaptively tune correction parameters based on live error data from hardware.

QEC transforms the dream of reliable quantum computation into a realistic engineering goal. It demonstrates that, despite the fragility of quantum states, information can be preserved indefinitely through clever redundancy and measurement. Together with error mitigation, it forms the foundation of fault-tolerant quantum computing, a future where algorithms can run for hours or days without being destroyed by noise.

Simulating noise models with Qiskit and Cirq

Understanding noise theoretically is valuable, but experiencing its impact through simulation provides deeper intuition. In real quantum devices, each qubit and gate is associated with measurable error probabilities that influence computational outcomes. To prepare for working with such imperfect systems, quantum frameworks such as Qiskit and Cirq enable users to simulate realistic noise environments and analyze how decoherence and operational errors affect quantum circuits.

By modeling noise in software, learners can observe how fidelity deteriorates, explore mitigation techniques, and design circuits that are robust under practical constraints. This bridges the gap between ideal quantum theory and real-world experimentation.

Noise simulation enables experimentation with imperfect quantum behavior, helping researchers understand, quantify, and manage the limitations of real hardware.

Significance of noise simulation

Before running programs on real quantum hardware, it is valuable to anticipate how noise will influence circuit performance. Simulating noise allows researchers to explore error behavior in a controlled environment, providing insight into how algorithms degrade under realistic conditions. These simulations also guide the design of more robust circuits and the development of mitigation techniques. The primary purposes of noise simulation are summarized as follows:

- **Prediction**: Estimating how real devices will behave before actual execution.
- **Validation**: Comparing simulated and experimental results to understand hardware imperfections.
- **Optimization**: Designing circuits and error mitigation strategies that tolerate noise effectively.

Even simple circuits can reveal the cumulative impact of decoherence. A Bell state circuit that ideally yields a 50–50 distribution may produce skewed results under noisy conditions. By simulating such effects, developers can evaluate circuit resilience without needing constant hardware access.

Simulating noise with Qiskit

Qiskit provides the Aer simulator, which includes configurable noise models mimicking the behavior of real IBM Quantum devices. The `NoiseModel` class allows users to define and inject realistic noise sources, such as depolarization, thermal relaxation, and readout errors, into a circuit simulation.

Here is an example introducing depolarizing noise in Qiskit:

```
from qiskit import QuantumCircuit, Aer, transpile, execute
from qiskit.providers.aer.noise import NoiseModel, depolarizing_error, thermal_relaxation_error
# Step 1: Create a simple circuit
qc = QuantumCircuit(2)
qc.h(0)
qc.cx(0, 1)
qc.measure_all()
# Step 2: Define a noise model
noise_model = NoiseModel()
depol_error = depolarizing_error(0.02, 2)   # 2% error on 2-qubit gates
noise_model.add_all_qubit_quantum_error(depol_error, ['cx'])
# Step 3: Run simulation with noise
backend = Aer.get_backend('qasm_simulator')
result = execute(qc, backend, noise_model=noise_model, shots=1024).result()
print(result.get_counts())
```

This example applies a small depolarizing error to the **controlled-NOT** (**CNOT**) **`cx`** gate, resulting in random bit-flips that degrade the entangled state's fidelity. Comparing results with and without the noise model shows how even minor imperfections distort ideal quantum distributions.

Simulating noise with Cirq

Cirq, developed by *Google Quantum AI*, includes an intuitive interface for adding stochastic noise channels directly to circuits. These channels probabilistically modify qubit density matrices, making Cirq well-suited for studying decoherence processes and gate errors.

Here is an example showing a depolarizing channel in Cirq:

```
import cirq
# Step 1: Define qubits and circuit
q0, q1 = cirq.LineQubit.range(2)
circuit = cirq.Circuit(
    cirq.H(q0),
    cirq.CNOT(q0, q1),
    cirq.measure(q0, q1)
)
# Step 2: Add depolarizing noise to the circuit
noisy_circuit = circuit.with_noise(cirq.depolarize(p=0.01))
# Step 3: Run the noisy simulation
simulator = cirq.DensityMatrixSimulator()
result = simulator.run(noisy_circuit, repetitions=1000)
print(result.histogram(key='0,1'))
```

Cirq's **`DensityMatrixSimulator`** tracks both pure and mixed states, capturing gradual decoherence and loss of purity, something that state vector simulators cannot represent. By adjusting the noise probability parameter, one can explore how errors propagate through the circuit.

Types of noise models

Different physical mechanisms contribute to noise in quantum hardware, and simulation frameworks model these effects using distinct mathematical channels. Each noise model captures a specific aspect of how qubits lose energy, coherence, or measurement accuracy. Understanding these models helps researchers choose the right simulation parameters for realistic experimentation. The major types of noise models are summarized in the following table:

Noise type	Description	Example application
Depolarizing noise	Randomly replaces a qubit's state with a maximally mixed state, representing loss of information.	Models control pulse errors in superconducting qubits.
Amplitude damping (T_1 decay)	Simulates energy loss from	1⟩|
Phase damping (T_2 decay)	Randomly destroys phase coherence without affecting energy levels.	Models dephasing from magnetic field fluctuations.
Readout noise	Models misclassification of qubit measurement outcomes.	Common in both ion trap and superconducting systems.

Table 5.3: *Common noise models and their physical interpretations*

Concept check: In practice, multiple noise channels act simultaneously. Realistic simulations often combine amplitude, phase, and readout errors to approximate full device behavior.

Visualizing noise effects

Noise affects measurement statistics and state fidelities. Visualization tools such as Qiskit's Aer noise analysis or Cirq's density matrix plotting help interpret how noise transforms quantum states.

Here are some examples:

- Without noise, a Bell state circuit yields count close to {'00': 512, '11': 512}.
- With depolarizing noise (2%), the distribution might shift to {'00': 470, '11': 460, '01': 45, '10': 49}, indicating random bit-flips.

Such comparisons reveal how even small error probabilities lead to significant distortions when circuits are repeated many times.

Learning outcomes from noise simulation

Hands-on experimentation with noise models transforms abstract concepts into practical understanding. By simulating realistic imperfections, learners gain experience in diagnosing, mitigating, and adapting to noise, skills essential for working with real quantum devices. The following outcomes summarize what can be achieved through guided noise simulation exercises:

- Quantify the impact of different error types on algorithm outcomes.
- Practice calibrating and mitigating measurement errors.
- Compare the robustness of algorithms such as Grover's search or **variational quantum eigensolver** (**VQE**) under varying noise levels.
- Understand how real quantum hardware behaves behind the scenes.

These exercises prepare readers for the realities of NISQ era experimentation, where careful modeling, rather than perfect isolation, is the key to progress.

Noise simulation transforms theory into experience. It allows learners to witness how quantum states degrade, how interference fades, and how small probabilities accumulate into major deviations. More importantly, it teaches that quantum computing today is an engineering discipline guided as much by error characterization as by algorithm design.

Working with NISQ devices

The current generation of quantum computers belongs to what researchers call the NISQ era. These are systems containing between tens and a few hundred qubits, powerful enough to perform meaningful experiments but not yet large or stable enough for fault-tolerant quantum computation.

Operating NISQ devices effectively requires both scientific awareness and engineering discipline. Developers must account for limitations in coherence time, connectivity, and gate fidelity while still extracting valuable computational results. This delicate balance defines the art of working with today's quantum machines.

The NISQ era is not a limitation; it is an opportunity to learn how quantum hardware behaves in reality, to innovate new algorithms, and to prepare for fault-tolerant systems of the future.

Characteristics of NISQ hardware

NISQ devices, though remarkable in capability, remain fundamentally constrained by current technological limits. Their behavior is shaped by physical and operational factors that determine which algorithms can be executed reliably. Understanding these characteristics helps developers design circuits that work within the practical boundaries of today's hardware. The key defining features of NISQ systems are outlined as follows:

- **Limited qubit count**: Devices typically range from 20 to 500-qubits. While impressive, this scale is insufficient for full error correction schemes, which may require thousands of qubits per logical qubit.
- **Short coherence times**: Qubits lose their quantum properties after microseconds or milliseconds, setting a strict limit on circuit depth.
- **Imperfect gate operations**: Each gate introduces a small probability of error, often between 0.1% and 1% per operation.
- **Restricted connectivity**: Not all qubits are directly connected; entangling gates can only be applied between specific pairs, requiring additional SWAP operations that further increase error.
- **Variable calibration**: Hardware parameters such as frequency, T_1, T_2, and error rates drift over time, requiring regular calibration.

Understanding device parameters

Before executing any quantum circuit, users should examine the hardware's calibration data. Both Qiskit and Cirq provide APIs to retrieve such details.

The most important parameters to consider are listed as follows:

- **T_1 (relaxation time)**: Duration before a qubit decays from $|1\rangle$ to $|0\rangle$.
- **T_2 (dephasing time)**: Duration over which the relative phase between $|0\rangle$ and $|1\rangle$ remains stable.
- **Gate error rates**: Average probability that a gate produces an incorrect result.
- **Readout errors**: Likelihood of measuring the wrong classical outcome.
- **Coupling map**: Defines which qubits can directly interact.

Let us look at an example in Qiskit:

```
from qiskit import IBMQ
IBMQ.load_account()
provider = IBMQ.get_provider(hub='ibm-q')
backend = provider.get_backend('ibm_nairobi')
# Display basic calibration data
backend_properties = backend.properties()
print(backend_properties.to_dict()['qubits'][0])
```

This code prints details for a specific qubit, including its T_1, T_2, and error probabilities. Such information helps users select optimal qubits and adjust circuit topology to minimize noise impact.

Strategies for reliable execution

Executing quantum programs on NISQ hardware requires a thoughtful balance between theoretical design and practical constraints. Because current devices are prone to drift and noise, successful experimentation depends on careful preparation, calibration, and execution strategies. The following best practices help ensure reliable and reproducible results when working with today's noisy quantum processors:

- **Optimize circuit depth**: Shorter circuits are less likely to lose coherence before completion. Use transpilation and circuit-optimization tools (e.g., `qiskit.transpile`) to reduce redundant operations.
- **Choose qubits strategically**: Select qubits with favorable calibration data. Many backends allow you to specify the exact layout for your circuit execution.
- **Characterize the backend regularly**: Hardware properties drift, so check calibration data before every run. Some providers publish daily updates accessible through their API dashboards.
- **Apply error mitigation techniques**: Use measurement calibration, ZNE, or readout error correction to improve accuracy without additional qubits.
- **Repetition and statistical averaging**: Execute circuits with large shot counts (e.g., 4,000–8,000) to average out random noise and obtain stable probability distributions.

Hybrid quantum and classical workflows

Because of hardware limitations, most practical quantum applications today rely on hybrid algorithms, in which quantum circuits handle computationally intensive subproblems while classical optimizers perform iterative updates.

Prominent examples

Some of the most effective hybrid frameworks are highlighted as follows:

- VQE for chemistry and materials modeling.
- **Quantum Approximate Optimization Algorithm** (**QAOA**) for combinatorial optimization.
- **Hybrid Quantum Machine Learning** (**HQML**) models for pattern recognition and feature encoding.

These algorithms are resilient to moderate noise and operate efficiently on current NISQ platforms. They illustrate how classical feedback loops can compensate for limited quantum coherence.

Interpreting real hardware results

When executing quantum circuits on physical devices, the results may deviate noticeably from ideal simulations. This is not a failure but an expected outcome in NISQ systems. The key is to interpret these imperfections meaningfully.

Guidelines for interpretation

The following guidelines help interpret experimental results from NISQ devices:

- Compare experimental histograms with noiseless simulator outputs.
- Identify systematic shifts (e.g., readout bias) versus random fluctuations.
- Use calibration and mitigation data to correct trends post-measurement.
- Document error rates and fidelity values when reporting or benchmarking results.

Working with NISQ devices is at the forefront of applied quantum computing. It demands creativity, adaptability, and continuous calibration. Despite their limitations, these systems have already achieved groundbreaking demonstrations, from quantum supremacy experiments to hybrid algorithmic breakthroughs.

The NISQ era reminds us that progress in quantum technology is incremental yet exponential; each small hardware improvement multiplies what algorithms can achieve. By learning to navigate and mitigate noise today, we prepare ourselves for the fault-tolerant quantum processors of tomorrow.

Conclusion

This chapter explored how real quantum hardware transforms theoretical qubits into physical systems governed by engineering and environmental constraints. We examined three major platforms, superconducting, ion trap, and photonic qubits, each balancing speed, stability, and scalability differently. The discussion on decoherence and noise highlighted how interactions, control imperfections, and external disturbances degrade quantum information. Through practical examples using Qiskit and Cirq, readers learned to simulate noise models, apply error mitigation, and interpret outcomes from noisy circuits. The introduction to QEC and surface codes outlined the path toward fault-tolerant computation, while the section on NISQ devices demonstrated how hybrid quantum–classical workflows enable progress despite hardware limitations. Together, these topics bridge theory and experiment, showing that understanding and managing noise is essential for advancing from today's noisy processors to tomorrow's reliable quantum computers. Building on this foundation, the next chapter shifts the focus from hardware concepts to practical implementation, introducing the programming tools and environments needed to begin hands-on exploration of quantum computing.

Questions

1. **What are the main physical implementations of qubits in quantum hardware?**

   Answer: The three leading implementations are superconducting qubits, trapped ion qubits, and photonic qubits. Each offers unique strengths; superconducting qubits for fast gates, ion traps for precision and long coherence, and photonic qubits for low decoherence and optical integration.

2. **What is decoherence, and why is it a major challenge?**

   Answer: Decoherence is the gradual loss of quantum superposition due to unwanted interactions with the environment. It causes qubits to behave classically, erasing the quantum advantage and limiting the duration of reliable computations.

3. **What are the two main processes that cause decoherence?**

   Answer: The two dominant processes are energy relaxation (T_1), where a qubit loses energy and returns to the ground state, and dephasing (T_2), where random phase fluctuations destroy interference patterns crucial for quantum operations.

4. **How do environmental and operational noise differ?**

   Answer: Environmental noise comes from external disturbances like temperature, magnetic fields, or cosmic rays, while operational noise arises from control imperfections, gate calibration errors, or readout inaccuracies during quantum operations.

5. **What is error mitigation in quantum computing?**

   Answer: Error mitigation refers to techniques that reduce the effect of noise on computational results without using additional qubits. It models and statistically or dynamically corrects noise to approximate ideal outputs on noisy hardware.

6. **How does QEC differ from error mitigation?**

   Answer: QEC actively detects and corrects errors by encoding information redundantly across multiple qubits, while error mitigation only reduces errors in measurement outcomes without modifying hardware or qubit count.

7. **What are surface codes, and why are they important?**

Answer: Surface codes are scalable two-dimensional error correction architectures that detect local errors using stabilizer measurements. They are fault-tolerant and compatible with superconducting chip layouts, making them key to building large-scale quantum computers.

8. **How can noise be simulated using Qiskit or Cirq?**

   Answer: Both platforms include built-in tools to model realistic hardware errors. Qiskit Aer uses customizable noise models, while Cirq applies stochastic noise channels within circuits, allowing users to analyze how errors affect results.

9. **What defines a NISQ device?**

   Answer: A NISQ device has 50–500 qubits but lacks full error correction. Despite being noisy, these systems enable real experiments, hybrid algorithms, and practical learning about hardware-level quantum behavior.

10. **Why is understanding noise essential for future quantum computing?**

    Answer: Mastering noise is crucial because it determines how reliably qubits can store and process information. Understanding, modeling, and mitigating noise lay the foundation for developing fault-tolerant quantum processors capable of performing large-scale computations.

Exercises

1. Simulate a superconducting qubit circuit using Qiskit. Create a two-qubit system with a Hadamard and CNOT gate to form a Bell state. Print the circuit diagram and describe how superconducting qubits implement these operations physically using microwave pulses.
2. Model depolarizing noise on the Bell circuit using Qiskit Aer's NoiseModel. Set a 2% error rate on the CNOT gate and compare the noisy result with the ideal case. Discuss how depolarizing noise alters the probability distribution of outcomes.
3. Implement amplitude and phase-damping channels using Cirq. Create a single-qubit circuit with a Hadamard gate, apply both noise channels, and visualize the effect on the qubit's Bloch sphere. Explain the relationship between T_1 and T_2 times and these damping effects.
4. Apply readout error mitigation in Qiskit. Construct calibration circuits using complete_meas_cal() and demonstrate how corrected results differ from raw measurement counts. Interpret what these reveals about measurement bias.
5. Design a three-qubit bit-flip code in Qiskit. Encode a logical qubit as $|\psi\_L\rangle=\alpha|000\rangle+\beta|111\rangle$, introduce a single-bit-flip error, and show how parity checks identify and correct the affected qubit.
6. Simulate a surface-code-style parity check by creating a 2×2 grid of qubits in Cirq. Implement stabilizer measurements and observe how local errors can be detected without directly measuring the logical state.
7. Investigate coherence-time effects by modeling circuits with increasing gate-to-gate delays. Use Qiskit's thermal relaxation noise to simulate decoherence and plot how the fidelity decreases as the delay increases.
8. Execute a small circuit on a real IBM Quantum backend (e.g., ibm_nairobi). Retrieve calibration data such as T_1, T_2, and gate error rates, and explain how they influence your choice of qubits for the experiment.
9. Explore a hybrid quantum–classical algorithm, such as the VQE, using Qiskit or Cirq. Introduce controlled noise and analyze how mitigation techniques affect convergence and result accuracy.
10. Reflect on the role of noise modeling in today's NISQ era. In a short paragraph, explain why understanding decoherence, noise simulation, and mitigation is essential for advancing toward fault-tolerant quantum computing.

CHAPTER 6
Getting Started with Python for Quantum Computing

Introduction

Quantum computing is entering an exciting phase where theory meets practice, and Python has become the language that bridges the gap. Unlike many programming languages that demand steep learning curves, Python offers a clear and intuitive syntax, making it accessible to beginners while powerful enough for advanced research. This is one of the reasons why leading quantum frameworks, such as *Qiskit* (*IBM Quantum*), *Cirq* (*Google Quantum AI*), and *Amazon Braket* (**Amazon Web Services** (**AWS**)), have adopted Python as their primary interface.

Getting started with quantum programming requires more than just writing code; it calls for a solid understanding of the tools and environments that support experimentation. Platforms like *Jupyter Notebook* and *Google Colab* enable the combination of live code, equations, explanations, and visualizations in a single workspace, an approach that is particularly useful when exploring quantum circuits and their probabilistic outcomes.

Equally important are the scientific libraries that power numerical computations and visual insights. NumPy provides the mathematical foundation for representing quantum states as vectors and applying quantum gates as matrices, while Matplotlib translates abstract probabilities into intuitive visualizations. Together, they help learners build confidence before moving on to advanced frameworks and real hardware.

This chapter provides a step-by-step pathway: revisiting Python essentials, setting up interactive environments, installing core **software development kits** (**SDKs**), and running your first quantum programs. By the end, you will not only understand how qubits are represented and manipulated but also gain practical experience in creating and visualizing simple quantum states, a critical first step toward mastering quantum algorithms.

Structure

The chapter covers the following topics:

- Python essentials for quantum programming
- Setting up Jupyter Notebook and Google Colab
- Installing and configuring Qiskit, Cirq, AWS Braket
- Using NumPy and Matplotlib for math and visualization
- Running basic Python scripts for quantum state representation

Objectives

This chapter introduces Python as the gateway to quantum programming, highlighting its simplicity, flexibility, and robust scientific ecosystem. Readers will explore how Python's core constructs, combined with libraries like NumPy and Matplotlib, form the mathematical backbone for representing qubit states, applying gates, and visualizing probabilistic outcomes. The chapter also guides learners in setting up Jupyter Notebook and Google Colab, providing interactive platforms to write, test, and document quantum programs effectively. With step-by-step instructions, readers will install and configure Qiskit, Cirq, and Amazon Braket SDKs, ensuring access to both simulators and real hardware. Hands-on exercises, such as building and simulating a Bell state, reinforce concepts of superposition and entanglement while validating the programming environment. By the end of this chapter, readers will have the foundational skills and tools needed to begin experimenting confidently with real quantum algorithms.

Python essentials for quantum programming

Python is the cornerstone of modern quantum computing development. Nearly every major quantum computing framework, such as Qiskit (by IBM), Cirq (by Google), and the Amazon Braket SDK (by AWS), uses Python as its primary programming interface. This widespread adoption is no coincidence: Python's clear syntax, high flexibility, and extensive scientific ecosystem make it the ideal language for both beginners and advanced researchers in the field.

It is essential to develop a strong command of Python's core language constructs, numerical computation libraries, and data visualization tools before diving into these specialized quantum libraries. These components form the mathematical and computational backbone on which quantum algorithms are designed, implemented, and executed.

This section revisits these Python fundamentals, serving as a conceptual bridge between traditional programming skills and the unique demands of quantum computing—including tasks such as representing qubit states, applying quantum gates, and visualizing their probabilistic behavior.

Python as an ideal language for quantum programming

Python plays a key role in the practical adoption of quantum computing by bridging high-level algorithm design and low-level quantum hardware execution. As quantum development increasingly depends on hybrid quantum–classical workflows, the choice of programming language directly affects accessibility, productivity, and ecosystem integration. Python's simplicity and strong scientific ecosystem make it well-suited for quantum researchers, engineers, and learners.

Python has emerged as the dominant language in quantum computing due to several compelling advantages that make it uniquely suited for this field:

- **Simple syntax**: Clear, readable syntax allows focus on quantum logic rather than low-level programming details.
- **Scientific ecosystem**: Libraries such as NumPy and Matplotlib support linear algebra, numerical computation, and visualization required for quantum systems.
- **Interoperability**: Integrates smoothly with Jupyter notebooks, cloud platforms, and machine learning frameworks for hybrid quantum–classical workflows.
- **Industry support**: Widely adopted by major quantum platforms, with strong open-source community maintenance.

Mastery of Python enables efficient adoption of quantum frameworks and supports a smooth transition from learning to practical quantum development.

Core Python concepts relevant to quantum computing

It is essential to master several core programming constructs that serve as the foundation for building and managing quantum code to program quantum systems effectively in Python.

These foundational Python features equip you with the essential tools to represent quantum data, control program flow, organize reusable code, and manage complex information structures, skills that are crucial for building reliable and scalable quantum applications:

- **Data types**: Understanding int, float, and especially complex is critical, as complex numbers represent qubit amplitudes. This allows you to model the real and imaginary components of quantum states.
- **Control flow**: Utilizing for and while loops for iteration, along with if...else statements for conditional logic, is crucial for constructing dynamic quantum experiments and automating repetitive runs.
- **Functions and modular code**: Writing reusable code blocks using def and importing external libraries with import helps maintain clarity and scalability as quantum projects grow in complexity.
- **Collections**: Data structures such as lists, tuples, and **dictionaries** (dictionary data type in Python) help store quantum states, simulation results, and mappings between qubits and classical bits.

Let us discuss an example demonstrating complex numbers for quantum amplitudes.

In quantum computing, each quantum state is described using probability amplitudes, which are often complex numbers. Python provides a built-in complex type, making it simple to represent and manipulate these values:

```
# Complex number representing a quantum amplitude
alpha = 0.6 + 0.8j
print("Real part:", alpha.real)
print("Imaginary part:", alpha.imag)
print("Magnitude:", abs(alpha))
print("Probability (|α|²):", abs(alpha)**2)
```

The output is as follows:

```
Real part: 0.6
Imaginary part: 0.8
Magnitude: 1.0
Probability (|α|²): 1.0
```

This complex number represents a valid quantum amplitude with a total probability of 1.

Using NumPy for linear algebra operations

Efficient numerical computation is fundamental to the implementation of quantum algorithms in practice. Since quantum computing heavily relies on vector and matrix manipulations involving complex numbers, a robust linear algebra library is essential. NumPy provides optimized, high-performance numerical routines, making it well-suited for representing quantum states and simulating quantum operations.

Linear algebra is the mathematical backbone of quantum computing. Every quantum operation can be described in terms of vectors and matrices:

- Qubit states are represented as column vectors.
- Quantum gates are represented as unitary matrices.
- Applying a gate to a state is performed by matrix–vector multiplication.

Using an efficient numerical library is essential because quantum states often involve complex numbers and multi-dimensional tensor products.

NumPy is the industry-standard Python library for numerical computing and is perfectly suited for these tasks.

The following NumPy capabilities are essential for quantum programming, as they provide the core mathematical operations needed to represent quantum states, apply gates, and build multi-qubit systems:

- **numpy.array**: Create vectors and matrices representing quantum states and gates.
- **numpy.dot() or @**: Perform matrix multiplication (used to apply gates to states).
- **numpy.kron()**: Compute the Kronecker (tensor) product, used to combine multiple qubits into larger systems.

- **dtype=complex**: Ensure support for complex-valued amplitudes, which are fundamental to quantum mechanics.

The following is an example that demonstrates the creation of Qubit states and applying a Hadamard gate (using NumPy). This script defines the |0⟩ and |1⟩ basis states, applies the Hadamard gate to |0⟩, and prints the resulting superposition state:

```
import numpy as np
# Define |0> and |1> basis states
zero = np.array([1, 0], dtype=complex)
one = np.array([0, 1], dtype=complex)
# Define the Hadamard gate
H = (1/np.sqrt(2)) * np.array([[1, 1],
                               [1, -1]], dtype=complex)
# Apply Hadamard to |0>
result = np.dot(H, zero)
print("Resulting state:", result)
```

The output is as follows:

```
Resulting state: [0.70710678+0.j 0.70710678+0.j]
```

This result represents the superposition state:

$$|\psi\rangle = \frac{1}{\sqrt{2}}(|0\rangle + |1\rangle)$$

Where the qubit is equally likely to be measured as *0* or *1*.

This principle of superposition is the foundation of quantum parallelism, which allows quantum computers to process many possibilities simultaneously.

Using Matplotlib for visualization

Quantum computing is inherently probabilistic. When you run a quantum circuit, you do not get a single deterministic answer—instead, you obtain counts of measurement outcomes across many repeated executions (shots). Interpreting these raw counts as probability distributions is critical for understanding how your circuit behaves. Matplotlib is a powerful and easy-to-use Python library for creating visualizations that make these results intuitive.

The following Matplotlib functions are especially useful in quantum programming, as they help transform raw numerical results into clear visual representations that make quantum behavior easier to interpret:

- **plt.bar()**: For plotting discrete probability histograms (common for qubit measurement results).
- **plt.plot()**: For visualizing continuous curves, such as wavefunctions or evolving amplitudes.
- **plt.title(), plt.xlabel(), plt.ylabel()**: For adding descriptive labels to make figures clear and publication-ready.

These functions allow you to transform abstract numerical results into visual insights.

The example here demonstrates the plotting of measurement probabilities. This script visualizes the measurement probabilities of |0⟩ and |1⟩ from the resulting state using a bar chart:

```
import matplotlib.pyplot as plt
# Probabilities of |0> and |1> from the previous state
probs = [abs(result[0])**2, abs(result[1])**2]
labels = ['|0⟩', '|1⟩']
plt.bar(labels, probs, color='teal')
plt.title("Measurement Probabilities")
```

```
plt.xlabel("Quantum States")
plt.ylabel("Probability")
plt.ylim(0, 1)
plt.show()
```

Function of the code: This code plots a bar chart showing the probabilities of measuring $|0\rangle$ or $|1\rangle$ for a single-qubit.

The resulting bar chart can be understood as follows:

- Two bars of equal height ($\approx$ 0.5 each) appear on the chart.
- This visually confirms that the qubit is in an equal superposition—it has a 50% chance of collapsing to either state upon measurement.

Putting it all together

You can simulate fundamental quantum behaviors even before using specialized quantum frameworks like Qiskit or Cirq by combining the computational power of NumPy with the visualization capabilities of Matplotlib.

This preliminary hands-on exposure strengthens conceptual understanding and bridges the gap between mathematical theory and practical quantum implementation.

This early hands-on practice is invaluable for learners because it helps them:

- Develop intuition about how quantum gates transform qubit states.
- Visualize probabilities rather than just interpreting abstract numerical arrays.
- Build confidence before transitioning to real quantum hardware or cloud-based platforms.

Setting up Jupyter Notebook and Google Colab

It is essential to setup a reliable and interactive development environment to begin programming quantum computers in Python. Quantum programming involves writing mathematical code, testing algorithms, visualizing circuit behavior, and documenting results, all of which are best supported by an environment that allows you to combine code, equations, narrative explanations, and visual outputs in a single document.

To support these requirements, developers commonly use interactive notebook-based environments that facilitate rapid experimentation and clear documentation.

Two of the most widely used platforms for this purpose are:

- **Jupyter Notebook**: A local, browser-based notebook interface.
- **Google Colab**: A cloud-based Jupyter environment hosted by *Google*.

Both platforms are widely adopted in the quantum computing community because they enable iterative experimentation, inline visualizations, and well-organized documentation of quantum programs.

Jupyter Notebook

This section provides a step-by-step guide to setting up and using these environments effectively, ensuring that you can quickly begin developing and testing quantum circuits.

Jupyter Notebook is an open-source, browser-based application that allows you to create and share interactive documents containing live code, mathematical equations, visualizations, and explanatory text. It has become the standard development environment for quantum programming because it enables students, educators, and researchers to prototype, test, and document code interactively—an essential workflow when experimenting with complex quantum algorithms.

The following capabilities make Jupyter Notebook especially well-suited for quantum programming, enabling an organized, interactive, and visually rich development experience:

- **Interactive, cell-based interface**: Execute code one cell at a time and view outputs immediately.
- **Language flexibility**: Primarily used with Python but supports many other programming languages.
- **Seamless integration**: Ideal for combining quantum circuits, mathematical formulas, and narrative text in the same file.
- **Compatibility**: Works smoothly with local installations of Qiskit, Cirq, and the Amazon Braket SDK.

Installation steps

Ensure you have Python and pip already installed on your system before installing. The installation steps are as follows:

1. Open a terminal or command prompt.
2. Install Jupyter Notebook with:
   ```
   pip install notebook
   ```
3. Launch Jupyter Notebook with:
   ```
   jupyter notebook
   ```
4. A new browser window will open at **http://localhost:8888/**, showing the Jupyter Notebook interface.

Creating and running a Notebook involves the following steps:

1. In the Jupyter interface, click **New | Python 3 (ipykernel)** to create a new notebook.
2. Enter Python code in the first cell.
3. Press *Shift* + *Enter* to execute the cell and move to the next one.

Google Colab

Google Colab (short for Colaboratory) is a cloud-based environment hosted by Google. It allows you to write and run code entirely in your web browser without installing any software locally. Colab is an excellent choice for beginners and students, especially when working on systems where installing large quantum libraries might be difficult or impractical because it removes setup barriers.

The following capabilities make Colab an accessible and convenient platform for beginners and students working on quantum programming:

- No installation or configuration required; everything runs in the cloud.
- Free access to hardware accelerators such as **central processing units** (**CPUs**), **graphics processing units** (**GPUs**), and **Tensor Processing Units** (**TPUs**).
- Seamless integration for file storage and synchronization.
- Support for major scientific and quantum libraries, including NumPy, Matplotlib, Qiskit, Cirq, and the Amazon Braket SDK.
- Built-in collaboration features allow multiple users to edit and comment on the same notebook in real-time.

Getting started with Google Colab involves the following steps:

1. Open a browser and go to **https://colab.research.google.com/**.
2. Sign in using your account.
3. Click **New Notebook** to create a blank notebook.
4. Install the required quantum libraries in the first cell. For example:
   ```
   !pip install qiskit
   !pip install cirq
   ```

These libraries will be installed and ready for use in subsequent cells of the notebook.

Managing notebooks in Google Colab is simple and flexible:

- Colab automatically saves your work to your *Google Drive* under a **`Colab Notebooks`** folder.
- You can also upload existing **`.ipynb`** files from your local machine.
- To export your work, go to **File** | **Download** | **.ipynb** or **.py**.

Choosing between Jupyter Notebook and Google Colab

When setting up an environment for quantum programming, the choice often comes down to Jupyter Notebook or Google Colab. Both platforms are widely used, but they cater to different needs. While Jupyter offers greater control and offline flexibility, Colab emphasizes accessibility and collaboration.

Recommendation: Beginners should start with Google Colab because it is simple, portable, and requires no setup.

Once you are comfortable with quantum programming, you can transition to Jupyter Notebook for advanced projects that require custom local configurations, persistent environments, or secure offline work.

For most learners, the selection depends on factors such as ease of setup, availability of computing resources, need for offline access, and project complexity. In practice, many quantum developers use both platforms at different stages of their workflow, Colab for quick experimentation and sharing, and Jupyter Notebook for controlled, reproducible local development.

Installing and configuring Qiskit, Cirq, AWS Braket

Before writing any quantum programs, you must install the software toolkits that provide circuit construction, simulation, and hardware access. These toolkits are commonly delivered as Python packages and can be installed directly in your notebook environment. A correctly configured SDK setup ensures that your code can run reliably on simulators first and later connect to cloud-based quantum devices when required.

Once you have setup your development environment using Jupyter Notebook or Google Colab, the next major step is to install the quantum computing SDKs.

These SDKs provide the essential tools needed to:

- Design and build quantum circuits.
- Run simulations on local backends.
- Execute code on real quantum hardware.

The three most widely used Python-based quantum SDKs in both industry and academia are:

- **Qiskit**: Developed for constructing and running circuits on IBM Quantum systems.
- **Cirq**: Developed for research-focused circuit construction, simulation, and noise modeling.
- **Amazon Braket SDK**: Offered by AWS to access multiple quantum hardware providers via the cloud.

Each of these frameworks supports local simulators (for cost-free testing) and remote hardware backends (for executing real experiments), making them indispensable tools for hands-on quantum learning and development.

Installing and configuring Qiskit

Qiskit is one of the most widely used and mature quantum computing frameworks available today. Developed by IBM, it is specifically designed for building, simulating, and executing quantum programs on both IBM Quantum hardware and local simulators. It has become the preferred choice in academia and industry due to its modular design, active community, and robust feature set.

Understanding the internal structure of Qiskit is helpful before proceeding with installation and usage. Its modular architecture allows developers to work at different abstraction levels, from low-level circuit construction to high-level algorithm design, making the framework flexible for both learning and advanced research.

Core modules of Qiskit

Qiskit is composed of four main modules, each serving a specific role:

- **Terra**: The foundational layer for building quantum circuits and managing execution on various backends.
- **Aer**: A high-performance simulation framework for testing and analyzing circuits locally.
- **Ignis**: Tools for noise modeling and error analysis, useful when working with real, noisy hardware.
- **Aqua**: A library of high-level quantum algorithms (now deprecated, but still referenced in legacy examples and tutorials).

Installation

You can install Qiskit using pip. In a terminal or a Jupyter Notebook/Google Colab cell, run:

```
pip install qiskit
```

This will download and install all the core modules and their dependencies. It may take a few minutes to complete, depending on your internet speed.

Tip for Google Colab: Prefix the command with `!` when running inside a notebook cell:

```
!pip install qiskit
```

Testing the installation

Use this minimal script to verify that Qiskit is working correctly:

```
from qiskit import QuantumCircuit
# Create a simple 2-qubit circuit
qc = QuantumCircuit(2)
qc.h(0)           # Apply Hadamard on the first qubit
qc.cx(0, 1)       # Apply CNOT with control=0 and target=1
print(qc)
```

The expected output is as follows:

```
     ┌───┐
q_0: ┤ H ├──■──
     └───┘┌─┴─┐
q_1: ─────┤ X ├
          └───┘
```

Seeing this circuit diagram confirms that Qiskit is installed correctly and ready to build quantum circuits.

You can optionally install Qiskit's visualization tools to enable enhanced circuit diagrams and plotting capabilities. This can be done using the command:

```
pip install qiskit[visualization]
```

Installing and configuring Cirq

Cirq is a Python library developed by Google for creating, simulating, and running quantum circuits. It is widely used in academic and research environments because of its flexibility, clean API, and support for custom gate definitions, noise modeling, and circuit optimization. Cirq is especially suited for experimenting with novel quantum algorithms at the research level.

Installation steps

To install Cirq, run the following command in your terminal or command prompt:

```
pip install cirq
```

If you are using Google Colab, prefix the command with **!**:

```
!pip install cirq
```

This will install the core Cirq library and its dependencies.

Testing the installation

Use this minimal script to verify that Cirq is installed and working correctly:

```
import cirq
# Define two qubits
q0, q1 = cirq.LineQubit.range(2)
# Create a simple circuit
circuit = cirq.Circuit(
    cirq.H(q0),
    cirq.CNOT(q0, q1)
)
print(circuit)
```

The output is as follows:

```
0: ───H───@───
          │
1: ───────X───
```

Seeing this output confirms that Cirq is successfully installed and able to construct quantum circuits.

Installing and configuring the Amazon Braket software development kit

Amazon Braket SDK is AWS's quantum computing platform. It provides cloud-based access to real quantum hardware from multiple leading providers, including:

- **IonQ**: Ion trap quantum systems.
- **Rigetti Computing**: Superconducting qubit processors.
- **Oxford Quantum Circuits** (**OQC**): Superconducting qubit systems.

In addition to real hardware access, Braket also includes a local simulator, which allows developers to design, test, and debug circuits cost-free before submitting them to physical devices.

Installation steps

To install the Braket SDK, run the following command in your terminal or command prompt:

```
pip install amazon-braket-sdk
```

If you are using Google Colab, prefix the command with **!**:

```
!pip install amazon-braket-sdk
```

This will install the SDK and its core dependencies.

Testing the installation

Use this minimal script to verify that the Braket SDK is installed correctly:

```
from braket.circuits import Circuit
# Create a small 2-qubit circuit
circ = Circuit().h(0).cnot(0, 1)
print(circ)
```

The output is as follows:

```
T  : |0|1|
q0 : -H-C-
        |
q1 : ---X-
T  = 2
```

If you see this circuit diagram, it confirms that the SDK is installed and able to build quantum circuits.

Verifying the development environment

After installing Qiskit, Cirq, and the Amazon Braket SDK, it is good practice to verify that all three SDKs are properly installed and accessible in your environment. This simple check ensures that your setup is ready for quantum development.

Before proceeding to more advanced quantum programs, it is important to quickly validate the installed libraries. This step helps identify missing dependencies or configuration issues early and ensures that the Python environment can successfully import all required quantum SDKs.

Verification script

Run the following code in a Jupyter Notebook cell, a Google Colab notebook, or any Python environment:

```
import qiskit, cirq, braket
print("Qiskit version:", qiskit.__qiskit_version__)
print("Cirq version:", cirq.__version__)
print(„Braket SDK version:“, braket.__version__)
```

Result: If all installations are successful, this script will print the version numbers of each library without raising any errors.

Seeing these version outputs confirms that your quantum programming environment is correctly setup and ready for building, simulating, and executing quantum circuits.

Using NumPy and Matplotlib for math and visualization

It is essential to understand how quantum states and operations are represented mathematically using classical linear algebra tools before working with specialized quantum SDKs such as Qiskit, Cirq, or the Amazon Braket SDK.

In quantum computing:

- Qubit states are represented as vectors.
- Quantum gates are represented as matrices.
- Applying a gate to a state involves matrix–vector multiplication.
- Measuring a qubit collapses it into a classical state ($|0\rangle$ or $|1\rangle$) with specific probabilities determined by its amplitudes.

To work with these mathematical objects in Python:

- NumPy is ideal for numerical computation and matrix operations, such as creating state vectors, building gate matrices, and performing tensor products.
- Matplotlib is used to visualize probability distributions, measurement histograms, and state amplitudes, helping to interpret the results of quantum computations.

This section introduces the core numerical and visualization techniques needed to build a strong intuition about how quantum states behave and how algorithms manipulate them.

Representing quantum states using NumPy

In quantum mechanics, each qubit is represented as a two-dimensional complex vector. The two fundamental basis states are:

$$|0\rangle = \begin{bmatrix}1\\0\end{bmatrix}, |1\rangle = \begin{bmatrix}0\\1\end{bmatrix}$$

A general qubit state can be expressed as:

$$|\psi\rangle=\alpha|0\rangle+\beta|1\rangle$$

Where α and β are complex numbers known as probability amplitudes, they must satisfy the normalization condition:

$$|\alpha|^2+|\beta|^2=1$$

This ensures that the total probability of measuring either $|0\rangle$ or $|1\rangle$ is always 1, which is a fundamental rule of quantum mechanics.

The following is an example demonstrating the definition of basic states and a superposition:

This script defines the $|0\rangle$ and $|1\rangle$ basis states as vectors and constructs their equal superposition, then prints all three states:

```
import numpy as np
# Define |0> and |1> basis states
zero = np.array([1, 0], dtype=complex)
one = np.array([0, 1], dtype=complex)
# Create a superposition state: (|0> + |1>) / √2
superposition = (1/np.sqrt(2)) * (zero + one)
print("Zero:", zero)
print("One:", one)
print("Superposition:", superposition)
```

The output is as follows:

```
Zero: [1.+0.j 0.+0.j]
One: [0.+0.j 1.+0.j]
Superposition: [0.70710678+0.j 0.70710678+0.j]
```

Applying quantum gates using NumPy

Quantum gates are unitary matrices that transform qubit states through matrix multiplication. Just as classical logic gates manipulate bits, quantum gates manipulate quantum state vectors to change the probabilities and phases of qubits.

One of the most important single-qubit gates is the Hadamard gate, which transforms the basis state $|0\rangle$ into an equal superposition of $|0\rangle$ and $|1\rangle$. This forms the foundation of quantum parallelism, where a qubit can exist in multiple states simultaneously:

$$H|0\rangle = \frac{|0\rangle+|1\rangle}{\sqrt{2}}$$

The following is an example demonstrating the application of the Hadamard gate (using NumPy).

This script applies the Hadamard gate to the $|0\rangle$ state, creating a balanced superposition and printing the resulting state vector:

```
import numpy as np
# Define Hadamard gate
H = (1/np.sqrt(2)) * np.array([[1, 1],
                               [1, -1]], dtype=complex)
```

```
# Apply Hadamard to |0>
new_state = np.dot(H, zero)
print("State after Hadamard:", new_state)
```

The output is as follows:

```
State after Hadamard: [0.70710678+0.j 0.70710678+0.j]
```

Computing measurement probabilities

The final step in most quantum algorithms is measuring the qubits after applying quantum gates. Measurement causes the quantum state to collapse into a classical bit value ($|0\rangle$ or $|1\rangle$) with a probability equal to the squared magnitude of its amplitude.

Mathematically, if a qubit's state is:

$$|\psi\rangle=\alpha|0\rangle+\beta|1\rangle$$

Then the probability of measuring each outcome is:

$$P(0)=|\alpha|^2, \qquad P(1)=|\beta|^2$$

The following example demonstrates the calculation of measurement probabilities.

This script computes the probabilities of measuring $|0\rangle$ or $|1\rangle$ by squaring the magnitudes of the state vector's amplitudes:

```
# Assuming new_state is the output of the Hadamard operation
prob_zero = abs(new_state[0])**2
prob_one = abs(new_state[1])**2
print("P(|0>):", prob_zero)
print("P(|1>):", prob_one)
```

The output is as follows:

```
P(|0>): 0.4999999999999999
P(|1>): 0.4999999999999999
```

This result shows that there is approximately a 50% chance of measuring $|0\rangle$ and a 50% chance of measuring $|1\rangle$. This aligns perfectly with the fact that the qubit was placed in a balanced superposition by the Hadamard gate.

Visualizing quantum states using Matplotlib

While numerical probabilities are precise, numbers alone can be difficult to interpret intuitively, especially when working with quantum states that involve complex amplitudes. Matplotlib helps overcome this challenge by enabling you to visualize probabilities as bar charts or histograms, making the behavior of qubits easier to understand at a glance. This is particularly useful for verifying whether a circuit has created the expected state (such as a balanced superposition).

The following example demonstrates the visualization of probabilities.

This script creates a bar chart to visually compare the measurement probabilities of $|0\rangle$ and $|1\rangle$ after applying the Hadamard gate:

```
import matplotlib.pyplot as plt
states = ['|0⟩', '|1⟩']
probs = [prob_zero, prob_one]
plt.bar(states, probs, color='navy')
plt.title("Measurement Probabilities After Hadamard Gate")
plt.xlabel("Quantum States")
plt.ylabel("Probability")
```

```
plt.ylim(0, 1)
plt.show()
```

The following points briefly explain the purpose of the visualization and how to read it:

- Plots the probabilities of measuring |0⟩ and |1⟩.
- Uses a bar chart to represent how likely each outcome is.

The following points describe the visual outcome that confirms the qubit is in an equal superposition state after applying the Hadamard gate:

- Two bars of equal height (~0.5).
- This visually confirms that the qubit is in an equal superposition state created by the Hadamard gate.

Combining multiple qubits

Real quantum algorithms rarely operate on single-qubits alone. Instead, they use multiple qubits combined into a larger quantum system. Mathematically, this is done using the tensor product (also called the Kronecker product) of individual qubit states.

For example, combining two qubits $|0\rangle \otimes |0\rangle$ produces a four-dimensional state vector representing all possible combinations of the two qubits.

The following example demonstrates the creation of a two-qubit |00⟩ state (using **numpy**):

```
import numpy as np
# Tensor product of |0> ⊗ |0>
two_qubit_zero = np.kron(zero, zero)
print(two_qubit_zero)
```

The output is as follows:

```
[1.+0.j 0.+0.j 0.+0.j 0.+0.j]
```

This is the four-element state vector representing the two-qubit basis state |00⟩:

$$|00\rangle = \begin{bmatrix} 1 \\ 0 \\ 0 \\ 0 \end{bmatrix}$$

Let us discuss an example that demonstrates the application of a Hadamard on the first qubit.

To apply a gate only on the first qubit of a multi-qubit system, use the tensor product of the gate with the identity matrix:

```
# Gate for first qubit only (H ⊗ I)
I = np.eye(2)
H_I = np.kron(H, I)
new_state = np.dot(H_I, two_qubit_zero)
print(new_state)
```

This transforms the system into:

$$\frac{|00\rangle + |10\rangle}{\sqrt{2}}$$

Here, the first qubit is in superposition, while the second qubit remains in |0⟩.

Running basic Python scripts for quantum state representation

This section transitions from environment setup to practical execution. By working through a simple example, you will confirm that the installed tools function correctly while gaining initial exposure to quantum state representation and measurement workflows.

With your environment setup and the essential libraries installed, you are now ready to write and execute your first quantum programs. This section provides a hands-on introduction to three fundamental tasks that form the backbone of quantum programming:

- Building a basic quantum circuit using Python-based quantum SDKs.
- Simulating the circuit on a local backend to verify its behavior.
- Retrieving and visualizing the measurement results to interpret the outcomes.

Completing this exercise will validate that your development setup is working correctly and give you your first practical experience in representing and manipulating quantum states, a crucial milestone before progressing to full-fledged quantum algorithms.

Creating and simulating a Bell state in Qiskit

The Bell state, also known as an **Einstein–Podolsky–Rosen (EPR)** pair, is the simplest and most iconic example of quantum entanglement.

It represents a pair of qubits whose outcomes are perfectly correlated, meaning they will always produce the same measurement result (00 or 11) even when separated. This makes the Bell state an ideal first experiment to verify that your quantum programming environment is setup correctly.

Creation of the basic Bell state

The Bell state is produced using two basic quantum gates:

- The **Hadamard** (H) gate on the first qubit; places it into an equal superposition of $|0\rangle$ and $|1\rangle$.
- The **Controlled-NOT** (CNOT) gate with the first qubit as control and the second as target, entangles the two qubits.

Mathematically, the transformation is:

$$|00\rangle \overset{H\otimes I}{\rightarrow} \frac{|00\rangle + |10\rangle}{\sqrt{2}} \overset{\text{CNOT}}{\rightarrow} \frac{|00\rangle + |11\rangle}{\sqrt{2}}$$

This final state is entangled: measuring one qubit immediately determines the outcome of the other.

Python script using Qiskit

This script builds a simple two-qubit entangled circuit, runs the simulation, and presents the measurement results:

```
from qiskit import QuantumCircuit, Aer, execute
from qiskit.visualization import plot_histogram
import matplotlib.pyplot as plt
# Create a circuit with 2 qubits and 2 classical bits
qc = QuantumCircuit(2, 2)
# Step 1: Apply Hadamard to the first qubit
qc.h(0)
# Step 2: Apply CNOT with control=0 and target=1
qc.cx(0, 1)
```

```
# Measure both qubits
qc.measure([0, 1], [0, 1])
# Simulate using the Local QASM simulator
simulator = Aer.get_backend('qasm_simulator')
job = execute(qc, simulator, shots=1024)
result = job.result()
counts = result.get_counts()
print("Measurement results:", counts)
# Plot histogram of results
plot_histogram(counts)
plt.show()
```

The expected output is as follows:

```
Measurement results: {'00': 503, '11': 521}
```

The resulting histogram displays nearly equal probabilities for the outcomes **00** and **11**, indicating that the two qubits are entangled and consistently collapse to the same value upon measurement.

The histogram will show two bars with almost equal heights for **00** and **11**. This confirms that the two-qubits are entangled—they always collapse to the same value.

Representing quantum states using state-vector simulation

In addition to measurement-based simulation, Qiskit also provides a state-vector simulator, which reveals the exact complex amplitudes of every basis state in a quantum system.

While measurement collapses the state into a definite classical outcome, the state-vector shows the full quantum superposition before any randomness is introduced. This offers deeper insight into the internal behavior of your quantum algorithm.

The following is an example demonstrating the viewing of the quantum state-vector (using Qiskit):

This script creates a two-qubit Bell state circuit, simulates it using the state-vector simulator, and prints the resulting state-vector to show the exact quantum state of the system:

```
from qiskit import Aer, QuantumCircuit, execute
# Build the Bell state circuit
qc = QuantumCircuit(2)
qc.h(0)
qc.cx(0, 1)
# Simulate using the statevector simulator
backend = Aer.get_backend('statevector_simulator')
result = execute(qc, backend).result()
state = result.get_statevector()
print("Statevector:", state)
```

Expected output:

```
Statevector: [0.70710678+0.j 0.+0.j 0.+0.j 0.70710678+0.j]
```

This output shows the Bell state represented as a vector of complex amplitudes:

$$\frac{|00\rangle + |11\rangle}{\sqrt{2}}$$

The interpretation of the state vector is as follows:

- The first and last elements correspond to the $|00\rangle$ and $|11\rangle$ states.
- Their equal amplitudes indicate 50% probability each, while the other basis states have amplitude 0.

Building the same circuit in Cirq

Just as with Qiskit, you can also use Cirq to create the same Bell state circuit.

Doing this allows learners to compare how different quantum frameworks implement the same quantum logic, reinforcing that the underlying principles remain consistent even though the syntax differs.

Before implementing the circuit, it is helpful to recognize that Cirq follows a slightly different programming style compared to Qiskit, particularly in how qubits, gates, and measurements are defined. Working through the Cirq version of the Bell circuit strengthens cross-framework understanding and improves portability of quantum programming skills.

The following example is of the Bell state circuit in Cirq.

This script creates a two-qubit Bell state using Cirq, simulates the circuit, and prints the measurement outcomes to verify entanglement:

```
import cirq
# Define two qubits
q0, q1 = cirq.LineQubit.range(2)
# Build the circuit
circuit = cirq.Circuit(
    cirq.H(q0),            # Hadamard on first qubit
    cirq.CNOT(q0, q1),      # CNOT from q0 to q1
    cirq.measure(q0, q1)    # Measure both qubits
)
# Simulate the circuit
sim = cirq.Simulator()
result = sim.run(circuit, repetitions=1024)
print("Results:\n", result.histogram(key=(q0, q1)))
print(circuit)
```

The sample output is as follows:

```
Results:
Counter({0: ~512, 3: ~512})
0: ───H───@───M───
          │
1: ───────X───M───
```

Notes: **The following points explain how to interpret the measurement results from Cirq when verifying the creation of a Bell state:**

- **In Cirq, measurement results are reported as decimal integers representing bitstrings:**

  0 represents the state 00.

  3 represents the state 11.

- **Seeing roughly equal counts for 0 and 3 confirms that the two qubits are entangled in a Bell state, just as they were in the Qiskit implementation.**

Building a sample circuit in Amazon Braket SDK

The Amazon Braket SDK allows you to design and visualize quantum circuits locally without immediately submitting them to cloud-based quantum hardware.

This is useful for quick prototyping and verification before running on real devices, which can be time-limited or cost-based.

The following demonstrates the creation of a Bell state circuit in Amazon Braket.

This script builds a two-qubit Bell state circuit using Braket by applying a Hadamard gate followed by a CNOT gate, then prints the circuit:

```
from braket.circuits import Circuit
# Create a simple Bell state circuit
bell = Circuit().h(0).cnot(0, 1)
print(bell)
```

The expected output is as follows:

```
T  : |0|1|
q0 : -H-C-
        |
q1 : ---X-
T  = 2
```

This output confirms that the Amazon Braket SDK is properly installed and can successfully build quantum circuits locally.

Conclusion

This chapter highlighted Python's central role in quantum programming and explained why it has become the preferred language for both learners and professionals. We revisited core Python concepts—such as data types, control flow, functions, and collections—that support structured and maintainable quantum code. Particular emphasis was placed on complex numbers, since probability amplitudes in quantum states are inherently complex-valued. We also explored how NumPy and Matplotlib provide the essential mathematical and visualization foundation required to represent quantum states as vectors, implement quantum gates as matrices, compute measurement probabilities, and interpret results through clear plots and histograms.

The chapter then focused on establishing a productive development workflow using interactive environments. Jupyter Notebook offers strong local control and reproducibility, while Google Colab provides fast, setup-free access with convenient collaboration and cloud execution. After configuring the environment, we installed and tested three widely adopted quantum SDKs—Qiskit, Cirq, and the Amazon Braket SDK—ensuring that readers can develop quantum circuits, run simulations cost-free, and later extend experiments to real quantum hardware. The verification steps confirmed that the complete toolchain is correctly configured.

Finally, through hands-on implementation of the Bell state across multiple frameworks, we gained practical insight into the foundational quantum principles of superposition and entanglement. Overall, the skills and setup established in this chapter provide a strong starting point for building larger circuits and progressing toward real-world quantum algorithms.

Questions

1. **What is quantum utility (QU) in quantum computing?**

   Answer: QU is a framework for evaluating whether a quantum algorithm provides a practical advantage over classical methods. It focuses on outcomes such as accuracy, efficiency, scalability, and robustness, rather than hardware specifications like qubit count or gate depth.

2. **Why are traditional metrics insufficient for measuring progress?**

   Answer: Metrics such as qubit count or gate fidelity show hardware growth but do not indicate whether a quantum program solves real problems effectively. QU addresses this gap by measuring actual problem-solving ability in meaningful contexts.

3. **What role do Qiskit patterns play in quantum programming?**

   Answer: Qiskit patterns provide structured templates that organize workflows into clear steps—problem definition, mapping, execution, post-processing, and evaluation—making quantum programs consistent, reproducible, and extensible.

4. **How do Qiskit patterns help avoid ad hoc development?**

   Answer: Without patterns, quantum code often becomes fragmented, difficult to debug, and hard to scale. Patterns enforce discipline by providing a shared structure, similar to design patterns in classical software engineering.

5. **What are the five stages of a Qiskit pattern workflow?**

   Answer: The stages are: (1) Problem definition, (2) Mapping, (3) Execution, (4) Post-processing, and (5) Evaluation using QU metrics.

6. **How does the Quantum Approximate Optimization Algorithm (QAOA) illustrate QU in optimization?**

   Answer: QAOA applied to Max-Cut demonstrates accuracy in cut values, potential efficiency gains, and scalability advantages compared to classical heuristics like simulated annealing, while maintaining robustness under noise.

7. **What is the significance of variational quantum eigensolver (VQE) in quantum chemistry?**

   Answer: VQE is used to estimate molecular ground-state energies, such as for H_2. Achieving results within chemical accuracy (~1.6 mHa) showcases meaningful QU and highlights the potential for quantum-assisted chemistry.

8. **How do QU and Qiskit patterns work together?**

   Answer: QU provides the benchmark for evaluating results, while Qiskit patterns offer the structured workflow. Together, they ensure that experiments are both rigorous and practically relevant.

9. **What challenges exist in measuring QU?**

   Answer: Challenges include benchmark selection bias, rapidly improving classical algorithms, hardware noise variability, scalability limits of current devices, and incomplete resource accounting.

10. **Why are case studies important in demonstrating QU?**

    Answer: Case studies like QAOA for optimization and VQE for chemistry show how QU metrics can be applied within structured Qiskit patterns, turning theory into reproducible, end-to-end workflows with real-world relevance.

Exercises

1. Implement a Qiskit script that solves a small Max-Cut problem using the QAOA. Compare the result with a classical simulated annealing solver. Reflect on whether QAOA demonstrates QU in this instance.
2. Use the chemistry workflow pattern in Qiskit to estimate the ground-state energy of molecular H_2 using the VQE. Compare your results with an exact diagonalization baseline. Discuss how accuracy is quantified in this context.
3. Study the scaling behavior of the QAOA by solving Max-Cut for graphs with 2, 4, and 6 nodes. Record solution quality and runtimes, and analyze trends that may indicate the potential for quantum advantage.
4. Design a workflow using Qiskit patterns for a new domain (e.g., portfolio optimization). Structure the implementation into five steps: problem definition, mapping, execution, post-processing, and evaluation.
5. On a noisy backend (e.g., IBM Quantum hardware or a noise simulator), run the VQE for molecular H_2 with and without error-mitigation techniques. Compare the results and reflect on the robustness dimension of QU.

6. Modify the QAOA ansatz by changing the number of layers (repetitions, reps). Record how solution quality and runtime vary, and discuss the trade-off between circuit depth and noise resilience.
7. Create a comparative table contrasting traditional quantum metrics (e.g., qubit count, circuit depth, fidelity) with QU metrics (accuracy, efficiency, scalability, and robustness). Summarize why QU-oriented metrics are more meaningful for real-world applications.
8. Use Matplotlib (or a similar visualization library) to plot the energy convergence curve of the VQE across optimization iterations. Explain how visualization aids interpretation during post-processing.
9. Write a Python function that accepts a Qiskit pattern workflow as input and outputs a structured QU profile—accuracy, efficiency, scalability, and robustness. Apply it to both the QAOA and the VQE experiments.
10. Write a short essay (300–400 words) discussing how QU and Qiskit patterns together support the transition of quantum computing from theory to practice. Use examples from optimization and quantum chemistry to support your argument.

Chapter 7
Programming with Qiskit from IBM

Introduction

Quantum computing is no longer confined to theory; it is now an area where learners and researchers can experiment directly with real systems. At the heart of this transformation is Qiskit, IBM's open-source **software development kit** (**SDK**). Written in Python, Qiskit offers a practical, intuitive, and powerful approach to designing quantum circuits, simulating their behavior, and executing them on actual quantum hardware. Its strength lies in simplicity: with only a few lines of code, users can explore concepts such as superposition, entanglement, and measurement that form the foundation of quantum computation.

One of Qiskit's greatest advantages is its complete ecosystem. It supports every stage of the workflow, circuit construction, visualization, error modeling, simulation, and execution on IBM's cloud-based processors. This integration makes Qiskit equally valuable in classrooms, research labs, and industry projects, offering both accessibility for beginners and depth for advanced exploration.

Flexibility is another hallmark of Qiskit. It can be installed locally for long-term projects requiring customization, or accessed instantly in cloud environments like *Google Colab* for quick experimentation and teaching. Its modular design—Terra for circuits, Aer for simulation, and the modern Runtime interface for hardware execution—ensures scalability as learners progress from basic examples to complex algorithms.

This chapter introduces Qiskit step-by-step, covering how to install it, create and visualize circuits, run programs on simulators, and ultimately, connect to real IBM Quantum devices. By the end, you will be equipped with the skills and confidence to begin practical quantum programming and lay the foundation for exploring advanced algorithms.

Structure

The chapter covers the following topics:

- Introduction and installing Qiskit
- Circuit construction and visualization
- Implementing Grover's algorithm
- Qiskit modules
- Simulation vs. real quantum hardware
- Case study on implementing quantum teleportation

Objectives

This chapter aims to equip readers with the knowledge and skills to use Qiskit, IBM's open-source framework for quantum programming, as a complete ecosystem for learning and experimentation. Readers will explore how Qiskit's modular components—Terra for circuit construction, Aer for high-performance simulation, and the runtime interface for accessing real IBM Quantum devices, work together to support the entire workflow from design to execution. The chapter guides learners through both local installation and cloud-based access via Google Colab, offering flexibility for beginners and advanced users alike. Practical examples, including the creation of Bell states and **Greenberger–Horne–Zeilinger** (**GHZ**) states, reinforce key concepts such as superposition and entanglement, while a hands-on implementation of Grover's algorithm introduces the power of amplitude amplification. By the end of this chapter, readers will have gained the confidence to construct, visualize, simulate, and execute quantum circuits, thereby bridging the gap between theoretical foundations and real-world applications.

Introduction and installing Qiskit

Qiskit, developed by IBM, is a leading open-source SDK that has become one of the most widely adopted frameworks in both academia and industry. Its strength lies in its versatility, equally accessible to beginners exploring the fundamentals of quantum programming and advanced researchers developing complex algorithms. By offering a unified environment for learning, experimentation, and discovery, Qiskit simplifies the journey into quantum computing.

A defining advantage of Qiskit is its comprehensive ecosystem, which supports the entire quantum workflow. From constructing and visualizing circuits to simulating algorithms on classical systems and executing programs on real quantum hardware, Qiskit integrates seamlessly with the IBM Quantum Experience. This connectivity makes it a practical tool not only for teaching but also for cutting-edge research.

With Qiskit, users can:

- Design and visualize quantum circuits in a step-by-step process.
- Simulate algorithms locally using high-performance classical backends.
- Execute programs on IBM's cloud-based quantum processors.
- Explore advanced applications in optimization, **quantum machine learning** (**QML**), and quantum chemistry.

Whether you are writing your first quantum program or experimenting with frontier algorithms, Qiskit provides the flexibility to grow from foundational concepts to advanced exploration. Its design reduces complexity, enabling learners, educators, and researchers to focus on creativity, innovation, and discovery in the rapidly evolving field of quantum computing.

Installation of Qiskit

Qiskit can be installed in two primary ways, depending on the user's needs and resources:

- **Local installation**: Recommended for long-term projects, research environments, and situations where you need more control over dependencies and custom configurations.
- **Cloud-based installation**: Ideal for beginners, classroom demonstrations, or short-term experimentation. Platforms like Google Colab allow users to get started instantly without worrying about setup or compatibility issues.

Local installation

Local installation provides a dedicated environment for long-term use and advanced experimentation. Before proceeding, ensure that the following prerequisites are met:

- Python 3.9 or later is installed on your system.
- Pip (Python package manager) is available.
- It is highly recommended to create and use a virtual environment (e.g., `venv` or `conda`) to avoid dependency conflicts with other Python packages.

The following steps show how to install Qiskit across major operating systems and how to verify the installation with a simple test program:

- **Windows**: Execute the following steps to install Qiskit:
    1. Download and install the latest version of Python (3.9+) from the official Python distribution.

2. During installation, select the option **Add Python to PATH** to simplify usage from the command prompt.
3. Open the command prompt and install Qiskit with:
   ```
   pip install qiskit
   ```
4. Verify the installation by running a test program:
   ```
   from qiskit import QuantumCircuit
   qc = QuantumCircuit(2)
   qc.h(0)
   qc.cx(0, 1)
   print(qc)
   ```

- **macOS**: Execute the following steps to install Qiskit:
  1. Install Python (3.9+) using Homebrew or from the official Python distribution.
  2. Open the **terminal** and run:
     ```
     pip install qiskit
     ```
  3. Verify installation using the preceding sample program provided.
- **Linux (Ubuntu/Debian-based)**: Execute the following steps to install Qiskit:
  1. Update the package list and ensure Python is installed:
     ```
     sudo apt update && sudo apt upgrade
     sudo apt install python3 python3-pip
     ```
  2. Install Qiskit using pip:
     ```
     pip install qiskit
     ```
  3. Test your installation by executing the verification program.
- **Verification output**: If installed correctly, the output of the test program will display the following circuit diagram:

```
     ┌───┐
q_0: ┤ H ├──■──
     └───┘┌─┴─┐
q_1: ─────┤ X ├
          └───┘
```

This confirms that Qiskit is ready for use.

Tip: **To enable advanced visualization features such as Bloch spheres, circuit drawings, and histograms, install the visualization package:**

```
pip install qiskit[visualization]
```

Cloud-based installation

While local installation provides flexibility and control, many learners and educators prefer a faster way to start using Qiskit without dealing with environment setup. For this purpose, cloud-based platforms offer a convenient solution. The most popular choice is Google Colab, which allows users to run Python code directly in their browser with no local installation required.

Colab provides free access to computational resources (including GPUs) and integrates easily with cloud storage, making it a practical environment for both teaching and collaborative projects. This approach is beneficial for:

- Beginners who want to experiment with Qiskit immediately.
- Instructors running workshops or classroom demonstrations.
- Researchers are conducting quick tests without configuring a full local setup.

The points here outline how to install Qiskit using Google Colab, highlight the advantages of cloud-based usage, and clarify when to choose cloud versus local installation.

Steps for cloud installation (Google Colab): Follow these steps to setup Qiskit on Google Colab:

1. Open Google Colab in your browser.
2. Create a new Python notebook.
3. In the first cell, install Qiskit using:
   ```
   !pip install qiskit[visualization] matplotlib
   ```
4. Once the installation completes, you can import Qiskit and begin writing code. For example:
   ```
   from qiskit import QuantumCircuit
   %matplotlib inline
   qc = QuantumCircuit(2)
   qc.h(0)
   qc.cx(0, 1)
   qc.measure_all()
   qc.draw('mpl')
   ```

Here, the **qc.draw('mpl')** function will generate a *graphical circuit diagram*, which is supported in Colab when the visualization tools are available.

Advantages of cloud-based installation: Key benefits of using Google Colab for Qiskit are:

- **No setup hassles**: Works immediately in the browser with a single installation command.
- **Portability**: Access your code from any device connected to the internet.
- **Collaboration**: Easily share notebooks with peers through cloud storage.
- **Scalability**: Suitable for workshops, hackathons, and short-term projects where time is limited.

Choosing between local and cloud installation: When to use local vs. cloud installation:

- Local installation is better suited for advanced users, research projects, or scenarios that require offline access and customization.
- Cloud-based installation is best suited for learners, quick experiments, or teaching environments where simplicity and speed are most important.

In practice, many learners begin with cloud installation to quickly explore Qiskit and later transition to a local setup for larger projects and advanced research.

First program in Qiskit

Once Qiskit has been successfully installed and verified, you are ready to write your first complete quantum program. A natural starting point is the creation of a Bell state, one of the most fundamental quantum states. Bell states are important because they demonstrate the principle of entanglement, where the measurement outcome of one qubit is directly correlated with the outcome of another, regardless of distance.

The following steps show how to build a Bell state circuit, simulate it, and interpret its measurement results:

1. **Bell state circuit**: The Bell state can be created using a two-qubit quantum circuit. The procedure involves:
   a. Applying a Hadamard gate (H) on the first qubit to create a superposition.
   b. Applying a CNOT gate (CX) with the first qubit as the control and the second qubit as the target entangles the two qubits.
   c. Measuring both qubits to observe the entanglement correlations:
      ```
      from qiskit_aer import AerSimulator
      ```

```
# Use the Qiskit Aer simulator
simulator = AerSimulator()
# Execute the circuit on the simulator
result = simulator.run(qc, shots=1024).result()
# Get the results
counts = result.get_counts()
print("Measurement results:", counts)
```

- **Expected circuit diagram (ASCII representation):**

```
     ┌───┐     ┌─┐
q_0: ┤ H ├──■──┤M├───
     └───┘┌─┴─┐└╥┘┌─┐
q_1: ─────┤ X ├─╫─┤M├
          └───┘ ║ └╥┘
c: 2/═══════════╩══╩═
                0  1
```

2. **Running the program**: The next step is to execute the circuit on a simulator backend to observe results. Qiskit provides the Aer simulator, which is suitable for initial testing and evaluation.

```
# Use the Qiskit Aer simulator
simulator = Aer.get_backend('qasm_simulator')
# Execute the circuit on the simulator
job = execute(qc, simulator, shots=1024)
# Get the results
result = job.result()
counts = result.get_counts(qc)
print("Measurement results:", counts)
```

3. **Expected output**: Running the circuit on a simulator with, say, `1024` shots will produce nearly equal counts for `00` and `11` (due to the Bell state), and no other outcomes in the ideal case. The exact numbers will vary run to run:

```
Example (will vary due to randomness):
Measurement results: {'00': 503, '11': 521}
```

The key point is that only `00` and `11` appear, with roughly 50% of each.

Note: **On real quantum hardware, small counts of 01 or 10 may appear due to noise and readout errors; in the ideal simulator, results concentrate on 00 and 11.**

This simple program demonstrates the core workflow in Qiskit:

1. Build a quantum circuit.
2. Simulate or execute it on a quantum device.
3. Measure and analyze the results.

The Bell state program is often considered the `Hello, World!` of quantum computing, as it introduces both superposition and entanglement in just a few steps.

Qiskit modules

Qiskit is designed as a modular framework, where each component is tailored to address a specific aspect of quantum computing. This modularity ensures flexibility, scalability, and clarity, allowing learners and researchers to engage with quantum programming at multiple levels of abstraction. Together, these modules form a comprehensive ecosystem, encompassing everything from building circuits to simulating them, analyzing noise, and applying advanced algorithms.

Before working on hands-on experiments, it is essential to understand the function of these modules. Having this foundation not only helps in writing effective quantum programs but also in interpreting results and debugging circuits with confidence.

Qiskit Terra as the quantum programming foundation

Qiskit Terra forms the core layer of the Qiskit framework. The name Terra, meaning *earth*, signifies its role as the foundation upon which the rest of Qiskit is built. Terra provides the fundamental tools required to:

- Construct quantum circuits step-by-step.
- Define and manipulate quantum operations (gates, measurements, classical registers).
- Optimize and transpile circuits so that they are compatible with specific hardware.
- Manage access to backends, whether they are classical simulators or real quantum processors available through the cloud.

In essence, Terra enables you to design, transform, and prepare circuits for execution in the quantum computing workflow.

Example: Creating a simple circuit with Terra

The following program illustrates how to create and display a simple circuit using Terra. The circuit applies a Hadamard gate to the first qubit and then measures both qubits:

```
from qiskit import QuantumCircuit
# Step 1: Create a quantum circuit with 2 qubits and 2 classical bits
qc = QuantumCircuit(2, 2)
# Step 2: Apply a Hadamard gate to the first qubit
qc.h(0)
# Step 3: Measure both qubits
qc.measure([0, 1], [0, 1])
# Step 4: Display the circuit
print(qc.draw())
```

Here is the ASCII circuit representation:

```
     ┌───┐     ┌─┐
q_0: ┤ H ├─────┤M├───
     └───┘┌────└┬┘───
q_1: ─────┤M─────────
          └──────────
c: 2/════════════════
          0   1
```

Key insight

This example highlights Terra's fundamental role, defining circuits at the gate level. While higher-level modules (such as Aqua) focus on applications, Terra keeps you close to the actual operations performed on quantum hardware. By working with Terra, users gain both flexibility and precision in circuit construction.

Qiskit Aer as a quantum simulation engine

Qiskit Aer is the simulation module of Qiskit, designed to provide high-performance classical simulators for quantum circuits. Since real quantum hardware is resource-limited and subject to noise, simulators play a vital role in testing, debugging, and validating algorithms before execution on actual devices.

Aer supports multiple simulation modes, each serving a unique purpose:

- **Statevector simulation**: Displays the exact amplitudes of all quantum states in the system. This mode is particularly useful for gaining deep insights into how circuits transform quantum states.
- **QASM simulation**: Mimics real hardware by generating measurement outcomes based on quantum probabilities. This mode is useful when testing algorithms that involve repeated measurements, such as variational quantum algorithms.

By using Aer, researchers can efficiently prototype circuits, understand their behavior in detail, and optimize them before committing to physical hardware execution.

Example: Simulating a circuit

The following example demonstrates how to simulate a simple Bell state circuit using both the **`statevector`** simulator and the QASM simulator:

```
from qiskit import QuantumCircuit
from qiskit_aer import AerSimulator
# Step 1: Create a 2-qubit circuit
qc = QuantumCircuit(2)
qc.h(0)            # Apply Hadamard to first qubit
qc.cx(0, 1)        # Apply CNOT with control=0 and target=1
# --- Statevector Simulation ---
sv_sim = AerSimulator(method='statevector')
qc_sv = qc.copy()
qc_sv.save_statevector()                 # tell Aer to save the statevector
sv_result = sv_sim.run(qc_sv).result()
statevector = sv_result.get_statevector()
print("Statevector:\n", statevector)
# --- QASM Simulation ---
qasm_sim = AerSimulator()
qc_qasm = qc.copy()
qc_qasm.measure_all()
qasm_result = qasm_sim.run(qc_qasm, shots=1024).result()
counts = qasm_result.get_counts()
print("Measurement Results:\n", counts)
```

The expected output is as follows:

- **Statevector simulation**: Displays the amplitudes of the Bell state:

  ```
  Statevector:
  [0.707+0.j, 0.+0.j, 0.+0.j, 0.707+0.j]
  ```

  This indicates an equal superposition of states $|00\rangle$ and $|11\rangle$.

- **QASM simulation**: Provides measurement counts that approximate a 50/50 distribution between 00 and 11:

  ```
  Measurement Results:
  {'00': 510, '11': 514}
  ```

Key insight

Qiskit Aer is indispensable for the development of quantum algorithms. While statevector simulation provides theoretical accuracy, QASM simulation delivers practical insights that mirror hardware behavior. By mastering both, learners can move seamlessly from abstract circuit design to realistic algorithm testing.

Qiskit Ignis for error and noise analysis

Real quantum devices are inherently noisy. Environmental interactions, gate imperfections, and measurement errors often impact quantum computations, resulting in outcomes that deviate from ideal simulations. This is one of the key challenges in practical quantum computing.

Qiskit Ignis was developed as a toolkit to address this challenge. The name *Ignis*, meaning *fire*, reflects its role in refining noisy computations.

Legacy Notice (2025) states that Qiskit Ignis is no longer actively developed and has been superseded by the Qiskit Experiments project (for calibration, characterization, benchmarking, and mitigation workflows) and by Qiskit Aer's noise modeling utilities (for simulated noise). Ignis remains historically important; however, for new projects, please use Qiskit Experiments and Qiskit Aer.

Historically, Ignis provided tools to:

- Model noise and errors in a controlled way.
- Mitigate imperfections through error correction and calibration routines.
- Study the impact of errors on the performance of quantum algorithms.

This is critical because algorithms that perform well under ideal conditions may yield very different results when run on real hardware. Ignis helps researchers design circuits that are robust against noise and test strategies for error resilience.

Modern usage of prefer Qiskit Experiments for device-level experiments and mitigation workflows, and Qiskit Aer for simulated noise studies; the following example uses legacy Ignis terminology purely for historical context.

Initializing a noise model

The following example demonstrates how to use Ignis with Qiskit Aer to simulate a noisy backend. Here, we introduce a simple depolarizing error to model imperfections in a CNOT gate:

```
from qiskit import QuantumCircuit
from qiskit_aer import AerSimulator
from qiskit.providers.aer.noise import NoiseModel, depolarizing_error
# Bell-state circuit
qc = QuantumCircuit(2, 2)
qc.h(0)
qc.cx(0, 1)
qc.measure([0, 1], [0, 1])
# Noise model: depolarizing error on 2-qubit gates
noise_model = NoiseModel()
error = depolarizing_error(0.05, 2)   # 5% error on CX
noise_model.add_all_qubit_quantum_error(error, ['cx'])
# Run with AerSimulator and noise
sim = AerSimulator()
result = sim.run(qc, shots=1024, noise_model=noise_model).result()
counts = result.get_counts()
print("Noisy Measurement Results:\n", counts)
```

Instead of a perfect 50/50 entanglement between `00` and `11`, the measurement results will show additional outcomes (`01`, `10`) caused by the depolarizing error. The following is the expected output:

```
Noisy Measurement Results:
{'00': 460, '11': 455, '01': 55, '10': 54}
```

This demonstrates how noise alters the output distribution, even in a simple two-qubit circuit.

The following components represent modern replacements for the legacy Ignis module, providing advanced tools for noise modeling, calibration, and error mitigation in contemporary Qiskit workflows:

- **Qiskit experiments**: Run calibration/characterization/mitigation routines on real backends and analyze results in a standardized way.
- **Qiskit Aer (noise)**: Construct and attach noise models (e.g., depolarizing, thermal relaxation, readout error) when simulating circuits. These supersede most Ignis workflows in modern Qiskit.

Key insight

Ignis is a powerful tool for bridging the gap between theoretical quantum circuits and realistic hardware performance. By allowing developers to simulate and analyze noise, Ignis helps in:

- Understanding how errors propagate in quantum algorithms.
- Designing strategies for noise mitigation.
- Preparing circuits that are more resilient when executed on actual quantum processors.

Qiskit Aqua for algorithms deprecated

Qiskit Aqua (algorithms for quantum applications) was Qiskit's high-level library dedicated to implementing quantum algorithms across diverse application domains.

Deprecation Notice (2025) declares that Qiskit Aqua has been removed from modern Qiskit distributions. Its functionality now resides in domain packages such as `qiskit-machine-learning`, `qiskit-optimization`, `qiskit-nature`, and `qiskit-finance`, as well as in `qiskit-algorithms` for general algorithm scaffolding. Attempting to import from `qiskit.aqua...` on current versions will raise `ImportError: No module named 'qiskit.aqua'`. Use modern packages for new code, or legacy packages for old tutorials.

Aqua provided ready-to-use functionalities for:

- **Machine learning**: Quantum classifiers, **support vector machines** (**SVMs**), and kernel methods.
- **Optimization**: Solving combinatorial optimization problems.
- **Chemistry**: Molecular simulations and ground state energy calculations.
- **Finance**: Portfolio optimization, option pricing, and risk analysis.

Historically, Aqua was designed to allow researchers and practitioners to explore quantum applications without needing to build algorithms from scratch.

However, Aqua has since been deprecated, and its functionalities have been migrated into domain-specific application modules such as:

- `qiskit-machine-learning`
- `qiskit-optimization`
- `qiskit-nature`
- `qiskit-finance`

Despite its retirement, Aqua remains important in two contexts:

- **Historical relevance**: Many tutorials, academic papers, and teaching materials still reference Aqua.
- **Conceptual foundation**: Aqua demonstrated how quantum algorithms could be applied to real-world domains, shaping the structure of today's specialized application libraries.

Legacy example (will not run on current Qiskit): The snippet here uses `qiskit.aqua.*` imports that have been removed. If you must run it, use a pinned legacy environment (e.g., an older version of Qiskit with `qiskit-aqua` 0.9.x) in an isolated virtual environment or conda environment.

The following example of *Legacy Aqua* usage illustrates how Aqua was used for a simple optimization problem using the **variational quantum eigensolver** (**VQE**) algorithm:

```
from qiskit import Aer
from qiskit.aqua.algorithms import VQE
```

```
from qiskit.circuit.library import TwoLocal
from qiskit.aqua.components.optimizers import COBYLA
from qiskit.aqua.operators import Z, I
# Step 1: Define a simple Hamiltonian (Z ⊗ I + I ⊗ Z)
hamiltonian = Z ^ I + I ^ Z
# Step 2: Choose a variational form (ansatz)
ansatz = TwoLocal(rotation_blocks='ry', entanglement_blocks='cz')
# Step 3: Define optimizer
optimizer = COBYLA(maxiter=100)
# Step 4: Initialize VQE with Aer simulator
backend = Aer.get_backend('statevector_simulator')
vqe = VQE(ansatz, optimizer=optimizer, quantum_instance=backend)
# Step 5: Run the algorithm
result = vqe.compute_minimum_eigenvalue(operator=hamiltonian)
print("Ground state energy: ", result.eigenvalue.real)
```

The expected output would be as follows:

```
Ground state energy: -2.0
```

This result corresponds to the lowest eigenvalue of the Hamiltonian, showing Aqua's ability to solve optimization and chemistry-related problems.

Modern equivalent (VQE) using current packages as:

```
# pip install qiskit qiskit-aer qiskit-algorithms
from qiskit.circuit.library import TwoLocal
from qiskit.quantum_info import SparsePauliOp
from qiskit_algorithms import VQE
from qiskit_algorithms.optimizers import COBYLA
from qiskit.primitives import Estimator
# Hamiltonian: Z ⊗ I + I ⊗ Z
H = SparsePauliOp.from_list([("ZI", 1.0), ("IZ", 1.0)])
# Variational ansatz and optimizer
ansatz = TwoLocal(rotation_blocks="ry", entanglement_blocks="cz")
optimizer = COBYLA(maxiter=100)
# VQE with Estimator primitive
vqe = VQE(Estimator(), ansatz, optimizer)
result = vqe.compute_minimum_eigenvalue(H)
print("Ground state energy: ", result.eigenvalue.real)
```

Specialized Qiskit application modules for building quantum applications

The following specialized Qiskit modules provide domain-focused tools and libraries that simplify the development of quantum applications across diverse areas such as machine learning, optimization, chemistry, finance, and algorithm design:

- **qiskit-machine-learning**: Classifiers, kernels, QSVMs, etc.
- **qiskit-optimization**: Combinatorial optimization (QAOA, etc.).
- **qiskit-nature**: Chemistry/physics (molecules, lattices).
- **qiskit-finance**: Portfolio problems, risk modeling.
- **qiskit-algorithms**: VQE, QAOA, and related algorithm scaffolds.

Qiskit Aqua played a pioneering role in making quantum algorithms accessible to non-specialists. While it is no longer actively developed, understanding Aqua is helpful for:

- Reading and interpreting earlier tutorials and research papers.
- Appreciating the evolution of Qiskit into domain-specific modules.
- Building a bridge between historical usage and modern application libraries in Qiskit.

Circuit construction and visualization

At the heart of quantum programming lies the quantum circuit—a structured sequence of gates, measurements, and operations applied to qubits. A quantum circuit defines how information is processed and transformed in a quantum computer. In Qiskit, circuits are intuitive to build, flexible to extend, and easy to visualize, making the framework particularly accessible to both learners and researchers.

Constructing circuits involves specifying the number of qubits and classical bits, applying quantum gates (such as the Hadamard or CNOT), and finally performing measurements. Qiskit's design allows these steps to be expressed in just a few lines of Python code, reducing the gap between abstract quantum concepts and practical experimentation.

Visualization plays a particularly significant role. While the mathematical foundations of quantum mechanics can be expressed in terms of linear algebra and complex amplitudes, these abstractions often remain difficult to grasp in practice. Circuit diagrams serve as a bridge:

- For learners, they make quantum processes tangible and easier to follow.
- For researchers, they provide a quick way to verify correctness and debug designs.
- For educators and authors, they create standardized illustrations suitable for teaching materials and publications.

In Qiskit, visualization is built directly into the framework, enabling circuits to be represented both in text-based ASCII form for quick checks in the console and in graphical form for clearer, publication-ready diagrams. This dual representation enhances understanding, collaboration, and communication in the field of quantum computing.

Creating a quantum circuit

To construct a quantum circuit in Qiskit, the first step is to define the number of qubits (quantum bits) and classical bits (used to store measurement outcomes). Once the registers are initialized, quantum gates can be applied to manipulate the qubits, followed by measurement operations to extract classical results.

Example: Creating a Bell state circuit

The Bell state is one of the simplest and most important examples of quantum entanglement. The following program demonstrates how to create this state using Qiskit:

```
from qiskit import QuantumCircuit
# Step 1: Create a quantum circuit with 2 qubits and 2 classical bits
qc = QuantumCircuit(2, 2)
# Step 2: Apply a Hadamard gate to the first qubit (superposition)
qc.h(0)
# Step 3: Apply a CNOT gate (control=0, target=1) to entangle the qubits
qc.cx(0, 1)
# Step 4: Measure both qubits
qc.measure([0, 1], [0, 1])
# Display the ASCII diagram of the circuit
print(qc.draw())
```

The expected ASCII output is:

```
     ┌───┐     ┌─┐
q_0: ┤ H ├──■──┤M├───
     └───┘┌─┴─┐└╥┘┌─┐
q_1: ─────┤ X ├─╫─┤M├
          └───┘ ║ └╥┘
c: 2/═══════════╩══╩═
                0  1
```

The explanation is as follows:

1. The Hadamard gate on the first qubit creates a superposition:

   $|0\rangle \rightarrow \frac{|0\rangle+|1\rangle}{\sqrt{2}}$

2. The CNOT gate then entangles the second qubit with the first, producing the Bell state:

   $\frac{|00\rangle+|11\rangle}{\sqrt{2}}$

3. Finally, the measurement operation collapses the qubits into classical outcomes, which will always be correlated—both qubits yield 0 or both yield 1.

Adding more gates

Qiskit supports a wide range of quantum gates, allowing programmers to build circuits of varying complexity. These include:

- Single-qubit gates such as the Hadamard (H), Pauli gates (X, Y, Z), and phase gates (S, T).
- Multi-qubit gates such as the CNOT, Toffoli (CCX), and SWAP.

By combining these gates, one can create advanced circuits and implement algorithms that demonstrate quantum properties such as superposition, entanglement, and interference.

Example: A three-qubit GHZ state circuit

The GHZ state is a three-qubit entangled state that generalizes the Bell state to multiple qubits. It illustrates how entanglement can extend beyond two qubits.

The GHZ state is defined as:

$$|\mathrm{GHZ}\rangle = \frac{|\mathbf{000}\rangle+|\mathbf{111}\rangle}{\sqrt{\mathbf{2}}}$$

```
from qiskit import QuantumCircuit
# Step 1: Create a quantum circuit with 3 qubits and 3 classical bits
qc = QuantumCircuit(3, 3)
# Step 2: Apply a Hadamard gate to the first qubit
qc.h(0)
# Step 3: Entangle the first and second qubits with a CNOT
qc.cx(0, 1)
# Step 4: Entangle the first and third qubits with another CNOT
qc.cx(0, 2)
# Step 5: Measure all qubits
qc.measure([0, 1, 2], [0, 1, 2])
# Display the ASCII diagram
print(qc.draw())
```

The expected ASCII circuit as:

```
     ┌───┐     ┌─┐
q_0: ┤ H ├──■──┤M├──
     └───┘  │  └╥┘
q_1: ───────X───╫─┤M├──
           ┌┴┐  ║
q_2: ──────┤ X ├─╫─┤M├──
           └───┘ ║
c: 3/════════════╩═════
                 0  1  2
```

The circuit's expected behavior can be described as follows:

- The Hadamard gate on qubit 0 creates a superposition.
- The first CNOT entangles qubit 1 with qubit 0.
- The second CNOT entangles qubit 2 with qubit 0, creating the GHZ state.
- Measurements will yield either 000 or 111 with nearly equal probability.

Tip (bitstring order in Qiskit): **The rightmost bit in a reported bitstring corresponds to classical bit 0 (little-endian). In this example, measuring [0,1,2] into [0,1,2] means the printed string 111 indicates all three-qubits measured 1.**

Visualizing circuits

Quantum circuits can often become complex, and visualization plays an important role in verifying, teaching, and publishing results. Qiskit provides multiple visualization options, each tailored for different purposes:

- **Text representation**: A quick inspection using `print(qc)` or `qc.draw()`. This displays the circuit in ASCII format, ideal for command-line checks.
- **Matplotlib visualization**: Produces clean graphical circuit diagrams using the mpl drawer. These diagrams are easy to interpret and suitable for use in books, presentations, or reports.
- **LaTeX visualization**: Generates high-quality figures through the LaTeX drawer. This is particularly useful for academic papers and teaching slides, where precision and aesthetics are crucial.

Prerequisites: Before running the code, ensure the following prerequisites are installed:

- **For Matplotlib diagrams**: `pip install qiskit[visualization] matplotlib`
- For the LaTeX drawer, install `pylatexenc` with `pip` and a TeX distribution (e.g., TeX Live/MiKTeX) for PDF and PNG outputs.

The following example demonstrates how to visualize a GHZ state circuit using Matplotlib:

```
# If needed (e.g., in Colab), install visualization support:
# !pip install "qiskit[visualization]" matplotlib
from qiskit import QuantumCircuit
# Create a 3-qubit GHZ state circuit
qc = QuantumCircuit(3, 3)
qc.h(0)
qc.cx(0, 1)
qc.cx(0, 2)
qc.measure([0, 1, 2], [0, 1, 2])
# In notebooks, ensure inline figures (optional in Colab/Jupyter)
# %matplotlib inline
# Render with Matplotlib
fig = qc.draw('mpl')
```

The expected output of the circuit visualization is:

- The Matplotlib visualization produces a neat and colorful diagram of the GHZ state circuit, where qubit wires are clearly shown, gates are appropriately spaced, and measurement operations are visually distinct.
- The diagram is publication-ready, making it suitable for textbooks, lecture slides, or research papers.

Simulation vs. real quantum hardware

One of Qiskit's greatest strengths lies in its flexibility: it allows circuits to be executed either on local simulators or on real quantum hardware via the *IBM Quantum Experience* cloud platform. Both approaches are integral to quantum learning and research, each serving complementary roles in the development process.

The following points explain the distinct roles of simulators, real quantum hardware, and how both contribute jointly to effective quantum learning and experimentation:

- **Simulators**: Simulators provide a fast, noise-free environment for building confidence in circuit design. They are invaluable for:
    - Testing and debugging algorithms before committing them to real devices.
    - Statevector analysis, where complete quantum state amplitudes can be inspected.
    - Rapid prototyping enables researchers to explore various circuit structures without hardware constraints.

Since simulators operate on classical computers, they allow learners to explore idealized quantum behavior and understand theoretical outcomes without the complications of real-world noise:

- **Real quantum hardware**: Executing circuits on real IBM Quantum devices introduces practical challenges that simulators cannot fully capture. These include:
    - Noise and decoherence cause errors in computation.
    - Qubit connectivity limitations require circuit transpilation and optimization.
    - Restricted qubit counts, reflecting the current technological limits of quantum processors.

While hardware results may deviate from ideal simulations, they are closer to true experimental practice, making them invaluable for understanding the realities of quantum computing:

- **Complementary roles**: Simulators and real hardware are not alternatives but rather complements in the quantum learning journey:
    - Start with simulators to validate ideas, explore idealized outcomes, and build foundational knowledge.
    - Progress to real hardware to study how algorithms behave under realistic conditions and to develop strategies for noise mitigation.

This dual approach ensures that learners and researchers can transition smoothly from theoretical models to practical implementations, gaining both conceptual clarity and experimental insight.

Using local simulators with Qiskit Aer

Qiskit Aer provides a suite of high-performance simulators that enable learners and researchers to test circuits without relying on physical quantum hardware. These simulators are extremely valuable in the early stages of learning, as they produce results that are free from hardware imperfections such as noise, decoherence, and connectivity constraints.

By working with simulators, one can validate circuit design, confirm expected outcomes, and debug algorithms efficiently before running them on real quantum devices.

The following example demonstrates how to run a Bell state circuit using Aer's QASM simulator, which mimics the probabilistic measurement outcomes of real hardware:

```
# If needed: pip install qiskit qiskit-aer
from qiskit import QuantumCircuit
from qiskit_aer import AerSimulator
# 1) Build the circuit
qc = QuantumCircuit(2, 2)
qc.h(0)
qc.cx(0, 1)
qc.measure([0, 1], [0, 1])
# 2) Run on Aer QASM simulator
sim = AerSimulator()
result = sim.run(qc, shots=1024).result()
counts = result.get_counts()
print("Simulation Results:", counts)
```

Let us discuss the expected output.

Running the circuit on a simulator (e.g., 1024 shots) yields nearly equal counts for the two Bell state outcomes. Exact numbers vary due to sampling:

```
Example (varies by run):
Simulation Results: {'00': ~50%, '11': ~50%}
```

In the ideal simulator, only **`00` and `11`** appear (~50% each). On real hardware, small fractions of 01 and 10 may also appear because of noise, decoherence, and readout errors.

Running on real IBM Quantum hardware

IBM provides free cloud-based access to real quantum processors through the IBM Quantum Experience platform. This allows learners and researchers to run the same circuits they design and test on simulators directly on physical qubits, offering hands-on experience with the challenges and realities of quantum computing.

Running circuits on real hardware is an important milestone. It exposes students to hardware-specific limitations, such as qubit connectivity, gate errors, and decoherence, and highlights the importance of circuit optimization and error mitigation.

IBM now recommends the Qiskit Runtime client instead of the legacy IBMQ provider. The Qiskit Runtime client handles authentication, device discovery, and the preferred primitives interface (e.g., **`SamplerV2`**, **`EstimatorV2`**).

Here are the steps to run on IBM Quantum hardware (Modern: Qiskit Runtime):

1. **Create an IBM Quantum account**: Register for an IBM Quantum account and obtain your API token from your account page.

2. **Install the Qiskit Runtime client**:

   ```
   pip install qiskit qiskit-ibm-runtime
   ```

   The older **`qiskit-ibm-provider`** is deprecated; use **`qiskit-ibm-runtime`**.

3. **Save and load your credentials (one-time save)**:

   ```
   from qiskit_ibm_runtime import QiskitRuntimeService
   # Save once (stores credentials under ~/.qiskit/qiskit-ibm.json)
   QiskitRuntimeService.save_account(
       channel="ibm_quantum_platform",    # use "ibm_cloud" if you run via IBM Cloud
       token="YOUR_API_TOKEN",
       set_as_default=True,
       overwrite=True
   ```

```
)
# In future sessions: just load
service = QiskitRuntimeService()
```

If your plan uses an instance/CRN, include it when saving the account.

4. **Choose a real backend**: Avoid hardcoding device names because systems are periodically retired or upgraded. Select an operational device programmatically:

```
backend = service.least_busy(operational=True, simulator=False)
print("Selected backend:", backend.name)
```

You can inspect available systems with `service.backends()`.

5. **Execute your circuit on hardware**:

   a. Simple job mode (**`backend.run`**).

   This mirrors older workflows but uses the Qiskit Runtime client. Always transpile to the target backend first:

```
from qiskit import QuantumCircuit, transpile
# Build a Bell-state circuit
qc = QuantumCircuit(2, 2)
qc.h(0)
qc.cx(0, 1)
qc.measure_all()
# Transpile to the device's native gate set and coupling map
tqc = transpile(qc, backend=backend, optimization_level=1)
# Submit to hardware
job = backend.run(tqc, shots=1024)
result = job.result()
counts = result.get_counts()
print("Hardware Results:", counts)
```

   Expected output: Nearly equal counts for 00 and 11, with small fractions of 01/10 due to noise and readout error (exact numbers vary).

   b. **Preferred modern path**: Runtime primitive (**`SamplerV2`**):

   `SamplerV2` is the recommended interface for sampling measurement outcomes. Convert the circuit to the device's ISA using a preset pass manager, then run with the primitive:

```
from qiskit import QuantumCircuit
from qiskit.transpiler.preset_passmanagers import generate_preset_pass_manager
from qiskit_ibm_runtime import SamplerV2 as Sampler
# 1) Build circuit
qc = QuantumCircuit(2, 2)
qc.h(0)
qc.cx(0, 1)
qc.measure_all()
# 2) Generate an ISA (hardware-native) circuit for the chosen backend
pm = generate_preset_pass_manager(backend=backend, optimization_level=1)
isa_circuit = pm.run(qc)
# 3) Run with SamplerV2
sampler = Sampler(backend)
job = sampler.run([isa_circuit], shots=1024)
res = job.result()
# 4) Get counts from the first circuit's publication (default register)
```

```
pub0 = res[0]
print("Hardware Results (Sampler):", pub0.data.meas.get_counts())
```

Key insight

Running circuits on IBM Quantum hardware offers invaluable experience:

- Simulators provide ideal, noise-free results.
- Real devices reflect practical challenges such as noise, decoherence, and limited connectivity.

Together, they provide a complete learning experience, bridging the gap between theory and experiment.

Implementing Grover's algorithm

Grover's algorithm is one of the landmark contributions to quantum computing, primarily because it offers a quadratic speedup for searching an unsorted database. In a classical setting, searching through N items requires O(N) steps, as each candidate must be checked individually. Grover's algorithm, however, can locate the desired item in approximately $O(\sqrt{N})$..

Intuition behind Grover's algorithm

Imagine you are trying to find a single marked entry in a large, unsorted list:

- **Classical approach**: Each item must be examined individually until the target is identified.
- **Quantum approach**: By using superposition, all items are explored simultaneously. Then, through clever interference, the probability of the correct answer is amplified while incorrect ones are suppressed.

This procedure can be broken down into four conceptual steps:

1. **Initialization**: Begin with an equal superposition over all possible states.
2. **Oracle**: Apply a special quantum operation that flips the phase of the marked state.
3. **Diffuser (amplitude amplification)**: Invert all amplitudes about their average, strengthening the marked state's presence.
4. **Measurement**: After approximately $\sqrt{N}$ repetitions, the marked state appears with high probability.

Example of Qubit Grover's algorithm

To make the concept concrete, let us implement Grover's algorithm for a two-qubit system. This corresponds to a database of four possible items (00,01,10,11), where the marked item is assumed to be 11.

The following steps outline how to construct and execute a two-qubit Grover's algorithm in Qiskit, beginning with library imports, defining the oracle and diffuser, and finally building the complete quantum circuit:

1. **Import libraries**:
```
from qiskit import QuantumCircuit, Aer, execute
from qiskit.visualization import plot_histogram
import matplotlib.pyplot as plt
```
2. **Define oracle for marked state (11)**:
```
def grover_oracle(circuit):
    # Flip both qubits
    circuit.x([0,1])
    # Apply CZ using H + CX + H decomposition
    circuit.h(1)
    circuit.cx(0,1)
```

```
    circuit.h(1)
    # Undo the flips
    circuit.x([0,1])
```

3. **Define the grover diffuser**:
```
 grover_diffuser ( circuit ):
    circuit.h([ 0 , 1 ])
    circuit.x([ 0 , 1 ])
    circuit.h( 1 )
    circuit.cx( 0 , 1 )
    circuit.h( 1 )
    circuit.x([ 0 , 1 ])
    circuit.h([ 0 , 1 ])
```

4. **Build the circuit**:
```
qc = QuantumCircuit(2, 2)
# Step 1: Initialization into superposition
qc.h([0,1])
# Step 2: Apply the Oracle
grover_oracle(qc)
# Step 3: Apply the Diffuser
grover_diffuser(qc)
# Step 4: Measurement
qc.measure([0,1], [0,1])
print(qc)
```

5. **Running the simulation**:
```
simulator = Aer.get_backend('qasm_simulator')
job = execute(qc, simulator, shots=1024)
result = job.result()
counts = result.get_counts()
print("Results:", counts)
plot_histogram(counts)
plt.show()
```

The expected output is as follows:

The histogram generated by the simulation will show a clear peak at state 11, which is the marked item. This verifies that Grover's algorithm successfully identified the target with high probability after just a single oracle–diffuser cycle in this two-qubit example.

Key insights

The following key insights can be drawn from Grover's algorithm:

- Grover's algorithm is a general-purpose algorithm, making it suitable for a wide range of black-box search problems.
- As the number of qubits grows, the search space expands exponentially, while Grover's advantage becomes increasingly significant.
- The algorithm elegantly demonstrates the power of superposition, quantum interference, and amplitude amplification.

Concept reinforcement: While small-scale demonstrations (such as this two-qubit example) are helpful for understanding, the true strength of Grover's algorithm is revealed only on larger quantum systems, where classical brute-force search quickly becomes infeasible.

Worked example on searching a 1000 item database

Scenario: You need to find a specific entry (e.g., a password) in an unsorted database with N=1,000 items. Each check (query to the oracle or lookup) takes the same unit of time.

The following points compare the efficiency of classical brute-force search with Grover's algorithm when applied to a database of one thousand items:

- **Classical search (brute-force)**:
    - **Expected checks**: $\approx N/2=500$ on average (worst case 1,000).
    - **Guarantee**: Only certain after checking all items or by chance earlier.
- **Grover's algorithm**:
    - **Iterations required**: $\lfloor \frac{\pi}{4}\sqrt{N} \rfloor \approx \lfloor \frac{\pi}{4} \times 31.62 \rfloor \approx 24\text{–}26$
    - **Each iteration**: One oracle call + a diffuser.
    - **Outcome**: High probability of measuring the target after ~*25* iterations.
- **Time comparison (unit cost per step)**:
    - **Classical**: ~*500* units expected, up to *1,000* worst case.
    - **Grover**: ~*25–32* units total.

Speedup: Roughly 15–20× fewer steps for N=1,000.

As N increases, the gap widens dramatically: classical scales as $O(N)$, Grover as $O(\sqrt{N})$.

Insight: On today's noisy hardware, errors reduce Grover's success probability. However, its asymptotic advantage remains, and as quantum devices scale, Grover's algorithm will become increasingly practical.

Case study on implementing quantum teleportation

Quantum teleportation transfers an unknown qubit state from *Alice* to *Bob*. This state, denoted as:

$$|\psi\rangle=\alpha|0\rangle+\beta|1\rangle,$$

is sent from Alice (qubit q_0) to Bob (qubit q_2) without physically moving a particle. The protocol uses three key steps:

1. Shared entanglement between Alice and Bob.
2. A Bell-basis measurement performed by Alice, and Bob.
3. Sending two classical bits that allow Bob to apply the required correction gates and reconstruct $|\psi\rangle$.

Registers: The quantum and classical registers used in the teleportation protocol are:

- **q_0 (Alice's input):** Holds the unknown state $|\psi\rangle$.
- **q_1 (Alice's half of the EPR pair):** Part of the entangled pair shared with Bob.
- **q_2 (Bob's half of the EPR pair):** Destination of $|\psi\rangle$.
- **c_0, c_1 :** Classical bits carrying Alice's two-bit measurement outcome to Bob.

Protocol overview

The quantum teleportation protocol proceeds through the following steps:

1. Prepare the unknown state on q_0: $|\psi\rangle$.
2. Create entanglement between q_1 and q_2: Apply H on q_1, then $CX(q_1$ "" → "" $q_2)$ → Bell pair $(|00\rangle+|11\rangle)/\sqrt{2}$.
3. Bell measurement (Alice): Apply , $CX(q_0$ " "→" " $q_1)$ then H on q_0; measure q_0, q_1 into c_0, c_1.

4. Classically controlled corrections (Bob on q_2):
   a. If c_1=1, apply X on q_2.
   b. If c_0=1, apply Z on q_2.

Result: q_2 becomes $|\psi\rangle$. Alice's q_0, q_1 become random and uncorrelated with $|\psi\rangle$.

Correction table (Alice | Bob): The correction operations Bob must apply based on Alice's measurement results are:

Alice result c_0,c_1	Bob's correction on q_2
00	I
01	X
10	Z
11	ZX (order Z then X; XZ is equivalent up to a global phase)

***Table 7.1**: Alice's outcomes and Bob's required correction operations*

Qiskit implementation using statevector and QASM

We teleport a general single-qubit state parameterized by Bloch angles θ,ϕ:

$$|\psi\rangle=\cos(\theta/2)|0\rangle+e^{i\phi}\sin(\theta/2)|1\rangle$$

The steps here demonstrate how to build and verify the quantum teleportation circuit in Qiskit:

1. **Build the circuit**:

```
from qiskit import QuantumCircuit, Aer, execute
import numpy as np
# Parameters for an arbitrary state |psi> (pick any angles you like)
theta = np.pi/3   # 60 degrees
phi   = np.pi/5   # 36 degrees
# Helper: prepare |psi> on q0 using ry(theta) and rz(phi)
def prepare_arbitrary_state(qc, q):
    qc.ry(theta, q)
    qc.rz(phi, q)
# 3 qubits (q0, q1, q2) and 2 classical bits (c0, c1)
qc = QuantumCircuit(3, 2)
# 1) Prepare unknown state on q0
prepare_arbitrary_state(qc, 0)
# 2) Create entanglement between q1 and q2 (EPR pair)
qc.h(1)
qc.cx(1, 2)
# 3) Bell measurement on Alice's side (q0, q1)
qc.cx(0, 1)
qc.h(0)
# Measure q0 -> c0, q1 -> c1
qc.measure(0, 0)
qc.measure(1, 1)
# 4) Classically controlled corrections on Bob's qubit q2
# NOTE on bit order:
# - With a 2-bit classical register [c0, c1], the integer value is little-endian:
#     value = c0 * 1 + c1 * 2
```

```
# - So: c1==1 corresponds to value 2 (0b10); c0==1 corresponds to value 1 (0b01).
qc.x(2).c_if(qc.cregs[0], 0b10)  # X if c1 == 1
qc.z(2).c_if(qc.cregs[0], 0b01)  # Z if c0 == 1
print(qc)
```

2. **Verify by statevector (conceptual check)**:

   Run a noiseless statevector simulation up to measurement to confirm the unitary parts behave as expected:

```
# Build a copy that stops before measurement/corrections
qc_unitary = QuantumCircuit(3)
prepare_arbitrary_state(qc_unitary, 0)
qc_unitary.h(1); qc_unitary.cx(1, 2)
qc_unitary.cx(0, 1); qc_unitary.h(0)
backend_sv = Aer.get_backend('statevector_simulator')
sv = execute(qc_unitary, backend_sv).result().get_statevector()
print("Statevector (pre-measurement):\n", sv)
```

3. **Interpretation**: The amplitudes encode a superposition over the four possible outcomes $c_0\, c_1 \in \{00,01,10,11\}$, where each branch maps Bob's q_2 to a corrected/uncorrected variant of $|\psi\rangle$. After we measure and correct, q_2 deterministically becomes $|\psi\rangle$.

4. **Run end-to-end (QASM) and inspect distributions**:

```
from qiskit.visualization import plot_histogram
import matplotlib.pyplot as plt
backend_qasm = Aer.get_backend('qasm_simulator')
job = execute(qc, backend_qasm, shots=2048)
res = job.result()
counts = res.get_counts()
print("Measurement outcomes on c0c1:", counts)
plot_histogram(counts)
plt.show()
```

5. **Expected results**: The classical results on $c_0\, c_1$ are roughly uniform over 00, 01, 10, 11 (≈25% each). Crucially, after the conditional corrections, q_2 holds $|\psi\rangle$ regardless of which outcome occurred.

Common pitfalls and troubleshooting

When implementing quantum teleportation, be mindful of the following common pitfalls and troubleshooting tips:

- **Missing classical controls**: If you apply `X/Z` unconditionally, q_2 will not equal $|\psi\rangle$ for all outcomes—use **`c_if`** and verify bit masks.
- **Bit-order confusion**: With two classical bits $[c_0, c_1]$, the integer value is little-endian: value =c_0·1+c_1·2. Keep this mapping consistent with the correction table.
- **Testing only basis states**: Always test a generic state (non-trivial θ, ϕ) to validate beyond $|0\rangle$ or $|1\rangle$.
- **On real hardware**: Expect noise (gate infidelity, readout error). Record counts and consider mitigation (measurement error mitigation, dynamical decoupling, noise-aware transpilation).

Conclusion

This chapter introduces Qiskit as a comprehensive and practical framework for quantum programming, emphasizing its ability to connect theoretical concepts with real-world experimentation. We examined the flexibility of installing Qiskit locally or through cloud-based platforms, such as Google Colab, making it accessible to both beginners and advanced users. The modular structure of Qiskit, Terra for building circuits, Aer for simulation, and the Qiskit

Runtime interface for hardware execution, was shown to provide an end-to-end environment for designing, testing, and running quantum programs. Through hands-on examples, we constructed Bell states and GHZ states, gaining practical insights into superposition and entanglement. The implementation of Grover's algorithm also highlighted the role of amplitude amplification in search problems. The quantum teleportation case study further illustrated how advanced protocols can be realized with Qiskit's tools. Together, these explorations established a strong foundation in programming, simulating, and executing circuits using IBM's quantum ecosystem.

Questions

1. **What is Qiskit, and why is it important for quantum programming?**

   Answer: Qiskit is IBM's open-source software development kit that allows users to design, simulate, and run quantum circuits. Its importance lies in providing a single, unified platform where learners and researchers can easily move from building circuits in Python to executing them on real IBM Quantum processors, making quantum computing both accessible and practical.

2. **How can Qiskit be installed?**

   Answer: Qiskit offers two convenient installation methods. It can be installed locally through Python and pip, which is ideal for long-term projects and advanced research that require customization. Alternatively, it can be setup instantly in cloud platforms like Google Colab, allowing beginners and educators to start coding without worrying about system configuration.

3. **What are the main modules of Qiskit, and what do they do?**

   Answer: The strength of Qiskit comes from its modular design. Terra provides the foundation for constructing and transpiling circuits, Aer delivers high-performance simulation tools that include noise modeling, and the Qiskit Runtime interface connects programs directly to IBM's quantum devices. Together, these modules cover the complete quantum computing workflow.

4. **Why is visualization an important feature in Qiskit?**

   Answer: Visualization makes quantum circuits easier to understand, debug, and communicate. In Qiskit, circuits can be represented as ASCII text for quick checks or as clean, graphical diagrams using Matplotlib and LaTeX for professional documentation, ensuring that both learners and researchers can clearly interpret circuits.

5. **What is the difference between running circuits on simulators and real hardware?**

   Answer: Simulators provide an ideal environment where results are free from errors and can be analyzed in detail, making them excellent for testing and debugging. Real hardware, however, introduces practical challenges such as noise, decoherence, and connectivity limits, but it reflects the actual conditions of quantum experiments and deepens practical understanding.

6. **What does creating a Bell state in Qiskit demonstrate?**

   Answer: Constructing a Bell state highlights two of the most fundamental principles of quantum computing: superposition and entanglement. It is often used as the first test in Qiskit because it confirms that the programming setup is correct while also demonstrating the unique correlations that only quantum systems can produce.

7. **How does Qiskit support larger experiments beyond simple circuits?**

   Answer: Qiskit is not limited to basic demonstrations; it also supports advanced algorithms and protocols. Users can implement Grover's search algorithm to explore quantum speedup or even perform quantum teleportation experiments, making it a versatile tool for both conceptual learning and applied research.

8. **Why is Grover's algorithm significant in the context of Qiskit?**

   Answer: Grover's algorithm demonstrates how quantum computing can outperform classical methods in searching unsorted data, reducing the required steps from N to roughly $\sqrt{N}$. Implementing it in Qiskit enables learners to observe the practical impact of amplitude amplification and quantum interference in solving real-world problems.

9. **How does Qiskit handle noise in quantum computation?**

   Answer: Qiskit addresses the issue of noise through Aer's noise simulation features and the modern Qiskit Experiments toolkit. These tools enable users to model realistic hardware errors, test mitigation techniques, and gain a deeper understanding of how imperfections affect algorithm outcomes, thereby bridging the gap between theory and practice.

10. **What is the key value of learning Qiskit for students and researchers?**

    Answer: Learning Qiskit offers a direct, hands-on approach to understanding quantum computing concepts while developing practical programming skills. It empowers students to visualize, simulate, and test their ideas, and gives researchers a robust environment to experiment with algorithms, making it one of the most valuable gateways into real-world quantum computing.

Exercises

1. Install Qiskit locally on your system and verify the installation by creating a simple 2-qubit circuit that includes a Hadamard gate and a CNOT gate. Print the ASCII diagram of the circuit and explain what the diagram represents.
2. Open Google Colab, install Qiskit using !pip install qiskit[visualization], and recreate the Bell state circuit. Run it on the QASM simulator with 1024 shots and generate a histogram to confirm entanglement.
3. Construct a GHZ state using Qiskit with three-qubits. Simulate the circuit on Aer's statevector simulator and display the amplitudes. Discuss how this extends the concept of entanglement beyond two-qubits.
4. Build a Bell state circuit and run it on both Aer's ideal simulator and a real IBM Quantum device using Qiskit Runtime. Compare the results and explain the impact of noise and hardware imperfections on the data.
5. Implement Grover's algorithm for a two-qubit search problem (target state = 11). Plot the histogram of results and explain how amplitude amplification leads to a peak in the marked state.
6. Write a Qiskit program to demonstrate quantum teleportation of an arbitrary single-qubit state. Simulate the protocol and verify that the final qubit matches the original state.
7. Explore Qiskit's visualization tools by drawing the GHZ state circuit using both ASCII (qc.draw()) and Matplotlib (qc.draw('mpl')). Reflect on the advantages of each representation for learning and communication.
8. Modify the Bell state circuit to create each of the four Bell states (Φ^+, Φ^-, Ψ^+, Ψ^-). Simulate and measure each case, noting how small circuit changes affect entanglement outcomes.
9. Design a noisy simulation by introducing a depolarizing error on CNOT gates using Aer's noise model. Run a Bell state circuit under this noise and analyze how the results differ from the ideal case.
10. Write a short reflection on how Qiskit's modular structure (Terra, Aer, and Runtime) supports the entire quantum computing workflow, and why this integration is valuable for both learners and researchers.

CHAPTER 8
Quantum Utility and Qiskit Patterns

Introduction

Quantum computing is entering a new phase where practical outcomes matter as much as theoretical breakthroughs. Early progress was often measured in terms of hardware metrics, such as qubit counts, circuit depths, and gate fidelities. While these achievements marked important milestones, they did not fully answer the central question now facing the field: *Does a quantum algorithm deliver better results than classical methods?*

This shift in perspective has given rise to the concept of **quantum utility** (**QU**). QU serves as a benchmark for practical advantage, focusing on whether a quantum program solves problems more effectively than the best available classical approaches. By emphasizing dimensions such as accuracy, efficiency, scalability, and robustness, QU ensures that research progress is judged not solely by novelty but by its real-world relevance and measurable impact.

Equally important is the ability to structure quantum applications consistently and reproducibly. This is where Qiskit patterns come into play. Much like design patterns in classical software development, Qiskit patterns provide modular workflows that guide developers from problem definition to evaluation and implementation. They help transform experimental prototypes into scalable, production-ready applications across domains such as optimization, chemistry, and machine learning.

This chapter introduces both QU and Qiskit patterns. You will learn how QU is defined and measured, how patterns bring workflow discipline, and how the two converge in end-to-end applications. Together, they provide a framework for building reproducible quantum programs and for evaluating whether those programs deliver genuine value in practice.

Structure

The chapter covers the following topics:

- Introduction to quantum utility concept and significance
- Measuring and interpreting quantum utility in practice
- Qiskit patterns design philosophy and workflows
- Building end-to-end quantum applications with patterns
- Case study on optimization and chemistry workflows

Objectives

This chapter introduces QU as a practical benchmark for evaluating quantum algorithms beyond theoretical potential. Readers will examine how QU emphasizes accuracy, efficiency, scalability, and robustness, moving the focus from hardware metrics to real-world outcomes. The chapter also explores Qiskit patterns, structured workflows that transform fragmented quantum experiments into reproducible, modular applications. Through examples in optimization, **Quantum Approximate Optimization Algorithm** (**QAOA**), and quantum chemistry [**variational quantum eigensolver** (**VQE**)], readers will see how QU and Qiskit patterns combine to build end-to-end quantum applications. These case studies highlight not only the scientific rigor of structured workflows but also their relevance in solving meaningful problems. By the end, readers will be able to critically assess quantum solutions and design workflows that balance innovation and practical utility.

Introduction to quantum utility concept and significance

Quantum computing is often celebrated for its theoretical breakthroughs, with landmark algorithms such as Shor's algorithm for factoring and Grover's algorithm for search demonstrating exponential and polynomial speedups over their classical counterparts. These milestones positioned quantum computing as a transformative paradigm with the potential to revolutionize domains such as cryptography, optimization, chemistry, and machine learning.

As the field matures, however, the guiding question has begun to shift. It is no longer sufficient to ask: *Can we implement this quantum algorithm?*

The more critical inquiry now is: *Does this quantum algorithm deliver useful results in practice?*

QU evaluates whether quantum programs provide practical advantages over classical methods, focusing on real-world performance rather than hardware metrics.

Understanding quantum utility

QU is a measure of practical advantage in quantum computing. Rather than relying on traditional hardware-focused metrics, such as circuit depth, gate counts, or qubit numbers, QU poses a more fundamental question:

Does the quantum program solve the problem more effectively than classical methods?

If the answer is yes, the algorithm demonstrates true utility and provides evidence of a practical advantage. If the answer is no, the algorithm remains primarily a theoretical exploration, valuable for research but not yet impactful in solving real-world problems.

QU evaluates quantum systems based on what they achieve, bridging theory and practical relevance by focusing on outcomes rather than specifications.

In practice, QU is evaluated through application-driven benchmarks that compare quantum workflows against the best available classical approaches under realistic conditions. This evaluation considers multiple dimensions—such as accuracy of results, computational efficiency, scalability to larger problem sizes, and robustness under noise—to determine whether a quantum solution delivers meaningful real-world value.

Significance of quantum utility

We are currently in the **noisy intermediate-scale quantum** (**NISQ**) era, where devices operate with tens to hundreds of qubits but remain constrained by decoherence, gate errors, and measurement noise. In such an environment, simple indicators such as qubit counts or circuit depths provide only a partial—and often misleading—picture of progress.

In this context, an outcome-oriented evaluation framework is essential to distinguish meaningful progress from incremental hardware improvements. QU provides this perspective by emphasizing end-to-end problem-solving performance rather than isolated device metrics. It encourages the community to evaluate quantum systems based on practical effectiveness, reproducibility, and scalability in real-world settings.

QU reframes evaluation from hardware specifications to real-world outcomes, encouraging researchers and practitioners to ask critical questions:

- *Does the quantum algorithm consistently outperform classical solvers on problems of realistic size?*

- *Are the observed improvements substantial enough to justify the added complexity of quantum execution?*
- *Can the results be replicated reliably, even in the presence of noise and hardware imperfections?*

By framing progress this way, QU separates genuine advances from overstated claims—highlighting algorithms with measurable utility as steps toward practical advantage, while others remain proofs of concept.

Most importantly, QU reorients the field toward real-world impact. It highlights domains where quantum methods show particular promise, including:

- **Optimization**: Applications in logistics, scheduling, and portfolio design.
- **Chemistry**: Accurate molecular simulations for materials science and drug discovery.
- **Machine learning**: Tasks such as classification, clustering, and kernel-based methods.

Through this lens, QU ensures that research progress is not judged solely by novelty but by its capacity to deliver tangible value.

Historical perspective

Early quantum progress focused on hardware metrics such as qubit count, circuit depth, and gate fidelity. While these measures were important engineering milestones, they offered limited insight into the real-world advantage over classical systems.

QU emerged to shift focus from technical specifications to practical outcomes, reflecting the field's growing maturity. By emphasizing measurable advantage, QU bridges theoretical promise and real-world impact, guiding both research and industry adoption.

This evolution mirrors the broader trajectory of computing technologies, where early progress is often measured by hardware capability before shifting toward application-level performance. As quantum hardware matured, the community increasingly recognized the need for evaluation metrics that reflect end-to-end usefulness rather than isolated device improvements.

Industry connection

The significance of QU extends beyond academia. Organizations such as *International Business Machines (IBM) Quantum* integrate QU into their strategy, using it to evaluate system performance and communicate progress in an outcome-oriented manner.

By emphasizing practical utility rather than abstract hardware metrics, these benchmarks help to:

- Guide ongoing research priorities.
- Accelerate industrial adoption.
- Shape the global roadmap for quantum technologies.

This industry validation establishes QU as a standard of accountability and progress, measuring quantum advances by real-world impact rather than just engineering milestones.

Dimensions of quantum utility

Rather than relying on a single performance indicator, QU adopts a holistic evaluation framework that captures both computational effectiveness and implementation practicality. This multi-faceted view is especially important in the NISQ era, where trade-offs between accuracy, resource usage, and noise resilience must be carefully balanced to assess real-world usefulness.

QU is a multi-dimensional measure that evaluates quantum algorithms by combining solution quality with practical feasibility. To determine whether a quantum approach delivers meaningful value, QU assesses performance across the following key dimensions:

- **Accuracy**: Does the algorithm produce higher-quality solutions than classical methods, such as chemical-level accuracy in simulations or superior optimization results?

- **Efficiency**: Can results be obtained with reduced computational cost or runtime, including overheads from compilation, transpilation, and error mitigation?
- **Scalability**: Does the algorithm's relative performance improve as problem size increases, even if small instances show limited advantage?
- **Robustness**: Can the algorithm maintain reliable performance on noisy quantum hardware, supported by effective error mitigation techniques?

Together, these dimensions ensure that quantum algorithms are evaluated for practical, reproducible, and scalable impact, establishing QU as a credible benchmark for real-world quantum computing progress.

Comparing traditional metrics and quantum utility

Early quantum progress was measured using hardware metrics such as qubit count, circuit depth, and gate fidelity. While important for engineering assessment, these measures offer limited insight into the real problem-solving advantage they offer over classical systems.

QU addresses this gap by shifting the focus from raw specifications to practical outcomes. The following comparison highlights the difference in perspective:

Traditional metric	Limitation	QU focus
Qubit count	Does not reflect actual problem-solving ability	Demonstrated advantage in real applications
Circuit depth	Hardware-dependent; ignores the quality of results	Efficiency and scalability of outcomes
Gate fidelity	Narrow, technical measure of performance	Robustness under realistic, noisy environments

***Table 8.1**: Comparison of traditional quantum metrics and QU focus areas*

Measuring and interpreting quantum utility in practice

Defining QU is only the first step; its real strength lies in the ability to measure and interpret it systematically. Without clear and consistent methods of evaluation, it would be impossible to distinguish between a quantum algorithm that serves merely as an academic demonstration and one that represents a genuine practical breakthrough. Systematic measurement ensures that claims of advantage are grounded in evidence, reproducible across platforms, and meaningful in real-world contexts.

To operationalize QU, practitioners must establish well-defined benchmarking procedures, standardized datasets, and fair classical baselines for comparison. Careful experimental design, including repeated trials, noise-aware evaluation, and transparent reporting of resource costs helps ensure that observed improvements reflect genuine algorithmic value rather than artifacts of implementation or experimental bias.

Framework for measuring quantum utility

Evaluating QU requires more than executing a quantum algorithm in isolation. Meaningful assessment demands side-by-side comparison with the best classical baselines, ensuring that both result quality and practical feasibility are evaluated under realistic conditions.

To make this evaluation systematic and reproducible, researchers typically follow a structured measurement pipeline that captures the full lifecycle of a quantum experiment, from problem formulation through execution and comparative analysis. This pipeline ensures that performance claims are supported by transparent, end-to-end evidence rather than isolated metrics.

The QU measurement pipeline is illustrated in *Figure 8.1*:

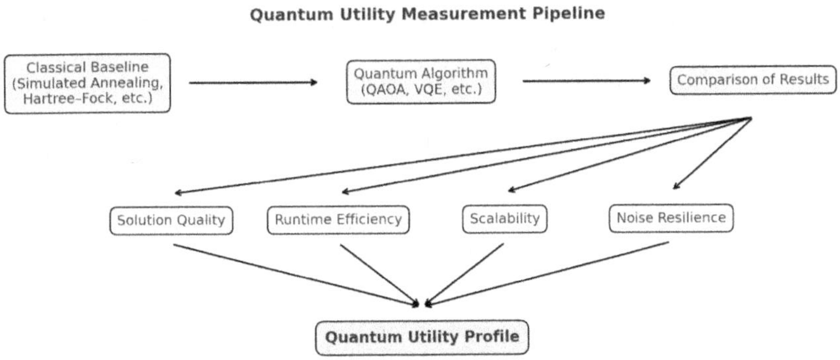

***Figure 8.1**: QU measurement pipeline*

A typical QU evaluation framework examines the following elements:

- **Solution quality**: Compare quantum results with classical solutions or verified benchmarks (e.g., molecular energies in chemistry or objective values in optimization).
- **Runtime efficiency**: Measure end-to-end execution time, including transpilation, hardware runs, and post-processing, and compare directly with classical solvers.
- **Scalability**: Analyze how performance changes as problem size increases, where genuine QU emerges if relative advantage grows for larger instances.
- **Noise resilience**: Compare performance on ideal simulators vs. real hardware, assessing noise impact and the effectiveness of error mitigation techniques.

Together, these steps ensure that QU is defined by demonstrable performance rather than theoretical promise alone.

The overall QU assessment can be viewed as a structured workflow, starting with classical comparisons, progressing through multi-dimensional evaluation, and concluding with a utility profile, as illustrated in *Figure 8.1*.

Practical example of optimization with QAOA

To illustrate how QU is assessed in real applications, it is useful to examine a representative optimization workflow where quantum and classical methods can be compared under identical conditions. The Max-Cut problem serves as a widely accepted benchmark for this purpose due to its clear objective function and well-established classical baselines.

A common way to evaluate QU in optimization is to use the QAOA on the Max-Cut problem, which aims to partition a graph to maximize the number of crossing edges.

The evaluation workflow for this QAOA-based Max-Cut example is summarized as follows:

- **Classical baseline**: Max-Cut is solved using classical heuristics, such as simulated annealing, to provide a reference benchmark.
- **Quantum method**: QAOA maps the problem to a parameterized quantum circuit, with parameters iteratively optimized by a classical optimizer.
- **Evaluation**: Performance is assessed by comparing cut quality, along with scalability and robustness under noise, against classical results.

If QAOA achieves better or sustained performance as problem size grows, it demonstrates positive QU, positioning QAOA as a practical testbed for real-world quantum advantage.

Practical example of chemistry with VQE

To complement optimization-based benchmarks, QU is also evaluated in quantum chemistry workflows where solution accuracy has direct scientific and industrial relevance. Molecular energy estimation provides a well-defined ground truth, making it an effective testbed for assessing whether quantum algorithms deliver meaningful practical value.

Another key demonstration of QU appears in quantum chemistry, where the VQE is used to estimate molecular ground state energies. A standard benchmark is the hydrogen molecule (H_2) due to its simplicity and well-known exact solution.

The QU evaluation workflow for the VQE-based chemistry example is summarized as follows:

- **Classical baseline**: Methods such as Hartree–Fock or exact diagonalization provide reliable reference energies.
- **Quantum method**: VQE maps the molecular Hamiltonian to qubits and uses a parameterized circuit (ansatz) with a classical optimizer to minimize energy.
- **Evaluation**: QU is assessed by how closely VQE approaches the exact ground state energy, with chemical accuracy (~1.6 millihartree) as a key threshold, along with robustness on noisy hardware.

When VQE achieves chemical accuracy—even under realistic noise—it demonstrates positive QU, highlighting its relevance for drug discovery, catalysis, and materials science.

Interpreting results

Measuring QU is only the first step; its meaningful interpretation is crucial. Not every numerical gain implies practical value, and QU must be applied as a rigorous benchmark, not a superficial label.

To avoid overstating progress, QU must be interpreted using careful, context-aware analysis rather than isolated numerical improvements. A disciplined evaluation helps distinguish genuine practical advantage from results that are statistically insignificant, problem-specific, or dependent on idealized assumptions.

Key principles for interpreting QU include:

- **Context matters**: The significance of improvement is domain-dependent; small gains may be trivial in toy problems but transformative in areas like finance or drug discovery.
- **Scaling is critical**: Quantum advantage often appears only at larger problem sizes, making scaling trends more important than isolated small instance results.
- **Hardware realism**: Results must hold on real, noisy hardware, not just ideal simulators, to claim genuine utility.

Applying these principles enables balanced, credible conclusions, clarifying where quantum algorithms already show promise, where limitations remain, and under what conditions real-world impact is achievable.

Challenges in measuring quantum utility

Although QU is conceptually well-defined, its practical evaluation poses significant challenges, requiring careful interpretation and scrutiny of advantage claims.

Key challenges include:

- **Benchmark bias**: Favorable problem instances can overstate utility; broad, representative benchmarks are essential.
- **Evolving classical baselines**: Rapid advances in classical methods make QU a moving target, not a fixed milestone.

- **Noise variability**: Fluctuating hardware errors degrade reproducibility.
- **Scalability limits**: Current devices limit testing to problem sizes where an advantage may emerge.
- **Resource accounting**: Ignoring overheads (compilation, error mitigation, repetitions) can inflate efficiency claims.

Together, these issues highlight the need for rigor, transparency, and caution. Acknowledging limitations alongside successes helps ensure QU remains a credible benchmark for genuine quantum progress.

Qiskit patterns design philosophy and workflows

Programming a quantum computer involves far more than simply writing circuits. To create real-world applications, developers need workflows that are consistent, modular, and reproducible. This is precisely where Qiskit patterns become essential, offering structured templates that transform fragmented experiments into well-organized, scalable applications.

Qiskit patterns promote a disciplined, workflow-driven approach to quantum application development by decomposing complex problems into well-defined stages. This structured methodology helps developers move systematically from problem formulation to performance evaluation while maintaining clarity, reusability, and scalability across different quantum use cases.

Understanding Qiskit patterns

Qiskit patterns are structured templates that guide developers in organizing quantum programs into well-defined stages. Rather than designing a new workflow from scratch for every experiment, patterns provide standardized blueprints that can be reused and adapted across multiple application domains, including optimization, chemistry, and machine learning.

By applying patterns, developers gain three critical advantages:

- **Consistency**: All workflows follow a predictable structure, making them easier to understand, maintain, and share.
- **Reproducibility**: Results can be reliably reproduced and independently verified, thereby strengthening the credibility of the experiments.
- **Extensibility**: New algorithms, hardware backends, and techniques can be incorporated with minimal adjustments, allowing workflows to evolve.

In this way, Qiskit patterns serve as a bridge between experimental prototyping and production-quality quantum applications, ensuring that workflows remain organized, scalable, and future-ready.

Significance of patterns

As quantum applications grow in complexity, the need for structured development practices becomes increasingly important. Patterns provide a systematic way to manage this complexity by promoting modular design, clear separation of concerns, and repeatable workflows that support both experimentation and production-grade development.

In the absence of structured approaches, quantum programs often devolve into ad hoc scripts that may work for small demonstrations but fail when scaled to real-world applications. Such unstructured development leads to several challenges:

- **Hard to scale**: Scripts built for a single experiment are rarely adaptable to larger or more complex problems.
- **Difficult to debug**: Without a clear workflow structure, identifying and fixing errors becomes time-consuming and error-prone.
- **Unreliable**: Small variations in coding style or execution order can affect reproducibility, undermining confidence in results.

Qiskit patterns address these challenges by introducing a software engineering discipline into quantum computing. Like classical design patterns, they provide shared structure and best practices, making quantum programs robust, reusable, and maintainable.

Design philosophy of Qiskit patterns

These guiding principles reflect the broader goal of bringing software engineering rigor into quantum application development. By embedding structure and best practices into the workflow itself, Qiskit patterns help teams build solutions that remain manageable as problem size, hardware diversity, and algorithmic complexity continue to grow.

Qiskit patterns are guided by four core principles that ensure workflows are robust, adaptable, and future-ready:

- **Modularity**: Break workflows into reusable components to improve maintainability and extensibility.
- **Reproducibility**: Enforce consistent structures across simulators and hardware to strengthen result reliability.
- **Abstraction**: Hide low-level details so developers focus on high-level logic, reducing complexity.
- **Extensibility**: Allow easy adaptation as algorithms and hardware evolve.

Together, these principles adapt classical software engineering best practices to quantum development, transforming isolated experiments into scalable, maintainable workflows.

Workflow structure of a Qiskit pattern

To ensure consistency across different application domains, Qiskit patterns formalizes the end-to-end development lifecycle into a clearly defined sequence of stages. This structured workflow helps practitioners systematically move from abstract problem formulation to measurable performance evaluation, while maintaining traceability and reproducibility throughout.

Every Qiskit pattern follows a five-step structured workflow, providing a consistent and repeatable approach for building quantum applications across domains such as optimization, chemistry, and machine learning:

- **Problem definition**: Clearly identify the domain and formulate the problem.

  Example: Defining the Max-Cut problem in optimization or the H_2 molecule in quantum chemistry.
- **Mapping**: Translate the problem into a quantum representation suitable for computation.

  Example: Expressing optimization tasks in **Quadratic Unconstrained Binary Optimization** (**QUBO**) form, or encoding a molecular Hamiltonian for chemistry simulations.
- **Execution**: Run the quantum algorithm on a chosen backend. Development is often done using simulators for speed and debugging, followed by execution on real quantum hardware for practical validation.
- **Post-processing**: Convert raw measurement outcomes into meaningful solutions.

  Example: Interpreting bitstrings as graph partitions in optimization, or extracting energy values from eigenstates in chemistry.
- **Evaluation**: Assess the performance of the workflow using QU metrics such as accuracy, runtime efficiency, scalability, and robustness.

By standardizing these steps, Qiskit patterns transforms quantum programming into a systematic and modular process, reducing complexity and enabling developers to focus on innovation rather than reinvention.

Example pattern structures

Concrete pattern instances help demonstrate how the abstract workflow translates into real application pipelines. By examining representative use cases across different domains, developers can better understand how to instantiate the pattern while preserving its structural discipline.

To illustrate how Qiskit patterns are applied in practice, consider the following domain-specific workflows:

- **Optimization pattern (QAOA)**: Define the problem | Map to QUBO | Run QAOA | Interpret bitstrings | Evaluate using QU.
- **Chemistry pattern (VQE)**: Define the molecule | Map the Hamiltonian | Run VQE | Extract energy values | Evaluate using QU.

These examples show how diverse applications can follow a common structured workflow while adapting domain-specific details. Adhering to such patterns ensures quantum programs are rigorous, reproducible, and engineering-ready, bridging research and production-quality development.

Building end-to-end quantum applications with patterns

Qiskit patterns reach their full potential when applied to complete, real-world workflows. By combining structured problem-solving steps with the concept of QU, developers can move beyond small-scale demonstrations and build applications that are both reproducible and practically meaningful.

In this section, we present two case studies—one in optimization using the QAOA, and another in chemistry using the VQE. Each example follows the five-step pattern flow:

1. Problem definition
2. Mapping
3. Execution
4. Post-processing
5. Evaluation (via QU)

These examples illustrate how Qiskit patterns offer a modular structure, while QU ensures rigorous benchmarking against classical methods.

QAOA-based optimization example

This example demonstrates how the Qiskit pattern workflow can be instantiated for a concrete optimization task. By walking through each stage—from problem formulation to QU evaluation, readers can observe how abstract workflow principles translate into an end-to-end, executable quantum application.

Problem definition

The Max-Cut problem is a well-known NP-hard challenge in combinatorial optimization. Given a graph, the objective is to divide its nodes into two sets so that the number of edges between the sets (the cut) is maximized.

This deceptively simple formulation has many practical applications, including:

- **Network design**: Maximizing bandwidth or minimizing interference between subnetworks.
- **Portfolio optimization**: Grouping assets into two balanced sets.
- **Logistics and routing**: Partitioning resources for efficient allocation.

Mapping

To implement Max-Cut on a quantum computer, the problem is first formulated as a QUBO and then mapped to a Hamiltonian that serves as the cost operator in QAOA. QAOA encodes this as a parameterized quantum circuit that alternates between a problem and a mixing Hamiltonian, with the parameters optimized classically to improve the solution.

Execution

QAOA implementation for the Max-Cut problem in Qiskit is as follows:

```
from qiskit_optimization import QuadraticProgram
from qiskit_optimization.algorithms import MinimumEigenOptimizer
from qiskit_algorithms import QAOA
from qiskit.primitives import Sampler
from qiskit.circuit.library import TwoLocal
# Step 1: Define Max-Cut problem (simple 2-node graph)
qp = QuadraticProgram()
qp.binary_var(‘x0’)
qp.binary_var(‘x1’)
qp.minimize(linear={‘x0’: 1, ‘x1’: 1}, quadratic={(‘x0’,’x1’): -1})
# Step 2: Setup QAOA with a two-layer ansatz
ansatz = TwoLocal(rotation_blocks=”ry”, entanglement_blocks=”cz”)
qaoa = QAOA(ansatz=ansatz, reps=2, sampler=Sampler())
# Step 3: Solve the problem
optimizer = MinimumEigenOptimizer(qaoa)
result = optimizer.solve(qp)
# Step 4: Post-process results
print(“Best solution:”, result.x)
print(“Objective value: “, result.fval)
```

The simplified QAOA circuit for the Max-Cut problem (two-qubits, two layers) is as follows:

```
         ┌─────────┐
q_0: ┤ Ry(θ1)  ├──■─────────■──
         └─────────┘  │         │
         ┌─────────┐  │         │
q_1: ┤ Ry(θ2)  ├──X──Ry(θ3)─X──
         └─────────┘
```

Post-processing

Measured bitstrings represent candidate graph partitions, with each string encoding node assignments and its cost value indicating cut quality. For a two-node graph, the bitstring 01 partitions the nodes into disjoint sets, yielding the maximum cut, and the minimum-cost solution identifies the optimal solution.

Evaluation using quantum utility

To determine whether QAOA demonstrates QU, its results must be compared against a classical baseline, such as simulated annealing or brute-force search.

Key aspects of evaluation include:

- **Solution quality**: Does QAOA find equal or better cut values?
- **Scalability**: Does performance improve as problem size grows?
- **Noise resilience**: Are results robust when executed on real quantum hardware rather than simulators?

If QAOA achieves comparable or superior performance under these criteria, it demonstrates positive QU in optimization.

VQE-based quantum chemistry example

This example illustrates how the Qiskit pattern workflow applies to quantum chemistry applications. By following the same structured stages used in optimization, the VQE workflow demonstrates how domain-specific problems can be systematically mapped, executed, and evaluated for QU in a reproducible manner.

Problem definition

In quantum chemistry, a central task is estimating a molecule's ground state energy, which determines stability, bonding, and reactivity. The H_2 serves as a foundational benchmark; success with H_2 enables extension to more complex systems in drug discovery, catalysis, and materials science.

Mapping

To simulate H_2 on a quantum computer, its molecular Hamiltonian is mapped to a qubit operator, commonly using the Jordan–Wigner transformation. This Hamiltonian is then used by VQE, which prepares parameterized quantum states and iteratively minimizes energy with a classical optimizer.

Execution

The VQE implementation for the H_2 molecule in Qiskit is as follows:

```
from qiskit_nature.second_q.drivers import PySCFDriver
from qiskit_nature.second_q.mappers import JordanWignerMapper
from qiskit_algorithms import VQE
from qiskit_algorithms.optimizers import COBYLA
from qiskit.circuit.library import TwoLocal
from qiskit.primitives import Estimator
# Step 1: Define the H₂ molecule at bond distance 0.735 Å
driver = PySCFDriver(atom="H .0 .0 .0; H .0 .0 .735", basis="sto3g")
qmolecule = driver.run()
# Step 2: Map Hamiltonian to a qubit operator
mapper = JordanWignerMapper()
hamiltonian = mapper.map(qmolecule.second_q_ops()["ElectronicEnergy"])
# Step 3: Setup VQE with a simple ansatz and optimizer
ansatz = TwoLocal(rotation_blocks= "ry", entanglement_blocks= "cz")
optimizer = COBYLA(maxiter=100)
vqe = VQE(Estimator(), ansatz, optimizer)
# Step 4: Solve the problem
result = vqe.compute_minimum_eigenvalue(hamiltonian)
# Step 5: Post-process results
print("Estimated ground state energy:", result.eigenvalue.real)
```

The simplified VQE circuit for the H_2 molecule (two-qubits) is as follows:

```
q_0: -Ry(θ1)-■-----------
             |
q_1: -Ry(θ2)-X--Ry(θ3)---
```

Post-processing

VQE outputs an estimate of the ground state energy of H_2, which is compared with classical reference methods such as Hartree–Fock or exact diagonalization. Achieving chemical accuracy (~1.6 millihartree) indicates strong effectiveness.

Evaluation using quantum utility

To claim QU, VQE must demonstrate that it has:

- **Accuracy**: Achieves energy values within chemical accuracy.
- **Noise resilience**: Maintains accuracy when executed on real hardware, despite noise.
- **Scalability**: Extends effectively to larger molecules, showing advantages over purely classical methods.

When these conditions are met, VQE demonstrates positive QU in chemistry, highlighting the promise of quantum computers to revolutionize molecular simulations.

Case study on optimization and chemistry workflows

The true strength of QU becomes most evident when it is applied within the structured workflows enabled by Qiskit patterns. In this section, we revisit two pivotal domains, optimization and chemistry, not to demonstrate code execution, but to examine how QU functions as a measurement framework. Unlike the end-to-end applications in section *Building end-to-end quantum applications with patterns*, the emphasis here is on interpreting outcomes through well-defined utility metrics, highlighting the practical significance of quantum approaches in real-world contexts.

Optimization case study using QAOA

This case study demonstrates how QU can be assessed in an end-to-end optimization workflow using Qiskit patterns. By examining empirical performance across accuracy, efficiency, scalability, and robustness, the example highlights how structured evaluation helps distinguish promising quantum behavior from purely theoretical results.

Context

Optimization problems, such as Max-Cut and portfolio design, are central to industries ranging from logistics to finance. These problems grow rapidly in size and complexity, making them excellent testbeds for evaluating whether quantum methods provide genuine real-world advantages.

Workflow with Qiskit patterns

Using the optimization pattern, the Max-Cut problem can be structured into the standard five-step flow:

1. **Problem definition**: Formulate the Max-Cut instance.
2. **Mapping**: Convert the problem into a QUBO form suitable for quantum processing.
3. **Execution**: Apply QAOA using a hybrid quantum–classical loop.
4. **Post-processing**: Interpret bitstrings as candidate graph partitions.
5. **Evaluation**: Compare results against classical baselines using QU metrics.

The following table presents key performance metrics observed during QAOA experiments, highlighting accuracy, efficiency, scalability, and robustness under varying conditions:

Metric	Observation
Accuracy	QAOA produced cut values that are close to or equal to those of classical heuristics, such as simulated annealing.
Efficiency	On small graphs, runtimes were comparable; scaling analysis suggested potential polynomial advantages with deeper circuits.
Scalability	As the number of nodes increased, QAOA maintained solution quality longer than classical solvers, which faced diminishing performance.

Robustness	On noisy hardware, error mitigation preserved acceptable performance, though variability across runs was observed.

***Table 8.2**: QU metrics applied to QAOA for optimization problems*

Max-Cut six-node graph mini case

To ground this discussion, consider a six-node Max-Cut instance.

The key observations from the Max-Cut six-node experiment are summarized as follows:

- **Simulator**: QAOA achieved cut values very close to the optimal solution.
- **Hardware**: Results showed mild degradation due to noise, but feasible solutions were still obtained.
- **Comparison**: QAOA maintained solution quality as the graph scaled, while simulated annealing degraded more quickly.

This mini case illustrates how QU metrics are applied in practice, highlighting both the promise and the current limitations of quantum optimization workflows.

Chemistry case study using VQE

This case study extends the QU evaluation framework to quantum chemistry, demonstrating how the same structured Qiskit pattern workflow can be applied beyond optimization tasks. By grounding the discussion in a well-understood molecular benchmark, the example highlights how QU metrics translate into scientifically meaningful performance assessment.

Context

Quantum chemistry is one of the most promising domains for quantum computing. A foundational benchmark is the estimation of the ground state energy of molecules. Even for a simple system like the H_2, classical methods can be resource-intensive when scaling to larger molecules, making this an ideal case for testing QU.

Workflow with Qiskit patterns

The following the chemistry pattern, the workflow for VQE unfolds as:

- **Problem definition**: Define the molecular system (H_2 at a fixed bond length).
- **Mapping**: Encode the molecular Hamiltonian into a qubit operator using the Jordan–Wigner transformation.
- **Execution**: Run VQE, alternating between a quantum circuit (state preparation) and a classical optimizer.
- **Post-processing**: Extract energy estimates from the quantum measurement results.
- **Evaluation**: Benchmark results against classical references such as Hartree–Fock or exact diagonalization, using QU metrics.

The following table summarizes the performance metrics observed in VQE experiments, emphasizing accuracy, efficiency, scalability, and robustness across both simulated and hardware implementations:

Metric	Observation
Accuracy	VQE achieved energies within chemical accuracy (≈1.6 mHa) of classical references on simulators.
Efficiency	On simulators, runtimes were competitive; on hardware, error mitigation increased costs but preserved meaningful results.
Scalability	Early experiments with larger molecules suggested that VQE scales more favorably than classical methods, though overheads remain significant.
Robustness	Noise caused fluctuations on hardware, but resilience was improved with shallow ansätze and error mitigation techniques.

***Table 8.3**: QU metrics applied to VQE for molecular energy estimation*

H_2 molecule ground state estimation mini case

To demonstrate, the ground state energy of H_2 was estimated:

- **Simulator**: The VQE produced values nearly identical to those obtained by exact diagonalization.
- **Hardware**: Despite noise, VQE results were within chemical accuracy after applying error mitigation.
- **Comparison**: While classical methods remain more efficient for H_2, VQE's scaling potential becomes increasingly attractive for larger molecules, where classical solvers face exponential growth.

This mini case highlights how Qiskit patterns and QU metrics together provide a structured, reproducible way to evaluate the relevance of quantum chemistry workflows.

These case studies in optimization (QAOA) and chemistry (VQE) show how QU, combined with Qiskit patterns, enables rigorous evaluation of quantum workflows. By using structured, reproducible patterns and assessing outcomes through accuracy, efficiency, scalability, and robustness, developers move beyond isolated demonstrations toward measurable progress. Although still early, these approaches outline clear pathways from academic experiments to industry-relevant quantum applications.

Conclusion

This chapter explored QU as a framework for measuring practical advantage in quantum computing, shifting the focus from hardware specifications to meaningful, application-level outcomes. By examining its core dimensions—accuracy, efficiency, scalability, and robustness, we established QU as a reliable and outcome-driven benchmark for evaluating the real-world relevance of quantum algorithms. Rather than relying solely on qubit counts or circuit depth, QU emphasizes whether quantum workflows deliver measurable improvements over classical baselines under realistic conditions.

In parallel, we introduced Qiskit patterns as structured, modular workflows that bring software engineering discipline to quantum application development. These patterns promote consistency, reproducibility, and extensibility, enabling developers to move systematically from problem definition through execution and evaluation. Through detailed examples, including the QAOA for combinatorial optimization and the VQE for molecular energy estimation, we demonstrated how QU and Qiskit patterns work together to support rigorous, end-to-end quantum experimentation.

The case studies further highlighted both the promise and current limitations of near-term quantum devices, particularly in the NISQ era. While clear large-scale quantum advantage remains an ongoing pursuit, the disciplined application of QU metrics combined with structured pattern-based workflows provides a credible pathway toward practical quantum impact. As hardware matures and algorithms evolve, this integrated framework will play a crucial role in guiding researchers and practitioners toward building scalable, industry-relevant quantum solutions.

Questions

1. **What is Qiskit, and why is it important for quantum programming?**

   Answer: Qiskit is IBM's open-source SDK for designing, simulating, and running quantum circuits. It provides a unified Python-based platform that lets users seamlessly transition from circuit development to execution on real quantum hardware, making quantum computing more accessible and practical.

2. **How can Qiskit be installed?**

   Answer: Qiskit can be installed locally via Python and pip for long-term, customizable projects, or used instantly on cloud platforms like Google Colab, enabling beginners to start without system setup.

3. **What are the main modules of Qiskit, and what do they do?**

   Answer: The strength of Qiskit lies in its modular architecture: Terra enables circuit construction and transpilation, Aer provides high-performance simulation with noise models, and Qiskit Runtime connects programs to real IBM Quantum devices—together supporting the end-to-end quantum workflow.

4. **Why is visualization an important feature in Qiskit?**

   Answer: Qiskit supports clear circuit visualization through ASCII text for quick inspection and Matplotlib/LaTeX diagrams for professional documentation, making circuits easier to understand, debug, and communicate.

5. **What is the difference between running circuits on simulators and real hardware?**

   Answer: Simulators offer error-free environments for testing and debugging, while real quantum hardware introduces noise and constraints but reflects practical experimental conditions and deepens real-world understanding.

6. **What does creating a Bell state in Qiskit demonstrate?**

   Answer: Constructing a Bell state demonstrates superposition and entanglement and is commonly used in Qiskit as a first test, verifying the correct setup while showcasing uniquely quantum correlations.

7. **How does Qiskit support larger experiments beyond simple circuits?**

   Answer: Qiskit supports advanced algorithms and protocols, enabling implementations such as Grover's search and quantum teleportation, making it useful for both conceptual learning and applied research.

8. **Why is Grover's algorithm significant in the context of Qiskit?**

   Answer: Grover's algorithm shows how quantum computing accelerates unsorted search, reducing the number of steps from N to $\sqrt{N}$. Implementing it in Qiskit lets learners observe amplitude amplification and quantum interference in practice.

9. **How does Qiskit handle noise in quantum computation?**

   Answer: Qiskit addresses noise through Aer's noise simulators and the Qiskit Experiments toolkit, enabling realistic error modeling, testing of mitigation techniques, and deeper insight into how hardware imperfections affect results—bridging theory and practice.

10. **What is the key value of learning Qiskit for students and researchers?**

    Answer: Learning Qiskit provides hands-on experience with quantum concepts and programming, enabling visualization, simulation, and experimentation, and serving as a powerful gateway to real-world quantum computing.

Exercises

1. Install Qiskit locally on your system and verify the installation by creating a simple 2-qubit circuit that includes a Hadamard gate and a CNOT gate. Print the ASCII diagram of the circuit and explain what the diagram represents.
2. Open Google Colab, install Qiskit using !pip install qiskit[visualization], and recreate the Bell state circuit. Run it on the (QASM) simulator with 1024 shots and generate a histogram to confirm the presence of entanglement.
3. Construct a (GHZ) state using Qiskit with three-qubits. Simulate the circuit on Aer's statevector simulator and display the amplitudes. Discuss how this extends the concept of entanglement beyond two qubits.
4. Build a Bell state circuit and run it on both Aer's ideal simulator and a real IBM Quantum device using Qiskit Runtime. Compare the results and explain the impact of noise and hardware imperfections on the data.

5. Implement Grover's algorithm for a two-qubit search problem (target state = 11). Plot the histogram of results and explain how amplitude amplification leads to a peak in the marked state.
6. Write a Qiskit program to demonstrate quantum teleportation of an arbitrary single-qubit state. Simulate the protocol and verify that the final qubit matches the original state.
7. Explore Qiskit's visualization tools by drawing the GHZ state circuit using both ASCII (qc.draw()) and Matplotlib (qc.draw('mpl')). Reflect on the advantages of each representation for learning and communication.
8. Modify the Bell state circuit to create each of the four Bell states (Φ^+, Φ^-, Ψ^+, Ψ^-). Simulate and measure each case, noting how small circuit changes affect entanglement outcomes.
9. Design a noisy simulation by introducing a depolarizing error on CNOT gates using Aer's noise model. Run a Bell state circuit under this noise and analyze how the results differ from the ideal case.
10. Write a short reflection on how Qiskit's modular structure (Terra, Aer, and Runtime) supports the entire quantum computing workflow, and why this integration is valuable for both learners and researchers.

CHAPTER 9
Programming with Cirq

Introduction

As quantum computing advances from theoretical exploration to experimental realization, the need for precise, transparent, and reproducible control has become increasingly important. While high-level frameworks like **Quantum Information Software Kit (Qiskit)** simplify quantum programming for beginners, *Google Cirq* offers a research-oriented environment that emphasizes fine-grained manipulation of qubits and gates. It enables developers and scientists to construct, simulate, and analyze quantum circuits at a level that mirrors real hardware operations.

Developed by the *Google Quantum AI* team, Cirq serves as both a powerful simulator and a gateway to physical quantum processors such as *Sycamore*—the platform behind Google's landmark demonstration of quantum supremacy. Its architecture gives users the flexibility to study gate behavior, design custom noise models, and experiment with complex quantum phenomena under controlled conditions.

Cirq's strength lies in its dual capacity: it enables ideal simulations for theoretical study and noisy simulations for realistic hardware evaluation. This capability enables researchers to investigate how decoherence, gate infidelity, and measurement errors impact circuit fidelity. By combining Cirq with visualization tools such as Matplotlib, users can interpret quantum results more intuitively through graphical analysis.

This chapter introduces the Cirq framework from installation to experimentation. You will learn how to build and execute circuits, apply noise models, implement a simplified version of Shor's factoring algorithm, and visualize outcomes effectively. Together, these skills form a comprehensive foundation for conducting practical, research-grade quantum programming using Cirq.

Structure

The chapter covers the following topics:

- Cirq framework basics and installation
- Building and executing circuits with Cirq API
- Simulation and noise models in Cirq
- Implementing Shor's factoring algorithm
- Circuit visualization with Cirq and Matplotlib

Objectives

This chapter introduces Cirq, a Python-based, research-grade framework for designing and simulating quantum circuits with high precision and control. It explains how Cirq differs from high-level platforms by enabling explicit control over qubits, gates, operation sequencing, and noise modeling. Through hands-on circuit construction, measurement analysis, and visualization using Cirq tools and Matplotlib, readers explore how decoherence and gate errors affect outcomes. A simplified implementation of Shor's factoring algorithm highlights Cirq's ability to manage complex multi-qubit operations and quantum interference. By the end of the chapter, readers can build, test, and visualize robust quantum circuits, effectively bridging theory with experimental realism in quantum computing.

Cirq framework basics and installation

Quantum computing increasingly emphasizes precision, control, and reproducibility alongside performance. While Qiskit focuses on accessibility through abstraction, Cirq, developed by Google Quantum AI, is a research-grade, open-source Python framework offering fine-grained control over gates, qubit layouts, and noise modeling—ideal for experimental analysis and circuit optimization.

Cirq operates as both a simulator and a hardware interface via the Google Quantum Engine, enabling access to processors such as Sycamore, and also underpins TensorFlow Quantum, bridging quantum computing with machine learning. Overall, Cirq supports research-level experimentation by providing precise control over quantum circuit execution and evolution.

Introduction to Cirq's core capabilities

Before exploring Cirq in detail, it is helpful to understand the core capabilities that distinguish it from other quantum programming frameworks. Cirq is designed with a strong emphasis on low-level circuit control, hardware-awareness, and research flexibility, making it particularly suitable for experimenting with near-term quantum devices and noise-aware workflows. Its Python-native design allows developers to construct, simulate, and analyze quantum circuits using familiar programming constructs while maintaining fine-grained control over qubit topology and gate operations.

Cirq is a Python-based framework developed by Google for flexible, research-oriented quantum programming. It enables precise design and simulation of quantum circuits with full control over qubits, gate operations, and noise modeling in a familiar Python environment. The following table highlights Cirq's key features and their practical benefits for developers and researchers:

Feature	Purpose and benefit
Pythonic design	Uses clear, native Python syntax, making it intuitive for developers and researchers familiar with Python.
Explicit qubit representation	Qubits are defined individually (using `LineQubit` or `GridQubit`), allowing precise control over their layout and connectivity.
Composable operations	Circuits are constructed from modular gate components such as H, X, and **Controlled-NOT** (**CNOT**) gates that can be easily combined and sequenced.
Noise and error modeling	Provides built-in noise channels, such as `DepolarizingChannel` and `AmplitudeDampingChannel`, to emulate real-world hardware imperfections.
Flexible simulation backends	Offers both ideal and noise-aware simulators, such as `Simulator` and `DensityMatrixSimulator`, for realistic experimentation.
Seamless integration	Integrates smoothly with tools like NumPy, Matplotlib, and TensorFlow Quantum for data analysis and hybrid quantum–classical workflows.
Hardware connectivity	Supports execution on Google's quantum processors via the Quantum Engine API, bridging the gap between simulation and real hardware.

***Table 9.1**: Key features of Cirq*

System requirements

Before proceeding with the installation, it is important to confirm that the computing environment satisfies the necessary software prerequisites. Ensuring compatibility at this stage helps prevent installation errors, dependency conflicts, and runtime issues when working with Cirq-based quantum programs.

Verify that your system environment meets the required prerequisites to avoid configuration issues and ensure a smooth setup before installing Cirq.

To prepare your environment for a successful Cirq installation, verify that your system meets the following requirements:

- **Operating system**: Windows 10 or newer / macOS 10.15 or newer / or any modern Linux distribution.
- **Python version**: 3.9 or above.
- **Pip**: Latest version (`python -m pip install --upgrade pip`).
- **Recommended packages**: NumPy, Matplotlib, and Jupyter Notebook for numerical operations and visualization.

Installing Cirq

Before beginning the installation process, it is useful to understand that Cirq supports multiple deployment environments depending on the user's needs. Whether the goal is long-term local development or quick cloud-based experimentation, Cirq provides a straightforward installation workflow that enables users to start building quantum circuits with minimal setup effort.

Cirq can be installed either locally for sustained development and experimentation or on cloud platforms such as Google Colab for quick setup, rapid prototyping, and classroom demonstrations.

Local installation

To install Cirq on a local machine, follow these step-by-step instructions:

1. Open a terminal or command prompt.
2. Install Cirq via pip:
   ```
   pip install cirq
   ```
3. Verify the installation:
   ```
   import cirq
   print("Cirq version:", cirq.__version__)
   ```
4. A printed version number (for example, `Cirq version: 1.4.0`) confirms a successful setup.

   (Optional) Install visualization and notebook support:
   ```
   pip install matplotlib notebook
   ```

Installation in Google Colab

Before running the installation commands, ensure that the Colab runtime is active and connected to the internet. This cloud-based environment eliminates the need for local configuration, allowing users to quickly setup Cirq and begin experimenting with quantum circuits directly from the browser.

Google Colab offers an easy-to-use, cloud-based setup that is ideal for quick experiments and instructional demonstrations.

To install Cirq, simply run the following commands in a Colab cell:

```
!pip install cirq
import cirq
print("Cirq ready in Colab:", cirq.__version__)
```

Testing the installation

After completing the installation, it is important to perform a quick functional check to ensure that Cirq and its dependencies are working correctly. A simple simulation helps verify that the environment is properly configured for quantum circuit creation and execution.

Verify Cirq by creating and simulating a simple Bell state circuit, which confirms correct qubit initialization, gate operations, and measurement functionality after installation. The following example demonstrates the verification process using a simple Bell state circuit:

```
import cirq
# Step 1 - Define two qubits
q0, q1 = cirq.LineQubit.range(2)
# Step 2 - Build the circuit
circuit = cirq.Circuit(
    cirq.H(q0),          # Create superposition on the first qubit
    cirq.CNOT(q0, q1),   # Entangle both qubits
    cirq.measure(q0, q1)
)
# Step 3 - Simulate
sim = cirq.Simulator()
result = sim.run(circuit, repetitions=1000)
print(result)
```

The expected output is as follows:

```
measurements: (q0, q1) = 00, 11, 00, 11 ...
```

Approximately half of the runs produce `00` and half `11`, confirming successful entanglement and a functional simulator.

Building and executing circuits with the Cirq API

Once Cirq is installed and verified, the next step is to design and execute quantum circuits, the fundamental building blocks of any quantum computation.

In Cirq, circuits are represented as ordered sequences of quantum operations, each acting on a specific set of qubits. These operations are grouped into moments, representing gates that can occur simultaneously without interference.

What distinguishes Cirq from many other frameworks is its explicit control: you can determine exactly which gate acts on which qubit and at what point in the timeline. This level of precision makes Cirq especially valuable for algorithm testing, hardware calibration, and research experiments that require reproducibility and transparency.

Defining qubits

In Cirq, qubits are not abstract placeholders, they are objects that can be positioned, connected, and directly manipulated.

This object-oriented representation gives Cirq a strong hardware-aware modeling capability, allowing developers to explicitly control qubit placement and connectivity. Such flexibility is especially important when designing circuits intended for specific quantum processors, where physical layout constraints and nearest-neighbor interactions must be considered.

Two of the most common types are shown in the following table:

Type	Description	Example
`LineQubit`	Qubits are arranged in a one-dimensional line, indexed sequentially (0, 1, 2, ...).	`q0, q1 = cirq.LineQubit.range(2)`
`GridQubit`	Qubits positioned on a two-dimensional grid are useful for mapping to real device topologies.	`q = cirq.GridQubit(1, 2)`

***Table 9.2**: Types of Qubit definitions in Cirq*

The following example shows how to create three linearly arranged qubits using Cirq's **LineQubit** class:

```
import cirq
qubits = cirq.LineQubit.range(3)
print(qubits)
```

The output is as follows:

```
[LineQubit(0), LineQubit(1), LineQubit(2)]
```

These qubits can now serve as the foundational elements for circuit construction.

Applying gates

Before examining specific gate operations, it is important to understand that Cirq treats quantum gates as composable, object-oriented primitives that can be programmatically attached to qubits. This design enables precise circuit construction, easy reuse of operations, and seamless integration with simulation and hardware backends.

Quantum gates are the fundamental operations that alter the state of qubits. In Cirq, these gates are implemented as Python objects, allowing users to apply them flexibly within circuits.

The following table lists some commonly used gates and their purposes:

Gate	Purpose	Syntax example
Hadamard (H)	Creates a superposition state.	**cirq.H(q0)**
Pauli-X (NOT)	Flips the qubit between $|0\rangle$ and $|1\rangle$.	**cirq.X(q1)**
CNOT (CX)	Entangles a control and target qubit.	**cirq.CNOT(q0, q1)**
Z-rotation	Applies a controlled phase shift.	**cirq.ZPowGate(exponent=0.5)(q0)**
Measurement	Collapses the qubit and records its classical value.	**cirq.measure(q0)**

***Table 9.3:** Common quantum gates in Cirq*

This snippet builds a Bell state circuit, entangling two-qubits and printing the **American Standard Code for Information Interchange** (**ASCII**) diagram:

```
q0, q1 = cirq.LineQubit.range(2)
bell_circuit = cirq.Circuit(
    cirq.H(q0),             # Create superposition
    cirq.CNOT(q0, q1),      # Entangle with q1
    cirq.measure(q0, q1)  # Measure both qubits
)
print(bell_circuit)
```

The expected output is as follows:

```
0: ───H───@───M───
          │   │
1: ───────X───M───
```

This ASCII diagram reveals how Cirq intuitively visualizes the circuit timeline.

Moments and operations

Cirq introduces the concept of moments to organize circuit execution into well-defined time steps, improving clarity and control.

Cirq groups quantum operations into moments, each representing a single logical time step, where gates act on disjoint qubits. This structure enforces correct sequencing and avoids gate conflicts. The following snippet prints each moment of a Bell state circuit to illustrate this time-based grouping:

```
for i, moment in enumerate(bell_circuit):
    print("Moment", i, ": ", moment)
```

The following is an example of the output:

```
Moment 0 : (H on q0)
Moment 1 : (CNOT on (q0, q1))
Moment 2 : (Measurement on (q0, q1))
```

This level of structure enables developers to insert, rearrange, or analyze gates with precision.

Executing circuits on a simulator

Understanding moments is essential for interpreting how Cirq schedules and organizes quantum operations over time. By grouping compatible gates into discrete layers, Cirq provides a clear temporal structure that helps developers reason about circuit depth, parallelism, and hardware constraints.

Cirq provides multiple simulation backends for running and testing circuits without quantum hardware, supporting debugging, visualization, and validation under both ideal and realistic conditions.

The following table summarizes the main simulators available in Cirq, along with their typical use cases:

Simulator	Description	Typical use
`cirq.Simulator`	Performs ideal statevector simulations.	Algorithm validation under perfect, noise-free conditions.
`cirq.DensityMatrixSimulator`	Models decoherence and environmental noise effects.	Realistic testing for **noisy intermediate-scale quantum** (**NISQ**) era circuits.
`cirq.CliffordSimulator`	Optimized for circuits composed of Clifford gates.	Research in quantum error-correction and stabilizer circuits.

***Table 9.4**: Executing circuits on a simulator*

The following example runs a Bell circuit on Cirq's **`Simulator 1024`** times to obtain measurement results:

```
sim = cirq.Simulator()
result = sim.run(bell_circuit, repetitions=1024)
print(result)
```

The sample output is as follows:

```
measurements:
q0=00...11...
q1=00...11...
```

Each repetition corresponds to one measurement of the circuit, producing binary outcomes that reflect quantum probabilities.

Analyzing measurement outcomes

After executing a quantum circuit, careful analysis of the measurement data is necessary to verify whether the circuit behaved as expected. Cirq provides convenient tools for aggregating repeated measurements, enabling developers to study statistical patterns and validate properties such as superposition and entanglement.

Measurement results are captured as histograms, indicating the frequency with which each outcome occurs across repeated runs. The following code computes a joint measurement histogram for **`q0`** and **`q1`**, showing how often each two-bit outcome occurs across shots:

```
hist = result.multi_measurement_histogram(keys=['q0', 'q1'])
print(hist)
```

The histogram might resemble:

```
{(0, 0): 518, (1, 1): 506}
```

This indicates approximately equal occurrences of 00 and 11, validating the entanglement between the two qubits.

Interpretation: The near-equal probabilities of 00 and 11 confirm that the qubits are perfectly correlated—a signature of the Bell state.

Parameterized circuits

Variational and hybrid quantum algorithms rely on tunable gate parameters, making parameterized circuits an essential capability in modern quantum programming.

Many quantum algorithms, particularly variational ones, require the ability to adjust gate parameters dynamically. Cirq provides symbolic parameters through SymPy integration.

Example (parameterized rotation): This example performs a parameterized rotation on a qubit, varying the angle θ and observing how the measurement outcomes change for different values of θ:

```
import sympy
theta = sympy.Symbol('theta')
param_circuit = cirq.Circuit(
    cirq.rx(theta)(q0),
    cirq.measure(q0)
)
sim = cirq.Simulator()
for t in [0, np.pi/2, np.pi]:
    result = sim.run(param_circuit, repetitions=100, param_resolver={theta: t})
    print(f"Theta = {t:.2f}: ", result.histogram(key='q0'))
```

Each value of theta yields a different probability distribution, allowing iterative tuning within hybrid quantum-classical workflows.

Saving and reusing circuits

Parameterized circuits are a key building block for modern hybrid quantum-classical algorithms such as the **variational quantum eigensolver** (**VQE**) and the **Quantum Approximate Optimization Algorithm** (**QAOA**). By allowing gate parameters to be tuned iteratively, Cirq enables flexible circuit optimization and supports adaptive workflows commonly used in near-term quantum computing.

Cirq supports serialization, enabling circuits to be saved, shared, and reloaded in JSON format. This feature ensures reproducibility, facilitates collaboration, and allows experiments to be seamlessly transferred across systems or shared with other researchers.

The following code saves a circuit to JSON and then reloads it, verifying reproducibility and making it easy to share or transfer experiments across environments:

```
# Save the circuit
cirq.to_json(bell_circuit, 'bell_circuit.json')
# Reload it later
loaded = cirq.read_json('bell_circuit.json')
print(loaded)
```

This is especially valuable when sharing experiments or version-controlled research workflows.

Example of creating a three-qubit GHZ state

Before constructing the circuit, it is useful to recognize that the **Greenberger-Horne-Zeilinger** (**GHZ**) state is a canonical benchmark for verifying multi-qubit entanglement and circuit correctness. Building this state in Cirq demonstrates how simple gate sequences can generate strong quantum correlations across multiple qubits.

A GHZ state demonstrates multi-qubit entanglement by correlating three or more qubits so that measuring one immediately determines the states of the others, illustrating a strong form of quantum correlation.

This code builds and runs a three-qubit GHZ circuit, then prints its measurement histogram, showing two dominant outcomes (000 and 111) that confirm full entanglement:

```
q0, q1, q2 = cirq.LineQubit.range(3)
ghz_circuit = cirq.Circuit(
    cirq.H(q0),
    cirq.CNOT(q0, q1),
    cirq.CNOT(q1, q2),
    cirq.measure(q0, q1, q2)
)
print(ghz_circuit)
sim = cirq.Simulator()
result = sim.run(ghz_circuit, repetitions=1024)
print(result.histogram(key='q0, q1, q2'))
```

Expected result: Only the outcomes 000 and 111 appear with nearly equal probability—demonstrating complete three-qubit entanglement.

Simulation and noise models in Cirq

In a perfect world, quantum gates would perform flawlessly, and qubits would remain coherent indefinitely. In reality, however, every quantum processor is influenced by noise—subtle disturbances arising from its interaction with the environment. These imperfections cause errors in gate operations, fluctuations in measurements, and a gradual loss of information, collectively known as decoherence.

To study and manage these imperfections before executing code on actual hardware, Cirq provides an advanced simulation environment. Through simulation, researchers can model how circuits behave under both ideal and noisy conditions, helping them to:

- Validate algorithm logic and expected outcomes.
- Quantify how noise affects performance and fidelity.
- Experiment with error-mitigation techniques in a controlled setting.

Importance of simulation

Before executing circuits on real quantum hardware, developers typically rely on simulation to validate correctness, study behavior under controlled conditions, and identify potential issues early in the workflow. This preparatory step reduces experimental uncertainty and helps ensure that hardware runs are both efficient and meaningful.

Simulation plays a pivotal role in quantum research and education, serving as a digital twin of real quantum hardware. It enables developers to:

- Test and debug algorithms safely without requiring access to cloud-based hardware.
- Analyze performance by measuring execution time, convergence, and scalability.
- Assess robustness against gate or measurement errors.
- Prototype hybrid workflows that combine classical and quantum components.

By simulating circuits under various conditions, one can predict how well an algorithm might perform on real devices—saving both time and experimental cost.

Simulation backends in Cirq

To support different levels of fidelity and performance, Cirq provides a range of simulation backends tailored to specific analysis needs. Selecting an appropriate simulator allows developers to balance speed, accuracy, and noise realism depending on the stage of quantum algorithm development.

Cirq offers multiple simulation backends that balance computational efficiency and physical realism, enabling circuit testing, debugging, and analysis under different conditions.

The following table highlights the main simulators and their ideal use cases:

Simulator	Description	Appropriate use cases
`cirq.Simulator`	Ideal statevector simulator with no noise.	Testing algorithms in a perfect environment.
`cirq.DensityMatrixSimulator`	Simulates mixed states and decoherence effects.	Studying noise and open-system dynamics.
`cirq.CliffordSimulator`	Optimized for Clifford-only circuits.	Exploring stabilizer codes and quantum error correction.

***Table 9.5**: Simulation backends in Cirq*

All simulators can execute circuits repeatedly (using shots) to generate measurement statistics comparable to real hardware runs.

Running an ideal simulation

Before introducing realistic noise models, it is useful to validate circuit behavior in a perfect simulation environment. Running an ideal simulation helps confirm that the circuit logic, gate sequencing, and measurement configuration are correct before moving to more complex, noise-aware experiments.

Let us begin by constructing a noise-free circuit that prepares a Bell state. The following code creates and runs a Bell state circuit on Cirq's simulator to verify ideal, noise-free operation:

```
import cirq
q0, q1 = cirq.LineQubit.range(2)
bell_circuit = cirq.Circuit(
    cirq.H(q0),
    cirq.CNOT(q0, q1),
    cirq.measure(q0, q1)
)
sim = cirq.Simulator()
result = sim.run(bell_circuit, repetitions=1000)
print(result.histogram(key='q0, q1'))
```

The typical output is as follows:

```
{(0, 0): 502, (1, 1): 498}
```

The outcomes `00` and `11` occur with nearly equal probability, confirming that the qubits are entangled—exactly as predicted in an ideal, noiseless environment.

Understanding quantum noise

Before modeling noise in circuits, it is important to recognize that real quantum hardware is inherently imperfect. Understanding the sources and mathematical representation of noise enables developers to design more robust algorithms and to interpret experimental results realistically.

Noise in quantum systems arises from several physical mechanisms. The main contributing factors include:

- **Decoherence**: Gradual loss of phase information as a qubit interacts with its environment.
- **Gate infidelity**: Small inaccuracies in the control pulses that implement quantum gates.
- **Measurement error**: Occasional misclassification of readout states.

To capture these imperfections mathematically, Cirq introduces noise channels—probabilistic transformations that describe how a qubit's state evolves under error.

The following table summarizes the key noise models available in Cirq:

Noise channel	Effect modeled	Syntax
Depolarizing	Randomly replaces the qubit's state with a mixed state.	`cirq.depolarize(p)`
Bit-flip	Flips $\|0\rangle \leftrightarrow \|1\rangle$ with probability p.	`cirq.bit_flip(p)`
Phase-flip	Introduces random phase inversion errors.	`cirq.phase_flip(p)`
Amplitude-damping	Simulates energy relaxation from $\|1\rangle$ to $\|0\rangle$.	`cirq.amplitude_damp(gamma)`

Table 9.6: *Noise channels in Cirq*

Each channel provides a simple yet physically meaningful model for understanding how real hardware deviates from theory.

Applying a global noise model

To study algorithm behavior under realistic hardware conditions, it is often useful to introduce a uniform noise profile across the entire circuit. Cirq provides convenient utilities for injecting global noise models, enabling controlled and repeatable experiments that approximate real device imperfections.

Cirq lets you apply uniform noise across all qubits with a single setting using **`ConstantQubitNoiseModel`**, making experiments consistently noisy for fair, reproducible comparisons.

The following code applies a uniform depolarizing noise model to all qubits, ensuring consistent, reproducible noisy conditions for simulation and analysis:

```
# 5% depolarizing noise applied globally
noise = cirq.ConstantQubitNoiseModel(cirq.depolarize(p=0.05))
noisy_circuit = bell_circuit.with_noise(noise)
print("Noisy Circuit:")
print(noisy_circuit)
```

The following is an excerpt of the output:

```
0: ──H──D(0.05)──@──D(0.05)──M──
                 │           │
1: ──────────────X───────────M──
```

Each **`D(0.05)`** indicates a depolarizing channel added after the corresponding gate—a concise way to visualize where noise enters the circuit.

Simulating noisy circuits

After introducing noise into the circuit, the next step is to simulate its impact on measurement outcomes. Running a noise-aware simulation helps quantify how real hardware imperfections can affect entanglement quality and overall algorithm reliability.

To examine the effect of noise on circuit behavior, the following code executes the noisy Bell state circuit using Cirq's **`DensityMatrixSimulator`** and displays how the measurement distribution changes under noise:

```
noisy_sim = cirq.DensityMatrixSimulator()
noisy_result = noisy_sim.run(noisy_circuit, repetitions=1000)
print(noisy_result.histogram(key='q0, q1'))
```

The example output is as follows:

```
{(0, 0): 415, (1, 1): 420, (0, 1): 82, (1, 0): 83}
```

Here, additional outcomes 01 and 10 appear because depolarizing noise occasionally disrupts the entanglement. This illustrates how real-world imperfections can blur ideal quantum correlations.

Creating custom noise models

Researchers often need to simulate multiple error sources together. Cirq supports this by allowing users to create custom composite noise models by subclassing the **NoiseModel** class, enabling combined effects such as depolarization and amplitude damping to be applied and analyzed within quantum circuits.

The following example demonstrates how to implement a custom composite noise model in Cirq:

```
from cirq import NoiseModel, depolarize, amplitude_damp
class CustomNoise(NoiseModel):
    def noisy_operation(self, operation):
        return [
            operation,
            depolarize(p=0.03).on_each(*operation.qubits),
            amplitude_damp(0.02).on_each(*operation.qubits)
        ]
custom_noise = CustomNoise()
noisy_circuit = bell_circuit.with_noise(custom_noise)
noisy_result = noisy_sim.run(noisy_circuit, repetitions=1000)
print(noisy_result.histogram(key='q0, q1'))
```

This model incorporates both random depolarization and energy relaxation, closely resembling the noise observed in superconducting qubits.

Visualizing the impact of noise

Noise effects are often easier to understand through visual comparison rather than raw numerical outputs. Graphical representations help reveal how quantum correlations degrade under realistic hardware conditions.

Visual analysis provides intuitive insight into how errors change quantum results. The following code plots side-by-side histograms for ideal and noisy runs, making the impact of noise on measurement outcomes easy to compare at a glance:

```
import matplotlib.pyplot as plt
ideal_counts = sim.run(bell_circuit, repetitions=1000).histogram(key='q0, q1')
noisy_counts = noisy_sim.run(noisy_circuit, repetitions=1000).histogram(key='q0, q1')
plt.subplot(1, 2, 1)
plt.bar([str(k) for k in ideal_counts.keys()], ideal_counts.values())
plt.title("Ideal Simulation")
plt.subplot(1, 2, 2)
plt.bar([str(k) for k in noisy_counts.keys()], noisy_counts.values(), color='orange')
plt.title("Noisy Simulation")
plt.tight_layout()
plt.show()
```

Interpretation: The ideal circuit produces two tall bars at `00` and `11`, whereas the noisy circuit shows smaller side bars for `01` and `10`. This graphical comparison clearly illustrates how decoherence and gate errors affect entanglement.

Measuring fidelity

Fidelity provides a quantitative measure of how well a quantum system preserves the intended state in the presence of noise and hardware imperfections. By comparing the ideal state produced in a noiseless simulation with the corresponding noisy output, researchers can objectively assess the quality of quantum operations and the effectiveness of error-mitigation strategies.

Fidelity quantifies how closely a noisy quantum state matches the ideal one. The following snippet computes the fidelity ⟨ψ | ρ | ψ⟩ by comparing the ideal Bell statevector with the noisy density matrix and evaluating their overlap:

```
import numpy as np
# Ideal final statevector
ideal_state = sim.simulate(bell_circuit).final_state_vector
# Noisy density matrix
rho = noisy_sim.simulate(noisy_circuit).final_density_matrix
# Fidelity calculation
fidelity = np.real(np.conj(ideal_state).T @ rho @ ideal_state)
print("State Fidelity:", fidelity)
```

Values close to 1.0 indicate excellent preservation of the target state, while lower values signify degradation due to noise.

Implementing Shor's factoring algorithm in Cirq

Among all quantum algorithms ever developed, Shor's algorithm stands as one of the most profound. Proposed by *Peter Shor* in 1994, it demonstrated that a quantum computer could factor large integers exponentially faster than the best known **classical methods**.

This single insight reshaped the landscape of computational mathematics and modern cryptography, since factoring large numbers is the security foundation of schemes like **Rivest-Shamir-Adleman** (**RSA**).

While a full-scale implementation of Shor's algorithm requires thousands of logical qubits and fault-tolerant gates, Cirq allows us to explore its core idea—quantum period finding—through a simplified demonstration.

This exercise highlights Cirq's capacity to model complex, multi-register quantum circuits and underscores the link between quantum interference and computational speedup.

Concept behind Shor's algorithm

This period finding capability is the core quantum advantage of Shor's algorithm. Classical algorithms must search for the period through repeated modular exponentiation, which becomes exponentially expensive for large integers. In contrast, the quantum approach evaluates many values simultaneously using superposition and then amplifies the correct periodic information through the **Quantum Fourier transform** (**QFT**). As a result, the algorithm converts a computationally hard factoring problem into an efficiently solvable quantum subroutine, demonstrating one of the most significant theoretical speedups known in quantum computing.

The classical task of factoring an integer N can be reframed as a period finding problem.

Shor's algorithm leverages this insight by transforming the problem into a form that quantum computers can solve efficiently through interference.

Algorithm overview

The algorithm overview of Shor's factoring procedure is summarized in the following steps:

1. Choose a random integer $a<N$ that is coprime to N.
2. Define the periodic function:

$$f(x)=a^x mod N$$

3. Find the period r such that $f(x+r)=f(x)$.
4. Use r to determine non-trivial factors of N as:

$$\gcd\,(a^{r/2} \pm 1, N)$$

5. Provided that *r* is even and $a^{r/2} \equiv/ -1(\text{mod} N)$.

The quantum component finds the period r exponentially faster than classical computation using superposition, modular exponentiation, and the QFT.

Quantum building blocks

Understanding these components helps in implementing and analyzing Shor's algorithm effectively. By structuring the algorithm into modular stages, developers can validate and optimize each part independently. Cirq supports this approach by allowing flexible construction and composition of these building blocks.

Shor's algorithm, like many quantum algorithms, is constructed from several fundamental building blocks. Each component serves a distinct purpose within the computation process, leveraging unique quantum mechanisms such as superposition, entanglement, and interference.

The following table outlines these core components and their respective roles:

Component	Purpose	Quantum mechanism
Superposition	Prepare all possible exponents simultaneously.	Hadamard gates are applied across control qubits.
Modular exponentiation	Encode $f(x)=a^x \bmod N$.	Implemented using controlled multiplication gates.
Inverse QFT	Extract the periodicity of *f(x)* through interference.	Achieved via a sequence of controlled phase rotations.

***Table 9.7**: Quantum building blocks of Shor's algorithm*

Cirq provides the flexibility to represent all three stages, allowing us to model the essence of Shor's approach within a manageable number of qubits.

Simplified demonstration

To make the working of Shor's algorithm concrete and accessible, we consider a small illustrative example that captures the essential idea of quantum period finding without requiring large-scale hardware. This simplified setup allows learners to observe how quantum interference reveals periodic structure, which is the key insight behind efficient factorization.

Factoring very large numbers (such as those used in RSA) is not feasible on today's small-scale quantum computers. However, we can illustrate the process using a toy example:

$$N=15, a=2$$

This configuration produces a period $r=4$, which will serve as the conceptual anchor for our demonstration.

Building the quantum circuit

To implement Shor's algorithm in Cirq, an eight-qubit quantum circuit is constructed, organized into functional sections that each perform a specific role in the computation. The key components include:

The first four-qubits act as the *exponent register*, which is placed in superposition to represent all possible exponents simultaneously.

The remaining four-qubits serve as the *function register*, storing the results of the modular exponentiation step.

This structure enables parallel evaluation of $f(x)=a^x \bmod N$, which underpins quantum speedup in factorization. The following code constructs an eight-qubit circuit in Cirq, applies superposition, performs modular exponentiation and the inverse QFT, and measures all qubits:

```
import cirq
import numpy as np
# Define qubits
qreg = cirq.LineQubit.range(8)
# Initialize circuit
circuit = cirq.Circuit()
# Step 1: Create superposition on the first four qubits
circuit.append(cirq.H.on_each(*qreg[:4]))
# Step 2: Simulated modular exponentiation (using CNOTs for simplicity)
for i in range(4):
    circuit.append(cirq.CNOT(qreg[i], qreg[i + 4]))
# Step 3: Apply inverse Quantum Fourier Transform (QFT⁻¹)
for i in range(3, -1, -1):
    circuit.append(cirq.H(qreg[i]))
    for j in range(i):
        circuit.append(cirq.CZPowGate(exponent=-1 / (2 ** (i - j)))(qreg[j], qreg[i]))
# Step 4: Measure all qubits
circuit.append(cirq.measure(*qreg, key='result'))
print(circuit)
```

The output (truncated ASCII diagram) is as follows:

```
0: ───H───@───────H───@───────────────M───
          │           │
1: ───H───@───────H───@───────────────M───
...
4: ───────────X───────────────────────M───
```

This structure encapsulates the essential logic of finding the quantum period. The Hadamard gates create superposition, the CNOTs mimic modular exponentiation, and the controlled-phase rotations simulate the inverse QFT.

Running the simulation

To verify the periodic behavior predicted by the simplified setup, we execute the constructed circuit on Cirq's ideal simulator and analyze the measurement statistics. This step confirms whether the quantum interference pattern correctly reveals the expected periodic structure.

We execute the circuit on Cirq's ideal simulator with 1,024 shots and collect a histogram of measurement outcomes for the exponent register. The following code runs the circuit on Cirq's ideal simulator for 1,024 shots and prints the measurement histogram for the exponent register:

```
sim = cirq.Simulator()
result = sim.run(circuit, repetitions=1024)
counts = result.histogram(key='result')
print(counts)
```

The following is an example output:

```
{0: 260, 4: 240, 8: 260, 12: 264}
```

These outcomes correspond to multiples of the true period $r=4$, appearing at regular intervals (0, 4, 8, 12).

Interpreting the results

The periodicity in the measurement outcomes arises from quantum interference. Each observed peak reflects a constructive interference pattern aligned with the period of the modular function $f(x)$.

From the period *r=4*, we can compute:

$$\gcd(a^{r/2}-1,N)=\gcd(2^2-1,15)=\gcd(3,15)=3$$

Thus, the non-trivial factors of *15* are correctly identified as *3* and *5*—validating the algorithm's logic.

Observation: Even in this simplified version, we witness the fundamental power of quantum computation: using interference patterns to reveal hidden periodicities, a feat that would require exponential effort classically.

Visualizing measurement outcomes

To better understand the periodic pattern revealed by the simulation, it is helpful to visualize the measurement distribution graphically. Plotting the results makes the repeating structure immediately apparent and supports intuitive interpretation of the period finding process.

We can use Matplotlib to visualize the distribution of the output. The following code renders a bar chart of measurement counts, making the distribution—and any periodic structure—easy to inspect at a glance:

```
import matplotlib.pyplot as plt
plt.bar(counts.keys(), counts.values())
plt.title("Measurement Outcomes - Simplified Shor's Algorithm")
plt.xlabel("Measured Value (decimal)")
plt.ylabel("Frequency")
plt.show()
```

Interpretation: The bar chart displays peaks at 0, 4, 8, and 12, visually confirming a period of 4. This visualization bridges the mathematical concept of periodicity with the physical behavior of quantum measurement.

Extending the model with noise

In real quantum hardware, environmental interactions and imperfect gate operations introduce errors that can affect algorithmic performance. To study how robust the simplified Shor demonstration is under realistic conditions, it is useful to incorporate a controlled noise model into the simulation.

To emulate more realistic conditions, we can apply a small depolarizing noise model. The following code adds depolarizing noise to simulate hardware imperfections and reruns the circuit to observe the changes in outcome:

```
noise = cirq.ConstantQubitNoiseModel(cirq.depolarize(p=0.02))
noisy_circuit = circuit.with_noise(noise)
noisy_result = sim.run(noisy_circuit, repetitions=512)
print(noisy_result.histogram(key='result'))
```

This introduces random disturbances that slightly distort the output frequencies, illustrating how real devices deviate from idealized outcomes—a crucial lesson for algorithmic resilience testing.

Circuit visualization with Cirq and Matplotlib

Quantum computing is often described as counterintuitive, and for good reason—its operations occur in a space that cannot be directly observed or perceived.

Visualization, therefore, becomes an indispensable tool for translating abstract quantum phenomena into interpretable, tangible insights.

Cirq provides built-in visualization capabilities for rendering circuits, displaying measurement results, and analyzing quantum states. When combined with Matplotlib, these tools enable researchers and learners to explore the interaction of gates, qubits, and measurements over time.

By mastering visualization, you move from writing quantum code to seeing quantum behavior, a critical skill for debugging, teaching, and research communication.

Viewing circuits in ASCII format

Before executing circuits on real hardware or advanced simulators, it is often helpful to quickly inspect the circuit structure in a lightweight, text-based form.

Cirq automatically produces ASCII circuit diagrams, enabling quick inspection and verification without a graphical interface. The following code displays a Bell state circuit using this text-based format:

```
import cirq
# Define qubits
q0, q1 = cirq.LineQubit.range(2)
# Create a Bell state circuit
bell_circuit = cirq.Circuit(
    cirq.H(q0),
    cirq.CNOT(q0, q1),
    cirq.measure(q0, q1)
)
print(bell_circuit)
```

The output is as follows:

```
0: ───H───@───M───
          │   │
1: ───────X───M───
```

This textual representation displays the full gate sequence, showing control–target relationships and measurement points.

HTML and rich visualization in notebooks

Modern notebook environments provide enhanced visual rendering that improves circuit readability and presentation quality.

When working in Google Colab or Jupyter Notebook, Cirq automatically renders circuits as interactive **Hypertext Markup Language** (**HTML**) diagrams when you simply type the circuit's name in a cell:

```
bell_circuit
```

This produces a neatly formatted, color-coded circuit where each operation is labeled and visually aligned. Such visualizations are ideal for teaching, presentations, and publications where readability and structure are important.

Customizing circuit displays

Cirq enables developers to customize the appearance of circuits by configuring diagram drawers or creating custom visual markers for gates. The following code customizes the circuit's text-based display by enabling Unicode characters, resulting in a clearer and more visually refined diagram:

```
drawer = bell_circuit.to_text_diagram_drawer(use_unicode_characters=True)
print(drawer)
```

This approach enhances formatting—aligning gates more precisely and supporting Unicode characters for better readability in printed material.

Visualizing measurement outcomes

Graphical inspection of measurement statistics provides an intuitive way to validate quantum behavior and detect correlations between qubits.

After executing a quantum circuit, the most direct way to understand its behavior is through measurement histograms. The following code runs the Bell circuit and plots a joint-measurement histogram, providing a quick visual summary of the outcome frequencies:

```
import matplotlib.pyplot as plt
sim = cirq.Simulator()
result = sim.run(bell_circuit, repetitions=1000)
hist = result.multi_measurement_histogram(keys=['q0', 'q1'])
# Plot histogram
plt.bar([str(k) for k in hist.keys()], hist.values())
plt.title("Measurement Outcomes for Bell State")
plt.xlabel("Measured States")
plt.ylabel("Frequency")
plt.show()
```

Interpretation: The histogram displays two dominant bars, typically for the outcomes 00 and 11. These correspond to the entangled Bell state, where both qubits always yield identical values.

Using plot_state_histogram() for quick visualization

For rapid and presentation-ready visualization, Cirq provides a built-in helper that automatically formats measurement histograms with minimal code.

Cirq also includes a convenient built-in method to visualize state probabilities more elegantly:

```
cirq.plot_state_histogram(result)
```

This function automatically labels the axes and formats probabilities, providing a professional-quality visualization for reports and lectures.

Plotting statevectors and amplitude probabilities

To gain deeper insight into quantum behavior, it is often useful to inspect the underlying statevector and visualize how probability mass is distributed across basis states.

Beyond measurement outcomes, you can visualize amplitudes, the core of quantum information, to understand how probability is distributed across basis states. This code simulates the Bell circuit and prints its final statevector, showing the complex amplitudes for each basis state:

```
state = sim.simulate(bell_circuit).final_state_vector
print(state)
```

The example of the output is as follows:

```
[0.707+0.j, 0.000+0.j, 0.000+0.j, 0.707+0.j]
```

These are the complex amplitudes for the states $|00\rangle$ and $|11\rangle$, each with probability 0.5. The following code plots the probability amplitudes of the Bell state as a bar chart, showing how the total probability is distributed across all basis states:

```
import numpy as np
probabilities = np.abs(state) ** 2
labels = ['00', '01', '10', '11']
plt.bar(labels, probabilities)
plt.title(„Probability Distribution of Bell State")
plt.ylabel(„Probability")
plt.show()
```

Interpretation: Two equal-height bars appear for $|00\rangle$ and $|11\rangle$—a visual confirmation of equal superposition and perfect correlation.

Visualizing quantum states on the Bloch sphere

For single-qubit states, the Bloch sphere provides an intuitive geometric representation of quantum behavior. Each point on the sphere represents a possible qubit state, with axes corresponding to the Pauli operators *X*, *Y*, and *Z*.

Cirq does not directly include a Bloch sphere plotter, but you can create one using Matplotlib. The following snippet computes a single-qubit Bloch vector from a statevector and renders it with Matplotlib, providing a quick geometric view of quantum state orientation:

```
from mpl_toolkits.mplot3d import Axes3D
def plot_bloch_vector(state):
    x = 2 * np.real(state[0] * np.conj(state[1]))
    y = 2 * np.imag(state[1] * np.conj(state[0]))
    z = np.abs(state[0])**2 - np.abs(state[1])**2
    fig = plt.figure()
    ax = fig.add_subplot(111, projection='3d')
    ax.quiver(0, 0, 0, x, y, z, color='r', arrow_length_ratio=0.2)
    ax.set_xlim([-1, 1]); ax.set_ylim([-1, 1]); ax.set_zlim([-1, 1])
    ax.set_xlabel('X'); ax.set_ylabel('Y'); ax.set_zlabel('Z')
    ax.set_title('Bloch Sphere Representation')
    plt.show()
# Example - |+⟩ state
plus_circuit = cirq.Circuit(cirq.H(q0))
plus_state = sim.simulate(plus_circuit).final_state_vector
plot_bloch_vector(plus_state)
```

Interpretation: The red arrow points along the +X axis, representing the |+⟩ state—a balanced superposition of |0⟩ and |1⟩. Bloch visualization vividly demonstrates how gate operations, such as the Hadamard gate, rotate qubit states around the sphere.

Comparing ideal and noisy simulations

A side-by-side comparison of ideal and noisy executions helps clearly reveal how hardware imperfections influence quantum circuit behavior.

Visualization is especially powerful when comparing the ideal vs. noisy execution of the same circuit. The following code compares the measurement outcomes of the same circuit under ideal and noisy conditions, plotting side-by-side histograms to visualize the effect of noise:

```
# Ideal circuit results
ideal_counts = sim.run(bell_circuit, repetitions=1000).histogram(key='q0, q1')
# Add noise
noise_model = cirq.ConstantQubitNoiseModel(cirq.depolarize(p=0.05))
noisy_circuit = bell_circuit.with_noise(noise_model)
noisy_counts = cirq.DensityMatrixSimulator().run(noisy_circuit, repetitions=1000).
histogram(key='q0, q1')
# Plot side-by-side comparison
plt.subplot(1, 2, 1)
plt.bar([str(k) for k in ideal_counts.keys()], ideal_counts.values())
plt.title("Ideal Circuit")
plt.subplot(1, 2, 2)
plt.bar([str(k) for k in noisy_counts.keys()], noisy_counts.values(), color='orange')
plt.title("Noisy Circuit")
plt.tight_layout()
plt.show()
```

Observation: The ideal plot shows only 00 and 11, whereas the noisy one displays additional outcomes, such as 01 and 10. This visualization makes decoherence and error accumulation instantly understandable.

Conclusion

This chapter presented Cirq as a research-oriented framework for designing and simulating quantum circuits with high precision, transparency, and hardware-aware control. Unlike higher-level SDKs that hide many execution details, Cirq encourages developers to think in terms of explicit qubits, gate placement, and time-ordered operations (moments). This emphasis is especially valuable for near-term quantum computing, where circuit depth, qubit connectivity, and noise behavior directly shape experimental outcomes.

Through hands-on examples such as the Bell state and the three-qubit GHZ state, readers observed how Cirq represents superposition and entanglement, and how measurement statistics can be interpreted using histograms. The chapter also highlighted parameterized circuits, showing how Cirq supports tunable gates that are essential in modern hybrid workflows, including variational and optimization-based algorithms. Moving beyond ideal execution, Cirq's noise channels and global/custom noise models were used to emulate realistic imperfections such as decoherence and gate infidelity. This enabled a practical comparison between ideal and noisy simulations and introduced fidelity as a quantitative way to judge how closely noisy results match intended states.

A simplified demonstration of Shor's algorithm further illustrated Cirq's ability to structure multi-register circuits and reveal periodic patterns through quantum interference, reinforcing why simulation and visualization are critical in understanding complex quantum behavior. Finally, circuit visualization in ASCII and notebook-based rendering, combined with Matplotlib plots, showed how abstract quantum results can be converted into clear, interpretable insights.

Overall, Cirq serves both as a powerful learning environment and as a practical research platform, helping readers bridge theoretical quantum concepts with experimental realism and reproducible implementation practices.

Questions

1. **What is Cirq, and why is it significant for quantum programming?**

   Answer: Cirq is Google's open-source Python framework for designing, simulating, and executing quantum circuits, offering fine-grained control over qubits, gates, and scheduling for experimental, hardware-level research and precise algorithm development.

2. **How can Cirq be installed?**

   Answer: Cirq can be installed locally with pip install cirq for sustained development, or quickly in Google Colab with !pip install cirq to enable immediate coding. Both options support simulation and circuit visualization.

3. **What distinguishes Cirq from Qiskit or other frameworks?**

   Answer: Unlike Qiskit, which emphasizes accessibility through abstraction, Cirq is built for research and experimentation, offering precise control over the order, timing, and placement of operations to model quantum hardware behavior realistically.

4. **What types of simulators does Cirq provide?**

   Answer: Cirq provides multiple simulators: the simulator for ideal statevector execution, the DensityMatrixSimulator for noise-aware mixed states, and the CliffordSimulator optimized for stabilizer circuits in quantum error-correction studies.

5. **How does Cirq model noise and errors?**

   Answer: Cirq provides built-in noise channels (e.g., depolarizing, bit-flip, amplitude damping) and supports global or custom noise models, enabling analysis of how decoherence and gate errors impact circuit performance.

6. **What does building a Bell state in Cirq demonstrate?**

   Answer: Creating a Bell state illustrates superposition and entanglement while also serving as a practical test to verify that Cirq's simulation and measurement processes function correctly.

7. **What is the purpose of implementing Shor's algorithm in Cirq?**

   Answer: Implementing Shor's algorithm showcases Cirq's capability to handle complex multi-qubit operations and quantum interference, demonstrating its ability to simulate quantum period finding for efficient integer factorization.

8. **Why is visualization important in Cirq?**

   Answer: Visualization clarifies abstract quantum operations. Cirq offers ASCII and HTML circuit diagrams and supports plots of measurement histograms, probability distributions, and Bloch sphere representations for clearer insight.

9. **How does Cirq help compare ideal and noisy simulations?**

   Answer: Cirq enables side-by-side simulations with and without noise, showing how decoherence and operational errors impact results and allowing evaluation of circuit fidelity and robustness.

10. **What is the key educational value of learning Cirq?**

    Answer: Learning Cirq builds a strong foundation in quantum programming through hands-on, research-level experimentation, strengthening understanding of circuit design, error behavior, and visualization while bridging theory with real-world practice.

Exercises

1. Install Cirq locally (pip install cirq) and verify it by creating a two-qubit circuit with Hadamard + CNOT. Print the ASCII diagram and explain the timeline symbols.
2. Run Cirq in Google Colab (!pip install cirq), recreate the Bell state, simulate with 1,024 repetitions, and plot a histogram. Explain how the results indicate entanglement.
3. Build a three-qubit GHZ circuit, simulate it, and plot outcomes using Matplotlib. Explain how GHZ extends entanglement beyond two qubits.
4. Apply global depolarizing noise using ConstantQubitNoiseModel, compare ideal vs. noisy histograms, and discuss decoherence effects.
5. Create a parameterized circuit with rx(θ), sweep θ values, record measurement changes, and relate this to hybrid optimization.
6. Implement a simplified Shor (N=15), analyze the histogram to find the period, and verify that the factors are 3 and 5.
7. Visualize states with Cirq + Matplotlib: plot Bell state probabilities and show the Bloch sphere for $|+\rangle$. Explain how visuals help interpretation.
8. Run the same Bell circuit on Simulator and DensityMatrixSimulator, then compare output fidelity under noise.
9. Serialize and reload a circuit using to_json() and read_json(), and explain how this improves reproducibility and collaboration.
10. Write a short reflection on how Cirq's transparency, noise modeling, and visualization support quantum research and advanced learning.

CHAPTER 10
Programming with AWS Braket

Introduction

As quantum computing moves from experimental curiosity to practical utility, scalable access to quantum hardware has become a central goal. While individual vendors like *IBM* and *Google* provide dedicated ecosystems, **Amazon Web Services** (**AWS**) takes a broader, hardware-agnostic approach through AWS Braket, a unified cloud platform that connects users to multiple quantum technologies within a single environment. Designed for both researchers and developers, Braket simplifies quantum experimentation by offering seamless integration between simulators, real quantum processors, and hybrid quantum–classical workflows.

AWS Braket's strength lies in its flexibility. It enables users to prototype algorithms on high-performance simulators, execute them on real hardware from providers such as *IonQ*, *Rigetti*, and *Oxford Quantum Circuits* (*QQCs*), and extend their workflows with classical optimization using AWS infrastructure. By combining accessibility, scalability, and cost transparency, Braket transforms quantum programming from an isolated research task into a reproducible, production-ready process.

This chapter provides a comprehensive guide to programming with AWS Braket. You will learn how to configure your AWS account, install and authenticate the Braket **software development kit** (**SDK**), and run your first quantum circuits on both simulators and real devices. The chapter further explores hybrid job execution, cost management, and performance optimization, culminating in a practical case study that demonstrates quantum–classical optimization using the **Quantum Approximate Optimization Algorithm** (**QAOA**).

Structure

The chapter covers the following topics:

- AWS Braket SDK setup and account configuration
- Hybrid classical and quantum workflows
- Case study on optimization with QAOA
- Running circuits on IonQ, Rigetti, and OQC
- Submitting jobs on AWS cloud infrastructure

Objectives

This chapter introduces AWS Braket, a cloud-based service that provides unified access to multiple quantum hardware providers and high-performance simulators. Readers learn to setup AWS, install and authenticate the Braket SDK, and run quantum circuits on simulators and real devices from IonQ, Rigetti, and QQC. The chapter highlights hybrid quantum–classical programming through Braket Hybrid Jobs, demonstrating integration of classical optimizers with quantum workflows. It also covers resource management, cost optimization, and monitoring using Amazon CloudWatch and Amazon S3. By the end, readers can configure, execute, and optimize quantum experiments in the AWS ecosystem, culminating in a practical implementation of QAOA for combinatorial optimization.

AWS Braket SDK setup and account configuration

Amazon Braket is the quantum computing service from AWS that provides a unified interface for designing, simulating, and executing quantum programs on both simulators and real hardware. Unlike vendor-specific frameworks such as Qiskit and Cirq, Braket enables access to multiple qubit technologies—ion-trap and superconducting within a single environment.

Braket connects to hardware from IonQ, Rigetti, and QQC, allowing researchers to compare architectures without changing SDKs. It also supports local simulators and managed hybrid workflows, combining quantum and classical computation on AWS. This section focuses on setting up the Braket SDK, configuring AWS access, and running a test circuit to validate the development environment.

Creating an AWS account

Before proceeding with the account creation steps, it is useful to understand that AWS Braket operates entirely within the AWS cloud ecosystem and relies on standard AWS identity, access, and billing mechanisms. Proper account configuration ensures that users can securely provision quantum resources and manage permissions required for executing Braket workloads.

To begin working with AWS Braket, you first need a valid AWS account. The process is straightforward and ensures you have access to all the tools needed to run both simulated and hardware-based quantum tasks. The steps below outline the account setup procedure:

1. **Sign up**: Visit **https://aws.amazon.com/** and create a new account using a valid and verified email address. This email will serve as your primary point of contact for account notifications and billing information.
2. **Billing details**: Provide the required payment details to activate your account. While AWS offers a Free Tier for Braket that includes limited usage on local simulators, running quantum tasks on actual hardware devices (such as those from IonQ or Rigetti) incurs costs based on the number of tasks executed.
3. **Region selection**: AWS Braket is currently supported in specific regions—such as **`us-east-1`** (N. Virginia), **`us-west-1`** (N. California), and **`eu-west-2`** (London). Selecting the region geographically closest to you helps reduce network latency and ensures faster task execution.
4. **Account verification**: Once you complete the verification process, you can sign in to the AWS Management Console, which serves as your control center for managing all AWS services, including Braket.

Configuring IAM permissions

AWS uses **Identity and Access Management** (**IAM**) to define and enforce user permissions, ensuring secure, controlled access to its services. Proper IAM configuration is a critical step before using AWS Braket, as it enables you to manage who can perform specific actions within your AWS environment.

Follow these steps to configure IAM for Braket access:

1. **Open the IAM console**: Navigate to the **AWS Management Console** | **IAM** | **Users** | **Add user** to begin creating a new user account.
2. **Create a user**: Assign a descriptive username, such as **`braket-user`**, and enable **Programmatic Access**. This allows the user to interact with AWS services using the **command-line interface** (**CLI**) or SDKs, which is essential for running Braket tasks.
3. **Assign permissions**: Attach the policy **`AmazonBraketFullAccess`** for complete Braket functionality, or define a custom policy to provide more granular control. A typical policy includes access to the following:
    - **braket:*** for creating and managing quantum tasks.
    - **s3:*** for storing quantum job results and related data.
    - **logs:*** for monitoring Braket activity through Amazon CloudWatch Logs.

4. **Download credentials**: Once the user is created, download the Access Key ID and Secret Access Key. These credentials are required for authentication when using AWS CLI or SDKs to run Braket jobs programmatically.

Installing the AWS Braket SDK

The AWS Braket SDK provides a Python-based interface for building, running, and analyzing quantum circuits. It can be installed either on your local system or in a cloud-based environment such as *Google Colab* or *Amazon SageMaker Studio Lab*, depending on your workflow preferences.

The SDK integrates with the broader AWS ecosystem and requires appropriate credential configuration to enable authenticated access to cloud resources. Depending on whether the user prioritizes ease of setup or environment control, the installation may be performed in a managed notebook environment or on a locally configured Python workspace.

Local installation

A local setup is particularly suitable for users who intend to integrate AWS Braket into existing Python projects, development environments, or automated workflows. It also allows customization of dependencies and versions, which can be beneficial for advanced experimentation and reproducible research.

To setup the SDK on your local machine, ensure that Python 3.9 or later is installed. Then, open your terminal or command prompt and execute the following command:

```
pip install amazon-braket-sdk amazon-braket-schemas boto3 matplotlib
```

Once the installation is complete, verify it by running the following Python commands:

```
import braket
print("AWS Braket SDK version:", braket.__version__)
```

This confirms that the SDK is correctly installed and ready to interact with AWS Braket services.

Cloud-based installation

If you prefer a cloud-based notebook environment such as Google Colab, you can install the SDK directly within the notebook cell. Prefix the installation command with an exclamation mark (`!`) to execute it as a shell command:

```
!pip install amazon-braket-sdk amazon-braket-schemas boto3 matplotlib
```

This setup is particularly useful for students, researchers, or developers who wish to experiment with Braket without configuring a local development environment.

Configuring AWS credentials

Your local environment must be authenticated with AWS before you can execute quantum tasks using AWS Braket. This ensures that your system has the proper permissions to access Braket resources securely. The recommended approach is to configure credentials using the AWS CLI.

The following step-by-step procedure outlines how to securely configure your local environment for authenticated access to AWS Braket services:

1. **Install the AWS CLI**:

   Begin by installing the AWS CLI using Python's package manager:

   ```
   pip install awscli
   ```

   The CLI provides a convenient interface for managing AWS services directly from your terminal.

2. **Run the configuration wizard**:

   Once installed, initialize the configuration setup by running:

   ```
   aws configure
   ```

You will be prompted to enter your credentials and preferences:

```
AWS Access Key ID [None]: <your_access_key>
AWS Secret Access Key [None]: <your_secret_key>
Default region name [None]: us-east-1
Default output format [None]: json
```

These settings are securely saved in your home directory at the following locations:

a. **~/.aws/credentials**: Stores your Access Key and Secret Key.

b. **~/.aws/config**: Stores your default region and output format.

3. **Test the configuration:**

To verify that your credentials are correctly configured and AWS Braket is accessible, run the following command:

```
aws braket get-device --device-arn arn:aws:braket:::device/quantum-simulator/amazon/sv1
```

If your configuration is successful, the command will return detailed information about the specified simulator device.

Testing the environment

Before proceeding to advanced quantum workloads, it is considered good practice to perform a quick functional check of the development environment. This preliminary validation helps detect configuration or permission issues early and ensures that the local setup can successfully communicate with the AWS Braket service endpoints.

With your credentials configured and the SDK installed, you can validate the setup by running a small circuit on an AWS-managed simulator. The following example prepares a Bell state and measures it 1,000 times:

```
from braket.circuits import Circuit
from braket.aws import AwsDevice
# Choose a simulator backend (Amazon SV1 state vector simulator)
device = AwsDevice("arn:aws:braket:::device/quantum-simulator/amazon/sv1")
# Build a Bell state circuit: |ψ⟩ = (|00⟩ + |11⟩) / √2
bell = Circuit().h(0).cnot(0, 1)
# Execute the circuit and collect results
task = device.run(bell, shots=1000)
result = task.result()
counts = result.measurement_counts
print("Measurement Results:", counts)
```

The following is an example output:

```
Measurement Results: {'00': 505, '11': 495}
```

The near-equal counts for `00` and `11`, with negligible results for other states, confirm successful Bell state entanglement. Small deviations from an exact 50–50 split arise from sampling randomness. Observing only these correlated outcomes also verifies that the environment is correctly installed and authenticated, and that it can execute jobs on AWS Braket.

Exploring the AWS Braket console

After setup and verification, users can explore the AWS Braket console, a centralized graphical interface that unifies Braket resources in a single dashboard. It enables intuitive interaction without direct coding, making it suitable for both beginners and advanced users.

The key sections of the console include:

- **Notebooks**: These are pre-configured Jupyter Notebook environments with the Braket SDK, dependencies, and sample notebooks already installed. They provide a ready-to-use workspace for building, visualizing, and executing quantum circuits without additional setup.
- **Devices**: This section lists all available quantum hardware and simulators, such as IonQ, Rigetti Computing, QQC, and the Amazon SV1 statevector simulator. You can check each device's status, queue availability, and pricing information to choose the optimal backend for your tasks.
- **Tasks**: The tasks dashboard serves as your monitoring center. It displays all submitted jobs, including their current states (queued, running, completed, or failed), along with direct links to results stored in Amazon S3.

Comparison with Qiskit and Cirq

AWS Braket, alongside Qiskit (IBM) and Cirq (Google), is a leading quantum programming platform. Although all three are Python-based and support quantum circuit design and execution, they differ in philosophy, ecosystem, and integration capabilities. The following table presents a comparative overview:

Aspect	Qiskit (IBM)	Cirq (Google)	AWS Braket (Amazon)
Primary goal	Education and research ecosystem	Research-grade fine control over hardware	Multi-vendor quantum cloud platform supporting diverse backends
Programming language	Python	Python	Python with AWS SDK integration
Hardware access	IBM Quantum devices	Google Sycamore (via Quantum Engine)	IonQ, Rigetti, OQC, and built-in simulators
Cloud integration	IBM Quantum Experience	Google Cloud Platform	AWS Management Console and Amazon S3
Hybrid workflows	Limited, for example, **variational quantum eigensolver** (**VQE**) and QAOA.	Experimental support	Fully managed Hybrid Jobs API enabling seamless quantum–classical execution
Cost model	Free (for simulators and limited hardware access)	Free (local simulators)	Pay-per-use model with a Free Tier for simulators

***Table 10.1**: Qiskit, Cirq, and AWS Braket comparison*

Running circuits on IonQ, Rigetti, and OQC

Once fully configured, AWS Braket allows users to execute quantum circuits on a range of real quantum hardware through a unified Python API. This abstraction removes the burden of learning multiple vendor-specific SDKs, enabling a consistent workflow for designing, submitting, and analyzing quantum experiments. With the same circuit definition, users can target hardware from IonQ (ion-trap systems with high fidelity), Rigetti (superconducting qubits optimized for fast gates), and QQC (compact, low-noise superconducting architectures).

A key advantage of Braket is seamless device switching: by changing only the device **Amazon Resource Name** (**ARN**), users can move between simulators and real **quantum processing units** (**QPUs**) without altering circuit logic. This design supports code reusability, systematic benchmarking across hardware platforms, and rapid experimentation, allowing researchers and developers to concentrate on quantum algorithms and performance analysis rather than low-level hardware details.

Building and executing quantum circuits

In AWS Braket, quantum circuits are represented using the **`Circuit`** class from the Braket SDK. This class provides a clear, Pythonic interface for composing quantum operations in a logical sequence. Each gate is added through a method call, making circuit construction intuitive and easy to follow.

The following example demonstrates the construction of a two-qubit Bell circuit:

```
from braket.circuits import Circuit
# Create a Bell state circuit
bell_circuit = Circuit().h(0).cnot(0, 1)
print(bell_circuit)
```

The output is as follows:

```
T  | 0 | 1 |
-------------
0  H   •
1      X
```

The circuit applies a Hadamard gate to qubit 0 to create a superposition, then a CNOT gate to entangle it with qubit `1`, producing a Bell state—a fundamental two-qubit entangled state used in many quantum communication and computation protocols.

This clear, concise representation in Braket helps visualize quantum operations step-by-step, making it particularly useful for teaching, debugging, and exploring quantum logic structures.

Executing on a simulator for quick verification

It is best practice to validate it on a simulator before deploying a circuit to real quantum hardware. Simulators allow you to verify circuit logic, identify syntax or gate errors, and understand expected output distributions without incurring hardware costs.

AWS Braket offers two primary simulation backends:

- **SV1 (statevector simulator)**: A high-performance, general-purpose simulator ideal for most small to medium-scale circuits.
- **TN1 (tensor network simulator)**: Optimized for circuits with limited entanglement, enabling efficient simulation of larger qubit systems.

The following example demonstrates the running of a bell circuit on the **`sv1`** simulator:

```
from braket.aws import AwsDevice
# Choose Amazon's managed simulator
simulator = AwsDevice("arn:aws:braket:::device/quantum-simulator/amazon/sv1")
# Execute the Bell state circuit
task = simulator.run(bell_circuit, shots=1000)
result = task.result()
print(result.measurement_counts)
```

The expected output (approximate) is as follows:

```
{'00': 504, '11': 496}
```

The results show roughly equal probabilities for **`00`** and **`11`**, confirming the successful generation of Bell state entanglement. Small variations in counts are due to the probabilistic nature of quantum measurement.

Running on IonQ hardware

After validating circuits on simulators, executing workloads on physical quantum processors provides insight into real device behavior, including noise, calibration variability, and queue dynamics. AWS Braket enables seamless access to third-party quantum hardware, allowing users to evaluate how algorithms perform under realistic experimental conditions.

IonQ systems use trapped-ion qubits controlled by precisely timed laser pulses. These platforms are known for long coherence times and high fidelity gates, making them well-suited for experiments in entanglement, small-scale algorithms, and cross-hardware benchmarking. The following example demonstrates how to submit a previously defined circuit to an IonQ QPU through AWS Braket:

```
from braket.aws import AwsDevice
# Select an IonQ QPU
ionq_device = AwsDevice("arn:aws:braket:::device/qpu/ionq/ionQdevice")
# Submit the Bell state circuit to IonQ hardware
task = ionq_device.run(bell_circuit, shots=100)
print("Task ID: ", task.id)
# Retrieve results when the task has completed
result = task.result()
print("IonQ Results:", result.measurement_counts)
```

The typical outcome (illustrative) is as follows:

```
{'00': 51, '11': 49}
```

You should expect near-equal counts for `00` and `11`, consistent with a Bell state measured in the computational basis. Minor deviations arise from finite sampling and real device noise (e.g., state-preparation and measurement errors, dephasing).

Running on Rigetti hardware

In addition to trapped-ion platforms, AWS Braket provides access to superconducting quantum processors that follow a different qubit implementation model. Exploring multiple hardware technologies helps users understand how device architecture influences circuit compilation, routing requirements, and overall algorithm performance.

Rigetti's Aspen-M series uses superconducting qubits arranged in lattice-style topologies because the device's connectivity map constrains two-qubit interactions; good results often require mindful qubit selection, shallow circuits, and the use of native gates.

The following example shows how the same Bell state circuit can be executed on a Rigetti superconducting quantum processor using AWS Braket:

```
from braket.aws import AwsDevice
# Select the Rigetti Aspen-M-3 QPU
rigetti_device = AwsDevice("arn:aws:braket:::device/qpu/rigetti/Aspen-M-3")
# Execute the same Bell circuit on hardware
task = rigetti_device.run(bell_circuit, shots=100)
print("Task ID: ", task.id)
# Wait for completion and fetch results
task.wait_for_completion()
result = task.result()
print("Rigetti Results:", result.measurement_counts)
```

The example output (illustrative) is as follows:

```
{'00': 47, '11': 45, '01': 5, '10': 3}
```

Most measurements appear in the correlated `00` and `11` outcomes expected for a Bell state, while small `01` and `10` counts result from readout and two-qubit gate errors typical of real quantum hardware.

Running on OQC hardware

QQC operates superconducting processors built on a proprietary coaxmon architecture, emphasizing compact layouts and low-noise control. While current OQC systems typically expose fewer qubits than some superconducting platforms, they offer stable, predictable performance, well-suited to education, benchmarking, and small-scale research workflows.

The following example demonstrates how to run the Bell state circuit on QQC device through AWS Braket:

```
from braket.aws import AwsDevice
# Select the OQC "Lucy" QPU
oqc_device = AwsDevice("arn:aws:braket:::device/qpu/oqc/Lucy")
# Execute the Bell state circuit on OQC hardware
task = oqc_device.run(bell_circuit, shots=100)
result = task.result()
print("OQC Results:", result.measurement_counts)
```

The sample output (illustrative) is as follows:

```
{'00': 52, '11': 48}
```

The results remain concentrated on `00` and `11`, consistent with a Bell state, while minor deviations from a 50–50 split arise from finite sampling and device-level noise such as readout and two-qubit gate errors.

Monitoring and managing quantum tasks

Efficient workload management is an essential aspect of cloud-based quantum computing, particularly when working with shared simulators and queued hardware resources. AWS Braket provides built-in mechanisms to observe task progress, handle asynchronous execution, and organize results for downstream analysis and automation.

Every job you submit through AWS Braket is tracked as an AWS quantum task with a unique **Task ID**. You can use this identifier to check status, wait for completion, and fetch results programmatically.

The following example illustrates how to programmatically query the execution status of a submitted quantum task using the AWS Braket SDK:

```
from braket.aws import AwsQuantumTask
# Query the current state of a previously submitted task
task_status = AwsQuantumTask(task.id).state()
print("Current status:", task_status)
```

Typical task states include **QUEUED**, **RUNNING**, **COMPLETED**, and **FAILED**. When a task finishes successfully, results—such as measurement counts and metadata—are automatically written to your configured Amazon S3 bucket, along with logs that support auditing and reproducibility.

Cross-device comparison

When selecting a backend for quantum experiments, it is important to recognize that no single hardware platform is universally optimal. Practical performance depends on factors such as circuit depth, qubit connectivity requirements, noise tolerance, and execution latency. A comparative view helps practitioners make informed decisions aligned with their specific algorithmic needs.

Each quantum hardware platform available through AWS Braket offers unique advantages based on its underlying physical implementation. The following table summarizes their key characteristics:

Feature	IonQ (trapped-ion)	Rigetti (Superconducting)	OQC (coaxmon)
Connectivity	All-to-all	Limited lattice topology	Moderate (topology optimized)
Coherence time	High (ms)	Medium (μs)	Medium-high (μs–ms)
Gate speed	Slower (ms)	Faster (ns)	Moderate
Error rates	Low	Moderate	Low
Ideal use case	Educational experiments, benchmarking	Variational algorithms, optimization	Stable demonstrations and testing

Table 10.3: *Comparison of IonQ, Rigetti, and OQC hardware features*

Hybrid classical and quantum workflows

As quantum hardware continues to evolve, current devices remain limited by noise, decoherence, and qubit count. This reality has given rise to the **noisy intermediate-scale quantum** (**NISQ**) era, where quantum processors are powerful but imperfect. To extract meaningful results under these constraints, researchers use hybrid quantum–classical workflows- a paradigm that combines the exploratory power of quantum computation with the stability and optimization strength of classical systems.

Amazon Braket provides a fully managed framework for building and running such workflows through its Hybrid Jobs feature. These jobs coordinate the interaction between classical optimizers executed on **central processing units** (**CPUs**) or **graphics processing units** (**GPUs**) and quantum circuits executed on QPUs. Together, they iteratively refine solutions to problems in optimization, chemistry, and machine learning.

Understanding hybrid workflows

A hybrid quantum–classical workflow is an iterative model in which quantum and classical systems interact. Quantum hardware explores complex solution spaces, while classical optimization guides the search. The workflow follows four key stages:

- **Initialize parameters**: A classical optimizer generates initial circuit parameters that control quantum gates or rotations.
- **Quantum evaluation**: The quantum processor executes the parameterized circuit and measures observables to produce an outcome value.
- **Classical update**: The classical algorithm updates parameters based on the measured result to improve the objective function.
- **Iteration**: The quantum evaluation stage and the classical update stage are repeated iteratively until convergence is achieved, meaning further parameter adjustments result in minimal improvement.

This loop combines quantum exploration of entangled state spaces with classical precision and optimization, enabling practical hybrid quantum computing.

AWS Braket Hybrid Jobs service

The AWS Braket Hybrid Jobs service offers a fully managed environment for building and running hybrid quantum–classical workflows. It allows users to execute an end-to-end Python program within a managed AWS container, while automatically handling orchestration, scheduling, resource provisioning, and secure communication between classical and quantum components.

Key features of the AWS Braket Hybrid Jobs service include:

- **Automatic orchestration**: Seamlessly manages coordination and data flow between classical optimization and quantum execution steps.
- **Pre-configured environments**: Provides ready-to-use containers with the Braket SDK and common scientific libraries, reducing setup effort.
- **Resource flexibility**: Supports both CPU and GPU instances, enabling cost–performance optimization based on workload needs.
- **Real-time monitoring**: Integrates with Amazon CloudWatch to track logs, metrics, and debug job execution.
- **Direct S3 access**: Automatically stores results, logs, and metadata in Amazon S3 for easy access and post-processing.

Workflow architecture

Hybrid quantum applications typically involve multiple coordinated stages spanning code preparation, resource allocation, execution, and result analysis. AWS Braket abstracts much of this operational complexity through a managed workflow model, enabling developers to focus on algorithm design rather than low-level infrastructure management. Understanding this high-level orchestration is essential before examining the individual components of a Hybrid Job.

A typical AWS Braket Hybrid Job consists of four core components that together define and manage the hybrid quantum–classical workflow:

- **Script definition (script.py)**: The main Python script that defines quantum circuits, the classical optimizer, and the feedback loop linking quantum results to parameter updates.
- **Device selection**: Specifies the target device ARN, which may be a simulator or hardware from IonQ, Rigetti, or QQC, influencing execution time, cost, and result fidelity.
- **Container setup**: Uses pre-configured AWS containers with the Braket SDK and scientific libraries, allowing selection of CPU or GPU instances to balance performance and cost.
- **Job submission**: Launches the workflow via the Hybrid Jobs API, which provisions resources, executes classical and quantum tasks, and enables monitoring and result retrieval through the Braket console, CLI, or Amazon CloudWatch.

Figure 10.1 shows the end-to-end workflow of an AWS Braket Hybrid Job, from script definition to execution and monitoring:

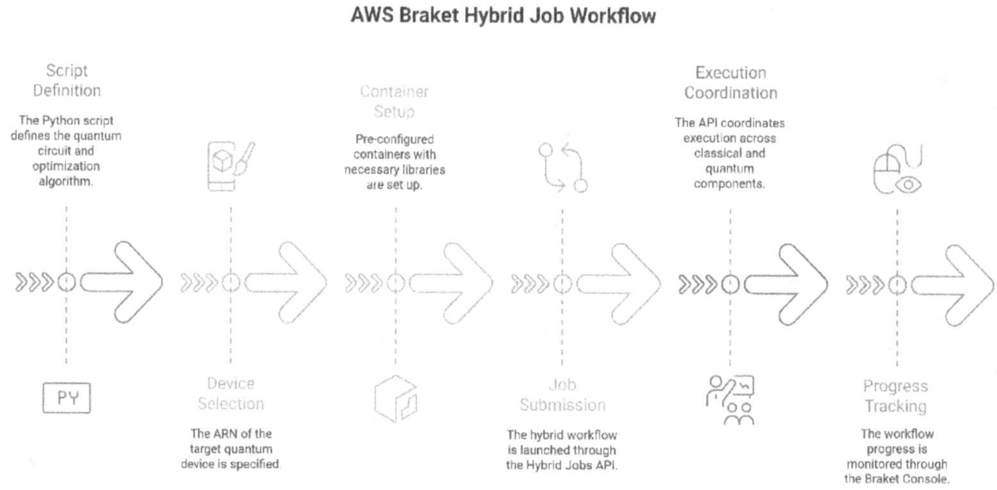

Figure 10.1: *AWS Braket Hybrid Job workflow from script to tracking*

Together, these components create a structured and automated workflow that bridges the classical and quantum domains—making it easier to prototype, test, and scale quantum-enhanced algorithms within AWS's managed ecosystem.

Example of a simple hybrid optimization loop

In practical quantum workflows, many near-term applications rely on parameterized circuits that are iteratively refined using classical feedback. AWS Braket Hybrid Jobs provide an integrated mechanism to coordinate this iterative process within a single managed execution environment. The following example illustrates how a minimal feedback-driven optimization can be structured using the Braket framework.

The following snippet demonstrates a minimal hybrid job: a classical optimizer tunes a single parameter (**theta**) in a one-qubit circuit to minimize a cost—here, the expectation of the Pauli-Z operator. The quantum step evaluates the circuit; the classical step updates (**theta**) using a finite-difference gradient:

```
# script.py
from braket.jobs import save_job_result
from braket.circuits import Circuit, Observable
from braket.aws import AwsDevice
import numpy as np
# Target device: Amazon SV1 simulator
device = AwsDevice("arn:aws:braket:::device/quantum-simulator/amazon/sv1")
def cost(theta):
    # One-qubit parametric circuit: RY(θ) on qubit 0
    circ = Circuit().ry(theta, 0)
    result = device.run(circ, shots=500).result()
    counts = result.measurement_counts
    # Estimate ⟨Z⟩ from counts: ⟨Z⟩ = P(0) - P(1) = 2*P(0) - 1
    p0 = counts.get("0", 0) / 500
    z_expectation = 2 * p0 - 1
    # Minimize cost; here we take cost = -⟨Z⟩
    return -z_expectation
# Random initialization
theta = np.random.random() * 2 * np.pi
# Simple gradient descent with finite differences
for _ in range(20):
    eps = 0.01
    grad = (cost(theta + eps) - cost(theta - eps)) / (2 * eps)
    theta -= 0.1 * grad  # Learning rate
# Persist final result for the job record
save_job_result({"Optimal θ": float(theta)})
```

Submit this job from a notebook using Hybrid Jobs:

```
from braket.jobs import AwsQuantumJob
job = AwsQuantumJob.create(
    source_module= "script.py",
    entry point= "script.py",
    device="arn:aws:braket:::device/quantum-simulator/amazon/sv1",
    job_name="simple-hybrid-demo",
    instance_type=" ml.m5.large"
)
print("Job ID:", job.arn)
```

Hybrid Jobs with parameterization

Parameterized quantum circuits form the foundation of many variational and hybrid quantum algorithms used in near-term devices. Efficient handling of tunable parameters enables repeated circuit evaluations without reconstructing the entire program, thereby improving optimization efficiency and experimental flexibility. AWS Braket supports this paradigm through built-in symbolic parameter features.

Hybrid workflows shine when your circuits use symbolic parameters—you vary a few numbers while keeping the circuit structure fixed. The Braket SDK provides this via **FreeParameter**, allowing you to define parameterized circuits that are compact, readable, and easy to optimize across many iterations.

The following example demonstrates how to construct and execute a parameterized quantum circuit using the **`FreeParameter`** feature in the AWS Braket SDK:

```
from braket.circuits import Circuit, FreeParameter
theta = FreeParameter("theta")
param_circuit = Circuit().ry(theta, 0)
print(param_circuit)
```

During optimization, you bind a numeric value to the placeholder without rebuilding the circuit:

```
from braket.aws import AwsDevice
device = AwsDevice("arn:aws:braket:::device/quantum-simulator/amazon/sv1")
# Bind a value (e.g., theta = 1.2) at run time
task = device.run(param_circuit, shots=500, inputs={"theta": 1.2})
result = task.result()
print(result.measurement_counts)
```

This approach keeps compilation overhead low and makes it straightforward to loop over many parameter values inside a Hybrid Job.

Integration with classical optimizers

Most practical hybrid quantum algorithms depend on tight coordination between quantum circuit evaluations and classical optimization routines. Efficient interoperability with established scientific computing frameworks is therefore essential for implementing scalable hybrid solutions. AWS Braket provides interfaces that facilitate this cross-stack integration within a unified workflow environment.

AWS Braket Hybrid Jobs works seamlessly with popular Python ecosystems, including SciPy, PyTorch, and TensorFlow (including TensorFlow Quantum). This lets you embed off-the-shelf optimizers such as **Constrained Optimization by Linear Approximation** (**COBYLA**), Adam, and **Simultaneous Perturbation Stochastic Approximation** (**SPSA**) directly into your hybrid job script, enabling classical machine learning tools to drive updates to your quantum parameters.

The following example illustrates how a classical optimization routine can be integrated with a quantum cost function within an AWS Braket hybrid workflow:

```
from scipy.optimize import minimize
def objective(params):
    # Wrap your quantum cost function; params is a 1-D array
    return cost(params[0])
result = minimize(objective, x0=[0.5], method="COBYLA")
print("Optimal parameter:", result.x)
```

In this pattern, the quantum step evaluates your parameterized circuit and returns a scalar loss, while the classical optimizer proposes the next parameter values because everything runs inside the managed Hybrid Jobs container, you can scale from quick experiments to longer runs without changing your code structure.

Practical considerations

As hybrid quantum applications transition from conceptual demonstrations to practical experimentation, careful operational planning becomes increasingly important. Beyond algorithm correctness, factors such as execution stability, resource efficiency, and reproducibility play a critical role in obtaining meaningful results on cloud-based quantum platforms.

Designing efficient hybrid quantum–classical workflows require balancing algorithmic design, hardware limitations, and cost efficiency. The best practices listed in the following table help ensure reliable results and efficient execution in the AWS Braket Hybrid Jobs environment:

Aspect	Best practice
Circuit depth	Keep circuits shallow (fewer than 100 gates) to minimize the effects of noise and decoherence. Deep circuits tend to accumulate gate errors, especially on NISQ hardware.
Optimizer choice	Choose robust optimizers such as SPSA, which perform well under noisy evaluations and limited measurement precision.
Resource selection	For lightweight optimization loops, select CPU instances (e.g., **`ml.m5.large`**). For machine learning or gradient-heavy workloads, opt for GPU instances (e.g., **`ml.p3.2xlarge`**) to accelerate classical computation.
Cost control	Always test on simulators first—like SV1 or TN1—before running on real QPUs. This helps verify logic and prevent unnecessary costs from failed hardware runs.
Logging and debugging	Enable Amazon CloudWatch logging for all hybrid jobs to trace execution steps, inspect intermediate values, and diagnose errors efficiently.

***Table 10.4**: Best practices for AWS Braket Hybrid Jobs*

By following these practices, developers can maximize the effectiveness of hybrid workflows, achieving a balance among quantum innovation, classical stability, and operational efficiency in real-world quantum applications.

Submitting jobs on AWS cloud infrastructure

Once a quantum circuit or hybrid workflow is designed, the next step is to submit it for execution on AWS Braket. Braket lets you run tasks either directly in your local Python environment or via the AWS Management Console. The platform manages every aspect of job execution—from queuing and routing tasks to QPUs or simulators, to collecting and storing results in your Amazon S3 bucket.

This section explains the end-to-end process for creating, submitting, and monitoring quantum jobs on AWS, including resource management and cost control strategies to ensure efficient, reproducible experimentation.

Before initiating job submission, users should ensure that the necessary permissions, storage configuration, and regional settings are correctly aligned with the selected execution backend. Proper pre-submission checks help prevent avoidable runtime failures and support smoother orchestration of quantum workloads within the AWS environment.

Quantum task model in AWS Braket

In AWS Braket, every quantum circuit execution—whether on a simulator or real hardware—is managed as a distinct quantum task. A quantum task encapsulates all the details of a single circuit run, including the target device, the number of measurement shots, and the location where results are stored. This unified model provides a consistent, streamlined experience across all backend types.

The typical quantum task workflow consists of four simple steps:

1. **Circuit definition**: Create a quantum program in Python by defining a circuit with gates, measurements, and optional parameters.
2. **Device selection**: Specify the target backend using its ARN, choosing either a simulator or a QPU from IonQ, Rigetti, or QQC.
3. **Task submission**: Submit the circuit via the **`run()`** method; after that, Braket handles queuing, scheduling, and secure execution.
4. **Result retrieval**: Access results via the task interface or console, with outputs automatically stored in Amazon S3 for analysis.

This model ensures that simulator and hardware executions use the same code structure, enabling a smooth progression from local prototyping to simulator validation and, finally, to real quantum hardware without requiring workflow changes. By encapsulating each execution as a quantum task, AWS Braket provides a modular, reproducible framework for managing quantum experiments, from simple test circuits to complex hybrid algorithms.

Submitting a simple quantum task

Executing a quantum circuit on AWS Braket is straightforward thanks to its unified quantum task model. Each submission, whether to a simulator or a QPU follows the same logical steps: define a circuit, choose a device, run the task, and collect results.

The following is an example showing the running of a Bell state circuit on the Amazon SV1 simulator:

```
from braket.circuits import Circuit
from braket.aws import AwsDevice
# Choose the simulator backend
device = AwsDevice("arn:aws:braket:::device/quantum-simulator/amazon/sv1")
# Define a simple Bell state circuit
bell = Circuit().h(0).cnot(0, 1)
# Submit the circuit as a quantum task
task = device.run(bell, shots=1000)
print("Task ID: ", task.id)
```

Once submitted, the task is queued for execution on the selected device. You can check its progress with:

```
print("Task Status:", task.state())
```

Common task states

Quantum tasks on AWS Braket progress through several predefined states, reflecting their position in the execution lifecycle. The following table summarizes these task states and their meanings:

Status	Meaning
CREATED	Task has been registered and is waiting to enter the device queue.
QUEUED	Task is in line awaiting execution.
RUNNING	Task is actively executing on the simulator or QPU.
COMPLETED	Task finished successfully; results are ready to retrieve.
FAILED	Task encountered an error, such as a timeout or permission issue.

***Table 10.5**: Common task states in AWS Braket and their corresponding descriptions*

When the task reaches the COMPLETED state, you can retrieve and view the results:

```
result = task.result()
print("Counts:", result.measurement_counts)
```

The typical output is as follows:

```
{'00': 507, '11': 493}
```

This outcome demonstrates the expected 50–50 probability distribution between $|00\rangle$ and $|11\rangle$, confirming the Bell state's entanglement.

Submitting hybrid jobs

For more complex quantum–classical workflows, AWS Braket provides the **`AwsQuantumJob`** interface. Unlike standard quantum tasks that execute a single circuit, hybrid jobs run longer scripts containing iterative loops, optimizer calls, and dynamic parameter updates. These jobs seamlessly combine classical computation with quantum execution under a fully managed framework.

The following example demonstrates the submission of a hybrid job:

```
from braket.jobs import AwsQuantumJob
job = AwsQuantumJob.create(
    source_module= "qaoa_demo",          # Folder or script containing your job
    entry_point="qaoa_demo:main",        # Entry function to be executed
    device="arn:aws:braket:::device/quantum-simulator/amazon/sv1",
    instance_type="ml.m5.large",         # Classical compute resource
    job_name="hybrid_qaoa_test",
    hyperparameters={"iterations": "50"}  # Optional job-specific parameters
)
print("Hybrid Job ARN:", job.arn)
```

Once submitted, the job appears under **Braket | Jobs** in the **AWS Management Console**, where you can:

- Monitor live execution logs.
- View CPU/GPU utilization.
- Track intermediate metrics and optimization progress.
- Retrieve outputs automatically stored in Amazon S3.

Monitoring jobs with CloudWatch

AWS Braket seamlessly integrates with Amazon CloudWatch, providing a powerful and centralized way to monitor your quantum tasks and hybrid jobs. CloudWatch offers real-time visibility into execution performance, system metrics, and error diagnostics—all accessible directly from the AWS Management Console.

You can track several key aspects of job execution:

- **Job duration**: Measure the total runtime of a job, including both quantum and classical phases. This helps identify bottlenecks or optimize long-running hybrid workflows.
- **Device queue time**: Observe how long each job spends waiting in the device queue before execution—useful for comparing availability and turnaround times across different QPUs and simulators.
- **Error logs**: Access detailed error reports, including stack traces, SDK configuration issues, or permission errors, to quickly diagnose and resolve failed executions.
- To view metrics visually, open CloudWatch from the AWS Management Console under: **Braket | Monitoring | CloudWatch Dashboard**.

Alternatively, you can retrieve logs programmatically using the AWS CLI:

```
aws logs get-log-events --log-group-name "/aws/braket/jobs" --log-stream-name "<job-id>"
```

This command returns execution logs for the specified job, helping you inspect step-by-step progress and identify potential runtime issues.

Retrieving and storing results in Amazon S3

All quantum tasks and hybrid jobs executed on AWS Braket automatically store their outputs in Amazon S3, ensuring persistent, organized, and easily accessible results. Each execution generates a structured collection of files, including measurement data, metadata, logs, and diagnostic information, stored within a dedicated S3 bucket.

By default, the output is written to a bucket following the naming convention:

```
amazon-braket-<account-id>-<region>
```

However, you can specify a custom S3 bucket and folder path at the time of task submission:

```
# Define a custom S3 destination
s3_folder = ("amazon-braket-123456789012", "MyResults/BellState")
# Submit a quantum task with explicit S3 destination
task = device.run(bell, shots=1000, s3_destination_folder=s3_folder)
```

After the job or task completes, you can retrieve results directly from S3 or use the Braket SDK's session interface to access them programmatically:

```
from braket.aws import AwsSession
session = AwsSession()
result = session.retrieve_job(job_arn=job.arn)
print(result)
```

The retrieved data typically includes:

- Measurement counts (**measurement_counts.json**).
- Execution metadata (device ARN, shot count, queue time, completion time).
- Logs and error reports for debugging or audit trails.

Cost estimation and resource management

Effective experimentation on cloud-based quantum platforms requires proactive cost planning alongside technical workflow design. Because hybrid jobs may involve multiple metered services operating concurrently, users should adopt budgeting and monitoring practices early in the development cycle to maintain predictable expenditure.

Running quantum experiments through AWS Braket involves costs that depend on the type of resource you use. AWS charges separately for simulators, quantum hardware tasks, and hybrid compute instances, allowing flexibility but also requiring careful budget monitoring.

Cost components

AWS Braket's pricing model includes separate cost components for simulation, hardware execution, and hybrid compute resources. The following points outline each component and its billing criteria.

- **Simulator usage**: Pricing depends on computation time and memory usage. Simulators are cost-effective for developing and testing circuits before deploying to hardware.
- **Quantum hardware tasks**: Hardware tasks are billed per shot, with rates varying across providers such as IonQ, Rigetti, and OQC.
- **Hybrid compute instances**: Hybrid jobs incur hourly charges based on the selected instance type (CPU or GPU) that runs your classical optimization and control logic.

Approximate 2025 pricing estimates

The following table provides approximate 2025 pricing for key AWS Braket resources, including simulators, quantum hardware, and hybrid compute instances:

Resource	Example	Pricing (per task/hour)
Amazon SV1 simulator	Statevector simulator	≈ $0.30 per minute of compute time
IonQ hardware	Trapped-ion device	≈ $0.01 per shot
Rigetti hardware	Superconducting processor	≈ $0.005 per shot
Hybrid instance (ml.m5.large)	CPU-based classical node	≈ $0.12 per hour

***Table 10.6**: Estimated 2025 pricing for major AWS Braket computational resources*

Best practices for cost management

Effective cost management in AWS Braket ensures efficient resource use and prevents unnecessary spending. The following best practices help control expenses while maintaining workflow quality.

- **Prototype on simulators first**: Validate and debug your circuits on SV1 or TN1 simulators before submitting them to real hardware. This minimizes failed or redundant hardware runs.

- **Scale up gradually**: Begin with a small number of shots or iterations to test stability. Increase task size only after confirming correctness and performance.
- **Optimize instance selection**: Match instance type to workload intensity—CPU instances for lightweight optimization loops and GPU instances for machine learning–driven hybrid algorithms.
- **Use AWS Billing tools**: Regularly monitor usage via **AWS Billing** | **Cost Explorer** or set spending alerts in the AWS console to track expenditures in real-time.

Best practices for efficient job execution

As quantum workloads scale in complexity and frequency, systematic execution strategies become essential for maintaining consistent performance across experiments. Establishing disciplined operational habits early helps researchers reduce variability, improve turnaround predictability, and make more effective use of shared quantum resources.

To achieve maximum performance, minimize latency, and ensure reproducibility when using AWS Braket, follow the best practices listed in the following table for efficient execution of both quantum tasks and hybrid jobs:

Category	Recommendation
Pre-run testing	Always validate circuits on simulators (e.g., SV1 or TN1) before submitting to real quantum hardware. This helps identify syntax errors, invalid gate operations, and logical bugs without incurring hardware costs.
Parallel execution	Run multiple smaller tasks in parallel instead of a single large job. This strategy reduces queue times, improves throughput, and allows partial results even if one task fails.
Region selection	Choose the AWS Region closest to your location or to the QPU's hosting region (such as `us-east-1` or `eu-west-2`) to reduce latency and improve execution efficiency.
Logging	Enable Amazon CloudWatch logging and review S3 outputs for every task. This ensures traceability, reproducibility, and easier debugging during iterative experiments.
Automation	Use Python automation scripts, AWS CLI, or AWS Step Functions to schedule recurring hybrid jobs, parameter sweeps, or nightly experiments automatically.

***Table 10.7**: Efficient execution of hybrid jobs*

By adhering to these recommendations, you can achieve faster turnaround, better cost control, and higher reproducibility, critical elements for scaling quantum research and hybrid algorithm development efficiently within AWS Braket's cloud environment.

Case study on optimization with QAOA

Optimization underlies many real-world challenges, from logistics and circuit design to chemical modeling, and is often formulated as combinatorial optimization problems with exponentially large search spaces. As problem size grows, classical algorithms face rapidly increasing computational costs, limiting their effectiveness.

QAOA offers a hybrid quantum–classical approach that alternates between quantum state evolution and classical parameter optimization. In this case study, QAOA is implemented on AWS Braket using Hybrid Jobs, enabling a unified and automated workflow that integrates quantum execution with classical optimization.

This case study demonstrates how variational optimization algorithms can be deployed in a cloud-native quantum environment to address representative combinatorial problems. The focus is on illustrating the end-to-end workflow—from problem encoding and parameter initialization to iterative optimization and result interpretation—using the managed capabilities of AWS Braket Hybrid Jobs.

Understanding QAOA

The QAOA is one of the most prominent hybrid algorithms designed for combinatorial optimization problems. It bridges quantum mechanics and classical optimization by representing a problem as a Hamiltonian, a mathematical construct that encodes the cost or energy of each possible solution configuration.

QAOA works by alternating between two types of quantum operations—each controlled by adjustable parameters:

- **γ**: Governs evolution under the cost Hamiltonian (H_C).
- **β**: Governs evolution under the mixing Hamiltonian (H_M).

These parameters are tuned iteratively to steer the quantum system toward configurations that minimize the cost function.

The general workflow of QAOA is as follows:

- **Define the problem Hamiltonian (H_C)**: Express the optimization problem as a cost Hamiltonian, where lower energy states correspond to better solutions.
- **Initialize the quantum state**: Start all qubits in an equal superposition using Hadamard gates, ensuring the algorithm explores all configurations simultaneously.
- **Apply parameterized unitaries**: Alternate between two parameterized unitary operators: one based on H_C (weighted by γ) and another based on H_M (weighted by β). This creates interference patterns that bias the system toward low-cost configurations.
- **Measurement and evaluation**: Measure the resulting quantum state to obtain bitstrings. Use these results to calculate the average cost (expectation value) of the observed solutions.
- **Classical parameter update**: Feed the measured cost into a classical optimizer, which updates the parameters (γ,β) to minimize the objective function.
- **Iteration and convergence**: Repeat the quantum–classical loop until the system converges to a configuration with minimum (or near-minimum) energy.

Formulating the Max-Cut optimization problem

To illustrate QAOA in practice, we use the Max-Cut problem—a classic benchmark for combinatorial optimization. Given an undirected graph, the goal is to partition the vertices into two sets so that the number of edges crossing the partition (i.e., with endpoints in different sets) is maximized.

Consider the four-node square graph:

```
(0)—(1)
 |   |
(3)—(2)
```

Here, the edge set is $E=\{(0,1),(1,2),(2,3),(3,0)\}$. We encode Max-Cut as a cost Hamiltonian whose low-energy states correspond to larger cuts. Using Pauli-Z operators Z_i acting on a qubit i, the standard Max-Cut Hamiltonian is:

$$H_C = \frac{1}{2}\sum_{(i,j)\in E} (1 - Z_i Z_j)$$

Intuition

For any edge (i,j), the term $\frac{1}{2}(1 - Z_i Z_j)$ evaluates to:

- *1* if qubits i and j are in opposite computational states (|0⟩ vs. |1⟩), meaning the edge is cut.
- 0 if they are in the same state, meaning the edge is not cut.

Thus, minimizing the energy (or equivalently maximizing the expected value when used as an objective) aligns with maximizing the number of cut edges. This direct correspondence makes Max-Cut an ideal testbed for QAOA's alternating applications of the cost and mixer unitaries.

QAOA implementation in AWS Braket

This section walks through a single-layer ($p = 1$) QAOA for Max-Cut using the Braket SDK, and shows how to run it as a Hybrid Job on the cloud simulator. We keep the code compact and emphasize the roles of the quantum circuit, the classical optimizer, and Braket's managed runtime.

The implementation begins by importing the required libraries and selecting the target execution device within AWS Braket:

1. **Prepare the environment**:

```
from braket.circuits import Circuit, Observable, FreeParameter
from braket.aws import AwsDevice
from braket.jobs import save_job_result
import numpy as np
# Target device: Amazon SV1 state-vector simulator
device = AwsDevice("arn:aws:braket:::device/quantum-simulator/amazon/sv1")
```

2. **Define the QAOA circuit**:

   We parameterize the cost and mixer layers with angles γ and β, and build a four-qubit Max-Cut instance on a square graph with edge **(0,1), (1,2), (2,3), (3, 0)**:

```
from braket.circuits import Circuit, FreeParameter
gamma = FreeParameter("gamma")
beta = FreeParameter("beta")
# Square graph edges
edges = [(0,1), (1,2), (2,3), (3,0)]
# QAOA layer for p = 1
qaoa = Circuit()
# 1) Equal superposition
for q in range(4):
    qaoa.h(q)
# 2) Problem unitary U_C(γ)
for i, j in edges:
    qaoa.cnot(i, j)
    qaoa.rz(2 * gamma, j)
    qaoa.cnot(i, j)
# 3) Mixer unitary U_M(β)
for q in range(4):
    qaoa.rx(2 * beta, q)
```

3. **Define the cost function**:

   We estimate the expected energy (H_C) from shot-based measurements. For each bitstring, we compute its Max-Cut value and take a frequency-weighted average. Next, we define a shot-based objective function that evaluates the parameterized circuit and returns the estimated Max-Cut energy.

```
def expected_cost(params):
    gamma_val, beta_val = params
    bound = qaoa.make_bound_circuit({"gamma": gamma_val, "beta": beta_val})
    result = device.run(bound, shots=1000).result()
    counts = result.measurement_counts
    energy = 0.0
```

```
    total = sum(counts.values())
    for bitstring, freq in counts.items():
        # Map '0' -> +1, '1' -> -1 for Z eigenvalues
        z = np.array([1 if b == '0' else -1 for b in bitstring])
        cost = sum((1 - z[i]*z[j]) / 2 for (i, j) in edges)
        energy += cost * (freq / total)
    return energy
```

4. **Classical optimization loop**:

   A classical optimizer searches for (γ,β) that minimizes the expected cost:

```
from scipy.optimize import minimize
import numpy as np
# Random initialization in [0, π)
init_params = np.random.uniform(0, np.pi, 2)
# Derivative-free optimizer suited to noisy objectives
result = minimize(expected_cost, init_params, method="COBYLA")
print("Optimal Parameters:", result.x)
print("Minimum Energy: ", result.fun)
```

   The sample output is as follows:

```
Optimal Parameters: [1.48, 0.73]
Minimum Energy: 1.02
```

5. **Submitting as a hybrid job**:

   Wrap the previous logic in a module (e.g., **`qaoa_script.py`** with a **`main()`** function) and submit it as a Hybrid Job so AWS Braket provisions the container, executes the optimization loop, and persists outputs to S3. Finally, the workflow can be packaged and submitted as a managed Hybrid Job to enable scalable execution on the AWS cloud:

```
from braket.jobs import AwsQuantumJob
job = AwsQuantumJob.create(
    source_module="qaoa_script",
    entry_point="qaoa_script:main",
    device="arn:aws:braket:::device/quantum-simulator/amazon/sv1",
    instance_type="ml.m5.large",
    job_name="maxcut-qaoa-demo"
)
print("Job ARN:", job.arn)
```

6. **Visualizing results**:

   After completion, visualize the outcome distribution and confirm that the dominant bitstrings encode valid Max-Cut partitions:

```
import matplotlib.pyplot as plt
counts = {'0000': 2, '0101': 480, '1010': 490, '1111': 28}
plt.bar(counts.keys(), counts.values())
plt.title("QAOA Output Distribution (Max-Cut)")
plt.xlabel("Bitstrings")
plt.ylabel("Counts")
plt.show()
```

   Expected result: Two prominent bitstrings (e.g., **`0101`**, **`1010`**) correspond to the two optimal partitions of the square graph.

7. **Interpreting quantum utility (QU)**:

QAOA's value in the NISQ regime is its balance of quality and efficiency. While it may not consistently beat the best classical solvers today, as devices scale and improve, QAOA can deliver QU—a problem-specific, measurable benefit in which the quantum–classical loop finds strong approximations faster or more economically than classical methods alone.

Braket helps because AWS Braket's Hybrid Jobs bring this pattern into a production-ready workflow: managed containers, direct access to QPUs/simulators, real-time logging, and automatic S3 archival, so you can focus on algorithm design, benchmarking, and reproducibility.

Conclusion

AWS Braket unifies access to diverse quantum hardware and simulators within a single cloud environment, enabling practical, scalable quantum experimentation. This chapter guided readers through setting up the Braket SDK, configuring AWS credentials, and executing quantum circuits on simulators and on real devices from IonQ, Rigetti, and OQC. It also introduced hybrid quantum–classical workflows that integrate classical optimization with quantum computation for solving complex problems efficiently. The case study on the QAOA demonstrated Braket's ability to support end-to-end optimization within managed AWS infrastructure. By applying these concepts, readers can now design, execute, and monitor quantum experiments seamlessly—bridging theory, hardware, and cloud computing in a unified platform.

Building on this foundation, the next chapter turns to variational and hybrid quantum algorithms designed for the NISQ era. It explores VQE for molecular energy estimation, QAOA for combinatorial optimization, and the integration of PennyLane with PyTorch for hybrid quantum–classical learning. Through implementations in Qiskit, Cirq, and AWS Braket, readers will see how quantum circuits and classical optimizers work together to address real-world problems in chemistry, finance, and logistics.

Questions

1. **What is AWS Braket, and why is it important for quantum computing?**

   Answer: AWS Braket is Amazon's cloud-based quantum computing service that allows users to design, simulate, and run quantum circuits on both simulators and real quantum hardware. It is significant because it unifies access to multiple hardware providers—such as IonQ, Rigetti, and OQC—within a single, consistent framework, promoting cross-platform experimentation and scalable quantum development.

2. **How can users install and configure the AWS Braket SDK?**

   Answer: The AWS Braket SDK can be installed using the command pip install amazon-braket-sdk amazon-braket-schemas boto3 matplotlib. After installation, users configure AWS credentials using aws configure, providing the Access Key, Secret Key, and Region. This setup securely links the local environment with AWS to run Braket tasks.

3. **What are the main quantum hardware options available in AWS Braket?**

   Answer: Braket provides access to several hardware backends: IonQ (trapped-ion qubits with high fidelity), Rigetti (superconducting qubits for fast gate operations), and OQC (coaxmon superconducting devices offering stability and low-noise). Each hardware type serves different research and educational purposes.

4. **What are Hybrid Jobs in AWS Braket?**

   Answer: Hybrid Jobs are managed workflows that combine quantum computation and classical optimization within a single execution pipeline. They enable iterative feedback loops—where the quantum circuit evaluates parameter values and the classical processor refines them—to solve optimization and machine learning problems efficiently.

5. **How are results stored and retrieved in AWS Braket?**

   Answer: All quantum tasks and hybrid job results are automatically saved in Amazon S3 buckets. Users can retrieve these outputs using the Braket SDK or directly from the AWS Console, ensuring persistent storage and easy access for analysis and reproducibility.

6. **What is the Quantum Task model in AWS Braket?**

   Answer: A Quantum Task represents a single circuit execution on a simulator or QPU. Each task is identified by a unique Task ID, allowing users to monitor its progress, retrieve results, and manage job states such as QUEUED, RUNNING, or COMPLETED within the Braket environment.

7. **What is the role of Amazon CloudWatch in Braket workflows?**

   Answer: Amazon CloudWatch provides real-time monitoring, logging, and alerting for quantum and hybrid jobs. It helps track runtime performance, detect failures, and analyze execution metrics, making it essential for large-scale and automated quantum experiments.

8. **How does AWS Braket support cost management?**

   Answer: AWS Braket charges separately for simulator usage, hardware tasks (per shot), and hybrid compute instances (per hour). To manage costs, users are advised to test on simulators first, scale gradually, and monitor usage through the AWS Billing Dashboard and Cost Explorer.

9. **What is the significance of the QAOA case study in this chapter?**

   Answer: The QAOA case study illustrates how AWS Braket enables hybrid quantum–classical optimization. It demonstrates parameter tuning, circuit execution, and cost minimization within a managed workflow, showcasing Braket's practical utility for NISQ-era problem solving.

10. **What core skills do readers gain from this chapter?**

    Answer: By completing this chapter, readers learn to setup and configure AWS Braket, build and execute quantum circuits, run hybrid workflows, analyze results via S3 and CloudWatch, and optimize algorithms like QAOA—developing a comprehensive foundation for quantum computing in the AWS ecosystem.

Exercises

1. Install the AWS Braket SDK locally, configure credentials, list available devices, and briefly explain each backend (IonQ, Rigetti, OQC, SV1).
2. Run AWS Braket in Google Colab, create a Bell state circuit, execute it on the SV1 simulator, plot the histogram, and confirm entanglement.
3. Execute the Bell circuit on real hardware (IonQ or Rigetti) and compare execution time and fidelity with simulator results.
4. Implement QAOA for a simple MaxCut problem, simulate it, plot energy convergence, and explain hybrid optimization.
5. Enable noise simulation, compare ideal vs noisy histograms, and discuss decoherence effects.
6. Build a parameterized circuit using FreeParameter, sweep SV1 values, and analyze changes in probability.
7. Create and simulate a three-qubit GHZ state on SV1 and explain multi-qubit entanglement.
8. Run a small Hybrid Job, record metrics, and explain classical–quantum orchestration.
9. Serialize and reload a circuit using IR methods and reflect on reproducibility and collaboration.
10. Write a brief reflection on how AWS Braket supports real-world quantum experimentation through multi-provider access and hybrid workflows.

CHAPTER 11
Variational and Hybrid Algorithms with Python

Introduction

Quantum computing has entered a new era where theory meets practice, enabling researchers and learners to explore real algorithms on accessible quantum devices. Within this evolving landscape, variational and hybrid quantum algorithms have become the most practical and impactful approaches for the **noisy intermediate-scale quantum** (NISQ) era. These algorithms seamlessly integrate quantum and classical computing, using quantum circuits to prepare parameterized states and classical optimizers to iteratively refine those parameters toward the lowest energy or optimal solution.

This chapter focuses on two foundational algorithms that embody this hybrid paradigm. The **variational quantum eigensolver** (**VQE**) is widely used in quantum chemistry to estimate molecular ground-state energies with remarkable efficiency. At the same time, the **Quantum Approximate Optimization Algorithm** (QAOA) is designed to tackle complex combinatorial optimization problems such as Max-Cut, scheduling, and routing. Both algorithms share a common iterative workflow: state preparation, measurement, and optimization making them suitable for current hardware capabilities.

Beyond these, the chapter introduces PennyLane with PyTorch, a powerful framework that bridges quantum computing with machine learning. Representing quantum circuits as differentiable layers enables gradient-based training similar to that in deep neural networks, thus enabling the development of hybrid quantum–classical learning models.

Through hands-on examples using Qiskit, Cirq, and AWS Braket, readers will learn to construct, train, and evaluate hybrid algorithms. By the end of the chapter, you will understand how these techniques bring quantum computing closer to real-world applications in chemistry, finance, and logistics, demonstrating the emerging potential of quantum advantage in practical domains.

Structure

The chapter covers the following topics:

- Variational quantum eigensolver
- Quantum Approximate Optimization Algorithm
- Using PennyLane with PyTorch for hybrid workflows
- Applications in chemistry, finance, and logistics
- Implementations with Qiskit, Cirq, and AWS Braket

Objectives

This chapter aims to equip readers with a clear understanding of variational and hybrid quantum algorithms that combine quantum state preparation with classical optimization. It focuses on two key methods: the VQE for estimating molecular energies and the QAOA for combinatorial optimization. Readers will learn how these algorithms operate through iterative quantum–classical feedback loops suited to NISQ devices. The chapter also introduces PennyLane with PyTorch, demonstrating how quantum circuits can serve as differentiable layers in deep learning models for hybrid training. Through practical examples using Qiskit, Cirq, and AWS Braket, learners will design, simulate, and optimize variational circuits on both simulators and real hardware. By the end of this chapter, readers will be able to implement VQE and QAOA workflows and apply hybrid approaches to real-world domains such as chemistry, finance, and logistics.

Variational quantum eigensolver

The VQE is one of the most significant hybrid algorithms designed for the NISQ era. Its primary goal is to estimate the ground-state energy of a quantum system, a fundamental problem in quantum chemistry, materials science, and molecular physics.

Traditional algorithms like **quantum phase estimation** (**QPE**) demand deep circuits and long coherence times, which are challenging to achieve with current hardware limitations. VQE offers a practical alternative by adopting a variational approach, where a parameterized quantum circuit (ansatz) generates trial quantum states, and a classical optimizer iteratively adjusts the parameters to minimize the system's energy expectation value.

Mathematically, the objective is defined as:

$$E(\theta) = \langle \psi(\theta) \mid \hat{H} \mid \psi(\theta) \rangle$$

Where $\hat{H}$ represents the Hamiltonian of the system and $|\psi(\theta)\rangle$ is the variational quantum state determined by parameters θ. The optimal set of parameters, θ^*, yielding the minimum-energy estimate, closely approximating the true ground-state energy.

VQE combines quantum expressivity with classical optimization, allowing today's noisy quantum processors to deliver chemically meaningful results efficiently—often in minutes rather than hours.

Workflow of VQE

The VQE functions through a hybrid feedback loop between a quantum processor and a classical computer. The two systems work together iteratively: quantum hardware prepares and measures states, while the classical processor refines parameters to minimize the system's energy. The following table outlines the sequential steps of the VQE, highlighting how quantum and classical operations interact during optimization:

Step	Operation	Executed on
1	Define molecular Hamiltonian ($\hat{H}$)	Classical
2	Construct a parameterized circuit (ansatz)	Quantum
3	Measure the expectation value ($\langle \hat{H} \rangle$)	Quantum
4	Update parameters using optimizer	Classical
5	Iterate until convergence	Quantum + classical

***Table 11.1**: Workflow of the VQE*

This iterative process continues until the classical optimizer determines the set of parameters that minimizes the energy expectation value, effectively approximating the system's ground-state.

Estimating the ground-state energy of H_2

To illustrate the VQE in practice, let us implement a simple workflow using Qiskit to estimate the ground-state energy of a **hydrogen molecule** (H_2). This example demonstrates the integration of quantum simulation with classical optimization to estimate molecular energy.

The VQE workflow for estimating the ground-state energy of H_2 can be organized into the following sequential steps:

1. Import libraries and define the molecule:

```
from qiskit_nature.second_q.drivers import PySCFDriver
from qiskit_nature.second_q.mappers import ParityMapper
from qiskit_nature.second_q.transformers import ActiveSpaceTransformer
from qiskit_nature.second_q.algorithms import GroundStateEigensolver, VQEUCCFactory
from qiskit.algorithms.optimizers import COBYLA
from qiskit.primitives import Estimator
from qiskit import Aer
# Hydrogen molecule setup
driver = PySCFDriver(atom='H .0 .0 .0; H .0 .0 .735', basis='sto3g')
problem = driver.run()
# Reduce to active space
transformer = ActiveSpaceTransformer(num_electrons=2, num_molecular_orbitals=2)
problem_reduced = transformer.transform(problem)
```

2. Map the Hamiltonian to qubits:

```
mapper = ParityMapper()
hamiltonian = mapper.map(problem_reduced.second_q_ops()["ElectronicEnergy"])
```

3. Define variational ansatz and optimizer:

```
from qiskit.circuit.library import TwoLocal
ansatz = TwoLocal(rotation_blocks='ry', entanglement_blocks='cz', reps=3)
optimizer = COBYLA(maxiter=200)
vqe_solver = VQEUCCFactory(Estimator(), ansatz=ansatz, optimizer=optimizer)
```

4. Compute the ground-state energy:

```
solver = GroundStateEigensolver(mapper, vqe_solver)
result = solver.solve(problem_reduced)
print("Ground-state energy:", result.total_energies[0])
```

The typical output is as follows:

```
Ground-state energy: -1.137 Hartree
```

This result closely approximates the exact ground-state energy obtained from classical quantum chemistry methods. It demonstrates that VQE, even when executed on NISQ hardware, can yield chemically accurate results within practical time and resource limits.

Key design choices in VQE

Designing an effective VQE requires carefully selecting components that balance repressibility, trainability, and hardware constraints. Thoughtful configuration helps minimize challenges such as barren plateaus, noise sensitivity, and overly deep circuits, all of which can significantly affect performance on near-term quantum devices.

The performance and accuracy of the VQE depend heavily on its design configuration. Each component, from the ansatz to the backend, plays a crucial role in determining convergence behavior, computational cost, and overall efficiency. The following table shows the key design components of the VQE, outlining common configuration options and their specific purposes in the algorithm:

Component	Options	Purpose
Ansatz	Hardware-efficient, **unitary coupled cluster** (**UCC**), RealAmplitudes	Defines the structure of the quantum circuit used to represent the trial wavefunction.

Optimizer	**Constrained Optimization by Linear Approximation (COBYLA), Simultaneous Perturbation Stochastic Approximation (SPSA), Adaptive Moment Estimation (ADAM), limited-memory Broyden-Fletcher-Goldfarb-Shanno Bound (L-BFGS-B)**	Adjusts circuit parameters to minimize the expectation value of the Hamiltonian.
Measurement strategy	Grouped Pauli measurements, adaptive sampling	Reduces measurement variance and shot noise during energy estimation.
Backend	Simulator or **quantum processing unit** (**QPU**) such as *IonQ* or *Rigetti*	Executes the circuit either in simulation or on real quantum hardware.

Table 11.2: *Key components, configuration choices, and functions in a VQE implementation*

Advantages and limitations

The VQE demonstrates strong potential for solving quantum chemistry problems on today's noisy hardware. However, like all hybrid algorithms, it offers both strengths and practical challenges that influence its performance and applicability.

The following points summarize the key advantages and limitations of VQE, outlining where it excels and the factors that can affect its efficiency in real-world implementations.

The advantages are as follows:

- Suitable for near-term noisy hardware, making it practical for today's NISQ devices.
- Produces physically meaningful results, such as accurate molecular ground-state energies.
- Highly modular, allowing easy adaptation to different systems, ansatz designs, or optimizers.

The limitations are as follows:

- Requires extensive circuit evaluations, resulting in high shot and computational overhead.
- Optimization landscapes can contain local minima (known as **barren plateaus**), which can slow convergence.
- Performance depends on initialization and the optimizer choice, which can affect the quality of the results.

Quantum Approximate Optimization Algorithm

The QAOA is a foundational hybrid quantum–classical algorithm designed to solve combinatorial optimization problems, such as Max-Cut, Traveling Salesman, and scheduling. These problems involve identifying the best configuration of binary variables that minimizes or maximizes a given cost function, an NP-hard challenge that becomes computationally intractable for classical systems as problem size increases.

QAOA bridges quantum computation and classical optimization by encoding the cost function into a problem Hamiltonian and then evolving a quantum system toward an approximate optimal solution. Its iterative structure resembles that of VQE, but it is optimized explicitly for discrete optimization landscapes.

Formally, QAOA aims to minimize the expected cost:

$$C(z) = \langle z \mid \hat{H}_C \mid z \rangle$$

Where $\hat{H}_C$ is the cost Hamiltonian encoding the objective function, and $|z\rangle$ represents a computational basis state corresponding to a potential solution.

QAOA's strength lies in its balance between quantum exploration and classical optimization, enabling near-term quantum devices to tackle real-world optimization problems effectively without the need for full-scale quantum error correction.

QAOA workflow

The QAOA follows a structured sequence of classical problem formulation and quantum state evolution. Understanding this workflow clarifies how information flows between classical computation and quantum circuit execution in each optimization cycle.

Like the VQE, the QAOA operates through an iterative quantum–classical feedback loop. The key distinction lies in how QAOA structures its problem (cost) Hamiltonian and mixing Hamiltonian, which together define the optimization landscape. The following table shows the step-by-step process of the QAOA, indicating which operations are executed on classical or quantum systems:

Step	Operation	Performed on
1	Define the cost Hamiltonian (H_c) for the optimization problem	Classical
2	Define mixing Hamiltonian ($H_M=\sum_i X_i$)	Classical
3	Initialize the quantum state	*((+\rangle^n))* using Hadamard gates
4	Apply alternating operators ($U_C(\gamma)$) and ($U_M(\beta)$)	Quantum
5	Measure expectation value and update (γ,β)	Classical
6	Repeat until convergence	Quantum + classical

***Table 11.3**: Workflow of the QAOA*

Mathematically, for a circuit depth p (number of layers):

$$|\psi(\gamma,\beta)\rangle = \prod_{k=1}^{p} e^{-i\beta_k H_M} e^{-i\gamma_k H_C} |+\rangle^{\otimes n}|$$

Example of solving the Max-Cut problem

This example demonstrates how a combinatorial optimization problem can be modeled as a quadratic program and solved using a hybrid quantum–classical approach. By combining graph construction, Hamiltonian encoding, and iterative parameter optimization, QAOA provides a structured pathway from problem definition to solution.

The following Qiskit example solves a 4-node Max-Cut instance using QAOA. We (1) build the graph and quadratic program, (2) configure QAOA on a simulator, and (3) retrieve the best cut.

The implementation proceeds through the following steps:

1. Define the graph and Hamiltonian:

```
import networkx as nx
from qiskit_optimization.applications import Maxcut
from qiskit_optimization.algorithms import MinimumEigenOptimizer
from qiskit.algorithms.minimum_eigensolvers import QAOA
from qiskit.algorithms.optimizers import COBYLA
from qiskit import Aer
# Create a 4-node cycle graph: (0-1-2-3-0)
G = nx.Graph()
G.add_edges_from([(0, 1), (1, 2), (2, 3), (3, 0)])
# Convert to a quadratic program for Max-Cut
maxcut = Maxcut(G)
qp = maxcut.to_quadratic_program()
```

2. Setup QAOA with a simulator backend:

```
# Optimizer and backend
```

```
optimizer = COBYLA(maxiter=150)
backend = Aer.get_backend('aer_simulator')
# Two QAOA layers (reps=2)
qaoa = QAOA(optimizer=optimizer, reps=2, quantum_instance=backend)
# Wrap QAOA as a minimum-eigenvalue optimizer for Max-Cut
algorithm = MinimumEigenOptimizer(qaoa)
result = algorithm.solve(qp)
print("Best solution:", result.x)
print("Max-Cut value:", result.fval)
```

The expected output is as follows:

```
Best solution: [1, 0, 1, 0]
Max-Cut value: 4.0
```

This bitstring corresponds to the optimal bipartition (e.g., {0,2} vs. {1,3}) that cuts all four edges in the cycle. It highlights how QAOA's alternating cost/mixer layers, tuned by a classical optimizer, efficiently locate high-quality solutions for discrete optimization.

Cost and mixing Hamiltonians

To understand how QAOA navigates the solution space, it is essential to examine the roles of the Hamiltonians that govern its evolution. These operators determine how the algorithm balances problem encoding with state exploration across successive layers.

In QAOA, two Hamiltonians define the algorithm's dynamics: the cost Hamiltonian encodes the problem's objective, while the mixing Hamiltonian enables exploration of different bitstring configurations.

Cost Hamiltonian:

$$H_C = \sum_{(i,j)\in E} \frac{1}{2}(1 - Z_i Z_j)$$

Mixing Hamiltonian:

$$H_M = \sum_i X_i$$

The circuit alternates between unitary operations derived from H_C and H_M, forming the basis of the QAOA ansatz:

```
from qiskit.circuit.library import QAOAAnsatz
from qiskit.circuit import Parameter
p = 1
gamma = Parameter('γ')
beta = Parameter('β')
ansatz = QAOAAnsatz(cost_operator=maxcut.to_ising()[0], reps=p)
ansatz.draw('mpl')
```

Parameter optimization

The performance of the QAOA depends heavily on identifying the optimal parameters (γ,β), which govern the evolution between the cost and mixing Hamiltonians. These parameters are tuned through iterative optimization processes using various classical strategies.

Common optimization approaches include:

- **Gradient-free methods**: COBYLA, Nelder–Mead robust against noise and suitable for small-scale, noisy devices.

- **Gradient-based methods**: ADAM, SPSA, provide faster convergence through parameter updates guided by gradient approximations.
- **Machine learning-inspired methods**: Bayesian optimization, reinforcement learning, leverage prior knowledge or adaptive exploration for improved parameter search.

Example implementation in Cirq

While high-level frameworks make algorithm construction more convenient, lower-level libraries such as Cirq offer finer control over individual gate operations and circuit structure. This added flexibility is especially valuable when experimenting with customized QAOA layers or analyzing the behavior of specific unitary transformations.

The following Cirq example demonstrates a minimal two-qubit QAOA implementation for a simple Max-Cut problem. It highlights how Cirq's gate-level flexibility enables precise experimentation with QAOA layers:

```
import cirq
import numpy as np
# Define qubits and parameters
q0, q1 = cirq.LineQubit.range(2)
gamma, beta = 1.2, 0.6
# Build a single-layer QAOA circuit
circuit = cirq.Circuit(
    cirq.H.on_each(q0, q1),  # Initialize in superposition
    cirq.ZZPowGate(exponent=-2 * gamma / np.pi).on(q0, q1),  # Cost Hamiltonian
    cirq.rx(2 * beta).on_each(q0, q1),  # Mixing Hamiltonian
    cirq.measure(q0, q1)
)
# Simulate and display measurement results
simulator = cirq.Simulator()
result = simulator.run(circuit, repetitions=1000)
print(result.histogram(key='0,1'))
```

The example output is as follows:

```
Counter({0: 502, 3: 498})
```

This circuit represents a single QAOA layer, alternating between cost and mixing unitaries. The output distribution reflects the optimal bitstring configurations, and Cirq's low-level control makes it ideal for customized, fine-grained QAOA experiments.

Advantages and limitations

The QAOA is one of the most promising approaches for solving complex combinatorial problems on today's quantum hardware. It effectively bridges quantum parallelism with classical optimization, offering a path toward near-term quantum advantage.

The following points summarize the main advantages and limitations of QAOA, highlighting its strengths in adaptability and scalability, as well as the practical challenges that affect its performance on NISQ devices.

The advantages are as follows:

- Solves complex optimization problems efficiently on current NISQ hardware.
- Easily adaptable to diverse cost functions across domains such as logistics, scheduling, and finance.
- Parameter-efficient and scalable with circuit depth (p), allowing gradual improvement in approximation quality.

The limitations are as follows:

- Highly dependent on parameter initialization, which can affect convergence speed and accuracy.
- Requires many circuit executions per optimization step, increasing computational cost.
- Sensitive to hardware noise, especially as circuit depth (p) increases.

Using PennyLane with PyTorch for hybrid workflows

In recent years, the line between quantum computing and machine learning has increasingly blurred, giving rise to hybrid quantum–classical learning frameworks. In these systems, quantum circuits function as parameterized models, analogous to layers in a neural network, and are optimized through classical gradient-based algorithms.

PennyLane, an open-source library developed by *Xanadu*, provides a seamless bridge between quantum programming and deep learning platforms like PyTorch and TensorFlow. This integration allows researchers and developers to train **quantum neural networks** (**QNNs**), perform variational optimization, and build end-to-end differentiable pipelines that operate directly on simulators or quantum hardware.

PennyLane transforms quantum computation into a differentiable function, enabling automatic gradient computation and backpropagation across hybrid models—mirroring the training dynamics of conventional deep learning architectures while harnessing the quantum advantage.

Core architecture of PennyLane

PennyLane is designed to unify quantum circuit execution with modern machine learning workflows. Its architecture emphasizes modularity and differentiability, allowing quantum computations to integrate seamlessly into classical optimization and deep learning pipelines.

A PennyLane workflow is organized into three essential layers, each handling a specific role in the hybrid quantum–classical computation pipeline:

- **Device layer**: Connects to quantum backends, either simulators or real QPUs, such as **`default.qubit`**, **`lightning.qubit`**, or **`braket.aws.qubit`**.
- **Quantum node (QNode)**: Defines a parameterized quantum function (circuit) that can be called like a standard Python function.
- **Interface layer**: Bridges PennyLane with classical machine learning frameworks such as PyTorch, TensorFlow, or JAX, enabling seamless integration with automatic differentiation and optimizers.

Each quantum circuit is wrapped inside a QNode, making it differentiable and directly compatible with classical optimization pipelines.

The following example shows a basic QNode:

```
import pennylane as qml
from pennylane import numpy as np
# Define device
dev = qml.device("default.qubit", wires=2)
# Define quantum node
@qml.qnode(dev)
def circuit(theta):
    qml.RY(theta, wires=0)
    qml.CNOT(wires=[0, 1])
    return qml.expval(qml.PauliZ(0))
print(circuit(0.3))
```

The output is as follows:

```
0.955336489
```

Building a quantum neural network with PyTorch

Building a QNN with PyTorch and PennyLane demonstrates how quantum computing can be seamlessly integrated into conventional deep learning frameworks. In this workflow, quantum circuits function as trainable layers within a classical neural network, enabling the model to learn from data using hybrid gradient-based optimization. The following steps demonstrate the complete process, from defining a quantum layer and integrating it with classical components to training the hybrid model using PyTorch's automatic differentiation engine:

1. **Import dependencies**:

```
import torch
import pennylane as qml
from torch import nn
n_qubits = 2
dev = qml.device("default.qubit", wires=n_qubits)
```

2. **Define a quantum layer**:

```
class QuantumLayer(nn.Module):
    def __init__(self):
        super().__init__()
        self.weights = nn.Parameter(0.01 * torch.randn(2))
    def forward(self, x):
        @qml.qnode(dev, interface="torch")
        def circuit(inputs, weights):
            qml.RY(inputs[0], wires=0)
            qml.RY(inputs[1], wires=1)
            qml.CNOT(wires=[0, 1])
            qml.RY(weights[0], wires=0)
            qml.RY(weights[1], wires=1)
            return qml.expval(qml.PauliZ(1))
        return circuit(x, self.weights)
```

3. **Integrate with a classical neural network**:

```
class HybridModel(nn.Module):
    def __init__(self):
        super().__init__()
        self.fc1 = nn.Linear(2, 2)
        self.quantum = QuantumLayer()
        self.fc2 = nn.Linear(1, 1)
    def forward(self, x):
        x = torch.tanh(self.fc1(x))
        x = torch.tensor([[self.quantum(x[0])]])
        x = self.fc2(x)
        return x
```

4. **Training the model**:

```
model = HybridModel()
optimizer = torch.optim.Adam(model.parameters(), lr=0.1)
for epoch in range(50):
    optimizer.zero_grad()
    inputs = torch.tensor([[0.2, 0.5]])
    target = torch.tensor([[0.8]])
    loss = (model(inputs) - target).pow(2).mean()
    loss.backward()
```

```
    optimizer.step()
    print(f"Epoch {epoch+1}: Loss = {loss.item():.4f}")
```

During training, PyTorch automatically backpropagates through the quantum circuit, allowing simultaneous updates of quantum parameters (rotation angles) and classical weights.

Hybrid optimization pipeline

Modern quantum machine learning relies on close coordination between quantum circuit evaluation and classical gradient-based learning. PennyLane enables this integration by embedding quantum nodes directly into differentiable machine learning workflows.

The hybrid optimization pipeline in PennyLane combines quantum computation and classical machine learning into a single end-to-end differentiable framework. The process can be summarized in four key stages:

1. **Quantum circuit forward pass**: The parameterized quantum circuit (QNode) is executed to generate expectation values that represent quantum features or predictions.
2. **Classical loss function**: The loss (such as **mean squared error** (**MSE**) or cross-entropy) is computed based on the difference between predicted and target values.
3. **Backpropagation**: Automatic differentiation using **`torch.autograd`** (or equivalent in TensorFlow/JAX) computes gradients with respect to both quantum and classical parameters.
4. **Parameter update**: A classical optimizer (e.g., Adam, **stochastic gradient descent** (**SGD**), or RMSProp) updates the weights of both subsystems for the next iteration.

Figure 11.1 shows the four stages of PennyLane's hybrid optimization loop—quantum circuit forward pass, loss computation, backpropagation, and parameter update—illustrating how quantum and classical components train together through iterative feedback:

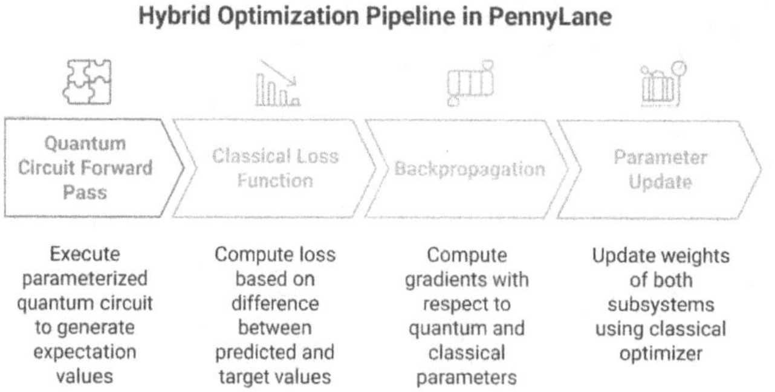

***Figure 11.1**: Hybrid optimization workflow in PennyLane*

Advantages of integrating PennyLane with PyTorch

Integrating PennyLane with PyTorch provides a unified framework for developing hybrid quantum–classical machine learning models. This collaboration enables quantum circuits to serve as differentiable layers in deep neural networks, combining the strengths of both paradigms for scalable, efficient learning.

The following table shows the major features and corresponding advantages of the PennyLane–PyTorch integration in hybrid quantum machine learning:

Feature	Advantage
End-to-end differentiability	Enables seamless backpropagation through both quantum and classical layers.

Hardware independence	Executes on simulators or real QPUs using Braket, IBM Q, or Xanadu Lightning without code changes.
Machine learning compatibility	Integrates directly with PyTorch optimizers and training loops.
Gradient control	Offers multiple differentiation methods, including parameter-shift, finite-difference, and adjoint-diff.
scalability	Supports mini-batch training and GPU acceleration for large hybrid models.

***Table 11.4**: Advantages of PennyLane and PyTorch integration*

Example applications of hybrid learning

The integration of quantum circuits into differentiable machine learning pipelines has opened new directions in quantum-enhanced modeling. By treating parameterized quantum circuits as trainable components, hybrid frameworks extend classical learning architectures into the quantum domain.

Hybrid quantum–classical learning frameworks enable a wide range of machine learning and optimization applications in which quantum circuits serve as differentiable models. Some representative examples include:

- **Quantum classifiers**: Replace classical hidden layers with quantum circuits for complex pattern recognition in image and signal classification tasks.
- **Quantum autoencoders**: Use variational circuits to efficiently compress and reconstruct quantum or classical data.
- **Quantum generative adversarial networks (GANs)**: Combine quantum generators with classical discriminators to produce synthetic datasets or simulate distributions.
- **VQE/QAOA enhancements**: Integrate deep learning optimizers such as ADAM or SGD to accelerate convergence in variational algorithms.

Applications in chemistry, finance, and logistics

Variational and hybrid quantum algorithms, particularly VQE and QAOA, have emerged as practical frameworks for solving real-world problems in the NISQ era. By combining quantum state preparation with classical optimization, these methods efficiently tackle computationally intensive tasks that classical approaches struggle with.

This section explores three key application domains- quantum chemistry, financial modeling, and logistics optimization, where hybrid algorithms are already demonstrating tangible potential and measurable performance gains.

Each of these domains employs a similar hybrid methodology- encode the problem as a Hamiltonian, implement it on a parameterized quantum circuit, and use classical optimization to steer the computation toward an optimal or low-energy configuration.

Quantum chemistry and molecular simulation

Predicting molecular ground-state energies is a fundamental challenge in quantum chemistry. Classical computational methods such as Hartree–Fock and coupled cluster theory become increasingly complex as molecular size increases, making them impractical for larger systems.

The VQE provides an efficient alternative by mapping the molecular electronic Hamiltonian to a qubit-based representation via encodings such as Jordan–Wigner or Bravyi–Kitaev. This allows quantum hardware to approximate molecular energies through variational optimization.

The typical workflow is as follows:

- Define the molecular structure (e.g., H_2, LiH, BeH_2).
- Convert the molecular Hamiltonian into its qubit equivalent.
- Construct a parameterized ansatz circuit (e.g., UCCSD).
- Use a classical optimizer to minimize the energy expectation value.

The following are some examples of use cases:

- **H_2**: VQE can estimate the bond-dissociation curve with near-chemical accuracy using only 4–6-qubits-well within the limits of current NISQ devices.
- **Larger molecules (LiH, BeH_2)**: AWS Braket provides access to scalable IonQ and Rigetti QPUs, allowing researchers to simulate energy surfaces for larger molecular systems.

Finance and portfolio optimization

Modern financial markets pose inherently complex optimization challenges such as risk minimization, asset allocation, and option pricing. These problems often take the form of quadratic or binary-constrained optimization problems, which are well-suited to **variational quantum algorithms** (**VQAs**) such as QAOA and VQE. Such algorithms enable the efficient exploration of vast solution spaces, making them attractive for quantitative finance and investment modeling.

The following example demonstrates the mean–variance portfolio optimization.

For a portfolio of N assets, the objective is to minimize overall risk while maximizing expected return, expressed as:

$$\text{Minimize: } w^T \Sigma w - \mu^T w$$

where w represents portfolio weights, Σ the covariance matrix of asset returns, and μ the expected returns vector.

By discretizing portfolio weights into binary variables, this formulation becomes a **quadratic unconstrained binary optimization** (**QUBO**) problem, which can be directly mapped onto a cost Hamiltonian for QAOA.

The implementation workflow is as follows:

1. Encode the expected returns (μ) and covariances (Σ) as Hamiltonian coefficients.
2. Apply QAOA to evolve the system under alternating cost and mixer Hamiltonians.
3. Measure resulting bitstrings and interpret them as optimal portfolio configurations:

```
# Simplified pseudo-code
H_cost = Σ_ij w_i w_j - μ_i w_i
# Apply QAOA with depth p=2
```

The following are the benefits:

- Quantum hardware explores multiple portfolio configurations in parallel.
- Variational optimization efficiently navigates non-convex risk landscapes.
- Seamless integration with PyTorch or TensorFlow allows adaptive retraining as market conditions evolve.

Logistics and combinatorial optimization

In logistics and operations research, companies constantly face the challenge of optimizing routes, schedules, and resource allocation, all of which are examples of NP hard combinatorial problems. Classical algorithms often become inefficient as problem size grows, making quantum approaches such as the QAOA a promising alternative.

QAOA provides a natural framework for addressing large-scale logistical problems, such as the **traveling salesman problem** (**TSP**), vehicle routing, and delivery network optimization, by encoding them as cost Hamiltonians that quantum circuits can efficiently explore.

The following example demonstrates the TSP:

- Represent each city as a node and each path as an edge associated with a travel cost.
- Encode the cost matrix into a Hamiltonian:

$$H_C = \sum_{i,j} c_{ij} Z_i Z_j$$

- The optimal route corresponds to the bitstring that minimizes H_C.

The implementation steps are as follows:

1. Convert the classical routing or distance matrix into a qubit Hamiltonian.
2. Initialize the parameters (γ, β) for QAOA.
3. Execute QAOA with a small circuit depth p on a quantum simulator or hardware backend.
4. Retrieve and decode bitstrings to determine the optimal travel order.

Cross-domain perspective

The versatility of variational and hybrid quantum algorithms lies in their ability to address problems across multiple disciplines using a unified computational framework. By translating diverse real-world challenges, whether in chemistry, finance, or logistics into Hamiltonian formulations, these algorithms leverage quantum systems for exploration and classical optimizers for refinement. The following table shows how variational and hybrid algorithms are applied across different domains, outlining their benefits and the platforms commonly used to implement them:

Domain	Algorithm used	Typical benefit	Example platform
Quantum chemistry	VQE	Molecular energy estimation with chemical accuracy	Qiskit Nature/AWS Braket
Finance	QAOA	Portfolio risk optimization and option pricing	Qiskit Finance/PennyLane
Logistics	QAOA/VQE	Route planning and resource allocation	Cirq/Braket Hybrid Jobs

***Table 11.5**: Cross-domain applications of hybrid quantum algorithms*

Implementations with Qiskit, Cirq, and AWS Braket

Each quantum programming environment—Qiskit (IBM), Cirq (Google), and AWS Braket (Amazon) provides distinct tools and integrations for implementing hybrid and variational quantum algorithms. Although their syntax and APIs differ, the underlying workflow remains conceptually identical, combining quantum circuit construction, classical optimization, and result interpretation within an iterative loop.

The following is the unified conceptual flow:

1. Construct a parameterized quantum circuit that defines the problem space.
2. Define a cost or objective function representing the quantity to minimize or maximize.
3. Apply a classical optimizer to update parameters and improve convergence.
4. Retrieve and analyze measurement results to evaluate algorithmic performance.

This section presents side-by-side implementations of VQE and QAOA using Qiskit, Cirq, and AWS Braket, illustrating how a single algorithmic concept can be executed across different quantum ecosystems.

Recognizing the cross-framework equivalence enables researchers to port experiments seamlessly, benchmark performance, and select the most efficient platform—whether for simulation, hardware access, or large-scale hybrid execution.

VQE implementation in Qiskit

The VQE is one of the most widely used hybrid algorithms for estimating molecular energies on near-term quantum devices. Qiskit provides an integrated ecosystem that connects quantum circuit construction, Hamiltonian mapping, and classical optimization into a unified chemistry workflow.

Qiskit Nature streamlines quantum chemistry workflows by coupling electronic-structure tooling with VQE. The following snippet sets up an H_2 molecule, maps its electronic Hamiltonian to qubits, and computes the ground-state energy with a variational solver:

```
from qiskit_nature.second_q.drivers import PySCFDriver
from qiskit_nature.second_q.mappers import ParityMapper
from qiskit_nature.second_q.algorithms import GroundStateEigensolver, VQEUCCFactory
from qiskit.algorithms.optimizers import COBYLA
from qiskit.primitives import Estimator
# Hydrogen molecule setup
driver = PySCFDriver(atom='H .0 .0 .0; H .0 .0 .735', basis='sto3g')
problem = driver.run()
# Map to qubit Hamiltonian
mapper = ParityMapper()
hamiltonian = mapper.map(problem.second_q_ops()["ElectronicEnergy"])
# Define ansatz and optimizer
optimizer = COBYLA(maxiter=200)
vqe_solver = VQEUCCFactory(Estimator(), optimizer=optimizer)
# Solve
solver = GroundStateEigensolver(mapper, vqe_solver)
result = solver.solve(problem)
print("Ground-state energy:", result.total_energies[0])
```

The expected output is as follows:

```
Ground-state energy: -1.137 Hartree
```

QAOA implementation in Qiskit

The QAOA can be efficiently implemented in Qiskit using its dedicated optimization module, which bridges classical problem modeling with quantum minimum-eigenvalue solvers. This integration enables a smooth transition from graph-based formulations to executable quantum circuits.

Qiskit Optimization streamlines combinatorial problems like Max-Cut by providing ready-to-use formulations and solvers. The following example builds a 4-node cycle graph, converts it to a quadratic program, and solves it with QAOA on the Aer simulator:

```
import networkx as nx
from qiskit_optimization.applications import Maxcut
from qiskit_optimization.algorithms import MinimumEigenOptimizer
from qiskit.algorithms.minimum_eigensolvers import QAOA
from qiskit.algorithms.optimizers import COBYLA
from qiskit import Aer
# Create graph (cycle of 4 nodes)
G = nx.Graph()
G.add_edges_from([(0,1), (1,2), (2,3), (3,0)])
# Build Max-Cut quadratic program
maxcut = Maxcut(G)
qp = maxcut.to_quadratic_program()
# Define QAOA solver
```

```
optimizer = COBYLA(maxiter=100)
backend = Aer.get_backend('aer_simulator')
qaoa = QAOA(optimizer=optimizer, reps=2, quantum_instance=backend)
# Solve
algorithm = MinimumEigenOptimizer(qaoa)
result = algorithm.solve(qp)
print("Best solution:", result.x)
print("Optimal value:", result.fval)
```

Typical outcome: A valid optimum for the 4-cycle is often a checkerboard partition, e.g., Best solution: [1, 0, 1, 0] with optimal value: 4.0.

VQE and QAOA in Cirq

While higher-level libraries abstract much of the algorithmic structure, Cirq provides a more granular programming model that allows researchers to explicitly construct and analyze each gate-level transformation. This level of control is particularly valuable when experimenting with custom variational circuits or studying algorithm behavior under controlled simulation settings.

Cirq exposes low-level circuit primitives and scheduling controls, making it ideal for research, custom ansatz, and noise-model experiments.

VQE example in Cirq (two-qubit toy Hamiltonian $H=Z_0Z_1$) is as follows:

```
import cirq, numpy as np
from scipy.optimize import minimize
# Qubits
q0, q1 = cirq.LineQubit.range(2)
# Ansatz: create entanglement, then a single tunable rotation
def build_circuit(theta):
    return cirq.Circuit(
        cirq.H(q0),
        cirq.CNOT(q0, q1),
        cirq.rx(theta).on(q0)
    )
# ⟨Z ⊗ Z⟩ expectation as the VQE cost
def expectation_zz(theta):
    sim = cirq.Simulator()
    result = sim.simulate(build_circuit(theta))
    state = result.final_state_vector
    # Z ⊗ Z on two qubits
    z = np.array([[1, 0], [0, -1]], dtype=complex)
    ZZ = np.kron(z, z)
    return np.real(np.vdot(state, ZZ @ state))
# Minimize energy (for H = Z0 Z1, energy = ⟨ZZ⟩)
res = minimize(lambda t: expectation_zz(t[0]), x0=[0.1], method="COBYLA")
print(„Optimal parameter:", res.x)
print(„Minimum energy:", expectation_zz(res.x[0]))
```

QAOA example in Cirq (two-node Max-Cut layer) is as follows:

```
import cirq, numpy as np
gamma, beta = 1.2, 0.7
q0, q1 = cirq.LineQubit.range(2)
circuit = cirq.Circuit(
```

```
    cirq.H.on_each(q0, q1),                                          # |+)^2
    cirq.ZZPowGate(exponent=-2 * gamma / np.pi).on(q0, q1),  # cost unitary
    cirq.rx(2 * beta).on_each(q0, q1),                               # mixer unitary
    cirq.measure(q0, q1)
)
sim = cirq.Simulator()
result = sim.run(circuit, repetitions=500)
print(result.histogram(key='0,1'))
```

Hybrid implementation with AWS Braket

When hybrid algorithms extend beyond short experiments and involve iterative optimization, coordinated execution across quantum and classical resources becomes increasingly important. AWS Braket addresses this need through its Hybrid Jobs framework, which manages both computation layers within a single, scalable cloud environment.

AWS Braket integrates quantum and classical components via Hybrid Jobs, enabling long-running optimization tasks to run seamlessly alongside managed compute instances. This setup eliminates the need for repeated submissions and manual synchronization between quantum and classical workflows:

```
from braket.jobs import AwsQuantumJob
job = AwsQuantumJob.create(
    source_module="vqe_module",
    entry_point="vqe_module:main",
    device="arn:aws:braket:::device/quantum-simulator/amazon/sv1",
    instance_type="ml.m5.large",
    job_name="vqe-h2-energy"
)
print("Job ARN:", job.arn)
```

Once launched, the Hybrid Job automatically provisions the classical environment, runs the quantum–classical feedback loop, and stores logs and results in your Amazon S3 bucket.

Comparative summary

Different quantum programming frameworks offer distinct strengths tailored to various stages of quantum algorithm development, from education and experimentation to scalable cloud-based execution. Understanding these differences helps researchers and developers choose the right tool for their specific objectives.

The following table shows a comparative overview of major quantum frameworks, highlighting their programming style, hardware accessibility, and most suitable use cases:

Framework	Programming style	Hardware access	Best use case
Qiskit	High-level modular API	IBM Q and simulators	Quantum chemistry, education
Cirq	Low-level circuit control	Google Sycamore and local devices	Research and algorithm testing
AWS Braket	Cloud-integrated hybrid execution	IonQ, Rigetti, *Oxford Quantum Circuits* (OQC)	Scalable hybrid workflows and optimization

Table 11.6: *Comparison of Qiskit, Cirq, and AWS Braket*

Conclusion

This chapter examined variational and hybrid quantum algorithms as the most practical computational paradigm for the NISQ era. Through the VQE and the QAOA, we explored how parameterized quantum circuits and classical optimization routines work together in an iterative feedback loop to solve energy estimation and combinatorial optimization problems. Rather than relying on deep, error-corrected quantum circuits, these methods strategically leverage shallow circuits combined with powerful classical optimizers, making them well aligned with current hardware capabilities.

Beyond foundational algorithmic principles, this chapter emphasized implementation across multiple ecosystems, including Qiskit, Cirq, PennyLane, and AWS Braket. These frameworks demonstrate that hybrid algorithms are not confined to theory but can be executed on simulators and real QPUs. The integration of PennyLane with PyTorch further illustrated how quantum circuits can function as differentiable components within modern machine learning workflows, opening new avenues in quantum-enhanced learning and optimization.

Importantly, variational methods embody a broader computational philosophy: quantum devices explore high-dimensional solution spaces, while classical systems guide convergence through optimization strategies. This synergy represents a realistic pathway toward quantum utility in domains such as chemistry, finance, and logistics. As quantum hardware matures, the principles and workflows introduced in this chapter will remain central to scalable quantum algorithm design. Mastering these hybrid techniques equips researchers and practitioners with the conceptual and practical tools necessary to translate quantum potential into measurable real-world impact.

Questions

1. **What are variational and hybrid quantum algorithms?**

   Answer: Variational and hybrid quantum algorithms combine quantum state preparation with classical optimization. A quantum circuit generates parameterized states, while a classical computer adjusts these parameters to minimize or maximize a cost function. This collaboration allows current noisy quantum devices to solve meaningful problems efficiently.

2. **What is the VQE used for?**

   Answer: VQE is primarily used in quantum chemistry to estimate the ground-state energy of molecules. It represents the system's Hamiltonian on qubits, prepares trial wavefunctions, and optimizes their parameters using classical algorithms to find the lowest energy configuration.

3. **How does the QAOA differ from VQE?**

   Answer: While VQE targets continuous problems, such as molecular energy estimation, QAOA focuses on discrete combinatorial optimization problems, such as Max-Cut, scheduling, and routing. Both follow hybrid workflows but differ in how they encode and minimize their respective Hamiltonians.

4. **Why are VQE and QAOA suitable for NISQ devices?**

   Answer: These algorithms use shallow, parameterized circuits that tolerate hardware noise better than deep quantum algorithms like QPE. Their iterative, measurement-based feedback loops make them practical for current-generation quantum processors.

5. **What role does classical optimization play in hybrid algorithms?**

   Answer: Classical optimizers such as COBYLA, SPSA, or Adam adjust quantum circuit parameters to minimize the expectation value of the Hamiltonian. This feedback mechanism ensures convergence toward optimal or near-optimal results, leveraging classical computational efficiency.

6. **How does PennyLane integrate with PyTorch in hybrid workflows?**

   Answer: PennyLane connects quantum circuits (QNodes) with PyTorch's automatic differentiation, allowing gradients to propagate through both quantum and classical layers. This enables end-to-end training of hybrid models using familiar machine learning techniques.

7. **What are the practical applications of VQE and QAOA?**

   Answer: VQE is widely used in quantum chemistry to simulate molecular structures and reaction dynamics, while QAOA finds applications in finance (portfolio optimization) and logistics (route planning and scheduling). Together, they demonstrate quantum computing's relevance to real-world industries.

8. **How do Qiskit, Cirq, and AWS Braket support hybrid algorithm development?**

   Answer: Qiskit offers high-level abstractions for chemistry and optimization problems. Cirq provides low-level circuit control for algorithm research and noise modeling. AWS Braket enables scalable, cloud-based hybrid execution using real quantum hardware.

9. **What are the main challenges in implementing hybrid algorithms?**

   Answer: Challenges include high measurement overhead, noisy qubits, and optimization difficulties like barren plateaus. Effective ansatz design, noise mitigation, and adaptive optimization strategies are key to overcoming these issues.

10. **What is the long-term significance of studying variational and hybrid algorithms?**

    Answer: These algorithms form the foundation for near-term quantum computing applications and will likely remain vital even as hardware improves. Mastering them prepares learners to design scalable quantum solutions that bridge quantum theory, machine learning, and real-world problem solving.

Exercises

1. Implement the VQE using Qiskit to estimate the ground-state energy of a H_2. Display the output energy and compare it with the theoretical reference value obtained from classical chemistry methods.
2. Construct a custom VQE ansatz in Qiskit or Cirq using rotation and entanglement gates of your choice. Experiment with different optimizers (COBYLA, SPSA, ADAM) and observe how each affects convergence and final accuracy.
3. Solve the Max-Cut problem using QAOA on a 4-node graph. Plot the histogram of the measured bitstrings and explain which configuration corresponds to the optimal partition.
4. Modify the QAOA implementation to increase circuit depth ($p = 1, 2, 3$) and compare how the approximation quality and runtime evolve with depth. Discuss the trade-off between accuracy and hardware noise.
5. Build a simple two-qubit QAOA circuit in Cirq, simulate it 1000 times, and analyze the probability distribution of outcomes. Explain how the parameters (γ, β) influence the solution space.
6. Integrate PennyLane with PyTorch to create a hybrid model that uses a quantum circuit as a trainable layer. Train it to approximate a simple nonlinear function [e.g., $y = \sin(x)$] and plot the learning curve.
7. Demonstrate gradient-based training in PennyLane by visualizing how quantum parameters change over epochs during optimization. Discuss how this process mirrors classical backpropagation.
8. Run a small VQE or QAOA circuit on AWS Braket's SV1 simulator. Compare the execution time and results with a local simulator, and reflect on the advantages of cloud-based quantum computation.
9. Introduce noise into a VQE simulation using Aer's noise models. Analyze how the presence of gate or measurement errors impacts convergence and accuracy.
10. Write a short reflection discussing how variational and hybrid algorithms bridge quantum and classical computation, and why they are considered the most practical approach for the current NISQ era.

CHAPTER 12
Quantum Cryptography and Security

Introduction

As global communication networks expand, safeguarding digital information has become critical to preserving privacy and trust. Traditional cryptographic systems—such as **Rivest–Shamir–Adleman** (**RSA**), **Diffie–Hellman** (**DH**) key exchange, and **elliptic curve cryptography** (**ECC**) rely on the computational difficulty of some mathematical issues to ensure security. However, with the rise of quantum computing, algorithms such as Shor's and Grover's threaten to dismantle these foundations by solving problems once considered intractable.

Quantum cryptography offers a transformative solution by securing information through the fundamental laws of physics rather than mathematical assumptions. It leverages quantum phenomena such as superposition, entanglement, and the no-cloning theorem to detect any attempt to intercept or observe a quantum transmission instantly. At the core of this approach lies **quantum key distribution** (**QKD**), a method that allows two parties to establish a secret key with unconditional security, even in the presence of an eavesdropper.

This chapter explores the principles and implementation of quantum cryptography, emphasizing the **Bennett–Brassard 1984** (**BB84**) protocol—the first and most widely adopted QKD scheme. Readers will simulate BB84 using Python and Qiskit, analyze its workflow, and observe how quantum mechanics ensures secure key exchange. The chapter also introduces **post-quantum cryptography** (**PQC**), which develops quantum-resistant algorithms for classical systems.

Together, QKD and PQC represent complementary approaches shaping the future of secure communication, one rooted in the physics of quantum systems, the other in advanced mathematics both essential for achieving quantum-safe security in the coming digital era.

Structure

The chapter covers the following topics:

- Basics of quantum cryptography
- BB84 protocol simulation with Python and Qiskit
- Applications in secure communication
- Quantum key distribution
- Post-quantum cryptography challenges

Objectives

This chapter introduces quantum cryptography as a transformative discipline that secures digital communication through the immutable laws of quantum mechanics rather than computational assumptions. Readers will explore how quantum principles: superposition, entanglement, and the no-cloning theorem enable unbreakable key exchange and real-time eavesdropping detection via QKD. The chapter examines QKD's operational framework, emphasizing the BB84 protocol, and demonstrates a step-by-step Python simulation using Qiskit, linking theory to implementation. It also presents PQC as a complementary defense against quantum attacks for classical systems. By the end, readers will understand how QKD and PQC together form the foundation for quantum-safe communication, ensuring long-term confidentiality and trust in an era of quantum computing.

Basics of quantum cryptography

Quantum cryptography represents one of the most groundbreaking applications of quantum mechanics to modern information security. Traditional encryption techniques rely on the difficulty of certain computations, such as factoring large numbers to protect data, assuming that these computations are practically impossible within reasonable time limits. Quantum cryptography challenges that notion by anchoring security in the laws of physics themselves rather than computational limits.

By exploiting uniquely quantum phenomena: superposition, entanglement, and the no-cloning theorem quantum cryptography guarantees that any attempt to intercept or observe a transmitted quantum state inevitably alters it. This natural detectability of intrusion forms the foundation of unconditional security, a feature no classical cryptographic method can claim.

In essence, while classical systems rely on unproven mathematical assumptions, quantum cryptography secures information through the fundamental behavior of nature.

Transition to quantum security

Classical cryptography secures today's digital systems using schemes such as RSA, DH, and ECC, which depend on the classical difficulty of problems like integer factorization and discrete logarithms. The emergence of Shor's algorithm threatens these foundations, as a sufficiently powerful quantum computer could efficiently solve such problems, undermining modern encryption.

Quantum cryptography adopts a fundamentally different model by relying on physical laws rather than computational hardness. Any attempt to measure or interfere with a quantum system introduces detectable disturbances, enabling real-time identification of eavesdropping and providing security rooted in the principles of quantum mechanics.

The following table outlines the key differences between classical and quantum cryptography, highlighting their contrasting security foundations and attack resistance:

Aspect	Classical cryptography	Quantum cryptography
Security basis	Mathematical complexity (e.g., factoring)	Laws of quantum mechanics
Guarantee type	Conditional—depends on computational limits	Unconditional—rooted in physics
Key exchange	Public-key systems [RSA, ECC, DH]	QKD
Eavesdropping detection	Absent; interception undetectable	Always detectable via state disturbance
Resistance to quantum attacks	Vulnerable to Shor and Grover algorithms	Immune by design

Table 12.1: *Comparison between classical and quantum cryptographic paradigms*

The following figure visually contrasts classical and quantum cryptography, showing how quantum approaches provide stronger, physics-based security than classical, computation-based methods:

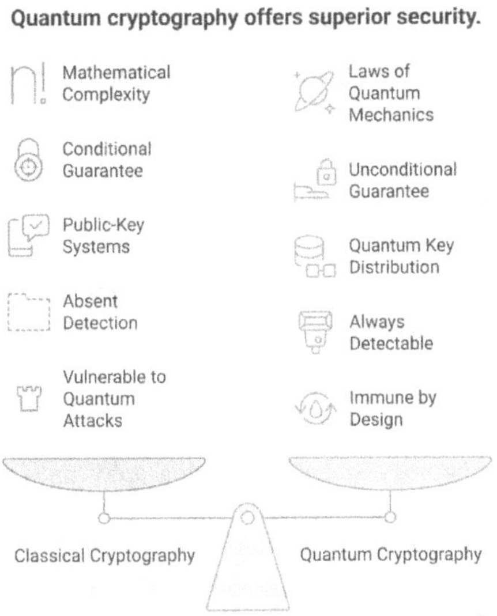

***Figure 12.1**: Classical and quantum cryptography security comparison*

Core principles of quantum cryptography

Quantum cryptography is fundamentally rooted in the laws of quantum mechanics rather than computational assumptions. Its security arises from intrinsic physical properties that govern the behavior of quantum systems.

The power of quantum cryptography stems from a few simple yet profound physical properties:

- **Superposition**: A qubit exists in a combination of $|0\rangle$ and $|1\rangle$, and measurement collapses it, exposing interception.
- **Measurement disturbance**: Observing a quantum state inevitably alters it, revealing eavesdropping through increased errors.
- **No-cloning theorem**: Unknown quantum states cannot be copied, preventing duplication attacks.
- **Entanglement**: Strong correlations between entangled qubits enable secure shared information.
- **Quantum randomness**: Quantum measurements generate truly unpredictable keys.

Together, these principles create a communication system that not only hides data but also exposes any unauthorized observation.

Components of a quantum cryptography system

A complete quantum cryptographic system consists of both physical hardware and logical protocol elements that function together to enable secure key exchange. Unlike traditional cryptographic frameworks, which rely solely on mathematical transformations, quantum cryptography integrates quantum transmission with classical coordination to detect and mitigate potential attacks.

A practical quantum cryptographic setup integrates both quantum and classical communication channels. The quantum channel carries information as individual photons, while the classical channel supports coordination and error correction.

The following table lists the main components of a quantum cryptographic system and briefly describes their roles in secure key distribution:

Component	Role and description
Quantum channel	Optical fiber or free-space link that transmits qubits encoded in photon states.
Classical channel	Publicly accessible medium for discussing measurement bases, errors, and key validation.
Sender (Alice)	Prepares and transmits photons representing bits in randomly chosen bases.
Receiver (Bob)	Measures each photon using randomly selected bases and records outcomes.
Eavesdropper (Eve)	Attempts interception; her measurements disturb quantum states, increasing the error rate.

Table 12.2: *Essential components in a quantum cryptographic communication system*

Advantages and limitations

As with any emerging security technology, quantum cryptography presents a combination of transformative benefits and practical constraints. While its security foundation is rooted in fundamental physical laws, real-world deployment requires addressing engineering, scalability, and cost considerations.

Quantum cryptography offers revolutionary security benefits, but its deployment also involves non-trivial technical challenges. The following table highlights the key advantages and limitations of quantum cryptography in practical communication systems:

Advantages	Limitations
Provides provably secure key exchange through QKD.	Requires specialized hardware (single-photon sources and detectors).
Detects any eavesdropping attempt automatically.	Signal loss and noise limit transmission distance (≈ 100–200 km via fiber).
Immune to quantum-computer attacks.	Equipment cost and maintenance remain high.
Enables long-term data confidentiality and authenticity.	Integration with classical networks requires careful engineering.

Table 12.3: *Advantages and limitations of quantum cryptography in secure communication systems*

Real-world implementations

Rapid progress in quantum communication technologies, particularly in single-photon generation, detection mechanisms, and optical transmission systems, has made it possible to implement quantum cryptographic protocols outside laboratory environments. These technological developments have encouraged governments, research laboratories, and telecommunications providers to experiment with secure quantum communication infrastructures in real-world networking scenarios.

Quantum cryptography has evolved from theory to reality. Several nations and industries have successfully demonstrated operational systems:

- **Fiber-based QKD links**: Deployed in metropolitan networks such as *Tokyo, Beijing,* and *Geneva,* supporting secure communication for banks and research institutions.
- **Satellite-based QKD**: *China Micius* satellite achieved intercontinental quantum key exchange, proving the feasibility of global-scale quantum communication.
- **Quantum network pilots**: Ongoing efforts—such as the *Beijing–Shanghai* backbone and *Europe EuroQCI* initiative—aim to create multi-node, continent-spanning quantum-secure infrastructure.

Quantum key distribution

At the heart of quantum cryptography lies QKD, a pioneering method that enables two parties to share a secret encryption key with absolute security, even over an insecure communication channel. Unlike conventional key exchange mechanisms that rely on mathematical problems, QKD derives its protection from the fundamental laws of quantum physics, ensuring that any attempt to intercept or observe the key becomes immediately detectable.

In practice, QKD allows two legitimate users—traditionally called Alice (the sender) and Bob (the receiver) to establish a shared random key using single-photons as carriers of information. If an eavesdropper (Eve) attempts to measure these photons, the act of observation will disturb their quantum state, revealing her intrusion. Once Alice and Bob confirm that their communication was free from tampering, the key they share can be used for secure encryption through classical algorithms such as the one-time pad or **Advanced Encryption Standard** (**AES**).

Fundamental concept and working principle

The purpose of QKD is not to transmit the encrypted message itself, but to generate and securely distribute a random secret key. This key can then be used in standard symmetric encryption.

A QKD session typically follows five essential stages. The following table summarizes the key stages of a QKD session, showing how quantum and classical operations work together to generate a secure shared key:

Stage	Quantum operation	Classical operation	Purpose
1. **Preparation**	Alice prepares qubits in random quantum states (bases).	—	Encode random bit values into photons.
2. **Transmission**	Qubits are sent through a quantum channel to Bob.	—	Deliver encoded quantum information.
3. **Measurement**	Bob measures each qubit using random bases.	—	Retrieve probabilistic bit outcomes.
4. **Sifting**	—	Alice and Bob publicly compare the bases used.	Keep only bits where bases match.
5. **Key distillation**	—	Apply error correction and privacy amplification.	Obtain the final shared secret key.

Table 12.4: *Typical workflow of a QKD process*

The following figure illustrates the main stages of the QKD process from qubit preparation to final key distillation:

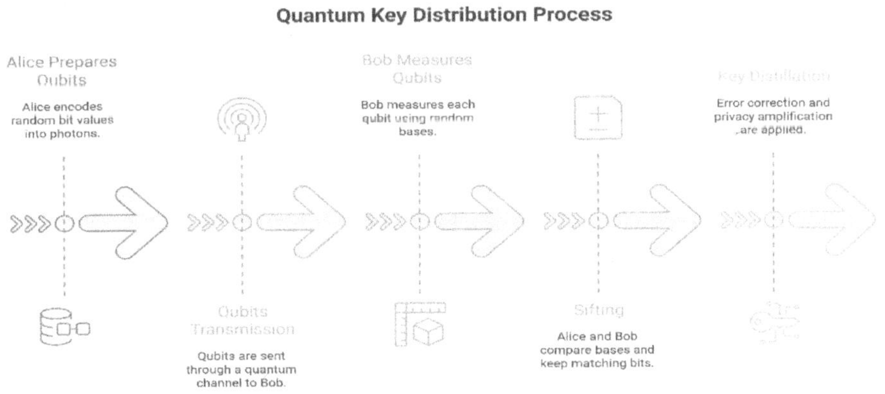

Figure 12.2: *QKD process overview*

Once the key is generated and verified, both users can confidently use it for secure communication, knowing that any eavesdropper would have been detected during transmission.

Security principles of QKD

QKD achieves security by leveraging the fundamental laws of quantum mechanics rather than relying on computational complexity. Unlike classical cryptographic systems, whose security depends on the difficulty of solving mathematical problems, QKD ensures that any attempt to intercept the transmitted quantum states inevitably leaves detectable traces in the communication channel.

The strength of QKD arises from three fundamental quantum principles:

- **No-cloning theorem**: It is impossible to create a perfect copy of an unknown quantum state. Eve cannot duplicate qubits without altering them.
- **Measurement disturbance**: Measuring a quantum state collapses it. Any observation by Eve inevitably changes the qubit's state, producing detectable anomalies.
- **Random basis selection**: Both Alice and Bob use randomly chosen measurement bases. Eve cannot correctly predict or align her basis choices, and her random guesses lead to measurable discrepancies.

Security in QKD is quantified through the **quantum bit error rate** (**QBER**), the proportion of mismatched bits detected after transmission.

If QBER $\leq 11\%$, communication is considered secure (noise within acceptable limits).

If QBER $> 11\%$, the key is discarded, as eavesdropping is highly probable.

Common QKD protocols

Over the years, several QKD protocols have been proposed, each refining the method of encoding and verifying quantum information. The following table presents some of the most widely used QKD protocols, outlining their core ideas, encoding methods, and practical applications in secure communication systems:

Protocol	Key idea	Encoding method	Practical use
BB84	First and foundational QKD protocol; uses random polarization bases.	Polarization or phase encoding.	Standard for most experimental and commercial systems.
Ekert 1991 (Ekert)	Based on quantum entanglement and Bell inequality violation.	Entangled photon pairs.	Used in quantum network and research experiments.
Bennett, 1992 (B92)	Simplified protocol using only two non-orthogonal states.	Minimal state encoding.	Useful for hardware-constrained systems.
Decoy-State QKD	Introduces variable photon intensities to detect multi-photon attacks.	Intensity modulation.	Enables secure long-distance QKD over optical fibers.

***Table 12.5**: Representative QKD protocols and their applications*

Hardware components in a QKD system

Implementing a QKD system requires specialized photonic and communication hardware capable of generating, transmitting, and measuring quantum states with high precision. These components work together to ensure that quantum information is exchanged reliably between the communicating parties while preserving the integrity of the quantum signals.

Practical implementation of QKD requires sophisticated optical components and precise synchronization between the sender and receiver. A standard setup includes:

- **Photon source**: Generates single or weak coherent photons to represent qubits.
- **Polarization or phase modulator**: Encodes classical bits into quantum states.
- **Quantum channel**: Fiber-optic or free-space link that transmits photons securely.
- **Single-photon detectors**: Measure incoming photons and record their states.
- **Classical channel**: Supports public discussion for basis comparison, error estimation, and post-processing.

In real-world scenarios, hardware imperfections, such as photon loss or detector inefficiency can affect reliability. However, these issues are typically mitigated using error correction and privacy amplification techniques during the key distillation phase.

Limitations and practical challenges

Despite its strong theoretical security guarantees, the deployment of QKD in real communication networks introduces several technical and operational challenges. These challenges arise from physical limitations of quantum signals, infrastructure requirements, and the complexity of integrating quantum communication systems with existing network architectures.

While QKD provides theoretically unbreakable security, it faces several practical and engineering challenges that must be addressed before widespread adoption:

- **Distance constraints**: Photon loss limits fiber-based QKD links to around 100–200 km.
- **High deployment costs**: Specialized equipment, such as single-photon detectors, remains expensive.
- **Integration complexity**: Combining QKD with existing communication infrastructure requires protocol-level standardization.
- **Side-channel vulnerabilities**: Hardware imperfections can leak information (e.g., detector timing attacks).

Ongoing research in **measurement-device-independent QKD** (**MDI-QKD**) and quantum repeaters aims to overcome these challenges, extending the practical range and reliability of quantum-secure communication.

BB84 protocol simulation with Python and Qiskit

While the earlier sections introduced the theoretical foundations of QKD, this section moves from concept to practice by exploring its most celebrated implementation, the BB84 protocol. Proposed by *Charles Bennett* and *Gilles Brassard* in 1984, BB84 remains the cornerstone of secure quantum communication.

Here, we examine both the logic and the practical workflow of BB84 and simulate it using Python and Qiskit. Through this exercise, readers will observe how two parties, Alice (the sender) and Bob (the receiver), can establish a shared secret key by exchanging qubits while detecting any eavesdropping attempt from Eve.

By the end of this section, you will understand the BB84 protocol end-to-end and gain hands-on experience in implementing it with Qiskit, bridging the gap between quantum theory and real-world experimentation.

Overview of the BB84 protocol

The BB84 protocol was the first to show that the laws of quantum mechanics alone can ensure secure key distribution. It uses polarized photons (or equivalent qubit states) transmitted in two different bases:

- **Rectilinear (+) basis**: $|0\rangle$ and $|1\rangle$
- **Diagonal (×) basis**: $|+\rangle = (|0\rangle + |1\rangle)/\sqrt{2}$ and $|-\rangle = (|0\rangle - |1\rangle)/\sqrt{2}$

Alice sends a random sequence of qubits encoded in these bases, and Bob measures them using his own randomly chosen bases. Afterward, they publicly compare which bases they used (not the bit values) and keep only the bits measured with matching bases—forming the sifted key.

If an eavesdropper (Eve) interferes, her measurement disturbs the qubits, producing detectable errors. By checking a small sample of bits, Alice and Bob can estimate the QBER to confirm whether the channel is secure.

Algorithmic workflow

To understand how QKD functions in practice, it is helpful to examine the sequence of operations performed during the protocol. The workflow combines quantum state transmission with classical communication steps to generate and verify a shared secret key.

The BB84 protocol operates through a sequence of well-defined steps that combine quantum and classical processes to establish a secure shared key. Each stage plays a specific role in detecting any eavesdropping attempt while maintaining synchronization between the sender and receiver.

The following table outlines these key steps in the BB84 workflow, summarizing their operations and purposes in the overall key distribution process:

Step	Operation	Purpose
1. **Key generation**	Alice chooses random bit values and random bases.	Introduces quantum randomness.
2. **Quantum transmission**	Alice encodes each bit as a photon/qubit and sends it.	Transfers information through the quantum channel.
3. **Measurement**	Bob measures each received qubit using random bases.	Retrieves probabilistic bit outcomes.
4. **Basis reconciliation**	Over a classical channel, Alice and Bob compare bases and discard mismatches.	Produces the sifted key.
5. **Error checking and distillation**	They test a small subset for errors, then apply corrections and privacy amplification.	Derive the final shared key.

Table 12.6: *Step-by-step summary of the BB84 workflow*

The following figure illustrates the complete BB84 QKD workflow, showing how quantum and classical processes combine to generate a shared secret key between Alice and Bob:

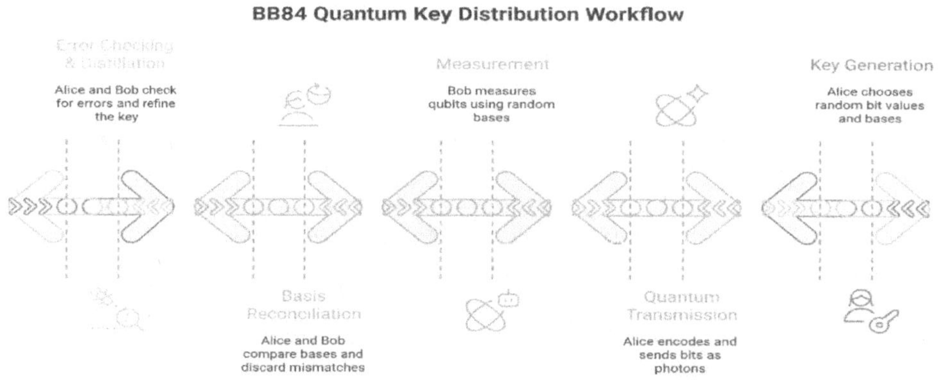

Figure 12.3: *BB84 QKD workflow stages*

Simulating BB84 in Python using Qiskit

To reinforce the BB84 workflow with a hands-on demonstration, the following example uses Qiskit's local simulator to model the core steps of encoding, measurement with random bases, and key sifting. This simulation represents an idealized scenario and is intended to help readers understand how basis alignment affects the final sifted key.

The following Python script simulates the BB84 process on Qiskit's local simulator:

```
# BB84 Simulation using Qiskit
from qiskit import QuantumCircuit, Aer, execute
import numpy as np
n = 16
rng = np.random.default_rng()
alice_bits = rng.integers(0, 2, n)
alice_bases = rng.integers(0, 2, n)  # 0 = rectilinear, 1 = diagonal
bob_bases   = rng.integers(0, 2, n)
```

```
backend = Aer.get_backend("qasm_simulator")
bob_results = []
for bit, a_basis, b_basis in zip(alice_bits, alice_bases, bob_bases):
    qc = QuantumCircuit(1, 1)
    if a_basis == 1: qc.h(0)
    if bit == 1: qc.x(0)
    if b_basis == 1: qc.h(0)
    qc.measure(0, 0)
    job = execute(qc, backend, shots=1, memory=True)
    bob_results.append(int(job.result().get_memory()[0]))
sift_mask = (alice_bases == bob_bases)
alice_sifted = alice_bits[sift_mask]
bob_sifted   = np.array(bob_results)[sift_mask]
print("Raw bits transmitted:", n)
print("Sifted key length:", len(alice_sifted))
print("Sifted key (Alice):", alice_sifted)
print("Sifted key (Bob):  ", bob_sifted)
```

In an ideal, noise-free simulation, Alice's and Bob's sifted keys match perfectly.

Modeling the eavesdropper Eve

To demonstrate how BB84 detects interception, the simulation can be extended with a simple eavesdropping strategy known as **intercept–resend**. In this attack, Eve measures each qubit using a randomly chosen basis and then prepares and forwards a new qubit based on her measurement outcome. It is because Eve does not know Alice's encoding basis that her intervention introduces errors that appear as an increased QBER when Alice and Bob compare a subset of their sifted key.

The following extension models an intercept-resend eavesdropper. Eve randomly measures and resends qubits, causing a measurable increase in QBER:

```
# Eve intercept-resend simulation
eve_bases = rng.integers(0, 2, n)
bob_results_eve = []
for bit, a_basis, e_basis, b_basis in zip(alice_bits, alice_bases, eve_bases, bob_bases):
    qc = QuantumCircuit(1, 1)
    if a_basis == 1: qc.h(0)
    if bit == 1: qc.x(0)
    # Eve measures
    if e_basis == 1: qc.h(0)
    qc.measure(0, 0)
    job = execute(qc, backend, shots=1, memory=True)
    eve_bit = int(job.result().get_memory()[0])
    # Eve resends
    qc = QuantumCircuit(1, 1)
    if e_basis == 1: qc.h(0)
    if eve_bit == 1: qc.x(0)
    if b_basis == 1: qc.h(0)
    qc.measure(0, 0)
    job = execute(qc, backend, shots=1, memory=True)
    bob_results_eve.append(int(job.result().get_memory()[0]))
sift_mask = (alice_bases == bob_bases)
alice_sifted = alice_bits[sift_mask]
```

```
bob_sifted_eve = np.array(bob_results_eve)[sift_mask]
qber = np.mean(alice_sifted != bob_sifted_eve)
print("Quantum Bit Error Rate (with Eve):", round(float(qber), 2))
```

Typical results show QBER ≈ 0.25, demonstrating that eavesdropping introduces a distinct, measurable error rate.

Sifted key to secret key transformation

The sifted key obtained after basis reconciliation may still contain transmission errors and potential information leakage due to noise or adversarial interference. Therefore, additional classical post-processing steps are required to ensure that both communicating parties obtain identical keys while eliminating any partial knowledge that an eavesdropper might possess.

Once Alice and Bob establish their sifted keys, they refine them through classical post-processing:

- **Error correction (information reconciliation)**: Align mismatched bits via parity checks.
- **Privacy amplification**: Apply universal hash functions to remove any partial knowledge an adversary might hold.
- **Authentication**: Verify message integrity using previously shared secret bits.

The outcome is a final secret key that is provably secure against all known attacks—classical or quantum.

Post-quantum cryptography challenges

While QKD offers security grounded in physical laws, most current digital systems still rely on classical cryptography such as RSA, DH, and ECC, which secure applications like online banking, **virtual private networks (VPNs)**, and blockchains. Their security depends on computational hardness—an assumption increasingly threatened by quantum computing.

PQC addresses this risk by developing new mathematical algorithms that run efficiently on classical computers while remaining secure against quantum attacks. Unlike QKD, PQC does not require specialized quantum hardware, making it more practical for large-scale deployment.

This section examines how quantum computing endangers existing encryption, introduces major families of PQC algorithms under standardization, and discusses the technical and organizational challenges of migration—highlighting a future where cybersecurity evolves through quantum-resilient algorithms alongside quantum communication technologies.

Quantum threat to classical encryption

For decades, digital security has rested on the assumption that some mathematical issues are infeasible to solve within any practical timeframe. Algorithms such as RSA, DH, and ECC depend on the hardness of integer factorization and discrete logarithms. However, with *Shor's algorithm* (1994), a powerful quantum computer could solve these problems in polynomial time, effectively dismantling modern public-key cryptography.

Grover's algorithm (1996) further compounds the threat by accelerating brute-force attacks, cutting the effective key strength of symmetric ciphers in half, making AES-256 comparable to AES-128 under quantum attack.

This looming reality defines the post-quantum era, where classical cryptography can no longer guarantee long-term confidentiality.

Understanding post-quantum cryptography

PQC develops encryption and signature schemes designed to resist both classical and quantum attacks while remaining deployable on existing hardware. Instead of relying on number-theoretic problems, PQC leverages alternative mathematical challenges with no known efficient quantum algorithms.

The following table summarizes the main families of post-quantum cryptographic algorithms, highlighting their representative schemes, underlying principles, and key advantages and limitations:

Cryptographic family	Representative schemes	Core idea	Strengths/limitations
Lattice-based	CRYSTALS-Kyber, Dilithium, FALCON	Security from high-dimensional lattice problems (LWE, SIS)	Efficient and versatile; moderate key sizes
Code-based	Classic McEliece	Based on error-correcting code decoding.	Long-term proven security; very large keys
Hash-based	SPHINCS+	Relies on one-way hash functions.	Simple and robust; slower signatures
Multivariate-polynomial	Rainbow (deprecated)	Solving nonlinear polynomial equations.	Compact signatures; some variants broken
Isogeny-based	SIKE (compromised 2022)	Hardness of elliptic curve isogenies.	Elegant theory; currently insecure

Table 12.7: *Major families of post-quantum cryptographic schemes*

Global standardization and industry momentum

To coordinate a global migration toward quantum-resistant security, the U.S. **National Institute of Standards and Technology** (**NIST**) launched an open competition in 2016.

After multiple evaluation rounds, the final selections (announced in 2024) are:

- **CRYSTALS-Kyber (FIPS 203)**: Standard for **key encapsulation mechanism**s (**KEMs**).
- **CRYSTALS-Dilithium (FIPS 204)**: Standard for digital signatures.
- **FALCON and SPHINCS**+: Designated as alternate signature schemes.

Parallel developments are underway worldwide:

- **European Union (ENISA)**: Building PQC migration frameworks for critical infrastructure.
- **India (Quantum Enabled Science and Technology (QuEST) initiative and National Quantum Mission (NQM))**: Supporting indigenous **research and development** (**R&D**) in PQC and quantum communication.
- **Japan and South Korea**: Integrating PQC algorithms into **Transport Layer Security** (**TLS**) 1.3, VPN, and 5G frameworks.

Implementation and migration challenges

Transitioning to PQC requires careful planning because many current security protocols were designed around classical cryptographic assumptions. As organizations prepare for a future where quantum computers may threaten existing encryption methods, upgrading cryptographic infrastructure must be done in a gradual and coordinated manner to ensure compatibility, security, and operational continuity.

Migrating to PQC is far more than a software update; it impacts every layer of global IT infrastructure. The following table outlines key infrastructure layers affected by the transition to PQC, along with their primary challenges and notable global initiatives addressing them:

Layer	Key challenge	Example initiative
Applications [TLS, Secure Shell (SSH), public-key infrastructure (PKI)]	Larger keys and slower handshakes affect performance.	Google–Cloudflare CECPQ2 hybrid TLS pilot.
Networks and (VPNs)	Firmware and hardware acceleration must support new primitives.	Cisco Quantum-Safe VPN project.

IoT and edge devices	Memory and power constraints hinder the implementation of PQC.	NIST Lightweight PQC program.
Enterprise and government	Certification, compliance, and staff training gaps.	NSA CNSA 2.0 Suite mandating quantum-resistant algorithms.

Table 12.8: *Real-world migration layers and global pilot programs*

Additional challenges include:

- **Performance overheads**: Larger keys increase bandwidth and storage demands.
- **Interoperability gaps**: Legacy protocols require hybrid extensions to support PQC.
- **Side-channel vulnerabilities**: Hardware implementations must prevent timing and power leaks.
- **Education and awareness**: Developers and administrators must learn new cryptographic paradigms.

Bridging quantum and classical worlds

As quantum technologies continue to evolve, modern security strategies increasingly consider a hybrid approach that integrates both quantum-based and classical cryptographic mechanisms. Rather than replacing existing systems entirely, this approach combines the strengths of quantum communication methods with advances in post-quantum algorithm design to build more resilient security architectures.

PQC and quantum cryptography address different aspects of security, yet complement one another perfectly:

- QKD secures the key exchange process using the physics of quantum mechanics.
- PQC secures data through quantum-resistant algorithms for encryption and authentication.

Together, they form a dual-layer defense that protects information both physically and mathematically.

Applications in secure communication

As quantum computing advances, securing communication networks has become a strategic necessity, as quantum threats endanger the foundations of digital trust across finance, government, healthcare, and critical infrastructure.

Quantum cryptography, especially QKD, provides physics-based security, while PQC strengthens classical systems against quantum attacks. Together, they enable intrusion detection, data protection, and long-term confidentiality.

This section highlights how QKD and PQC are transforming real-world domains—such as finance, defense, telecom, and cloud systems—and how their combined use is shaping a quantum-safe digital ecosystem.

Quantum-secured networks

QKD has emerged as the backbone of next-generation secure communication networks. By integrating quantum channels with classical fiber networks, these systems enable the exchange of encryption keys with provable physical security.

Prominent global deployments include:

- **China's Beijing–Shanghai backbone network**: Over 2,000 km of fiber interconnecting government, finance, and research institutions, forming the world's largest operational quantum network.
- **Tokyo QKD network**: A multi-vendor testbed led by Japan's **National Institute of Information and Communications Technology** (**NICT**), verifying interoperability across commercial systems.
- **EuroQCI**: An EU-wide initiative integrating terrestrial and satellite QKD to achieve continent-scale quantum-secure connectivity by 2030.

Securing financial transactions

Financial institutions manage data whose confidentiality directly influences national and corporate stability. Quantum cryptography enhances this security by providing keys that cannot be intercepted or reconstructed.

Banks and payment networks employ QKD-generated session keys to continuously refresh symmetric encryption, such as AES, preventing long-term key exposure. Notable trials by JPMorgan Chase, Banco Bilbao Vizcaya Argentaria (BBVA), and Chinese financial institutions have shown that QKD-based encryption offers both low latency and high throughput, making it suitable for real-time trading environments.

Government and defense communication

Government and defense sectors are among the earliest adopters of quantum-secure communication technologies due to the critical need to protect sensitive strategic information. Quantum cryptographic systems are increasingly being explored to safeguard military coordination, diplomatic exchanges, and intelligence communication networks against both present-day cyber threats and future quantum enabled attacks.

In military and diplomatic domains, communication secrecy is critical. Quantum technologies offer an unparalleled level of assurance: even a theoretically infinite adversary cannot extract information undetected:

- **India's Defence Research and Development Organisation (DRDO) QKD trials**: Demonstrated 100 km fiber-based secure links between research facilities.
- **U.S. DARPA quantum network**: Among the earliest quantum communication testbeds connecting multiple labs via entanglement.
- **NATO QSC and ESA missions**: Exploring satellite-enabled QKD for secure command channels.

Commercial and industrial adoption

Beyond government and research environments, interest in quantum-secure communication is rapidly expanding across commercial sectors that manage highly sensitive digital information. Organizations operating critical infrastructure and data-intensive services are exploring these technologies to strengthen long-term confidentiality and resilience against emerging cyber threats.

Quantum-secure communication is no longer limited to laboratories. Major industries are incorporating it to safeguard sensitive operational data. The following table presents key industry sectors adopting quantum-secure communication, illustrating practical applications and the advantages achieved through their implementation:

Sector	Application	Advantage
Healthcare	Protection of genomic and patient data in telemedicine and cloud storage.	Ensures compliance with HIPAA and GDPR.
Energy grids	Secure command channels between distributed control centers.	Prevents cyber-induced blackouts.
Telecommunications	Quantum-safe 5G/6G backbone encryption.	Provides forward-compatible network confidentiality.
Cloud computing	Integration of QKD-derived keys into data-at-rest encryption.	Enables tamper-proof cloud key management.

***Table 12.9**: Industry applications of quantum-secure communication*

Hybrid cryptographic transition

Given the diversity of modern digital systems and infrastructure, a gradual transition toward quantum-resilient security is considered the most practical strategy. Hybrid cryptographic frameworks allow organizations to integrate emerging quantum-safe mechanisms while maintaining compatibility with existing classical security protocols.

No single cryptographic approach can secure every system. The foreseeable path forward is hybridization, where QKD and PQC operate in tandem:

- **QKD**: Generates keys with physics-guaranteed secrecy.
- **PQC**: Provides authentication and digital signatures immune to quantum algorithms.
- **Classical crypto**: Ensures backward compatibility and speed for legacy systems.

This layered design ensures continuous protection during the global transition from classical to quantum-resilient infrastructure.

Future of quantum-safe communication

The next decade will witness the convergence of quantum and classical networks into integrated quantum-secure ecosystems. Advancements in quantum repeaters, entanglement distribution, and satellite QKD will enable secure, global data exchange—forming the backbone of the quantum internet.

Quantum cryptography, once a theoretical concept, now stands as the foundation of next-generation cybersecurity, ensuring that communication remains confidential not just for years, but for decades to come.

As research and industrial efforts continue to mature, collaboration among governments, academia, and technology providers will play a crucial role in shaping standards, deployment models, and interoperable quantum-secure infrastructures. These coordinated initiatives will help ensure that future communication systems remain resilient against both classical and quantum-enabled cyber threats.

Conclusion

This chapter examined quantum cryptography as a groundbreaking advancement in securing communication through the principles of quantum mechanics. By contrasting it with classical cryptography, we saw how QKD provides unconditional security rooted in physical laws rather than computational complexity. The BB84 protocol, explored in both theory and simulation using Python and Qiskit, demonstrated how secure key exchange can detect and withstand eavesdropping attempts. We also discussed the growing threat posed by quantum computers to conventional encryption and introduced PQC as a complementary safeguard for classical infrastructures. Together, QKD and PQC form the foundation of quantum-safe security, combining physics-based protection with algorithmic resilience. Ultimately, this chapter emphasized that the future of cybersecurity lies in integrating these two paradigms: bridging quantum and classical systems to ensure long-term confidentiality, authenticity, and trust in the era of quantum communication.

Questions

1. **What is quantum cryptography, and how does it differ from classical cryptography?**

   Answer: Quantum cryptography secures communication using the laws of quantum mechanics instead of mathematical complexity. While classical cryptography relies on computational hardness (e.g., factoring large numbers), quantum cryptography ensures security through physical principles such as superposition and measurement disturbance, making eavesdropping inherently detectable.

2. **What is QKD?**

   Answer: QKD is a method that allows two parties to share a secret encryption key using quantum states, usually photons. Its unique feature is that any attempt to intercept or measure the qubits alters their state, alerting the legitimate users to potential eavesdropping.

3. **What makes the BB84 protocol significant in quantum cryptography?**

   Answer: The BB84 protocol, introduced by Bennett and Brassard in 1984, was the first QKD scheme demonstrating that secure key exchange is possible solely through quantum physics. It uses randomly chosen polarization bases to detect eavesdropping and generate a shared secret key.

4. **How can the BB84 protocol be simulated using Python and Qiskit?**

   Answer: In Qiskit, the BB84 protocol can be simulated by encoding qubits in random bases, transmitting them, and performing random measurements. The process shows how Alice and Bob can establish a sifted key while detecting any interference caused by an eavesdropper (Eve).

5. **What is the QBER, and why is it important?**

   Answer: QBER represents the percentage of mismatched bits between Alice and Bob's keys after transmission. A low QBER indicates secure communication, while a high QBER suggests noise or eavesdropping, prompting key rejection.

6. **What are the limitations of practical QKD systems?**

   Answer: QKD systems face challenges such as limited transmission distances (typically 100–200 km in fiber), high equipment costs, and integration issues with classical infrastructure. Research into quantum repeaters and satellite QKD aims to overcome these barriers.

7. **How does PQC differ from quantum cryptography?**

   Answer: PQC focuses on developing new mathematical algorithms that resist attacks from quantum computers while still running on classical hardware. In contrast, quantum cryptography uses quantum hardware and physics-based principles for secure key exchange.

8. **Why are lattice-based algorithms like CRYSTALS-Kyber and Dilithium leading PQC candidates?**

   Answer: Lattice-based algorithms offer strong security backed by hard mathematical problems and are efficient enough for real-world deployment. Their balance of performance, scalability, and theoretical soundness makes them prime candidates for standardization.

9. **How do QKD and PQC complement each other in ensuring quantum-safe security?**

   Answer: QKD provides physical-layer protection through quantum mechanics, while PQC offers software-level defense through quantum-resistant algorithms. Together, they create a layered approach that secures both communication channels and stored data.

10. **What does the future of quantum-secure communication look like?**

    Answer: The future lies in hybrid cryptographic architectures that combine QKD, PQC, and classical encryption. Advancements in satellite QKD, quantum repeaters, and international initiatives like EuroQCI and India's NQM are paving the way for the quantum internet, enabling secure global communication networks.

Exercises

1. Implement the BB84 QKD protocol in Qiskit by generating random qubits, assigning random bases to Alice and Bob, and printing the sifted keys that form their shared secret.
2. Extend the BB84 simulation to include an eavesdropper (Eve) who performs an intercept–resend attack and calculate the QBER to detect intrusion.
3. Demonstrate the no-cloning theorem in Qiskit by attempting to copy an unknown qubit state, showing that measurement collapses it, and proving cloning is impossible.
4. Construct a complete QKD workflow using Python arrays that performs the five stages: preparation, transmission, measurement, sifting, and key distillation—and display the final shared key.
5. Visualize photon polarization states used in QKD by plotting rectilinear (+) and diagonal (×) bases with Matplotlib and explaining how mismatched bases lead to discarded bits.
6. Compare classical and quantum cryptography by creating a table that shows the differences in key exchange, security basis, and resistance to quantum attacks.

7. Simulate a noisy quantum channel in BB84 by introducing bit-flip errors and plotting how increasing noise affects the QBER and overall key reliability.
8. Research any NIST-approved PQC algorithm, such as CRYSTALS-Kyber or Dilithium, and summarize its mathematical foundation and security advantages.
9. Design a hybrid cryptographic architecture combining QKD and PQC to illustrate how physical and mathematical defenses work together in quantum-safe communication.
10. Write a 200-word reflection on quantum-safe communication, explaining how quantum cryptography and PQC ensure long-term data security in the quantum era.

Chapter 13
Quantum Machine Learning

Introduction

As **artificial intelligence** (**AI**) continues to evolve, the frontier of computational innovation is now being shaped by its intersection with quantum computing. Traditional **machine learning** (**ML**) systems rely on classical processors to identify patterns and optimize predictions, yet they face inherent limitations when handling exponentially large datasets or deeply nonlinear relationships. Quantum computing offers a transformative alternative, operating through principles such as superposition, entanglement, and interference to explore solution spaces far beyond classical reach.

Quantum ML (**QML**) emerges at this intersection, combining the data-driven adaptability of AI with the powerful representational capacity of quantum mechanics. In QML, information is encoded in quantum states, manipulated by **parameterized quantum circuits** (**PQCs**), and optimized using hybrid algorithms that seamlessly integrate with classical learning frameworks. This synergy enables models to capture complex correlations with fewer parameters and potentially achieve exponential speed-ups for certain tasks.

This chapter introduces the foundations and practical applications of QML, emphasizing implementation through PennyLane and PyTorch. Readers will explore key topics such as quantum data encoding methods, building quantum classifiers, and designing hybrid classical–quantum architectures, culminating in a hands-on binary classification case study. The chapter concludes with an overview of emerging QML applications across domains such as finance, healthcare, and data science, highlighting their growing real-world relevance.

By bridging classical and quantum paradigms, QML represents a critical step toward the next-generation of intelligent systems—where computation and cognition intertwine at the quantum level to drive unprecedented performance and discovery.

Structure

The chapter covers the following topics:

- Quantum data encoding methods
- Building quantum classifiers with PennyLane and PyTorch
- Hybrid classical–quantum models
- Case study: Binary classification task
- Applications of QML in AI and data science

Objectives

This chapter introduces QML as the convergence of AI and quantum computation, where quantum principles such as superposition, entanglement, and interference enhance learning and pattern recognition. Readers will learn how classical data is encoded into qubits using basis, amplitude, and angle encoding techniques, forming the foundation for quantum models. The chapter guides learners through building and training quantum classifiers and hybrid classical–quantum models using PennyLane and PyTorch, demonstrating how data encoding learn complex relationships within data. A practical binary classification case study illustrates the full QML workflow, from encoding to optimization. Finally, readers will explore real-world applications of QML across finance, healthcare, and data science. By the end, they will understand how QML bridges classical AI and quantum computing, unlocking new pathways for intelligent, high-performance learning systems.

Quantum data encoding methods

In classical ML, information is expressed in numerical form vectors, matrices, and tensors that capture measurable features of data. Quantum computing, however, operates on an entirely different foundation. Instead of manipulating numbers directly, quantum algorithms act on quantum states, which exist in a continuous, complex space governed by superposition and entanglement.

To make classical data compatible with this framework, we must first transform it into quantum form. This process, known as quantum data encoding or feature mapping, determines how numerical information is represented within qubits. The effectiveness of this mapping profoundly influences a quantum model's ability to learn patterns, generalize from examples, and exploit the unique computational advantages of quantum mechanics.

In essence, quantum data encoding bridges the classical world of information and the quantum world of computation. The quality of this bridge directly affects both performance and interpretability. In this section, we explore several encoding strategies—basis encoding, amplitude encoding, angle (rotation) encoding, and hybrid (entanglement-based) encoding, each offering a distinct balance between simplicity, expressiveness, and hardware feasibility.

Importance of encoding

Quantum algorithms rely on state preparation as their first and most crucial step. Every computation begins by embedding data into quantum states, which then evolve under controlled gate operations. The way these states are initialized, i.e., how we encode the data, determines the model's learning capacity and computational reach.

An ideal encoding should achieve three goals:

- **Efficiency**: Representing large datasets with minimal qubits and shallow circuit depth.
- **Expressivity**: Enabling the circuit to represent rich, nonlinear relationships between features.
- **Trainability**: Allowing smooth parameter updates during optimization without vanishing gradients.

To put it simply, encoding defines the quantum model's language of understanding. If the encoding is too simple, the model may fail to learn complex patterns; if it is too intricate, the circuit may become too noisy or unstable to train effectively.

Basis encoding

Basis encoding is the most direct and intuitive method of embedding classical data into quantum states. In this approach, each binary feature (0 or 1) of a classical vector is mapped to a qubit's computational basis state:

$$0| \ |0\rangle, 1| \ |1\rangle$$

The full vector is represented by the tensor product of all qubit states, forming a multi-qubit basis state such as $|101\rangle$.

This method reflects the binary structure of digital information and is especially suitable for representing categorical or logical data.

The mathematical representation is as follows:

$$|x\rangle = |x_0 x_1 \ldots x_{n-1}\rangle, x_i \in \{0,1\}$$

Each qubit begins in the $|0\rangle$ state and is flipped to $|1\rangle$ using a Pauli-X gate whenever the corresponding feature equals 1.

The following is an implementation example:

```
import pennylane as qml
from pennylane import numpy as np
dev = qml.device("default.qubit", wires=3)
@qml.qnode(dev)
def basis_encoding(bits):
    for i, bit in enumerate(bits):
        if bit == 1:
            qml.PauliX(wires=i)
    return qml.state()
data = [1, 0, 1]
print(basis_encoding(data))
```

This circuit initializes three-qubits and applies Pauli-X gates to the first and third qubits, generating the quantum state $|101\rangle$.

The advantages of this approach are as follows:

- Extremely simple and transparent representation.
- Minimal gate count and low noise sensitivity.
- Ideal for binary or Boolean datasets.

The following are the limitations:

- Requires one-qubit per bit—inefficient for large datasets.
- Cannot represent continuous-valued data without prior discretization.

Amplitude encoding

Amplitude encoding represents a more compact and elegant approach. Instead of assigning one-qubit to each feature, it encodes an entire vector of classical values into the amplitudes of a quantum state. Through superposition, a small number of qubits can capture exponentially large data spaces.

In this scheme, the features of a normalized vector x determine the probability amplitudes of the quantum state:

$$|\psi\rangle = \sum_{i=0}^{2^n-1} x_i \, | \, i\rangle, \text{where} \sum_i |x_i|^2 = 1$$

This allows a system of only n qubits to represent 2^n features.

The following is an implementation example:

```
import pennylane as qml
from pennylane import numpy as np
dev = qml.device("default.qubit", wires=3)
@qml.qnode(dev)
def amplitude_encoding(data):
    qml.AmplitudeEmbedding(features=data, wires=range(3), normalize=True)
    return qml.state()
data = np.array([0.5, 0.1, 0.4, 0.2, 0.3, 0.7, 0.1, 0.1])
print(amplitude_encoding(data))
```

Here, a three-qubit circuit encodes eight features in the system's amplitude space, using quantum superposition to represent multidimensional data compactly.

The advantages of this method are as follows:

- Encodes high-dimensional data with exponential efficiency.
- Makes full use of the quantum state's amplitude space.
- Theoretically ideal for large-scale feature representation.

The limitations are as follows:

- State preparation circuits can be complex and hardware-intensive.
- Sensitive to noise and requires precise normalization.
- Currently more practical for simulation than for physical devices.

Angle or rotation encoding

Angle encoding, also known as **rotation encoding**, is one of the most practical and widely used data embedding methods for current quantum devices. Instead of storing data in amplitudes, it translates each classical feature into a rotation angle that acts on a qubit's statevector.

For instance, a feature value x_i can be encoded by rotating a qubit around the y-axis:

$$|\psi(x_i)\rangle = R_Y(x_i)|0\rangle$$

The resulting position of the qubit on the Bloch sphere represents the encoded value geometrically.

The following is an implementation example:

```
import pennylane as qml
from pennylane import numpy as np
dev = qml.device("default.qubit", wires=3)
@qml.qnode(dev)
def angle_encoding(data):
    for i, value in enumerate(data):
        qml.RY(value, wires=i)
    return qml.state()
data = np.array([0.2, 1.0, 0.6])
print(angle_encoding(data))
```

Each rotation corresponds to a feature value, embedding numerical information as qubit orientations on the Bloch sphere.

The following are the advantages of this encoding technique:

- Hardware-efficient and natively supported on most quantum processors.
- Smoothly differentiable, ideal for gradient-based optimization.
- Produces shallow circuits, suitable for **noisy-intermediate scale quantum** (**NISQ**)-era computation.

The limitations are as follows:

- One-qubit required per feature.
- No inherent inter-feature correlation (must be added through entanglement).
- Feature values must be appropriately scaled within a limited range.

Hybrid and entanglement-based encodings

Hybrid encoding schemes combine multiple encoding strategies to capture both feature magnitude and correlation. By introducing entanglement between qubits, they create intricate interdependencies among features that mimic nonlinear interactions in classical neural networks.

For example, an encoding circuit might first apply angle rotations to represent individual features, then use CNOT or CZ gates to entangle qubits, allowing information to spread across the quantum system.

The following is an implementation example:

```
@qml.qnode(dev)
def hybrid_encoding(data):
    # Step 1 - Apply angle encoding
    for i, val in enumerate(data):
        qml.RY(val, wires=i)
    # Step 2 - Add entanglement
    qml.CNOT(wires=[0, 1])
    qml.CNOT(wires=[1, 2])
    return qml.state()
```

This encoding design provides notable strengths for complex data modeling but also introduces specific computational challenges.

The advantages are as follows:

- Captures nonlinear correlations between input features.
- Enhances expressivity without increasing data dimensionality.
- Highly customizable for specific learning tasks.

The limitations are as follows:

- Greater circuit depth and optimization complexity.
- May experience gradient instability in deeper configurations.
- More demanding for error-prone hardware.

Comparative summary

Each encoding approach discussed so far offers a distinct balance between expressivity, efficiency, and hardware feasibility. To consolidate these insights, it is useful to compare their key characteristics side by side and understand where each method best fits within a QML pipeline. The following table compares the main quantum data encoding techniques, outlining their key features and suitable applications:

Encoding type	Features per n qubits	Circuit depth	Expressivity	Hardware feasibility	Typical use
Basis	N	Very low	Low	Excellent	Binary/Categorical data
Amplitude	2^n	High	Very high	Challenging	High-dimensional continuous data
Angle	N	Low	Moderate	Excellent	Continuous features, variational circuits
Hybrid/ Entanglement	Variable	Medium–high	Very high	Moderate	Nonlinear, correlation-driven tasks

***Table 13.1**: Comparison of quantum data encoding techniques*

Building quantum classifiers with PennyLane and PyTorch

Once data have been successfully encoded into quantum states, the next step is to train a quantum circuit to learn from them. This learning process forms the foundation of QML, an emerging discipline in which quantum systems perform tasks traditionally handled by classical algorithms, such as classification, regression, and clustering.

In classical ML, models such as logistic regression or neural networks learn decision boundaries that separate different classes of data. In QML, this idea is implemented using data encoding (PQCs), whose gate parameters are optimized through iterative training. By adjusting rotation angles and entanglement patterns, the quantum circuit effectively becomes a quantum classifier, a system that learns to distinguish between classes encoded in quantum states.

In this section, we will construct a simple yet powerful hybrid quantum-classical classifier using PennyLane and PyTorch, illustrating how both frameworks seamlessly integrate to form an end-to-end learning pipeline.

Concept of quantum classifiers

Quantum classifiers represent an emerging class of ML models that use quantum circuits to perform classification tasks. By exploiting quantum phenomena such as superposition and entanglement, these models can transform input data into higher-dimensional representations, potentially revealing patterns that are difficult to capture using purely classical methods.

At their core, quantum classifiers operate like classical models that map input features to predicted labels, except that the computation happens in a quantum Hilbert space rather than Euclidean space. A quantum classifier generally consists of three major components:

- **Feature encoding**: Classical input data are embedded into quantum states through encoding circuits (as discussed in the previous section).
- **Variational circuit**: A trainable quantum circuit applies parameterized gates and entanglement to transform the encoded states.
- **Measurement and optimization**: The circuit's output probabilities are measured, compared with true labels, and optimized using gradient descent.

The learning process involves repeatedly adjusting the quantum circuit's parameters θ to minimize a cost function, typically the binary cross-entropy loss or **mean squared error** (**MSE**), depending on the task.

Structure of a quantum classifier

A quantum classifier can be viewed as a sequence of transformations that convert classical input data into a measurable quantum output used for prediction. The process typically involves encoding classical features into quantum states, applying a trainable quantum circuit to process the information, and finally measuring the resulting quantum state to obtain a classification outcome.

Let us formalize the structure. Given an input feature vector x, the model performs the following transformations:

$$\mathbf{x} \; \overset{\text{Encoding}}{|} \; |\psi(\mathbf{x})\rangle \; \overset{U(\theta)}{|} \; |\varphi(\mathbf{x},\theta)\rangle \; \overset{\text{Measurement}}{|} \; \hat{y}$$

Here:

- $|\psi(x)\rangle$ represents the encoded quantum state.
- $U(\theta)$ denotes the parameterized quantum circuit.
- $\hat{y}$ is the measured expectation value corresponding to the model's prediction.

During training, the model minimizes the cost function:

$$L(\theta) = \frac{1}{N}\sum_{i=1}^{N} (\hat{y}_i - y_i)^2$$

Where y_i are true labels and $\hat{y}_i$ are quantum predictions.

Building the quantum classifier with PennyLane

PennyLane allows us to define trainable **quantum nodes** (QNodes) that behave like differentiable layers and are fully compatible with PyTorch or TensorFlow optimizers.

Let us begin with a simple two-qubit classifier that uses angle encoding for binary input features:

1. **Import dependencies**:
```
import pennylane as qml
from pennylane import numpy as np
import torch
from torch import nn
import torch.optim as optim
```
2. **Define the quantum device**:
```
n_qubits = 2
dev = qml.device("default.qubit", wires=n_qubits)
```
3. **Construct the QNode**: The following QNode encodes two features into rotation angles and applies a trainable variational layer:
```
@qml.qnode(dev, interface="torch")
def quantum_circuit(inputs, weights):
    # Encoding classical features into qubit rotations
    for i in range(n_qubits):
        qml.RY(inputs[i], wires=i)

    # Adding trainable variational layer
    qml.RY(weights[0], wires=0)
    qml.RY(weights[1], wires=1)
    qml.CNOT(wires=[0, 1])

    # Measurement (expectation value)
    return qml.expval(qml.PauliZ(1))
```
4. **Integrate with PyTorch**: We now wrap this QNode inside a PyTorch layer, allowing it to participate in standard training loops:
```
class QuatumClassifier(nn.Module):
    def __init__(self):
        super().__init__()
        self.weights = nn.Parameter(0.01 * torch.randn(2))

    def forward(self, x):
        return torch.stack([quantum_circuit(x_i, self.weights) for x_i in x])
```
5. **Training the model**: Let us train the model on a small binary dataset (for example, XOR-type data):
```
# Sample dataset
X = torch.tensor([[0., 0.], [0., np.pi/2], [np.pi/2, 0.], [np.pi/2, np.pi/2]])
Y = torch.tensor([[0.], [1.], [1.], [0.]])
# Model and optimizer
model = QuantumClassifier()
optimizer = optim.Adam(model.parameters(), lr=0.1)
loss_fn = nn.MSELoss()
# Training loop
epochs = 30
for epoch in range(epochs):
    optimizer.zero_grad()
    output = model(X)
    loss = loss_fn(output, Y)
```

```
        loss.backward()
        optimizer.step()
        print(f"Epoch {epoch+1}: Loss = {loss.item():.4f}")
```

Over several epochs, the model's parameters are tuned so that the circuit correctly learns to classify input states based on their encoded features.

Understanding the learning process

Training a quantum classifier is conceptually similar to training a neural network—but the learning happens in quantum state space. Each update step slightly modifies the rotation angles or entanglement structure within the quantum circuit. As a result, the shape of the decision boundary evolves not in a linear or planar form, but across multidimensional quantum manifolds defined by interference patterns.

This is one of the reasons QML can potentially surpass classical ML in pattern recognition: the nonlinear transformations occur naturally within quantum mechanics, rather than being explicitly engineered through additional layers or activations.

Advantages and limitations

Every hybrid quantum–classical classifier exhibits unique strengths and trade-offs that influence its effectiveness across different learning scenarios. The following table summarizes the major advantages and limitations of hybrid quantum classifiers based on key aspects such as representation, integration, and scalability:

Aspect	Advantage	Limitation
Representation	Learns nonlinear relationships using fewer parameters.	Requires careful circuit design to avoid barren plateaus.
Integration	Seamlessly integrates with classical ML frameworks.	Gradient noise and hardware errors can hinder convergence.
Scalability	Well-suited for NISQ devices and small datasets.	Large-scale training remains computationally expensive.

***Table 13.2**: Advantages and limitations of hybrid quantum classical classifiers*

Practical considerations

Implementing and training quantum classifiers in real-world scenarios requires careful attention to certain technical and experimental details. These considerations help ensure model stability, reproducibility, and compatibility with available hardware.

The following points outline key practical aspects to keep in mind when designing and deploying hybrid quantum–classical models:

- **Normalization of inputs**: Always normalize feature values to fall within valid rotation ranges (usually 0 to π).
- **Choice of measurement operator**: The observable (e.g., Pauli-Z or Pauli-X) influences the classifier's decision boundary.
- **Optimizer sensitivity**: Quantum circuits may require smaller learning rates due to oscillatory loss landscapes.
- **Hardware deployment**: For real-device execution, replace **`default.qubit`** with **`qiskit.ibmq`** or another hardware backend in PennyLane.

Hybrid classical–quantum models

In most real-world scenarios, the data we work with images, text, financial signals, or sensor readings are far too large and complex to be processed entirely on a quantum device.

At the same time, classical deep learning models have matured, excelling at extracting useful patterns and features from such data.

The natural next step, therefore, is to combine the strengths of both paradigms:

- Classical models perform efficient feature extraction using well-established architectures such as convolutional or dense layers.
- Quantum models handle the higher-level representation learning and decision-making tasks using data encoding.

This combination forms a hybrid classical–quantum model—a system in which classical and quantum components interact seamlessly within a single training loop. Such hybrid systems are not only feasible on today's NISQ hardware but also pave the way toward more powerful quantum-enhanced learning architectures.

In practice, hybrid models typically integrate classical neural networks with quantum circuits through a shared optimization process. Classical components process the input data and pass intermediate representations to the quantum circuit, which performs parameterized transformations and produces measurement outcomes. These outcomes are then fed back into the classical optimizer, enabling end-to-end training using gradient-based methods.

Concept of hybrid learning

In a hybrid model, information flows between the classical and quantum domains in a coordinated fashion. The typical workflow can be summarized as:

- **Classical preprocessing**: Input data (e.g., images or vectors) are scaled, normalized, and possibly reduced in dimension through a classical neural network.
- **Quantum encoding**: The processed features are encoded into qubits using one of the techniques discussed in *Section 13.1* (e.g., angle or amplitude encoding).
- **Quantum computation**: A parameterized quantum circuit acts as a learnable transformation that generates expressive quantum features.
- **Classical postprocessing**: Measurement results from the quantum circuit are fed back into a classical layer to produce the final prediction.

This architecture allows the model to utilize quantum expressivity without being constrained by the limited qubit counts available in current hardware.

Power of hybrid models

Hybrid architectures are valuable because they strike a balance between accessibility and innovation.

The classical portion manages large-scale numerical processing, while the quantum portion introduces non-classical correlations and interference effects that enrich the model's representational space.

In other words, classical components perform what they do best—efficient computation—and quantum circuits add an extra layer of learning capacity that classical models cannot easily replicate.

This synergy allows hybrid models to remain practical on current quantum hardware while still exploring the advantages of quantum-enhanced learning. By combining classical scalability with quantum state transformations, these systems create richer feature representations that may improve performance in certain classification, optimization, and pattern recognition tasks.

Architecture of a hybrid model

A hybrid quantum–classical model integrates conventional neural network layers with data encoding within a single computational pipeline. In this architecture, classical processors handle data preprocessing and intermediate feature transformations, while quantum circuits operate as specialized layers that process encoded quantum states and produce measurement outcomes used for prediction.

A generic hybrid quantum-classical workflow can be visualized as follows:

Input data | Classical layers | Quantum circuit | Output prediction

Each component contributes a distinct function. The following table outlines the key stages in a hybrid quantum–classical workflow, highlighting their primary functions and representative examples:

Stage	Function	Example
Classical frontend	Feature extraction	Dense or convolutional layers
Quantum layer	Nonlinear transformation and entanglement	Parameterized quantum circuit
Classical output layer	Decision or regression	Fully connected neuron

Table 13.3: *Key stages and functions in hybrid quantum classical workflow*

This layered structure ensures full differentiability, allowing both quantum and classical parameters to be jointly optimized using backpropagation.

Implementation example with PennyLane and PyTorch

The following example demonstrates a simple end-to-end hybrid workflow where a small classical network prepares intermediate features, a quantum circuit acts as a learnable layer, and the measured output is passed back to a classical layer for prediction. This compact illustration is intended to clarify how quantum and classical components can be trained together within a single optimization loop.

To illustrate this architecture, let us construct a small hybrid classifier that combines a classical neural network with a quantum circuit:

1. **Define the QNode**:

```
import pennylane as qml
from pennylane import numpy as np
import torch
from torch import nn
import torch.optim as optim
n_qubits = 2
dev = qml.device("default.qubit", wires=n_qubits)
@qml.qnode(dev, interface="torch")
def quantum_layer(inputs, weights):
    # Encode classical outputs into qubit rotations
    for i in range(n_qubits):
        qml.RY(inputs[i], wires=i)

    # Trainable quantum transformation
    qml.CNOT(wires=[0, 1])
    for i in range(n_qubits):
        qml.RY(weights[i], wires=i)
    return qml.expval(qml.PauliZ(1))
```

2. **Combine with classical layers**:

```
class HybridModel(nn.Module):
    def __init__(self):
        super().__init__()
        self.fc1 = nn.Linear(4, 2)  # Classical preprocessing
        self.q_weights = nn.Parameter(0.01 * torch.randn(2))  # Quantum parameters
        self.fc2 = nn.Linear(1, 1)  # Classical output layer
    def forward(self, x):
        x = torch.tanh(self.fc1(x))  # Classical transformation
        q_out = torch.stack([quantum_layer(sample, self.q_weights) for sample in x])
        return torch.sigmoid(self.fc2(q_out.unsqueeze(1)))
```

3. **Training the hybrid model**:

```
# Sample XOR dataset
X = torch.tensor([[0., 0., 0., 0.],
                  [0., np.pi/2, 0., np.pi/2],
                  [np.pi/2, 0., np.pi/2, 0.],
                  [np.pi/2, np.pi/2, np.pi/2, np.pi/2]])
Y = torch.tensor([[0.], [1.], [1.], [0.]])
model = HybridModel()
optimizer = optim.Adam(model.parameters(), lr=0.1)
loss_fn = nn.MSELoss()
for epoch in range(20):
    optimizer.zero_grad()
    output = model(X)
    loss = loss_fn(output, Y)
    loss.backward()
    optimizer.step()
    print(f"Epoch {epoch+1}: Loss = {loss.item():.4f}")
```

This hybrid network passes classical features through a linear layer, encodes them into a quantum circuit, and then feeds the quantum measurement back into a final classical neuron for classification.

Advantages of hybrid architectures

Hybrid architectures combine the strengths of classical and quantum models, enabling efficient learning while leveraging the unique capabilities of both computational paradigms. A comparative view helps clarify how each approach performs across key dimensions of scalability, expressivity, feasibility, and interpretability.

The following table compares the characteristics of classical, quantum, and hybrid models across key performance metrics:

Feature	Classical models	Quantum models	Hybrid models
Scalability	Excellent	Limited by qubits	Moderate, scalable frontend
Expressivity	Moderate	High (nonlinear)	Very high (combined)
Hardware feasibility	Fully mature	Early stage	Near-term practical
Interpretability	High	Moderate	Balanced and tunable

Table 13.4: *Comparison of classical, quantum, and hybrid model characteristics*

Challenges and considerations

Although hybrid quantum–classical models offer a practical pathway for implementing QML on current hardware, their design and deployment require careful consideration of both computational and hardware-related factors.

Developers must balance the capabilities of classical processing with the limitations of available quantum devices to ensure stable and efficient model training.

While hybrid systems are powerful, designing them involves certain challenges:

1. **Interface overhead**: Transferring data between classical and quantum environments can introduce latency.
2. **Gradient noise**: Hybrid training is sensitive to noisy gradients due to stochastic quantum measurements.
3. **Hardware constraints**: Limited qubit counts restrict the number of quantum features that can be encoded.
4. **Model interpretability**: Understanding how classical and quantum layers interact can be non-trivial.

Despite these challenges, hybrid systems remain the most viable near-term solution for deploying QML applications.

Case study: Binary classification task

To connect the concepts of quantum encoding and hybrid architectures with real-world implementation, let us consider a binary classification task, one of the simplest yet most informative experiments in QML.

Binary classification lies at the heart of many practical problems, such as spam detection, medical diagnosis (disease vs. healthy), and sentiment analysis (positive vs. negative). In the quantum setting, it helps us visualize how a PQC learns to separate two classes of data using quantum interference and entanglement.

In this case study, we will build a complete quantum classifier for a two class dataset using PennyLane integrated with PyTorch, showcasing how encoding, circuit design, and optimization work together in a learning loop.

The objective is to train the model so that it can correctly assign class labels based on patterns present in the input features. By iteratively adjusting the parameters of the quantum circuit and the associated classical components, the hybrid model gradually learns a decision boundary that separates the two classes. This example illustrates how quantum circuits can participate in practical ML workflows alongside classical optimization techniques.

Problem overview

Before implementing the classifier, it is helpful to clearly define the objective of the learning task and the sequence of operations involved in the quantum workflow. The goal is to design a model that can learn patterns from input features and accurately assign them to one of two categories based on the information encoded in quantum states.

Our goal is simple: given a small dataset with two numerical features per sample, we want the model to classify each instance into one of two classes, represented by output labels 0 and 1.

To achieve this, we will:

1. Encode each input sample into a quantum state.
2. Apply a parameterized quantum circuit to transform that state.
3. Measure the output expectation value.
4. Train the parameters so the measured output approximates the correct class label.

This pipeline provides a hands-on understanding of how **variational quantum classifiers (VQCs)** operate.

Data preparation

We begin with a simple binary dataset—for example, an **exclusive OR (XOR)** like pattern. The XOR problem is a classic benchmark because it cannot be linearly separated in classical space, yet can be effectively learned in a quantum Hilbert space due to natural nonlinear mappings.

The following snippet defines a small two-feature dataset and its corresponding binary labels. The inputs are expressed as rotation-friendly values so they can be directly used for angle encoding in the quantum circuit.

```
import torch
from pennylane import numpy as np
# Input features (two per sample)
```

```
X = torch.tensor([
    [0.0, 0.0],
    [0.0, np.pi / 2],
    [np.pi / 2, 0.0],
    [np.pi / 2, np.pi / 2]
])
# Target Labels
Y = torch.tensor([[0.], [1.], [1.], [0.]])
```

Each feature pair will be encoded into two-qubits using angle encoding, where each value determines a rotation around the y-axis.

Designing the quantum classifier

The classifier uses a two-qubit quantum circuit with a simple variational design. The goal is to allow the circuit to learn class separation through rotation and entanglement.

The following PennyLane QNode defines the core variational quantum circuit used for classification. It encodes the two input features using rotation gates, applies entanglement to capture feature interactions, and returns an expectation value that serves as the model's prediction signal.

```
import pennylane as qml
import torch
from torch import nn, optim
# Quantum device
dev = qml.device("default.qubit", wires=2)
@qml.qnode(dev, interface="torch")
def quantum_circuit(inputs, weights):
    # Encode features into qubits
    qml.RY(inputs[0], wires=0)
    qml.RY(inputs[1], wires=1)
    # Add entanglement
    qml.CNOT(wires=[0, 1])
    # Parameterized layer
    qml.RY(weights[0], wires=0)
    qml.RY(weights[1], wires=1)
    qml.CNOT(wires=[1, 0])
    # Measurement
    return qml.expval(qml.PauliZ(1))
```

This structure introduces both local rotations (for individual feature learning) and entanglement (for feature correlation), enabling nonlinear decision boundaries in quantum space.

Integrating with PyTorch

To train the quantum model using familiar deep learning tools, the quantum circuit must be integrated into a classical ML framework. PennyLane provides interfaces that allow QNodes to interact directly with libraries such as PyTorch, enabling automatic differentiation and parameter optimization within a unified training loop.

We now wrap the quantum circuit inside a PyTorch model so it can be trained using standard optimizers:

```
class QuantumClassifier(nn.Module):
    def __init__(self):
        super().__init__()
        self.weights = nn.Parameter(0.01 * torch.randn(2))
```

```
    def forward(self, x):
        return torch.stack([quantum_circuit(x_i, self.weights) for x_i in x])
```

This model acts like any PyTorch layer but internally performs quantum computation through PennyLane.

Training the model

Once the model structure is defined, training follows the same iterative optimization process used in classical ML. At each epoch, the quantum circuit produces predictions, the loss is computed against the true labels, and gradients are used to update the trainable circuit parameters.

We will train the classifier using MSE loss and the Adam optimizer, gradually adjusting the quantum gate parameters to minimize the prediction error:

```
model = QuantumClassifier()
optimizer = optim.Adam(model.parameters(), lr=0.1)
loss_fn = nn.MSELoss()
epochs = 30
for epoch in range(epochs):
    optimizer.zero_grad()
    output = model(X)
    loss = loss_fn(output, Y)
    loss.backward()
    optimizer.step()
    print(f"Epoch {epoch+1}: Loss = {loss.item():.4f}")
```

During training, the optimizer updates the rotation gate parameters. As these angles change, the measurement outcomes shift, refining the circuit's ability to distinguish between the two classes.

Visualizing the learning outcome

After training, we can examine how well the model has learned to classify the data.

If the loss converges and outputs approach `[0, 1, 1, 0]`, the circuit has effectively discovered a quantum decision boundary separating the two classes.

This can also be visualized by plotting the circuit's output probability surface across the input feature space, an effective way to show how the quantum model bends the input space to achieve separability.

In practice, visualization helps validate whether the learned model generalizes beyond the training samples. By evaluating the trained circuit on a grid of input values and plotting the corresponding prediction surface, we can observe regions where the model predicts class 0 or class 1. A clear separation between these regions indicates that the hybrid quantum classifier has learned a meaningful decision boundary.

Discussion and observations

The results obtained from this case study highlight how even small quantum circuits can participate in practical learning workflows when integrated with classical optimization methods. Although the example uses a simplified dataset, it demonstrates the essential training dynamics and interpretability of VWCs.

This experiment demonstrates several key takeaways:

- **Simplicity meets power**: A minimal circuit with two qubits can learn nonlinear relationships that require multiple neurons in classical networks.
- **Hardware readiness**: Such models can be executed on real *IBM Quantum* or *IonQ* hardware by replacing the simulator backend.

- **Interpretable workflow**: Each gate corresponds to a learnable transformation, providing insights into how features interact.

Applications of QML in AI and data science

QML is no longer an abstract research pursuit, it is quickly becoming a practical framework that blends quantum principles with established data science workflows. The fusion of quantum mechanics and AI introduces new ways to process information, optimize models, and uncover patterns hidden in complex data.

By exploiting superposition, entanglement, and interference, QML algorithms can explore exponentially growing data spaces. This capability enables powerful applications in classification, pattern recognition, optimization, and simulation—core areas of modern AI and data science.

As quantum computing platforms continue to evolve, researchers and industry practitioners are actively exploring how QML techniques can enhance data-driven decision-making across diverse domains. From healthcare analytics and financial forecasting to materials discovery and intelligent automation, quantum-enhanced learning models are being investigated as potential tools for addressing computational challenges that are difficult for classical methods alone.

Quantum-enhanced pattern recognition

Pattern recognition is fundamental to every learning system. Classical algorithms analyze data using linear or kernel-based mappings, but quantum models can project features into a vast Hilbert space, where class boundaries naturally become separable.

Example application (quantum kernels): **quantum support vector machines** (**QSVMs**) use quantum feature maps to calculate similarities between data points. Instead of computing inner products in a classical kernel space, a quantum processor measures overlaps between quantum states:

$$k(x_i,x_j)=|\langle\psi(x_i)|\psi(x_j)\rangle|^2$$

Such kernels have been shown to outperform classical kernels on certain synthetic and small-scale image datasets by efficiently revealing nonlinear correlations.

Quantum optimization and learning

Optimization is the backbone of ML, from adjusting weights in neural networks to minimizing loss functions. Quantum algorithms like the **Quantum Approximate Optimization Algorithm** (**QAOA**) and **variational quantum eigensolver** (**VQE**) approach optimization differently: by encoding objective functions into Hamiltonians and evolving them toward energy minima.

In data science, this quantum driven optimization is valuable for:

- **Portfolio optimization**: Balancing risk and return in financial assets.
- **Feature selection**: Identifying minimal yet informative feature subsets.
- **Hyperparameter tuning**: Searching non-convex parameter spaces faster than exhaustive classical methods.

Quantum neural networks

Quantum neural networks (**QNNs**) mimic the layer-based structure of classical deep networks but replace neurons with parameterized quantum gates. Each layer performs a unitary transformation on qubits, with trainable parameters adjusted through gradient-based optimization.

Applications include:

- **Image recognition**: Encoding pixel intensities as rotation angles and learning compressed visual features.
- **Time-series prediction**: Modeling sequential data using quantum recurrent structures.
- **Signal classification**: Identifying noise patterns in radar or biomedical data.

QNNs are particularly effective when integrated with 13, enabling differentiable training on hybrid processors.

Quantum data analysis and clustering

Data-clustering techniques aim to group similar data points based on distance metrics. Quantum computing introduces new perspectives through algorithms such as Quantum k-Means, which estimate distances based on quantum-state overlaps rather than Euclidean distances.

Benefits include:

- **Higher-dimensional mapping**: Each qubit combination defines a multidimensional data projection.
- **Parallel similarity computation**: Quantum parallelism evaluates all pairwise distances simultaneously.
- **Reduced computation time**: Theoretical speed-ups for large-scale datasets once scalable hardware becomes available.

Example implementation concept: In a quantum k-means workflow, data vectors are encoded via amplitude encoding, and the quantum circuit computes state fidelities to determine cluster centroids. Hybrid iterations refine cluster assignments classically.

Quantum natural language processing

An emerging frontier in AI is **quantum natural language processing** (**QNLP**), which leverages the compositional structure of quantum states to represent meaning and grammar.

In QNLP, words are represented as quantum vectors and grammatical rules as tensor operations, aligning naturally with quantum entanglement and tensor product mathematics.

Potential applications include:

- Semantic analysis and text classification.
- Context-aware chatbots that exploit quantum correlations for nuanced inference.
- Quantum-enhanced embedding models for large-scale linguistic datasets.

Real-world sectors adopting QML

QML is steadily moving from theoretical exploration to practical adoption. Many industries are beginning to integrate QML techniques to solve computationally intensive optimization, prediction, and decision-making problems that classical systems struggle with.

The following table highlights several real-world sectors where QML is being explored, along with its major application areas and the advantages it offers:

Sector	Application area	Quantum benefit
Finance	Portfolio optimization, fraud detection	Faster combinatorial optimization and anomaly detection
Healthcare	Genomic pattern mining, drug discovery	Efficient molecule-energy estimation and pattern learning
Cybersecurity	Intrusion detection, key distribution analysis	Quantum-safe learning and encryption resilience
Manufacturing	Process control, fault prediction	Quantum sensors and predictive maintenance
Transportation	Traffic forecasting, logistics optimization	Real-time route optimization via QAOA

***Table 13.5**: Emerging industry sectors and applications adopting QML*

Challenges and future directions

Although QML has demonstrated encouraging theoretical and experimental progress, the field is still in an early stage of technological maturity. Continued research is required to improve algorithm design, hardware stability, and scalable learning frameworks that can operate effectively on near-term quantum devices.

Despite its promise, QML faces challenges:

- **Hardware limitations**: Noise and limited qubit counts constrain circuit depth.
- **Data encoding overhead**: Mapping high-dimensional data to quantum states remains resource-intensive.
- **Model interpretability**: Understanding the learned quantum parameters remains an open research area.

However, ongoing innovations in error mitigation, quantum feature maps, and cloud-based quantum services are rapidly reducing these barriers.

Conclusion

This chapter explored QML as a transformative convergence of AI and quantum computing. By comparing classical and quantum paradigms, we observed how quantum principles such as superposition, entanglement, and interference expand the representational and computational power of learning systems. Through step-by-step demonstrations using PennyLane and PyTorch, readers learned to encode classical data into quantum states, design PQCs, and train hybrid classical–quantum classifiers that capture nonlinear correlations with minimal resources.

The binary classification case study illustrated that even small quantum circuits can achieve meaningful learning outcomes, demonstrating how quantum models can discover complex decision boundaries in high-dimensional state spaces. By integrating classical neural network layers with quantum circuits, hybrid architectures allow practical experimentation with quantum-enhanced learning while leveraging the strengths of classical optimization and data processing.

The discussion of real-world QML applications further highlighted its growing relevance across sectors such as finance, healthcare, cybersecurity, manufacturing, and data science. In these domains, quantum algorithms offer new possibilities for pattern recognition, optimization, and predictive modeling that may eventually surpass the capabilities of purely classical approaches.

At the same time, the chapter acknowledged important challenges facing QML, including hardware noise, limited qubit counts, and the complexity of encoding large datasets into quantum states. Continued progress in quantum hardware, error mitigation techniques, and hybrid algorithm design will play a critical role in overcoming these limitations.

Ultimately, QML represents more than a technological innovation, it marks a paradigm shift toward intelligent systems that combine classical efficiency with quantum expressivity. As quantum technologies mature, QML is expected to become an essential component of next-generation AI systems, enabling new forms of discovery, optimization, and data-driven intelligence.

Questions

1. **What is QML?**

   Answer: QML is the integration of quantum computing and ML, where quantum systems process data to identify patterns and optimize models. It leverages quantum properties like superposition and entanglement to enhance computational efficiency and represent complex relationships beyond classical limits.

2. **How does QML differ from classical ML?**

   Answer: Classical ML operates on numerical data using linear algebra and optimization, while QML encodes data into quantum states and manipulates them through quantum circuits. This allows QML to explore exponentially larger feature spaces, offering potential speed-ups and richer model expressivity.

3. **What are the main methods of encoding data into quantum states?**

   Answer: Common encoding techniques include basis encoding, amplitude encoding, angle (rotation) encoding, and hybrid or entanglement-based encoding. Each method balances circuit depth, qubit efficiency, and expressivity depending on the data type and learning task.

4. **What is a PQC?**

   Answer: A PQC is a quantum circuit with tunable parameters—such as rotation angles that can be optimized during training. It functions like the weight layers of a neural network, allowing the quantum system to learn decision boundaries from data.

5. **Why are hybrid classical–quantum models important?**

   Answer: Hybrid models combine the scalability of classical networks with the expressive power of quantum circuits. They allow large datasets to be preprocessed classically, while the quantum layer captures complex, nonlinear correlations in reduced feature spaces—making them ideal for near-term quantum devices.

6. **What tools are commonly used to implement QML?**

   Answer: Frameworks such as PennyLane, Qiskit ML, and TensorFlow Quantum enable seamless integration of quantum circuits with classical ML libraries like PyTorch and TensorFlow, supporting differentiable training and hybrid workflows.

7. **What was demonstrated in the binary classification case study?**

   Answer: The chapter's case study used PennyLane and PyTorch to build and train a two-qubit quantum classifier on an XOR dataset. It illustrated how parameterized quantum gates can learn nonlinear decision boundaries through quantum entanglement and measurement outcomes.

8. **What are the main advantages of QML?**

   Answer: QML offers exponential data representation, natural nonlinearity, and potential quantum speed-ups for optimization tasks. It also enables new types of kernels, clustering, and feature mappings that classical methods cannot efficiently reproduce.

9. **What challenges currently limit QML deployment?**

   Answer: The main challenges include limited qubit counts, circuit noise, complex state preparation, and high data encoding overhead. Additionally, training stability and interpretability remain active research areas as hardware continues to mature.

10. **Which industries are adopting QML?**

    Answer: Sectors such as finance, healthcare, cybersecurity, manufacturing, and transportation are experimenting with QML for optimization, risk modeling, pattern recognition, and predictive analytics—demonstrating its growing practical significance in the AI ecosystem.

Exercises

1. Implement basis, amplitude, and angle encoding in PennyLane by encoding a three-feature classical vector into quantum states and printing the resulting amplitudes to observe how each encoding method represents data.

2. Construct a two-qubit PQC in PennyLane integrated with PyTorch to perform binary classification. Train the model with the Adam optimizer and display the loss per epoch to verify convergence.
3. Design a hybrid classical–QNN that combines a classical preprocessing layer with a quantum layer implemented in PennyLane. Train the hybrid model on XOR data and explain how the classical and quantum layers collaborate during optimization.
4. Reproduce the binary classification case study from this chapter using PennyLane and Matplotlib. Visualize the learned probability surface and discuss how quantum interference and entanglement contribute to the formation of nonlinear decision boundaries.
5. Create a comparative table listing the advantages, limitations, and applications of basis, amplitude, angle, and hybrid encodings, and explain which method is most practical for NISQ-era devices.
6. Implement a QNN using PennyLane's qml.qnn module for a two-feature dataset. Train the model and plot accuracy versus epochs, comparing the results with those of a classical neural network.
7. Replace the Adam optimizer in your QML training loop with the **simultaneous perturbation stochastic approximation** (**SPSA**) optimizer and analyze differences in convergence under noisy conditions.
8. Simulate a noisy quantum environment using PennyLane's default.mixed device and plot how varying noise levels affect classification accuracy. Discuss the need for error mitigation techniques in real QML implementations.
9. Research a real-world QML application in finance, healthcare, or cybersecurity. Summarize the dataset, the approach, and the performance benefits achieved with quantum models.
10. Write a 200-word reflection explaining how QML bridges classical AI and quantum computation, highlighting its current challenges, future potential, and role in developing next-generation intelligent systems.

CHAPTER 14
Quantum Simulation Projects

Introduction

Quantum simulation stands at the heart of what makes quantum computing truly transformative. While many quantum algorithms remain in the experimental stage, simulation offers a tangible path toward solving real scientific challenges—modeling the behavior of molecules, materials, and physical systems at the atomic and subatomic level. Traditional computational approaches in chemistry, physics, and materials science often struggle to accurately capture these phenomena. As system complexity increases, the computational resources required grow exponentially, making precise modeling nearly impossible even for the most powerful supercomputers.

Quantum computers, however, operate according to the same laws that govern the systems they aim to simulate superposition, entanglement, and interference. This natural alignment allows them to represent and process information in ways that classical systems cannot. By encoding molecular and material properties directly into qubits, quantum devices can efficiently approximate ground-state energies, reaction mechanisms, and quantum phase transitions, unlocking insights that were once out of reach. Algorithms such as the **variational quantum eigensolver** (**VQE**) and **quantum phase estimation** (**QPE**) exemplify this potential, combining quantum experimentation with classical optimization to achieve remarkable precision.

This chapter introduces the principles, workflows, and applications of quantum simulation through hands-on projects using Python-based frameworks like Qiskit, Cirq, and **Amazon Web Services** (**AWS**) Braket. Readers will build and analyze simulations across multiple domains from molecular energy estimation to spin system modeling, connecting abstract quantum theory with practical experimentation. Ultimately, this chapter shows how quantum simulation transforms computation into a virtual laboratory, bridging theory and discovery to accelerate innovation across science and engineering.

Structure

The chapter covers the following topics:

- Molecular simulation using VQE in Qiskit
- Quantum simulation on AWS Braket
- Hands-on simulation labs with Python
- Spin system modeling using Cirq
- Applications in chemistry, physics and material science

Objectives

This chapter introduces quantum simulation as one of the most impactful near-term applications of quantum computing, enabling researchers to model molecular, physical, and material systems at a quantum-mechanical level. Readers will learn how quantum algorithms such as the VQE and QPE are used to estimate molecular energies and simulate particle interactions with high precision. The chapter provides practical guidance on implementing simulation projects using Python-based frameworks—including Qiskit, Cirq, and AWS Braket that integrate classical optimization with quantum state evolution. Through hands-on examples, learners will construct molecular models, explore spin system dynamics, and perform cloud-based simulations on real or emulated hardware. Finally, readers will examine key scientific domains—chemistry, physics, and materials science to understand how quantum simulation accelerates discovery and innovation. By the end of this chapter, they will recognize how quantum simulation transforms computation into a virtual laboratory, bridging theory and experimentation to solve complex real-world problems.

Molecular simulation using VQE in Qiskit

Quantum simulation represents one of the most powerful and practical applications of quantum computing in the near-term. Among all scientific domains, quantum chemistry stands out as a natural beneficiary of this technology. Traditional computational chemistry techniques, such as Hartree–Fock and Coupled-Cluster methods, exhibit exponential scaling with increasing molecular complexity. Even for small molecules, accurately estimating electronic structures and ground-state energies demands enormous computational resources.

Quantum computers, however, can directly model molecular systems because the underlying physics of electrons and qubits both follow the laws of quantum mechanics. This natural alignment allows qubits to represent electron configurations, enabling efficient energy estimation. The VQE has emerged as the leading approach for performing such simulations on **noisy intermediate-scale quantum** (**NISQ**) devices. It combines quantum state preparation with classical optimization to compute a molecule's ground-state energy with remarkable accuracy.

In this section, readers will explore how VQE operates, understand its quantum–classical workflow, and implement a step-by-step simulation in Python using Qiskit to estimate the molecular energy of a simple system, such as the **hydrogen molecule** (H_2).

Concept of Variational Quantum Eigensolver

The VQE is a hybrid algorithm that merges the strengths of both quantum and classical computation. It is designed to solve for the ground-state energy of a quantum system—the lowest possible energy that satisfies Schrödinger's equation.

The process begins with a parameterized quantum circuit, known as an **ansatz**, which generates a quantum state $|\psi(\theta)\rangle$ depending on a set of tunable parameters θ. The expectation value of the system's Hamiltonian H with respect to this state gives the estimated energy:

$$E(\theta)=\langle\psi(\theta)|H|\psi(\theta)\rangle$$

According to the variational principle, this energy is always greater than or equal to the true ground-state energy E_0. By iteratively adjusting the parameters θ through a classical optimizer, the algorithm gradually minimizes $E(\theta)$ until it converges to E_0.

VQE workflow and architecture

The VQE is a hybrid quantum–classical algorithm used to estimate the ground-state energy of quantum systems. It combines parameterized quantum circuits with classical optimization techniques, enabling complex quantum problems to be addressed using relatively shallow circuits that are compatible with NISQ devices.

The VQE operates as a collaborative loop between a quantum processor and a classical computer. Each plays a distinct role:

- The quantum computer prepares and measures quantum states to evaluate energy.
- While the classical computer updates the parameters that define those quantum states.

This synergy allows VQE to work effectively even on today's noisy, small-scale quantum devices.

The overall workflow can be summarized in the following stages:

- **Problem definition (Hamiltonian construction)**: The molecular Hamiltonian is derived from quantum-chemical principles and describes the total energy of the system. Using Qiskit's Molecule and

FermionicOperator modules, the Hamiltonian is expressed in terms of qubit operations through a process known as **mapping**.

- **Ansatz preparation**: A parameterized quantum circuit (ansatz) is built to represent the trial wavefunction $|\psi(\theta)\rangle$. Common choices include **Unitary Coupled-Cluster Singles and Doubles** (**UCCSD**) excitations or hardware-efficient ansätze optimized for NISQ devices.
- **Quantum evaluation:** The quantum circuit prepares the state and measures the expectation value of each term in the Hamiltonian. These measurements estimate the system's total energy for the current parameter set.
- **Classical optimization:** A classical optimizer e.g., **Constrained Optimization by Linear Approximation** (**COBYLA**), **simultaneous perturbation stochastic approximation** (**SPSA**), or gradient descent adjusts the parameters θ to minimize the measured energy.
- **Iteration and convergence:** Quantum evaluation and classical optimization repeat iteratively until the difference between consecutive energy estimates becomes negligible. The final minimized energy approximates the molecule's ground-state energy.

The following figure illustrates the VQE workflow, showing the interaction between quantum and classical steps in energy estimation:

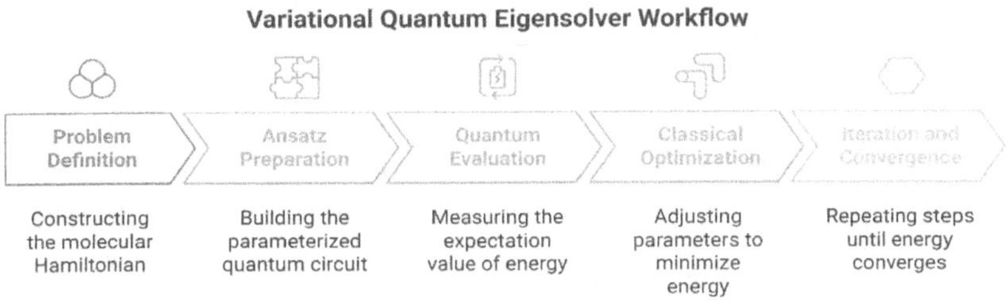

Figure 14.1: *VQE workflow for ground-state energy estimation*

The following table summarizes the functional roles of each component involved in a typical VQE workflow, showing how classical and quantum processes integrate within the hybrid loop:

Stage	Quantum role	Classical role
Hamiltonian setup	Encodes molecular structure into a qubit Hamiltonian	Parses chemistry data and builds an operator form
Ansatz construction	Prepares a quantum state	Defines parameterized circuit structure
Measurement	Computes expectation values	Collects and aggregates measurement outcomes
Optimization	—	Updates parameters to minimize energy
Convergence	Validates energy precision	Checks for stability in the final energy

Table 14.1: *Functional roles of quantum and classical components in the VQE workflow*

Implementation of VQE in Python using Qiskit

To truly appreciate how the VQE functions, it helps to build it step-by-step. In this section, we will simulate the H_2 using Qiskit Nature, a specialized module for quantum chemistry applications. The goal is to compute the ground-state energy of H_2 using the VQE algorithm and compare it with the theoretical energy obtained from classical methods.

This hands-on exercise illustrates how Python serves as a bridge between chemistry, physics, and quantum computing, allowing researchers to run molecular simulations on both local simulators and real *IBM Quantum* hardware.

To understand how the VQE operates in practice, we implement the workflow step-by-step using Qiskit. The following sequence demonstrates how the molecular Hamiltonian is constructed, mapped to qubits, and optimized through a hybrid quantum–classical loop to estimate the ground-state energy of the H_2.

1. **Import required libraries**: We begin by importing the necessary Qiskit modules for simulation, optimization, and molecular modeling:

```
from qiskit import Aer
from qiskit.utils import QuantumInstance
from qiskit.algorithms import VQE
from qiskit_nature.drivers import PySCFDriver
from qiskit_nature.problems.second_quantization.
electronic import ElectronicStructureProblem
from qiskit_nature.converters.second_quantization import QubitConverter
from qiskit_nature.mappers.second_quantization import ParityMapper
from qiskit.circuit.library import TwoLocal
from qiskit.algorithms.optimizers import COBYLA
```

2. **Define the molecular system**: We specify the geometry of the H_2, setting the atomic positions and units. **PySCFDriver** constructs the molecular electronic Hamiltonian:

```
driver = PySCFDriver(atom='H .0 .0 .0; H .0 .0 0.735', unit='Angstrom', basis='sto3g')
problem = ElectronicStructureProblem(driver)
```

3. **Map the problem to qubits**: Quantum computers cannot directly operate on electron-based Hamiltonians. We convert the molecular Hamiltonian into a qubit Hamiltonian using the **ParityMapper**:

```
mapper = ParityMapper()
converter = QubitConverter(mapper=mapper)
qubit_op = problem.second_q_ops()
main_op = converter.convert(qubit_op[0], num_particles=problem.num_particles)
```

4. **Define ansatz and optimizer**: We define a parameterized quantum circuit (ansatz) and select a classical optimizer. The **TwoLocal** circuit is hardware-efficient and well-suited to NISQ devices. The code for the same is as follows:

```
ansatz = TwoLocal(rotation_blocks='ry', entanglement_
blocks='cz', entanglement='full', reps=3)
optimizer = COBYLA(maxiter=200)
```

5. **Setup and run VQE**: We initialize a quantum backend and run the hybrid optimization loop to estimate the ground-state energy:

```
backend = Aer.get_backend('statevector_simulator')
quantum_instance = QuantumInstance(backend)
vqe_solver = VQE(ansatz=ansatz, optimizer=optimizer, quantum_instance=quantum_instance)
result = vqe_solver.compute_minimum_eigenvalue(main_op)
print("Estimated Ground-State Energy (Hartree):", result.eigenvalue.real)
```

6. **Interpret the results**: Once executed, the VQE outputs an energy value close to the true ground-state energy of the H_2 molecule (~–1.137 Hartree). Slight deviations occur due to circuit depth, optimization limits, and numerical precision.

Practical considerations

Implementing VQE in real or simulated environments requires careful attention to several practical factors. These considerations ensure that the molecular energy estimations remain stable, reproducible, and hardware-compatible.

The following guidelines are recommended when designing and executing VQE simulations:

- **Hamiltonian complexity**: The accuracy of results depends on how precisely the molecular Hamiltonian is represented. Simplified basis sets like STO-3G work for demonstrations but may not capture all electron correlations.
- **Ansatz design**: A deeper ansatz improves expressivity but increases circuit depth and noise. For NISQ devices, hardware-efficient circuits often outperform chemistry-inspired ones.
- **Optimizer choice**: Different optimizers behave differently under noisy or high-dimensional landscapes. SPSA and COBYLA are preferred for stability with few function evaluations.
- **Measurement shots**: Increasing the number of shots per circuit improves accuracy but adds to runtime. A typical range of 1,000–5,000 shots balance precision and efficiency.
- **Noise and hardware realism**: When deploying on real quantum hardware, include noise models using Qiskit Aer's NoiseModel to reflect realistic device conditions.
- **Convergence tuning**: Stopping criteria (tolerance values) should be carefully defined- too loose and the model may underfit; too strict and it may never converge.

The following figure highlights key factors that influence the accuracy and efficiency of VQE simulations:

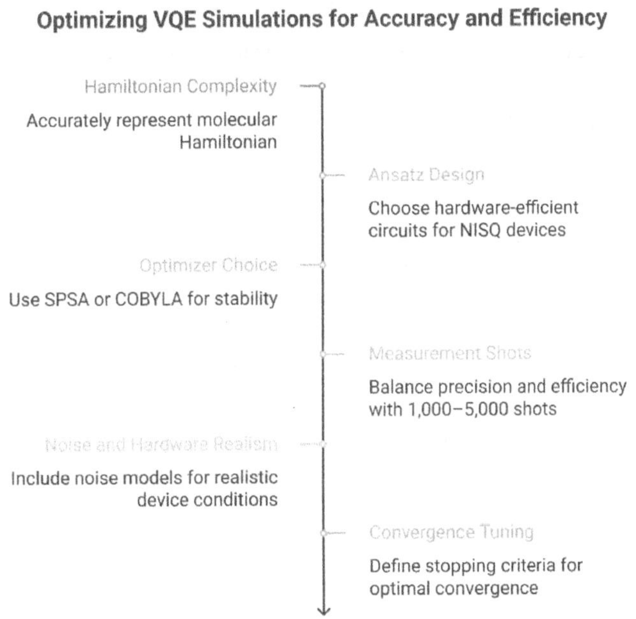

***Figure 14.2**: Key parameters for optimizing VQE performance and convergence*

Advantages and limitations

The VQE stands as one of the most practical algorithms for near-term quantum computers. Its hybrid design leverages the best of both quantum and classical worlds, making it highly adaptable for real chemical and physical simulations. However, like all NISQ-era algorithms, it faces trade-offs between scalability, accuracy, and hardware feasibility.

The following table highlights the primary advantages and limitations of VQE, emphasizing how it balances theoretical capability with current technological constraints:

Aspect	Advantages	Limitations
Scalability	Compatible with small to medium quantum devices; scales better than full quantum phase estimation.	Still limited by qubit count and circuit depth on noisy hardware.
Accuracy	Achieves near chemical precision for small molecules.	Sensitive to noise and optimizer convergence; may require repeated runs.
Flexibility	Supports multiple ansatz designs and classical optimizers.	Performance depends heavily on parameter initialization.
Hardware compatibility	Runs efficiently on today's NISQ hardware using shallow circuits.	Real hardware noise can degrade accuracy without error mitigation.

***Table 14.2**: Advantages and limitations of the VQE algorithm*

Mini project on molecular energy estimation using VQE

Hands-on projects help bridge theoretical understanding with real computational practice. In this mini-project, you will simulate the H_2 using the VQE approach in Qiskit and analyze how quantum–classical collaboration achieves accurate molecular energy estimation.

The exercise emphasizes not just coding, but the scientific interpretation behind each step, how a quantum algorithm mimics the physics of molecular systems.

Objective: Estimate the ground-state energy of the H_2 molecule using VQE and compare it with the reference value obtained through classical computational methods.

Project workflow: Follow these key stages, mirroring a real hybrid simulation setup:

1. **Define the molecular structure**: Use Qiskit's `PySCFDriver` to specify the hydrogen atoms and generate the molecular Hamiltonian.
2. **Map to qubits**: Convert the electronic Hamiltonian into a qubit operator using the `ParityMapper` or Jordan–Wigner encoding.
3. **Design the ansatz**: Build a parameterized quantum circuit using `TwoLocal` or UCCSD to represent the molecule's wavefunction.
4. **Select an optimizer and backend**: Choose an optimizer such as SPSA or COBYLA, and run the circuit on the `statevector_simulator` or a real IBM Quantum backend.
5. **Compute and analyze results**: Execute the VQE algorithm, record the estimated ground-state energy, and compare it against the classical benchmark (~–1.137 Hartree for H_2).

Expected output: The simulation should output a value close to the theoretical ground-state energy, confirming that the hybrid VQE algorithm successfully captures molecular properties using only a few qubits.

Spin system modeling using Cirq

Spin systems are fundamental to understanding the behavior of quantum materials, magnetism, and condensed matter physics. From modeling magnetic interactions in lattices to simulating superconducting qubits, spin Hamiltonians provide an ideal framework for exploring how quantum particles interact at microscopic levels.

In classical physics, modeling such systems quickly becomes infeasible as the number of particles increases, the state space grows exponentially. However, quantum computers naturally represent spin states through qubits, where each qubit corresponds to a spin-½ particle.

Using Cirq, Google's open-source quantum framework, researchers can efficiently construct and simulate these spin systems. In this section, we will focus on modeling simple spin chain systems (like the Ising model) to understand how quantum interactions and entanglement evolve across qubits.

To analyze spin interactions quantitatively, physicists represent the system using a mathematical operator known as a Hamiltonian. The Hamiltonian encodes the total energy of the system and determines how the quantum state evolves over time. By expressing spin interactions in Hamiltonian form, we can translate physical models of magnetism into quantum circuits that can be simulated on quantum computing frameworks such as Cirq.

Understanding spin Hamiltonians

A spin Hamiltonian describes how spins interact under magnetic or coupling influences.

One of the simplest and most studied is the Ising Hamiltonian, defined as:

$$H = -J\sum_{i} Z_i Z_{i+1} - h\sum_{i} X_i$$

Here:

- J represents the coupling strength between neighboring spins.
- h is the external magnetic field.
- Z_i and X_i denote Pauli operators acting on the ith qubit.

The ground-state configuration of this system depends on the balance between magnetic alignment (driven by J) and quantum fluctuations (driven by h).

Building the Ising model in Cirq

Once the Hamiltonian describing the system is defined, the next step is to construct a quantum circuit that approximates its behavior. In practice, this involves mapping the interaction terms of the Hamiltonian to quantum gates that act on qubits representing individual spins. Cirq provides a flexible programming environment for implementing these operations and simulating the resulting dynamics.

Let us now build and simulate a simple two-qubit Ising system using Cirq.

1. **Import libraries**:
```
import cirq
import numpy as np
```
2. **Define qubits and parameters**: We represent two spin-½ particles using Cirq□s **`GridQubit`**:
```
# Define two qubits
q0, q1 = cirq.LineQubit.range(2)
# Define model parameters
J - 1.0    # coupling strength
h = 0.5    # magnetic field
```
3. **Construct the Ising Hamiltonian**: We simulate the evolution of the Ising Hamiltonian using the corresponding quantum gates:
```
# Define the circuit
circuit = cirq.Circuit()
# Apply Z-Z interaction term
circuit.append(cirq.CZ(q0, q1)**J)
# Apply X-rotation to simulate magnetic field
circuit.append(cirq.rx(2 * np.pi * h).on_each(q0, q1))
# Measure both spins
circuit.append(cirq.measure(q0, q1, key='result'))
print(circuit)
```
4. **Execute the simulation**:
```
simulator = cirq.Simulator()
```

```
result = simulator.run(circuit, repetitions=1000)
print(result.histogram(key='result'))
```

The histogram shows the frequency of each spin configuration, revealing how the system evolves under the combined effects of interactions and magnetic fields.

Interpretation and discussion

After executing the circuit multiple times, the measurement outcomes can be analyzed to understand how the simulated spin system behaves under different interaction strengths. The resulting probability distribution of spin configurations reflects the competition between coupling interactions and external magnetic influences in the Hamiltonian.

The results provide insights into quantum correlations, configurations where spins tend to align or anti-align depending on the strength of J and h:

- For large J and small h, spins prefer alignment (ferromagnetic behavior).
- For large h, quantum fluctuations dominate, causing random orientations (paramagnetic behavior).

By adjusting these parameters, one can explore quantum phase transitions—changes in ground-state properties driven purely by quantum effects.

Practical considerations

Although the basic spin chain simulation is conceptually straightforward, implementing reliable quantum simulations requires careful attention to computational and physical constraints. Factors such as circuit depth, noise modeling, and parameter exploration influence both the accuracy of the simulation and the insights that can be extracted from the results.

When implementing spin system simulations in Cirq, certain experimental and technical factors must be managed carefully to ensure accuracy, scalability, and meaningful interpretation of results. The following points outline key practical considerations for effective simulation design and analysis:

- **Circuit depth**: Keep circuits shallow to minimize simulation overhead on classical backends.
- **Noise modeling**: Cirq supports realistic noise channels (`cirq.depolarize`) for testing robustness.
- **Scalability**: Extend simulations to larger spin chains using `cirq.GridQubit.rect()`.
- **Parameter sweeps**: Automate multiple runs with varying J and h to study system behavior.

Quantum simulation on AWS Braket

Cloud-based quantum computing has become a cornerstone for modern research and experimentation. AWS Braket, Amazon's quantum computing service, provides a unified platform to design, simulate, and execute quantum algorithms on real hardware from multiple providers, including *IonQ*, *Rigetti*, and *QuEra*.

For scientists and engineers, Braket serves as a gateway to powerful simulators and physical quantum processors, without requiring on-premises quantum hardware. Its Python SDK integrates seamlessly with popular libraries such as PennyLane, Qiskit, and Cirq, making it an ideal environment for prototyping quantum simulations and variational algorithms.

In this section, we will build and run a simple quantum simulation on AWS Braket, illustrating how cloud-based platforms extend the reach of quantum research in chemistry, physics, and materials science.

Overview of the AWS Braket environment

Cloud-based quantum platforms have significantly simplified access to quantum computing resources. Instead of requiring dedicated laboratory infrastructure, researchers and developers can now design, simulate, and execute quantum circuits through scalable cloud environments. AWS Braket is one such platform that integrates quantum hardware, classical compute resources, and development tools into a unified ecosystem.

AWS Braket provides a hybrid interface that connects classical computing resources with quantum backends. It offers two main modes of operation:

- **Local simulator**: Allows users to prototype algorithms using built-in simulators, such as statevector (SV1) or density matrix (DM1).
- **Quantum hardware access**: Enables execution on real devices offered by multiple vendors superconducting, trapped-ion, or neutral-atom systems.

Architecture highlights: AWS Braket's architecture connects quantum and classical resources through a unified cloud framework. The following highlights outline its key structural features:

- Python-based SDK accessible through Amazon SageMaker or any local Jupyter environment.
- Integration with Amazon S3 for storing circuit definitions and results.
- Job management through Amazon Braket Jobs for scalable hybrid workloads.

Setting up and running a simulation

Once the development environment is configured, users can begin constructing quantum circuits and executing them on either simulators or real quantum hardware. AWS Braket provides a straightforward workflow for creating circuits, selecting a backend device, running simulations, and retrieving measurement results for analysis.

The following example demonstrates how to create, simulate, and retrieve results from a quantum circuit on AWS Braket:

1. **Install and import libraries**:
```
!pip install amazon-braket-sdk
from braket.circuits import Circuit
from braket.aws import AwsDevice
from braket.devices import LocalSimulator
```
2. **Create a quantum circuit**:

   Here we define a simple two-qubit Bell state circuit:
```
# Define circuit
circuit = Circuit().h(0).cnot(0, 1)
print(circuit)
```
3. **Choose a backend**:

   Braket supports both local simulators and real quantum hardware.

   To run locally:
```
device = LocalSimulator()
result = device.run(circuit, shots=1000).result()
print(result.measurement_counts)
```
   To run on a real device (e.g., IonQ):
```
# Uncomment to execute on hardware
# device = AwsDevice("arn:aws:braket:::device/qpu/ionq/ionQdevice")
# result = device.run(circuit, shots=1000).result()
```
4. **View results**:

   The output displays measurement counts showing the characteristic correlations of an entangled Bell state ($|00\rangle$ and $|11\rangle$ outcomes dominating).

Advantages of using AWS Braket

While AWS Braket primarily serves as a development and execution platform for quantum algorithms, its cloud-based design also offers practical benefits for experimentation, collaboration, and scalability. By integrating classical and quantum resources within a single environment, researchers can rapidly prototype algorithms and transition from simulation to hardware execution.

AWS Braket simplifies scaling experiments and resource management. Its advantages extend beyond convenience to practical research applications.

The following table summarizes key benefits and current limitations of using AWS Braket for quantum simulations:

Aspect	Advantages	Limitations
Accessibility	Provides cloud-based access to multiple hardware types.	Requires AWS credentials, and usage costs apply.
Integration	Seamless integration with Qiskit, Cirq, and PennyLane.	Limited offline operation capabilities.
Performance	High-performance simulators for large circuits.	Simulator limits may apply for very deep circuits.
Scalability	Supports batch jobs and hybrid workflows via Braket Jobs.	Network latency can affect iterative experiments.

***Table 14.3**: Advantages and limitations of quantum simulation on AWS Braket*

Applications in chemistry, physics, and material science

Quantum simulation is not merely an academic pursuit—it has become a practical tool for solving some of the hardest scientific problems in chemistry, physics, and materials science. These fields involve complex quantum interactions that are computationally expensive or even impossible to simulate using classical methods.

Quantum computers, by directly modeling quantum states, enable scientists to study molecular reactions, electronic properties, and material behaviors with unprecedented precision. From predicting chemical reaction pathways to discovering new superconducting materials, quantum simulation bridges theory and experimentation, opening doors to discoveries that traditional computation can only approximate.

Across multiple scientific disciplines, quantum simulation enables researchers to investigate microscopic processes that determine the macroscopic behavior of molecules, materials, and physical systems. By leveraging qubits to represent quantum states directly, scientists can model interactions that are extremely difficult to compute with classical algorithms. The following sections highlight how quantum simulation techniques are applied in three major domains—quantum chemistry, physics, and materials science demonstrating their potential to accelerate scientific discovery and technological innovation.

Applications in quantum chemistry

Quantum chemistry seeks to understand how atoms and molecules interact at the subatomic level. Accurate energy estimation is essential for determining bond strengths, reaction dynamics, and molecular stability.

Quantum algorithms such as the VQE and QPE allow direct simulation of molecular Hamiltonians the mathematical representations of molecular energy.

Quantum algorithms like VQE enable diverse chemical applications, from molecular energy estimation to catalyst design. The following use cases highlight how quantum simulation techniques are transforming modern computational chemistry:

- **Molecular energy estimation**: Compute ground-state energies of small molecules like H_2, LiH, or BeH_2.

- **Reaction pathway analysis**: Model potential energy surfaces to predict reaction mechanisms.
- **Catalyst design**: Simulate quantum effects in catalysts to improve efficiency in chemical manufacturing.

Applications in physics

In physics, quantum simulation helps decode phenomena that arise from the collective behavior of many interacting particles. Classical physics breaks down when systems become highly entangled or exhibit quantum correlations—scenarios naturally modeled by qubits.

Quantum simulation extends beyond chemistry into fundamental areas of physics. The following key domains highlight how quantum algorithms help uncover new insights into the structure and behavior of physical systems:

- **Condensed matter physics**: Study spin systems (Ising and Heisenberg models) to understand magnetism and quantum phase transitions.
- **Quantum thermodynamics**: Explore how energy, entropy, and coherence interact in nanoscale systems.
- **Superconductivity and topological states**: Use quantum computers to model exotic phases of matter that exhibit zero resistance or protected edge states.

Applications in material science

Material science relies heavily on understanding electron behavior and lattice dynamics within solids. Quantum simulations can predict structural, thermal, and electrical properties before materials are even physically synthesized.

Quantum simulations enable researchers to design and analyze next-generation materials with atomic precision. The following applications illustrate how quantum computing accelerates innovation in material science:

- **Battery materials**: Simulate ionic transport in solid electrolytes to design more efficient batteries.
- **Photonic materials**: Model light–matter interactions for quantum sensors and optical devices.
- **Nanomaterials**: Study molecular adsorption and electron transport in nanostructures such as graphene or carbon nanotubes.

The following table summarizes major application areas of quantum simulation across scientific domains, along with their core objectives and quantum advantages:

Domain	Application focus	Quantum advantage
Chemistry	Molecular energy estimation, reaction prediction	Exponential speed-up in solving electronic structures
Physics	Spin models, superconductivity, thermodynamics	Accurate modeling of many-body quantum systems
Material science	Battery and nanomaterial design	Predictive modeling of material properties and stability

Table 14.4: *Key scientific domains benefiting from quantum simulation*

Hands-on simulation labs with Python

To truly understand the power of quantum simulation, hands-on experimentation is essential. This section provides guided simulation labs that connect theoretical concepts to practical execution using Python-based frameworks such as Qiskit, Cirq, and AWS Braket.

Each lab focuses on a key application area—chemistry, spin systems, and materials—demonstrating how quantum algorithms model natural systems in ways classical computing cannot. Students are encouraged to execute, modify, and analyze these simulations to deepen their intuition about how quantum algorithms emulate the physical world.

To make the learning process structured and experiential, the following laboratory exercises guide students through progressively more complex simulations. Each lab demonstrates how a different quantum computing framework can be used to model physical systems and analyze their behavior through quantum circuits. By completing these exercises, students gain practical familiarity with algorithm implementation, circuit construction, and interpretation of simulation results.

Lab 1 on molecular energy estimation using VQE in Qiskit

The first laboratory exercise introduces molecular simulation using the VQE. This hybrid quantum–classical algorithm is widely used in quantum chemistry to estimate molecular ground-state energies using shallow circuits suitable for current quantum hardware.

Objective: Compute the ground-state energy of the H_2 molecule using the VQE algorithm.

Procedure: Follow these steps to setup and run a VQE simulation in Qiskit for estimating the ground-state energy of H_2:

1. Use `PySCFDriver` in Qiskit to define molecular geometry.
2. Map the molecular Hamiltonian to qubits using `ParityMapper`.
3. Implement a VQE solver with the `TwoLocal` ansatz and COBYLA optimizer.
4. Run the simulation and record the estimated energy in Hartree units.
5. Compare your result with the theoretical ground-state energy (–1.137 Hartree).

Expected outcome: Students should observe that VQE provides near-exact energy values with minimal circuit depth, demonstrating its efficiency for NISQ hardware.

Lab 2 on two-qubit spin system simulation using Cirq

The second lab shifts focus from molecular chemistry to quantum physics by exploring spin systems. Spin models such as the Ising model are fundamental in condensed matter physics and provide a simple yet powerful framework for studying quantum interactions and magnetic behavior.

Objective: Model an Ising spin chain using Cirq to study quantum correlations and magnetic behavior.

Procedure: Follow the following steps to construct and simulate a two-qubit Ising spin system in Cirq, exploring how variations in coupling and magnetic field influence spin behavior:

1. Define two `LineQubit` representing spin-½ particles.
2. Construct the Ising Hamiltonian using CZ and RX gates.
3. Vary the coupling constant J and magnetic field h.
4. Measure spin correlations across multiple iterations.
5. Plot energy or probability distributions to visualize spin alignment trends.

Expected outcome: Students will observe ferromagnetic and paramagnetic behaviors emerging naturally from the quantum circuit's evolution.

Lab 3 on quantum circuit execution on AWS Braket

The third lab demonstrates how quantum circuits can be executed within a cloud-based quantum computing environment. AWS Braket enables users to run circuits on simulators as well as real quantum hardware, allowing researchers to observe how algorithms behave under realistic experimental conditions.

Objective: Run a Bell state simulation on AWS Braket's `LocalSimulator` and retrieve measurement outcomes.

Procedure: Follow these steps to run a Bell state simulation on AWS Braket, verifying entanglement using both local and hardware backends.

1. Install the Amazon Braket SDK.
2. Build a two-qubit Bell state circuit using **`h(0)`** and **`cnot(0, 1)`**.
3. Run the simulation on the **`LocalSimulator`** backend.
4. View and analyze the measurement histogram to verify entanglement.
5. Optionally, run the same job on a real IonQ or Rigetti backend.

Expected outcome: The output distribution should predominantly display $|00\rangle$ and $|11\rangle$ results, confirming entanglement generation.

Lab 4 on material property simulation as an open challenge

The final lab is designed as an open exploration exercise that encourages students to apply the concepts learned in the previous labs. Rather than following a fixed procedure, students are invited to design their own small quantum simulation experiment and investigate how system parameters influence physical behavior.

Objective: Design a simple quantum circuit to model the electron configuration of a custom molecule or solid-state structure.

Procedure: Follow these steps to design and execute a custom material or molecular simulation, optimizing circuit parameters to observe energy and system behavior variations:

1. Select a molecule (e.g., LiH or CH_4) or lattice structure.
2. Define its Hamiltonian and encode it using an appropriate mapping scheme.
3. Choose either Qiskit, Cirq, or Braket as your simulation environment.
4. Optimize circuit depth and parameters to achieve greater accuracy.
5. Visualize how energy levels change as parameters (bond angles, fields, etc.) vary.

Expected outcome: Students will gain hands-on experience in quantum modeling, observing how small parameter variations affect system stability and energy.

Conclusion

This chapter presented quantum simulation as a cornerstone of practical quantum computing, demonstrating how algorithms such as the VQE and QPE address the limitations of classical computational models. Through step-by-step projects using Qiskit, Cirq, and AWS Braket, readers learned how to simulate molecular systems, spin interactions, and material properties with quantum-level precision. The chapter emphasized how hybrid quantum–classical workflows combine quantum state evolution with classical optimization, enabling the efficient study of complex physical systems even on current NISQ hardware.

By integrating conceptual explanations with practical implementation examples, the chapter illustrated how quantum simulation serves as a bridge between theoretical quantum mechanics and real-world experimentation. Readers explored how algorithms such as VQE can estimate molecular ground-state energies, how spin systems can be modeled using circuit-based quantum frameworks, and how cloud platforms such as AWS Braket extend access to powerful simulators and emerging quantum processors.

The chapter also highlighted the growing impact of quantum simulation across multiple scientific disciplines, including chemistry, physics, and materials science. From predicting molecular reactions and designing catalysts to modeling magnetic systems and discovering advanced materials, quantum simulation offers a powerful tool for accelerating scientific discovery. As quantum hardware continues to mature and error mitigation techniques improve, the methods introduced in this chapter will become increasingly scalable and impactful. Ultimately, quantum simulation transforms computation into a virtual laboratory, enabling researchers to explore complex quantum phenomena and drive innovation across science and engineering.

Questions

1. **What is quantum simulation?**

   Answer: Quantum simulation is the use of quantum computers to model physical, chemical, or material systems whose behavior follows quantum mechanics. It enables researchers to replicate and analyze complex interactions at the atomic or subatomic level that classical computers cannot efficiently handle.

2. **Why is quantum simulation considered a near-term application of quantum computing?**

   Answer: Unlike many quantum algorithms requiring fault-tolerant hardware, quantum simulation can deliver useful results on today's NISQ devices. It focuses on small, physically meaningful problems—such as molecular energies—that align well with current hardware capabilities.

3. **What makes quantum simulation superior to classical simulation methods?**

   Answer: Classical methods approximate quantum systems through heavy computation, often limited by exponential scaling. Quantum simulators, by contrast, use qubits governed by the same quantum principles—superposition and entanglement—to model systems more naturally and efficiently.

4. **What is the VQE?**

   Answer: The VQE is a hybrid quantum–classical algorithm used to find the ground-state energy of molecules or materials. It combines a parameterized quantum circuit (ansatz) for state preparation with a classical optimizer that iteratively minimizes energy.

5. **How does the QPE algorithm complement VQE?**

   Answer: While VQE is suited for noisy and near-term devices, QPE is a more precise, long-term algorithm that estimates eigenvalues of a unitary operator—offering exact results on fault-tolerant quantum computers.

6. **Which tools are used for implementing quantum simulations?**

   Answer: Popular frameworks include Qiskit for molecular energy estimation, Cirq for spin system modeling, and AWS Braket for scalable, cloud-based quantum experiments across multiple hardware platforms.

7. **What scientific domains benefit most from quantum simulation?**

   Answer: Quantum simulation has significant applications in chemistry (molecular energy computation), physics (spin and thermodynamic modeling), and materials science (designing batteries, catalysts, and nanomaterials).

8. **How do hybrid quantum–classical workflows improve simulation accuracy?**

   Answer: Hybrid workflows leverage quantum hardware for state preparation and measurement, while classical processors handle optimization and convergence, resulting in efficient, noise-resilient computations.

9. **What challenges limit large-scale quantum simulations today?**

   Answer: Current limitations include limited qubit counts, gate errors, decoherence, and restricted circuit depth. These factors constrain simulation size and precision, but they are rapidly improving with advances in hardware and error mitigation techniques.

10. **What future potential does quantum simulation hold?**

    Answer: Quantum simulation will revolutionize scientific research by enabling virtual experimentation, allowing scientists to design molecules, discover materials, and study quantum phenomena directly through computation, driving innovation across science and technology.

Exercises

1. Implement the VQE in Qiskit to estimate the ground-state energy of the H_2. Use the PySCFDriver and ParityMapper, and compare your computed energy with the theoretical value (–1.137 Hartree).
2. Modify your VQE simulation to include different optimizers (e.g., SPSA, COBYLA, or L-BFGS-B) and analyze how convergence behavior and accuracy vary across optimizers.
3. Construct a two-qubit Ising spin system in Cirq using CZ and RX gates. Vary the coupling constant (J) and magnetic field (h) to observe how the resulting spin correlations change.
4. Run the Ising model simulation on Cirq's noise simulator (cirq.depolarize) and visualize how increasing noise affects the system's energy and probability distribution.
5. Create a Bell state circuit in AWS Braket and execute it on both the LocalSimulator and a real IonQ backend. Compare the measurement histograms to confirm entanglement and hardware noise effects.
6. Design a custom molecular simulation in Qiskit for a molecule such as LiH or BeH_2 using VQE. Adjust the bond length and plot the total energy as a function of the interatomic distance.
7. Simulate a three-qubit spin chain in Cirq using GridQubit.rect() and measure correlations to explore emergent quantum behavior in larger systems.
8. Research a real-world application of quantum simulation in chemistry, physics, or materials science, such as catalyst design or superconductivity modeling and summarize its objectives and outcomes.
9. Create a comparative table summarizing the advantages, limitations, and use cases of Qiskit, Cirq, and AWS Braket for quantum simulation.
10. Write a 200-word reflection discussing how quantum simulation serves as a bridge between theory and experimentation, explaining its impact on accelerating discovery in molecular chemistry, condensed matter physics, and materials research.

CHAPTER 15
End-to-end Mini Projects

Introduction

Quantum computing moves from theory to meaningful practice when ideas are developed into complete, working applications. While earlier chapters introduced individual algorithms, frameworks, and tools, genuine understanding emerges when these elements are integrated into end-to-end projects that address realistic computational challenges. This chapter is designed to make that transition clear by transforming abstract quantum concepts into practical workflows through mini projects based on search, optimization, and classification.

Each project in this chapter represents a distinct quantum paradigm. Grover's algorithm demonstrates how quantum search can efficiently navigate constrained solution spaces, as illustrated through a Sudoku solving application. The **Quantum Approximate Optimization Algorithm** (**QAOA**) shows how quantum methods can support financial decision-making through portfolio optimization. **Quantum neural networks** (**QNNs**), implemented with PennyLane and PyTorch, highlight the growing intersection of quantum computing and **machine learning** (**ML**) by applying hybrid models to image classification tasks. Together, these projects reveal how different quantum approaches can be tailored to different classes of real-world problems.

Beyond algorithm execution, this chapter emphasizes the broader engineering process involved in building quantum applications. Readers will explore how to define a problem, encode data into quantum states, select an appropriate algorithm, design circuits, integrate classical optimization, and evaluate performance under realistic conditions. In this way, the chapter not only teaches how quantum algorithms work, but also how they are developed, tested, and refined as complete systems.

By the end of this chapter, learners will have moved beyond isolated examples to a more holistic understanding of quantum application development. They will gain the confidence to connect theory, implementation, and evaluation in ways that reflect emerging research and industry practice.

Structure

The chapter covers the following topics:

- Quantum Sudoku solver with Grover's algorithm
- Portfolio optimization with QAOA on AWS Braket
- Quantum image classification with PennyLane and PyTorch
- Project design, implementation and testing
- Applying theory to end-to-end applications

Objectives

This chapter presents end-to-end quantum mini projects as a practical approach to applying quantum computing principles in real-world scenarios. Readers will learn how algorithms such as Grover's algorithm, the QAOA, and QNNs can be developed, executed, and tested within complete project frameworks. The chapter provides comprehensive guidance on designing, implementing, and evaluating quantum workflows that combine both quantum and classical components. Using Python-based frameworks such as Qiskit, PennyLane, and **Amazon Web Services** (**AWS**) Braket, learners will build hands-on projects that demonstrate quantum applications across multiple domains—constraint satisfaction through Grover's search, portfolio optimization using QAOA, and image classification with hybrid QNNs. Through detailed algorithmic walkthroughs and stepwise code implementations, readers will connect theory to experimentation by developing fully functional quantum solutions. Finally, the chapter emphasizes how project design, testing, and integration form the foundation for scalable and reproducible quantum applications. By the end of this chapter, readers will understand how to transform theoretical algorithms into end-to-end, deployable systems, bridging the gap between quantum theory and practical engineering.

Quantum Sudoku solver with Grover's algorithm

Sudoku is one of the most recognizable logic puzzles of the modern age. A 9×9 grid, divided into smaller 3×3 sub-grids, must be filled with digits 1 to 9 so that no number repeats in any row, column, or block. Though it appears playful, Sudoku is, in fact, a constraint satisfaction problem□a category well-known for its combinatorial complexity.

In classical computation, solving Sudoku often relies on backtracking, constraint propagation, or heuristic search methods. However, as the puzzle size grows, the number of possible configurations increases exponentially, leading to long computational times.

Here, quantum computing offers a remarkable alternative. By leveraging the principles of superposition and amplitude amplification, Grover's algorithm can explore multiple possibilities simultaneously, providing a quadratic speedup over classical search algorithms.

In this project, we will design a Quantum Sudoku solver using Grover's algorithm in Qiskit. To keep the problem manageable on today's **noisy intermediate-scale quantum** (**NISQ**) hardware, we will work with a simplified 4×4 Sudoku grid. The goal is not merely to solve Sudoku but to demonstrate how a quantum search algorithm can navigate a constrained solution space efficiently.

Algorithmic background

At the heart of Grover's algorithm lies a simple yet powerful idea: it identifies one or more marked solutions among N possible candidates in roughly i iterations—a significant improvement over the linear scaling of classical search.

Let us briefly review the core steps:

1. **Initialization**: All possible states are created in equal superposition, representing every potential Sudoku configuration simultaneously.
2. **Oracle operation**: A specially designed oracle flips the phase of the correct solutions, marking them as desirable outcomes.
3. **Diffusion operator**: Also called the inversion about the mean, this step amplifies the amplitudes of the marked states so they stand out in subsequent measurements.
4. **Measurement**: Finally, the quantum state is measured, and the correct solution appears with the highest probability.

When applied to Sudoku, the oracle encodes the puzzle's logical constraints—ensuring that no two identical numbers appear in the same row, column, or sub-grid. Each valid Sudoku configuration corresponds to one of Grover's marked states.

Implementation steps

To implement a quantum Sudoku solver, the puzzle must first be reformulated in a way that can be processed by a quantum search algorithm. Instead of examining candidate solutions sequentially, the quantum approach represents many possible configurations simultaneously within a superposition of states. Grover's algorithm can then be used to iteratively amplify the probability of valid configurations that satisfy the puzzle's constraints.

Let us now translate this concept into an executable plan. The workflow in *Figure 15.1* summarizes how Grover's algorithm is applied to Sudoku, showing the transition from puzzle constraints to quantum-state preparation, search, and measurement.

The following sequence of steps outlines how to prepare a simplified Sudoku puzzle for quantum search and how Grover's algorithm is used to identify the correct solution configuration.

1. **Simplify the Sudoku board**: We begin with a 4×4 Sudoku puzzle. Each cell can hold a value from 1 to 4, but representing all possibilities directly would require numerous qubits. To stay efficient, we encode cells as binary variables to represent possible placements.
2. **Encode logical constraints**: Sudoku rules—unique numbers per row, column, and block—are expressed as Boolean conditions. These logical relationships ensure that:
    a. Each row contains four unique numbers.
    b. Each column contains four unique numbers.
    c. Each 2×2 block has no repetition.

   These Boolean expressions can later be converted into quantum gates to form the oracle circuit:

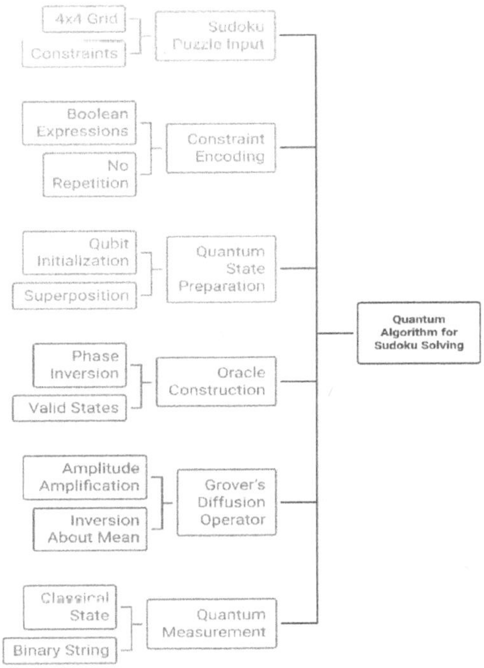

***Figure 15.1**: Workflow of the quantum Sudoku solver using Grover's algorithm*

3. **Design the oracle**: The oracle acts as the gatekeeper of Sudoku rules. It identifies valid Sudoku states—those satisfying all encoded conditions—and flips their quantum phase. In our simplified example, we use placeholder logic to demonstrate the mechanism, but in an advanced setup, each rule would correspond to a dedicated set of quantum gates.
4. **Apply Grover's diffusion operator**: This operator increases the probability amplitude of valid configurations while suppressing those of invalid configurations. By inverting about the mean, it magnifies the amplitude of the marked states—effectively guiding the system closer to the solution.

5. **Run the algorithm**: The oracle and diffusion operations are alternated several times. Each iteration increases the probability that the correct Sudoku configuration will appear when the quantum state is measured. The exact number of iterations is roughly $\pi/4 \times \sqrt{N}$, where N is the total number of possible states.

6. **Measure the outcome**: Finally, measurement collapses the quantum superposition into a classical state. The resulting binary string corresponds to the most probable Sudoku configuration. By decoding this string, you can reconstruct the 4×4 Sudoku grid.

Code walkthrough

To better understand how the solver operates in practice, it is useful to examine a compact circuit implementation that mirrors the main stages of Grover's algorithm. The code here does not attempt to solve the full complexity of Sudoku, but it demonstrates how a constrained search problem can be expressed through quantum circuit construction and simulated step-by-step.

The following program illustrates a prototype Sudoku solver using Qiskit. Although simplified, it captures the essential spirit of Grover's search: preparation, marking, amplification, and measurement:

```
from qiskit import QuantumCircuit, Aer, transpile, execute
from qiskit.visualization import plot_histogram
# Step 1: Define number of qubits for a simplified 4x4 Sudoku encoding
n_qubits = 8  # Simplified binary representation
qc = QuantumCircuit(n_qubits, n_qubits)
# Step 2: Initialize superposition of all states
qc.h(range(n_qubits))
# Step 3: Construct a simple illustrative oracle
qc.cz(0, 1)
qc.cz(2, 3)
# Step 4: Apply Grover's diffusion operator
qc.h(range(n_qubits))
qc.x(range(n_qubits))
qc.h(n_qubits - 1)
qc.mct(list(range(n_qubits - 1)), n_qubits - 1)
qc.h(n_qubits - 1)
qc.x(range(n_qubits))
qc.h(range(n_qubits))
# Step 5: Measure the results
qc.measure(range(n_qubits), range(n_qubits))
# Execute the circuit
simulator = Aer.get_backend('qasm_simulator')
job = execute(transpile(qc, simulator), backend=simulator, shots=1024)
result = job.result()
counts = result.get_counts()
plot_histogram(counts)
```

Let us now interpret what is happening here:

1. The Hadamard layer creates the superposition of all possible Sudoku states.
2. The CZ gates simulate a basic oracle by introducing phase shifts.
3. The diffusion block amplifies valid states.
4. Finally, measurement converts the quantum state back to classical information.

Output and interpretation

When this circuit runs on the simulator, it produces a histogram showing different binary outcomes. Each binary string represents a possible Sudoku configuration. The tallest bar in the histogram corresponds to the valid configuration identified by Grover's algorithm.

Even though this is a simplified implementation, it demonstrates how quantum interference helps focus computational effort on correct answers, rather than brute-forcing through all possibilities.

In a complete Sudoku solver, the oracle would encode all puzzle constraints with much greater precision, and the amplified output state would correspond to a fully valid board configuration. Nevertheless, this prototype provides an important conceptual foundation by showing how quantum search can narrow the solution space and highlight the most promising candidate states through amplitude amplification.

Portfolio optimization with QAOA on AWS Braket

Every investor dreams of maximizing returns while minimizing risk—a problem at the heart of portfolio optimization. In finance, constructing an optimal portfolio involves deciding how much to invest in each asset to reduce overall risk while increasing expected profit. The challenge arises because the relationships among assets (their correlations) create an enormous search space of possible investment combinations.

Classical algorithms handle this through numerical methods such as quadratic programming or Monte Carlo simulations. However, as the number of assets grows, these approaches become computationally expensive. Quantum computing offers a new path forward through the QAOA, which blends classical optimization with quantum mechanics to efficiently tackle discrete combinatorial problems.

In this section, we will use AWS Braket, Amazon's quantum cloud platform, to implement a portfolio optimization model using QAOA. You will see how quantum circuits can represent financial decision variables, how expectation values encode portfolio cost, and how classical optimizers guide the quantum model toward an optimal investment strategy.

Algorithmic background

To apply QAOA effectively, the optimization problem must first be expressed in a form suitable for quantum processing. Many practical optimization tasks including scheduling, logistics, and financial portfolio selection can be reformulated as binary decision problems. By representing these decisions with qubits and translating the objective function into a Hamiltonian, the problem becomes compatible with a variational quantum circuit that can explore the solution space through parameterized quantum operations.

The QAOA was designed to solve problems expressible as the minimization of a cost function over binary variables. It alternates between two unitary operations:

- **Problem unitary ($U_{(}C_{)}$)**: Encodes the cost function into a Hamiltonian whose ground state corresponds to the optimal solution.
- **Mixer unitary ($U_{(}B_{)}$)**: Introduces transitions among states to explore the solution landscape.

These operations are parameterized by angles (γ, β). The algorithm repeats p layers of these unitaries, measuring the system's expectation value after each round. A classical optimizer [such as **Constrained Optimization by Linear Approximation** (**COBYLA**) or **simultaneous perturbation stochastic approximation (SPSA)**] then adjusts γ and β to minimize the expected cost.

When applied to portfolio optimization, the cost Hamiltonian includes:

- **Expected return**: Representing reward (to be maximized).
- **Risk**: Represented by asset correlations.
- **Budget constraint**: Limiting the number of assets chosen.

QAOA treats these factors as energy contributions in a quantum system. By minimizing the total energy, we identify the optimal portfolio configuration.

Implementation steps

Implementing a QAOA-based solution involves translating classical financial variables into a quantum optimization framework. The process begins with defining the portfolio objective, continues with constructing the corresponding quantum circuit, and concludes with iterative parameter optimization through a hybrid quantum–classical workflow.

Let us now see how this concept translates into practice:

1. **Define the portfolio problem**: Assume we have four assets. Each qubit represents a decision:

   $|0\rangle$ means do not include the asset, $|1\rangle$ means include the asset.

   We define two key matrices:

   - **Expected returns (r)**: potential gains per asset.
   - **Covariance matrix (Σ)**: representing correlations (risk) among assets.

   Our objective is to maximize returns while keeping total risk to a minimum. *Figure 15.2* summarizes the flow of portfolio optimization in QAOA, mapping traditional financial variables into their quantum equivalents through **quadratic unconstrained binary optimization** (**QUBO**) formulation and Hamiltonian construction:

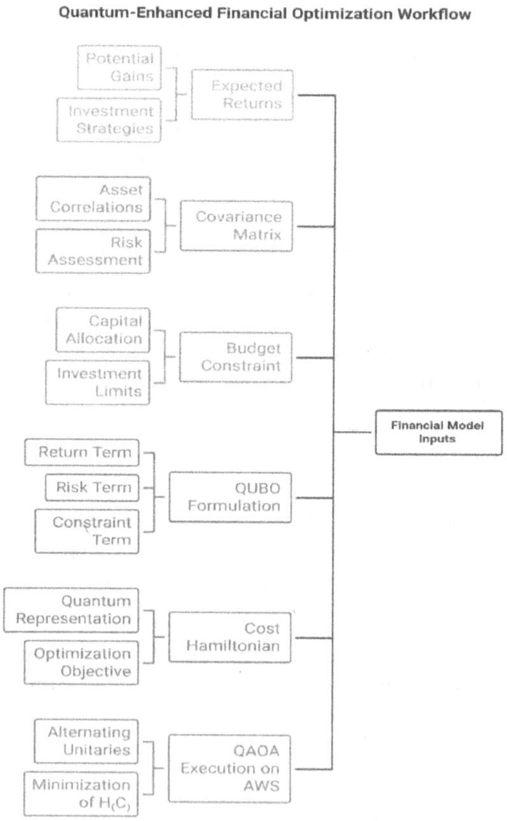

***Figure 15.2:** Quantum-enhanced financial optimization workflow*

2. **Convert to a QUBO**: The optimization objective can be expressed as:

$$C(x) = -r^T x + q x^T \Sigma x$$

Where r is the returns vector, Σ the covariance matrix, q a risk-aversion parameter, and x a binary vector of investment decisions.

This QUBO is mapped to a cost Hamiltonian $H_{(C)}$, where each term corresponds to a Pauli-Z operator acting on a qubit.

3. **Setup AWS Braket and QAOA circuit**: AWS Braket allows running hybrid quantum–classical workflows across multiple devices [*IonQ, Rigetti, Oxford Quantum Circuits* (*OQC*), etc.]. The following is a simplified demonstration using Braket's Python **software development kit** (**SDK**) and PennyLane integration:

```
from braket.circuits import Circuit
from braket.aws import AwsDevice
from braket.devices import LocalSimulator
from pennylane import qnode, numpy as np
import pennylane as qml
# Step 1: choose device (local simulator for testing)
device = LocalSimulator()
# Step 2: define problem parameters
n_qubits = 4
returns = np.array([0.10, 0.07, 0.12, 0.05])
covariance = np.array([
    [0.005, 0.002, 0.001, 0.000],
    [0.002, 0.004, 0.002, 0.001],
    [0.001, 0.002, 0.006, 0.003],
    [0.000, 0.001, 0.003, 0.005]
])
risk_factor = 0.5
# Step 3: define QAOA circuit
@qml.qnode(qml.device("braket.local.qubit", wires=n_qubits))
def qaoa_circuit(gamma, beta):
    # initial superposition
    for i in range(n_qubits):
        qml.Hadamard(wires=i)
    # problem unitary (simplified)
    for i in range(n_qubits):
        qml.RZ(2 * gamma * (risk_factor * covariance[i][i] - returns[i]), wires=i)
    # mixer unitary
    for i in range(n_qubits):
        qml.RX(2 * beta, wires=i)
    return qml.expval(qml.PauliZ(0))
# Step 4: run optimization loop
gamma, beta = 0.5, 0.5
result = qaoa_circuit(gamma, beta)
print("Expectation value:", result)
```

This snippet initializes qubits, applies the problem and mixer unitaries, and evaluates the cost. In a full implementation, a classical optimizer iteratively updates γ and β to minimize the expected cost until convergence.

4. **Optimize parameters**: Using an optimizer like COBYLA, Nelder–Mead, or SPSA, we iteratively adjust the parameters (γ, β) to reduce the expected portfolio cost.

Each iteration follows:

a. Run the circuit with currents γ and β.

b. Measure the expectation value of $H_(C)$.

c. Update parameters toward a lower cost.

5. **Measure and interpret results**: After convergence, the measurement results show the probability of each bitstring configuration. Each string corresponds to a combination of assets. The bitstring with the highest probability represents the optimal portfolio.

   For instance, a measurement result 1010 means assets 1 and 3 should be included, while 2 and 4 should be excluded.

Results and discussion

Running the previous setup on the AWS Braket local simulator yields an expectation value landscape that gradually converges as the parameters are tuned.

You will notice how specific combinations dominate the measurement histogram—these represent low-risk, high-return portfolios given your defined parameters.

When executed on Braket's real quantum hardware, slight variations occur due to device noise, yet the overall probability distribution retains its characteristic peaks near optimal portfolios.

While the example presented here uses a simplified circuit and a small number of assets, the same approach can scale to larger financial models by incorporating additional qubits and more detailed risk constraints. As quantum hardware improves and hybrid optimization techniques mature, algorithms like QAOA may provide increasingly competitive solutions for complex financial decision-making problems.

Quantum image classification with PennyLane and PyTorch

Image classification is one of the most successful applications of classical ML. CNNs already power everything from medical imaging to self-driving cars. However, as datasets grow and architectures become more complex, energy consumption and training time increase.

Quantum ML (**QML**) proposes a new paradigm. By encoding image features into quantum states and exploiting properties such as entanglement and superposition, a quantum circuit can, in principle, capture richer correlations using fewer parameters.

In this section, we will build hybrid quantum–classical image classifiers using PennyLane integrated with PyTorch:

1. We start with a binary classification task—distinguishing between the digits 0 and 1.
2. Then we extend the model to a multi-class task — classifying digits 0 through 3.

The aim is not just to train a model but to understand how quantum layers can replace or complement classical neural components in deep learning pipelines. *Figure 15.3* illustrates the end-to-end hybrid process, showing how classical preprocessing integrates with quantum feature encoding and variational circuits to achieve image classification.

Algorithmic background

QNNs combine variational quantum circuits with classical ML techniques to form a hybrid learning model. In this approach, the quantum circuit serves as a trainable feature-transformation layer, while classical optimization algorithms guide the learning process by adjusting the circuit parameters. This framework allows quantum circuits to learn patterns in data in a manner analogous to classical neural networks.

At the heart of our classifier lies the QNN—a **parameterized quantum circuit** (**PQC**) whose rotation angles serve as neural network weights.

Each training step follows a hybrid loop:

- **Data encoding**: Classical pixel intensities are embedded into qubit rotations.
- **Variational circuit**: Parameterized gates (e.g., RY, RZ) transform the encoded state; entangling gates capture feature correlations.
- **Measurement**: Expectation values of Pauli-Z operators form the circuit's output vector.
- **Classical optimization**: PyTorch's backpropagation (via PennyLane's automatic differentiation) updates both quantum and classical parameters.

For multi-class problems, multiple QNN heads or a softmax layer map quantum outputs to several categories.

The overall learning pipeline integrates classical preprocessing, quantum feature extraction, and classical optimization. The workflow illustrated in *Figure 15.3* summarizes how image data flows through the hybrid quantum–classical classifier:

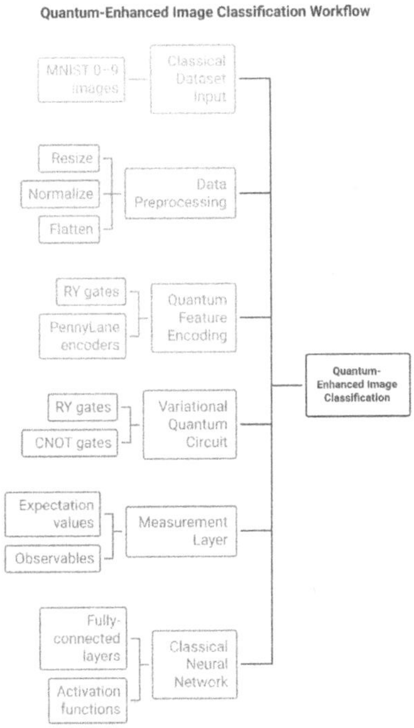

***Figure 15.3**: Quantum-enhanced image classification workflow*

Implementation steps

Building a hybrid quantum classifier involves several stages, including data preparation, quantum circuit construction, integration with a classical neural network framework, and iterative training. The following steps outline how these components are assembled into a working model:

The implementation begins with dataset preparation and continues through circuit construction and model training.

1. **Prepare the dataset**: We use the **Modified National Institute of Standards and Technology** (**MNIST**) dataset, downsampled to 4 × 4 pixels for fast quantum encoding.

   For binary classification, select only the digits *0* and *1*; for multi-class classification, include digits 0–3.

   The following Python snippet prepares the dataset and filters the relevant digit classes for training the hybrid model:

```
from torchvision import datasets, transforms
from torch.utils.data import DataLoader, Subset
transform = transforms.Compose([
    transforms.Resize((4,4)),
    transforms.ToTensor(),
    transforms.Normalize((0.5,), (0.5,))
])
dataset = datasets.MNIST(root="./data", train=True, download=True, transform=transform)
binary_idx = [i for i, (img, label) in enumerate(dataset) if label in [0,1]]
multi_idx  = [i for i, (img, label) in enumerate(dataset) if label in [0,1,2,3]]
```

2. **Build the quantum circuit**: We define a variational circuit that rotates each qubit according to encoded pixel values and introduces entanglement:

```
import pennylane as qml
from pennylane import numpy as np
n_qubits = 4
dev = qml.device("default.qubit", wires=n_qubits)
@qml.qnode(dev, interface="torch")
def quantum_circuit(inputs, weights):
    # Encode image features
    for i in range(n_qubits):
        qml.RY(inputs[i], wires=i)
    # Entangle neighboring qubits
    for i in range(n_qubits-1):
        qml.CNOT(wires=[i, i+1])
    # Trainable rotations
    for i in range(n_qubits):
        qml.RY(weights[i], wires=i)
    # Measure expectation
    return [qml.expval(qml.PauliZ(i)) for i in range(n_qubits)]
```

3. **Integrate with PyTorch**: Now, let us wrap the quantum circuit as a PyTorch layer and append classical layers for classification:

```
import torch
from torch import nn
class HybridQNN(nn.Module):
    def __init__(self):
        super().__init__()
        self.q_weights = nn.Parameter(torch.randn(n_qubits))
        self.fc = nn.Linear(n_qubits, 1)  # binary output
    def forward(self, x):
        q_out = []
        for sample in x:
            qc_out = quantum_circuit(sample, self.q_weights)
            q_out.append(qc_out)
        q_out = torch.stack(q_out)
        return torch.sigmoid(self.fc(q_out))
```

For multi-class tasks, modify the final layer:

```
self.fc = nn.Linear(n_qubits, 4)   # outputs for digits 0-3
```

4. **Training and evaluation**:

```
model = HybridQNN()
criterion = nn.BCELoss()
optimizer = torch.optim.Adam(model.parameters(), lr=0.01)
for epoch in range(5):
    for images, labels in DataLoader(Subset(dataset, binary_idx), batch_
size=16, shuffle=True):
        images = images.view(-1, 4)  # flatten 4x4 into 4 features
        optimizer.zero_grad()
        output = model(images)
        loss = criterion(output.squeeze(), labels.float())
        loss.backward()
        optimizer.step()
    print(f"Epoch {epoch+1}, Loss: {loss.item():.4f}")
```

Results and discussion

After several epochs, the binary classifier begins to separate digits 0 and 1 with increasing confidence. Extending the model to multi-class (digits 0–3) requires only changing the output dimension and using **`CrossEntropyLoss`** instead of binary loss.

When plotted, the decision boundaries show how quantum embeddings introduce subtle curvature, patterns a purely linear classifier might miss. Although the circuit presented here is intentionally compact, it demonstrates how quantum circuits can serve as learnable components within modern ML pipelines. With larger datasets, deeper circuits, and improved quantum hardware, hybrid QNNs may provide new opportunities for pattern recognition tasks where classical models struggle to capture complex correlations.

Project design, implementation and testing

Every successful quantum project, whether it solves a puzzle, optimizes a portfolio, or classifies images, follows a well-structured pipeline, from conceptual design to rigorous testing. In classical software engineering, this process is second nature. However, in quantum application development, project design introduces new considerations: circuit depth, noise resilience, hardware compatibility, and quantum–classical interfacing.

This section explores how to plan, design, implement, and test end-to-end quantum projects effectively. Using lessons from the previous case studies—Grover's Sudoku solver, portfolio optimization with QAOA, and quantum image classification—we will establish a systematic methodology that can be applied to a wide range of quantum problem domains.

Algorithmic background

While each quantum algorithm has unique mathematical foundations, its implementation follows a general life cycle analogous to classical project engineering, with key stages:

1. **Problem formulation**: Define the challenge in terms of data, constraints, and desired outcomes.
2. **Quantum mapping**: Translate the classical objective into a Hamiltonian or circuit representation.
3. **Algorithm selection**: Choose the most appropriate quantum algorithm (e.g., Grover's, VQE, QAOA, QNN).
4. **Circuit construction**: Encode data into qubits, apply quantum operations, and design measurement schemes.

5. **Simulation and debugging**: Run circuits on simulators to test correctness before hardware execution.
6. **Hybrid integration**: Combine quantum and classical elements for real-world applicability.
7. **Testing and validation**: Evaluate accuracy, convergence, and robustness under different configurations.

The lifecycle described above can be visualized as an iterative workflow in which quantum circuit design, classical optimization, and experimental validation continuously inform one another. The architecture in *Figure 15.4* illustrates how these components interact within a typical hybrid quantum–classical development pipeline:

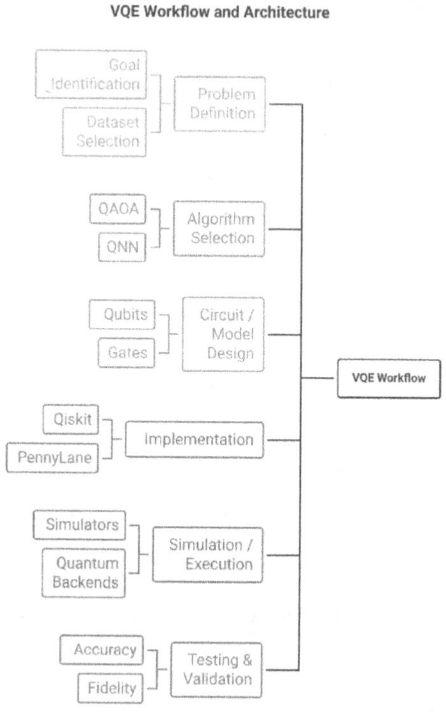

***Figure 15.4**: VQE workflow and architecture*

Implementation steps

After establishing the algorithmic framework, the next stage is translating these conceptual stages into a practical development process. This involves organizing the problem definition, circuit design, optimization strategy, and testing procedures into a structured workflow that can be implemented using quantum programming frameworks.

Let us walk through the process step-by-step using a generalizable design workflow:

1. **Define the problem statement**: Begin with a clearly articulated question. For example:
   a. *Can Grover's algorithm speed up Sudoku search?*
   b. *Can QAOA produce efficient asset allocations?*
   c. *Can hybrid QNNs classify handwritten digits?*

   The formulation should specify input data, desired outputs, and evaluation metrics (e.g., accuracy, loss function, energy minimization).

2. **Design the quantum workflow**: The workflow design integrates three core perspectives:
   a. **Data perspective**: How data (e.g., pixel values, risk matrices, Sudoku cells) is encoded into qubits.
   b. **Algorithmic perspective**: What algorithm or variational form drives computation?

   c. **Execution perspective**: Where and how the circuit runs—local simulators for testing, hardware for deployment.

   A typical quantum workflow can be visualized as:

```
Classical Input → Data Encoding → Quantum Circuit Execution → Measurement →
Classical Postprocessing
```

3. **Implement incrementally**: Implementation should follow a layered approach. Begin with small, verifiable components:
   a. Test data preprocessing functions.
   b. Verify single-qubit encodings.
   c. Expand gradually to multi-qubit entanglement.
   d. Introduce optimization or training loops only after circuit correctness is validated.
4. **Integrate classical components**: Most real-world quantum applications are hybrid by nature. Classical elements handle:
   a. Optimizer updates (COBYLA, Adam, SPSA).
   b. Loss evaluation and visualization.
   c. Dataset batching and performance tracking.
   d. These elements communicate with quantum circuits via frameworks such as PennyLane, Qiskit Runtime, or AWS Braket SDK.
5. **Perform testing and verification**: Testing in quantum systems extends beyond verifying output correctness. It includes:
   a. **Functional testing**: Ensuring each circuit block performs as intended.
   b. **Statistical testing**: Comparing simulation results across multiple shots to detect anomalies.
   c. **Noise analysis**: Measuring how device noise or gate errors affect accuracy.
   d. **Performance benchmarking**: Comparing runtime and fidelity across simulators and hardware backends.
   e. **Regression testing**: Re-running known configurations to ensure updates do not degrade performance.
6. **Evaluate results and iterate**: Evaluate results against the problem objectives. For example:
   a. **Sudoku**: Validate if the bitstring corresponds to a valid grid.
   b. **QAOA**: Compare computed returns vs. known optimal portfolios.
   c. **QNN**: Assess accuracy and loss trends on test data.
   d. Iterate by refining encodings, adjusting hyperparameters, or modifying circuit depth based on observed performance.

Code design template

Although specific implementations vary across frameworks, most quantum software projects follow a similar modular structure. The template below outlines a reusable pattern for organizing quantum circuits, optimization loops, and evaluation functions in a clear and extensible manner.

Here is a simplified pseudocode structure applicable to most quantum projects:

```
# Step 1 - Define problem and data
data = load_data()
params = initialize_parameters()
# Step 2 - Create quantum device
dev = qml.device("default.qubit", wires=n_qubits)
```

```
# Step 3 - Build variational circuit
@qml.qnode(dev)
def circuit(inputs, weights):
    encode(inputs)
    apply_ansatz(weights)
    return measure()
# Step 4 - Define cost function
def cost(weights):
    return expectation_value(circuit, data, weights)
# Step 5 - Optimize
opt = qml.GradientDescentOptimizer(stepsize=0.1)
for i in range(epochs):
    weights = opt.step(cost, weights)
    log_results(i, weights, cost(weights))
```

Results and testing insights

When testing your quantum project, you will notice results vary depending on hardware and noise levels. On simulators, outcomes should match theoretical expectations; on hardware, deviations often arise from gate infidelities or decoherence.

Comparing both environments helps evaluate quantum robustness on how well the algorithm tolerates real-world imperfections.

For this reason, it is important to evaluate results not only in terms of accuracy but also in terms of stability and reproducibility. Repeating experiments across different noise models, circuit depths, and parameter settings provides deeper insight into how reliably the quantum workflow performs under varying computational conditions.

Applying theory to end-to-end applications

Building end-to-end quantum applications marks the moment when theory and experimentation converge. By this stage, learners have explored three representative domains—search (Grover's Sudoku), optimization (QAOA Portfolio), and ML (quantum image classification)—each illustrating a different facet of quantum computation.

Now, the challenge lies in integrating theory, design, and evaluation into a unified workflow that reflects how modern quantum solutions are developed in research and industry.

Unlike classical programming, where an algorithm can be neatly encapsulated in code, quantum application development demands a systems-thinking mindset. One must consider circuit scalability, noise models, data encoding schemes, and hybrid orchestration between classical and quantum processors.

This section synthesizes these aspects into a methodological blueprint for translating theoretical insight into practical, deployable quantum projects.

Algorithmic background

Before examining specific implementations, it is useful to recognize that most quantum algorithms follow a common operational pattern. Regardless of the application domain, quantum workflows involve encoding classical information into qubits, transforming those states through quantum gates, and extracting probabilistic outcomes through measurement.

Across all quantum paradigms, the same foundational pillars apply:

- **Representation of information**: How data is encoded: amplitude, angle, or qubit-wise feature mapping.
- **Computation via unitary evolution**: How algorithms transform these encodings through parameterized

oracles or Hamiltonians.

- **Measurement and statistical interpretation**: How quantum outputs translate into classical results.
- **Hybrid feedback loop**: How classical optimizers adjust circuit parameters based on measurement outcomes.

Each end-to-end solution reuses these stages but contextualizes them differently—Grover's algorithm treats constraints as oracles, QAOA treats energy minima as portfolios, and QNNs treat expectation values as class probabilities.

Integration of concepts

The three quantum projects, Grover's search, QAOA optimization, and QNN illustrate how different quantum algorithms can complement one another, connecting search, optimization, and learning into a unified framework for applied quantum computing. The following table summarizes how these three projects complement one another, showcasing their respective goals, techniques, and educational outcomes:

Quantum approach	Primary goal	Core technique	Educational outcome
Grover's search	Constraint satisfaction	Oracle and amplitude amplification	Understanding quantum search
QAOA optimization	Minimizing risk and maximizing return	Variational circuit and hybrid optimization	Linking quantum physics to decision science
QNN	Pattern recognition and classification	Variational encoding and gradient descent	Bridging quantum and deep learning

***Table 15.1**: Integration of quantum projects and their educational impact*

Together, they provide a panoramic view of how quantum mechanics can enhance classical computation from deterministic search to probabilistic reasoning and learning.

Figure 15.5 brings together all three mini projects discussed in this chapter, highlighting how Grover's algorithm, QAOA, and quantum image classification integrate through shared workflows and cloud execution environments.

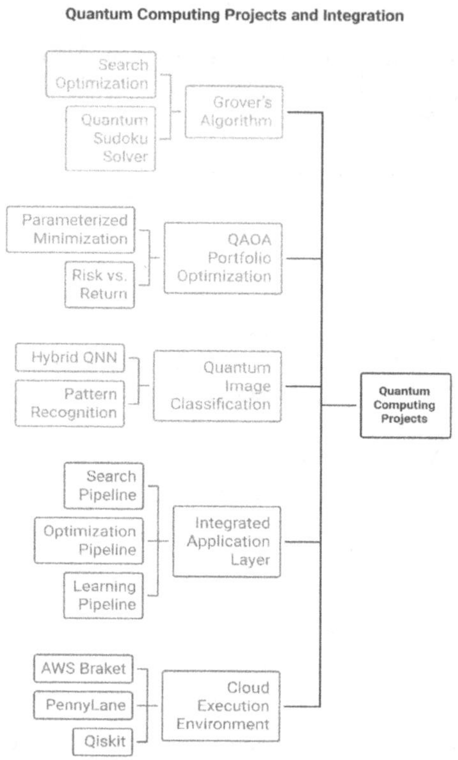

Figure 15.5: *Quantum computing projects and integration*

Implementation path for end-to-end projects

To move from isolated experiments to complete applications, follow this structured approach:

1. **Define a cross-domain objective**: Design a project that combines multiple quantum techniques. Example: Use Grover's algorithm to generate candidate portfolios, then QAOA to refine them for optimal return, and finally apply a QNN to predict risk patterns based on historical data.
2. **Develop a unified data model**: Ensure that all algorithms share compatible data representations. For instance, a normalized vector of financial metrics can serve as both an input for QAOA's Hamiltonian and as training data for a QNN.
3. **Orchestrate execution environments**: Use cloud platforms like *AWS Braket*, *IBM Quantum*, or *Xanadu Cloud* to manage hybrid execution. You might run Grover's search on a simulator, QAOA on Rigetti hardware, and the QNN training loop on a GPU-accelerated classical host—all within one pipeline.
4. **Testing and performance monitoring**: Monitor both classical metrics (accuracy, loss, runtime) and quantum metrics (circuit depth, fidelity, noise rates). Visualization dashboards can track how each iteration of a hybrid loop converges toward the desired outcome.
5. **Reflect and iterate**: After achieving a working prototype, evaluate which aspect of quantum advantage truly appeared:

   a. Faster convergence? b. Better generalization? c. Lower computational cost?

   Document lessons learned about algorithm tuning, encoding efficiency, and hybrid orchestration.

Case study integration example

This example demonstrates how different quantum algorithms can work together within a single application pipeline. Rather than solving a problem with one technique, the workflow distributes tasks across search, optimization, and learning stages.

Consider integrating the three earlier projects into one demonstrative ecosystem:

1. **Input phase: Sudoku encoding**: Grover's circuit generates valid configurations (analogous to feasible financial portfolios).
2. **Optimization phase: QAOA**: Among feasible states, QAOA minimizes risk or energy, refining toward the best solution.
3. **Evaluation phase: QNN**: The QNN classifies output states as optimal, sub-optimal, or invalid based on learned patterns.

The outcome: a pipeline that performs logical search, optimization, and evaluation entirely within a quantum-inspired framework.

Testing and validation

Before deploying a quantum application, it is essential to verify that each module behaves as expected. Initial testing should be performed on simulators to validate circuit logic and parameter settings before executing the workflow on real quantum hardware.

Testing integrated projects extends to:

- **Cross-module consistency**: Ensure Grover's outputs feed correctly into QAOA inputs.
- **Statistical robustness**: Verify repeated runs yield similar distributions despite quantum randomness.
- **Scalability checks**: Gradually increase qubit counts and observe performance trade-offs.
- **Hardware deployment**: Validate simulator-derived parameters on real quantum devices.

Reflection on learning and practice

Working through these projects helps learners move beyond theoretical understanding toward practical quantum development. It reinforces how algorithm design, experimentation, and hybrid computation combine to produce meaningful quantum applications.

Completing these projects reveals a deep truth about the evolving landscape of quantum technology: quantum programming is as much about mindset as it is about mathematics.

It teaches:

- How to decompose complex problems into quantum-friendly representations.
- How to collaborate across classical and quantum domains.
- How to tolerate uncertainty, probabilistic outcomes, and continuous experimentation.

Conclusion

This chapter presented end-to-end quantum mini projects as a bridge between theoretical understanding and practical implementation, illustrating how diverse quantum algorithms can be applied to real-world computational challenges. Through step-by-step projects using Qiskit, PennyLane, and AWS Braket, readers explored the design and execution of applications across three important domains: search, optimization, and classification. These domains were represented through Grover's algorithm, the QAOA, and QNNs, each demonstrating a distinct paradigm of quantum computation.

A key theme throughout the chapter has been the role of hybrid quantum–classical workflows. Because current quantum devices operate in the NISQ era, successful applications often rely on collaboration between quantum circuits and classical optimization methods. By combining quantum state preparation and measurement with classical parameter tuning and data processing, these hybrid approaches enable meaningful experimentation even with today's hardware limitations.

Equally important is the emphasis on project design, testing, and validation. Developing quantum applications requires more than implementing an algorithm; it involves careful problem formulation, thoughtful data encoding, circuit design, and iterative evaluation. Through the structured methodologies presented in this chapter, readers learned how to construct reproducible workflows that can be adapted to different application domains.

Ultimately, these end-to-end projects demonstrate that quantum computing is evolving from a purely theoretical discipline into a practical engineering field. By integrating algorithmic insight, software frameworks, and experimental evaluation, researchers and developers can build scalable quantum solutions that address increasingly complex problems. As quantum hardware continues to advance, the skills and methodologies developed through projects like these will play a crucial role in shaping the future of quantum-enabled technologies.

Questions

1. **How does Grover's algorithm achieve a quadratic speedup over classical search?**

   Answer: Grover's algorithm achieves a quadratic speedup by using amplitude amplification. It initializes a uniform superposition of all possible states, applies an oracle to mark valid solutions, and then uses the diffusion operator to amplify the amplitude of those marked states. After roughly $\sqrt{N}$ iterations, the probability of measuring the correct solution becomes significantly higher than in classical search.

2. **What is the mathematical representation of the QAOA cost Hamiltonian in portfolio optimization?**

   Answer: The QAOA cost Hamiltonian H_C is derived from the QUBO form:

   $$C(x) = -r^T x + q x^T \Sigma x$$

   where r is the expected returns vector, Σ is the covariance matrix, and q is the risk-aversion coefficient. This expression is mapped to a Hamiltonian by replacing binary variables with Pauli-Z operators, allowing quantum circuits to minimize the cost function through energy expectation values.

3. **How does data encoding differ in Grover's, QAOA, and QNN-based implementations?**

   Answer: Data encoding plays a crucial role in quantum algorithms because it determines how classical information is represented within quantum circuits. Different algorithms use different encoding strategies depending on the nature of the problem they are designed to solve.

   a. **Grover's algorithm**: Encodes discrete logical conditions as Boolean oracle functions.

   b. **QAOA**: Encodes continuous optimization terms (returns, risk) into a cost Hamiltonian.

   c. **QNNs**: Encode analog data, such as pixel intensities, into qubit rotation angles (RY or RX gates), allowing smooth gradient-based learning. This diversity in encoding reflects the algorithm's underlying computational objective—search, optimization, or learning.

   This diversity in encoding reflects the algorithm's underlying computational objective—search, optimization, or learning.

4. **What role does parameter optimization play in hybrid quantum–classical algorithms?**

   Answer: Parameter optimization fine-tunes circuit parameters (like γ and β in QAOA or rotation weights in QNNs) using classical optimizers such as COBYLA, SPSA, or Adam. The quantum processor evaluates the cost or loss function, and the classical processor updates parameters iteratively—forming a feedback loop that enables efficient convergence even on noisy hardware.

5. **How does Grover's algorithm contribute to problem-solving?**

   Answer: Grover's algorithm efficiently identifies valid solutions within large search spaces using amplitude amplification, offering a quadratic speedup compared to classical brute-force search methods.

6. **What role does QAOA play in quantum optimization?**

   Answer: QAOA models optimization problems as Hamiltonians and uses PQCs to minimize cost functions—balancing exploration and exploitation through hybrid classical optimization.

7. **How do QNNs enhance ML?**

   Answer: QNNs embed classical data into quantum states and use entanglement to capture complex feature relationships, enabling efficient pattern recognition with fewer parameters than classical deep networks.

8. **How is gradient computation handled in hybrid QNN models?**

   Answer: Gradients in hybrid QNNs are computed using the parameter-shift rule, which evaluates the circuit twice—once at $\theta+\pi/2$ and once at $\theta-\pi/2$. This allows differentiation of quantum expectation values with respect to circuit parameters, enabling seamless integration with classical frameworks like PyTorch for backpropagation.

9. **How do hybrid quantum–classical workflows improve performance?**

   Answer: They divide computation between quantum and classical processors—quantum systems handle state preparation and measurement, while classical systems manage optimization and parameter tuning, ensuring efficiency and scalability.

10. **What factors affect circuit depth and fidelity in end-to-end quantum projects?**

    Answer: Circuit depth and fidelity are influenced by gate count, entanglement structure, noise levels, and hardware connectivity. Deeper circuits increase expressivity but are more susceptible to decoherence and gate errors. Balancing depth with device capabilities is crucial for maintaining high-fidelity results on NISQ hardware.

Exercises

1. Implement Grover's algorithm in Qiskit to solve a simplified 3×3 Sudoku puzzle. Construct an oracle that encodes valid number placements and verify the solution using measurement histograms from the QASM simulator.
2. Modify your Grover circuit to include multiple valid solutions. Observe how the number of marked states affects the number of optimal Grover iterations and the resulting probability distribution.
3. Construct a QAOA-based portfolio optimization model in AWS Braket or PennyLane. Use three assets with a defined returns vector and covariance matrix, and compare the optimized bitstring with the classical minimum-risk solution.
4. Experiment with different optimizers (e.g., COBYLA, SPSA, Adam) in your QAOA implementation. Plot the cost function convergence curves for each optimizer and analyze how the convergence rate and accuracy vary.
5. Design and train a simple QNN (QNN) in PennyLane integrated with PyTorch to classify binary digits (0 and 1) from a 4×4 MNIST dataset. Evaluate model accuracy and visualize loss reduction over epochs.
6. Extend your QNN model for a multi-class task (digits 0–3). Compare accuracy trends between binary and multi-class setups and discuss how circuit depth and qubit count influence training stability.
7. Integrate the three quantum projects into a hybrid workflow: use Grover's algorithm to generate candidate solutions, QAOA to optimize among them, and a QNN to classify or evaluate the quality of final results.

8. Simulate noise effects on your Grover or QAOA circuits using Qiskit's noise models or AWS Braket's depolarization parameters. Examine how increased noise affects the probability of success and solution fidelity.
9. Create a comparative table summarizing the resource requirements (qubits, depth, iterations) and performance of Grover's, QAOA, and QNN projects. Highlight their strengths and trade-offs in the context of NISQ era quantum computing.
10. Write a 200-word reflection explaining how end-to-end quantum projects bridge theory and implementation, and how hybrid workflows can accelerate the development of scalable quantum applications across different domains.

Chapter 16

Artificial Intelligence and Quantum Computing

Introduction

Artificial intelligence (**AI**) and **quantum computing** (**QC**) are transforming modern computation, and their convergence marks a pivotal stage in this evolution. Through accessible Python frameworks such as Qiskit Machine Learning, PennyLane, and TensorFlow Quantum, learners can now build, train, and evaluate intelligent quantum models that merge data-driven reasoning with the physical principles of superposition and entanglement.

This integration enables powerful hybrid workflows. AI models enhance quantum systems through intelligent calibration, noise mitigation, and optimization, while quantum processors contribute exponential representational capacity to AI tasks such as classification, sampling, and generative modeling. The result is a collaborative ecosystem **Quantum AI** (**QAI**), where classical and quantum algorithms co-learn in unified pipelines.

Modern toolkits make this exploration practical. You can simulate circuits locally or run them on real quantum backends via the cloud, using classical optimizers and differentiable quantum layers in tandem. Such flexibility supports both teaching and advanced research, bridging theoretical principles with executable experimentation.

This chapter introduces the AI-Quantum Convergence by examining its motivation, core algorithms, and hybrid architectures. It guides you through **quantum neural networks** (**QNNs**), quantum-inspired learning methods, and AI-driven quantum optimization, complemented by case studies and Python labs. By the end, you will understand how AI and QC together form a foundation for the next-generation of intelligent, adaptive, and scalable computational systems.

Structure

The chapter covers the following topics:

- AI-Quantum Convergence
- Quantum-inspired AI algorithms
- Building advanced quantum neural networks
- Case studies and Python labs
- Symbiosis between AI and quantum computing
- Hybrid AI-Quantum architectures
- AI for quantum system optimization
- Challenges and future research directions

Objectives

This chapter aims to help readers understand the convergence of AI and QC as a unified framework for intelligent computation. It introduces how AI techniques such as machine learning and optimization can enhance quantum system performance, and how quantum algorithms can accelerate and enrich AI models. Readers will explore hybrid architectures such as the **variational quantum classifier** (**VQC**) and the QNN, learning how classical and quantum layers collaborate within adaptive feedback loops. Hands-on Python labs using Qiskit Machine Learning and PennyLane demonstrate key concepts including data encoding, hybrid optimization, and AI-driven quantum calibration. The chapter also examines quantum-inspired algorithms that bring quantum principles to classical systems. By the end, readers will gain the conceptual and practical skills needed to design, simulate, and analyze AI-Quantum workflows for next-generation intelligent systems.

AI-Quantum Convergence

In the contemporary landscape of computational science, two frontiers have independently reshaped the way machines perceive, learn, and reason: AI and QC. AI, rooted in the ambition to replicate human intelligence through algorithms and data, has evolved from symbolic reasoning to deep neural networks capable of generating text, recognizing images, and translating languages. QC, in contrast, draws its strength from the counterintuitive principles of superposition, entanglement, and interference, enabling information to be processed in fundamentally new ways.

Today, these two domains are no longer isolated. Their intersection—often referred to as QAI—marks the beginning of a transformative era in computational thinking. While AI provides models that learn from data, QC introduces a new substrate that can accelerate learning, explore vast search spaces simultaneously, and capture correlations that remain hidden to classical systems. This convergence forms the intellectual foundation for the remainder of this chapter.

Parallel revolutions converging toward a shared vision

The trajectories of AI and QC have long run in parallel.

Early AI systems of the 1950s and 1960s were purely symbolic, relying on hand-crafted rules and deterministic logic. By the 1980s, the emergence of connectionism and neural networks shifted attention toward statistical learning. Around the same period, physicists such as *Richard Feynman* and *David Deutsch* were articulating the theoretical possibility of quantum machines that could simulate nature more efficiently than any classical computer.

For decades, these developments progressed independently—AI, hungry for computational power, and QC, struggling for physical realization. The modern era of cloud-accessible quantum hardware and high-performance AI accelerators has finally made it possible for these two revolutions to meet. Their union is not accidental but inevitable: data-driven intelligence requires exponential resources, and quantum mechanics naturally provides exponential representational capacity.

The significance of the convergence

The merging of AI and QC is driven by more than technological curiosity; it arises from their shared potential to overcome classical computational limitations.

The synergy between AI and QC can be understood through four foundational principles each representing a distinct yet interdependent pillar of this convergence. *Figure 16.1* illustrates the four cornerstones driving the AI-Quantum relationship:

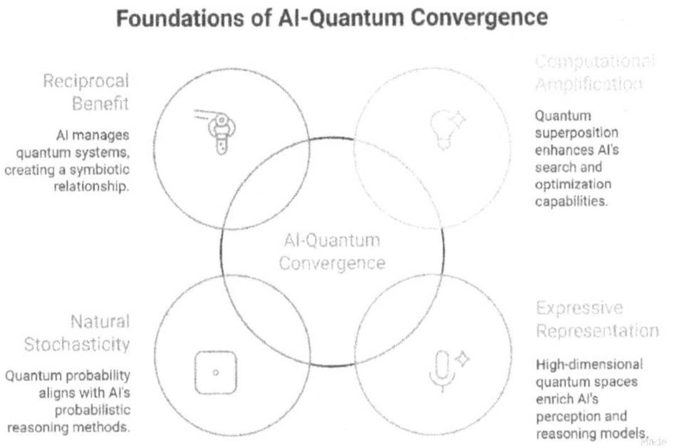

***Figure 16.1**: Foundations of AI-Quantum Convergence*

The convergence is transformative rather than additive, reshaping learning, reasoning, and optimization across computing paradigms:

- **Computational amplification**: Quantum superposition enables parallel evaluation of many possibilities, offering potential speed-ups for search, optimization, and sampling central to AI.
- **Expressive representation**: High-dimensional quantum state spaces encode complex correlations that are difficult for classical representations to capture.
- **Natural stochasticity**: Inherent quantum probabilism aligns naturally with Bayesian reasoning, reinforcement learning, and generative models.
- **Reciprocal benefit**: Quantum resources enhance AI, while AI techniques optimize quantum systems by calibrating qubits, reducing noise, and improving control—forming a truly symbiotic relationship.

Milestones in AI-Quantum integration

The evolution of AI and QC reflects a gradual convergence from symbolic reasoning to intelligent quantum architectures. The following table summarizes key milestones highlighting this progression:

Era	Dominant trend	Representative breakthroughs
1950–1990	Symbolic AI and rule-based reasoning	No quantum integration; classical inference systems
2000–2015	Data-driven machine learning	First theoretical analyses of quantum speed-ups for learning
2015–2020	Birth of **quantum machine learning (QML)**	VQC, quantum annealer optimization
2020–Present	AI-Quantum co-evolution	AI-controlled quantum calibration, hybrid deep–quantum architectures

***Table 16.1**: Milestones in AI-Quantum integration*

This chronology highlights how incremental theoretical curiosity matured into practical frameworks such as TensorFlow Quantum, PennyLane, and Qiskit Machine Learning, where quantum circuits are treated as differentiable components within larger AI models.

Toward cognitive quantum systems

The ultimate vision extends beyond algorithmic acceleration. Researchers now imagine cognitive quantum systems—integrated environments in which perception, reasoning, and control operate coherently across classical and quantum layers.

Such systems could analyze complex sensory data, encode it into quantum representations for high-dimensional inference, and interpret the outcomes through classical neural or symbolic components. The result would be a continuum of intelligence rather than a dichotomy between classical and quantum computation.

Example of classical feature encoding into a quantum state

Classical data can be represented in quantum form through simple encoding operations. The following code shows how a numerical feature is mapped to a qubit amplitude using Qiskit:

```
from qiskit import QuantumCircuit, Aer, execute
import numpy as np
# Classical data point mapped to quantum amplitude
theta = np.pi / 6
qc = QuantumCircuit(1)
qc.ry(2 * theta, 0)    # rotation encodes the feature value
backend = Aer.get_backend('statevector_simulator')
state = execute(qc, backend).result().get_statevector()
print("Encoded state amplitudes:", state)
```

This circuit shows how a single numerical feature can be encoded into a qubit's amplitude, forming a basic quantum data embedding step and a foundation for QML pipelines.

Symbiosis between AI and quantum computing

The relationship between AI and QC is not one of dependency but of mutual reinforcement. Each domain enhances the other's potential—AI provides adaptive intelligence to manage complex quantum systems, while QC offers a fundamentally new substrate to accelerate and enrich learning.

This symbiosis represents a co-evolution of computational paradigms, blending data-driven reasoning with the physical principles of quantum mechanics.

In practice, this interaction enables AI to analyze quantum experimental data, identify system patterns, and support intelligent optimization. At the same time, QC introduces new computational possibilities that can enhance complex learning and optimization tasks.

Bidirectional flow of benefits

The relationship between AI and QC is reciprocal, with each enhancing the other. AI improves quantum system performance, while QC expands the capabilities of AI models, creating a continuous cycle of innovation.

This reciprocal exchange creates a feedback loop in which improvements in quantum hardware expand AI capabilities, while advances in AI enable more efficient monitoring, control, and optimization of quantum systems.

AI empowering QC

Quantum hardware is powerful but fragile, with qubits prone to decoherence, noise, and instability. Machine learning techniques, such as reinforcement learning, Bayesian optimization, and neural control are increasingly used to calibrate, stabilize, and improve quantum operations.

AI contributes to QC through:

- **Error diagnosis and correction**: Deep neural networks detect and classify noise patterns to support real-time error mitigation.
- **Pulse sequence optimization**: Reinforcement learning agents tune microwave pulse parameters to maximize fidelity during quantum gate execution.

- **Hardware calibration**: Regression models predict qubit drift, enabling dynamic recalibration without manual intervention.
- **Quantum compiler optimization**: Graph neural networks and evolutionary algorithms optimize circuit layouts to minimize gate depth and cross-talk.

These applications transform quantum hardware development from manual trial-and-error to data-driven automation, drastically shortening calibration cycles.

Quantum computing empowering artificial intelligence

QC provides new computational resources that can enhance AI capabilities by manipulating exponentially large state spaces, supporting high-dimensional feature learning, probabilistic reasoning, and global optimization.

Key contributions include:

- **QML**: Algorithms like **quantum support vector machine** (**QSVM**) and VQC use superposition to evaluate decision boundaries across large feature spaces.
- **Quantum-accelerated sampling**: Quantum annealing and amplitude estimation reduce the cost of sampling in probabilistic models.
- **QNNs**: **Parameterized quantum circuits** (**PQCs**) function as trainable layers within hybrid learning models.
- **Quantum Boltzmann machines**: Quantum states encode probability distributions, enabling faster convergence and richer representations.

Together, these advances redefine AI as a hybrid quantum–classical ecosystem, where quantum logic extends the scope of learnable patterns.

AI and QC form a two-way innovation loop: AI enhances quantum systems through intelligent control and calibration, while quantum computation extends AI's learning capacity and representational power.

Figure 16.2 illustrates this bidirectional enhancement, showing how each domain empowers the other to achieve greater efficiency, adaptability, and intelligence:

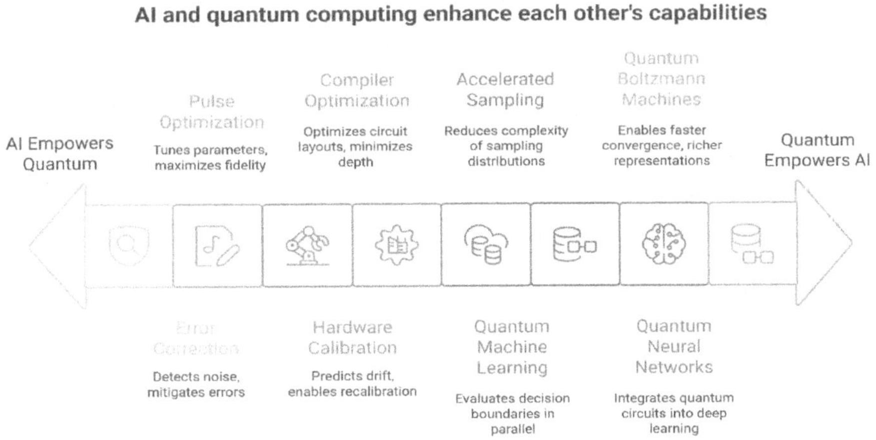

***Figure 16.2**: AI and QC enhance each other's capabilities*

Comparative summary of two directions of symbiosis

The collaboration between AI and QC is best understood through their complementary roles—each advancing the other's effectiveness in a shared computational ecosystem.

The following table summarizes the two primary directions of symbiosis, comparing how AI supports quantum operations and how quantum technologies enhance AI capabilities:

Perspective	Role of AI	Role of QC	Outcome
AI for QC	Learns to control and optimize quantum systems	Provides physical substrate for experimentation	Higher system fidelity and reduced noise
QC for AI	Consumes quantum-generated insights	Offers speed-ups and richer state representations	Accelerated and enhanced learning models

***Table 16.2**: Comparative summary of the two directions of symbiosis*

This comparison underscores the relationship's reciprocal nature.

AI sustains the operational operation of quantum systems, while quantum mechanics enriches the AI conceptually and computationally.

Emerging hybrid workflow

Hybrid AI-Quantum workflows integrate classical machine learning with quantum computation in a coordinated system. Classical algorithms prepare and manage data, while quantum circuits perform specialized transformations using quantum properties such as superposition and entanglement. This collaboration allows both technologies to complement each other within a unified learning process.

Modern research increasingly treats AI and QC as interlocking modules rather than separate technologies. A typical hybrid workflow progresses through the following stages:

1. **Data pre-processing**: Classical AI filters, normalizes, and encodes data into quantum-compatible formats (e.g., amplitude or angle encoding).
2. **Quantum computation**: The quantum circuit performs transformations, learning, or optimization tasks within the high-dimensional Hilbert space.
3. **Measurement and post-processing**: The resulting quantum states are measured and converted to classical probabilities or feature vectors.
4. **AI-based interpretation**: Machine learning models interpret the output—classifying patterns, tuning hyperparameters, or evaluating success criteria.

The synergy lies in the feedback loop: AI refines the quantum model based on performance metrics, while quantum computation provides AI with richer data representations.

Illustrative example of AI-driven calibration feedback

AI can support quantum hardware calibration by learning patterns from previous measurements and predicting system drift. By analyzing calibration data, machine learning models help anticipate changes in qubit behavior and assist in maintaining stable quantum operations.

AI techniques can enhance the reliability of quantum hardware by learning from calibration data to predict and correct system drift. The following code demonstrates a simple regression model that forecasts qubit drift, illustrating how AI aids automated quantum system calibration:

```
import numpy as np
from sklearn.linear_model import LinearRegression
# Example: AI model predicting qubit drift from noisy calibration data
np.random.seed(42)
time = np.arange(0, 100)
drift = 0.01 * time + np.random.normal(0, 0.05, 100)
model = LinearRegression().fit(time.reshape(-1, 1), drift)
```

```
predicted_drift = model.predict([[120]])  # forecast for future cycle
print(f"Predicted drift at t=120: {predicted_drift[0]:.4f}")
```

This simple regression example illustrates how a classical AI model can forecast qubit drift from calibration data, enabling automated adjustments to maintain gate fidelity in a real quantum processor.

Quantum-inspired AI algorithms

While the physical realization of large-scale quantum computers remains an ongoing pursuit, the mathematical ideas behind quantum mechanics have already begun to influence classical algorithm design. This emerging field, known as **Quantum-inspired AI**, adapts the principles of superposition, entanglement, and probabilistic interference to classical computing environments. These algorithms do not require qubits or cryogenic hardware; instead, they emulate quantum behavior to achieve superior performance in optimization, search, and pattern recognition tasks.

Quantum-inspired approaches represent a practical bridge between present-day AI systems and the quantum algorithms of the near future allowing researchers to experiment with quantum-like logic while remaining within the scalability of classical processors.

Essence of quantum inspiration

Quantum-inspired computing bridges the gap between classical algorithms and quantum principles. It applies key ideas from quantum mechanics to design more adaptive and efficient computational methods.

The term quantum-inspired describes algorithms that borrow concepts from quantum theory without executing on quantum hardware. Such methods may simulate amplitude-like probability weights or an interference-style combination of solutions.

These algorithms rely on three key analogies:

- **Superposition as parallel search**: Candidate solutions are explored collectively rather than sequentially.
- **Entanglement as correlation modeling**: Variable dependencies are captured through correlated updates.
- **Measurement as probabilistic selection**: Outcomes are obtained via stochastic sampling.

Together, these analogies translate quantum ideas into effective strategies for classical algorithm design.

Prominent quantum-inspired algorithms

Several classical optimization and learning techniques have been redesigned using quantum-inspired ideas to improve exploration and solution quality.

Many classical AI and optimization methods have been reinterpreted through quantum-inspired principles, producing algorithms that mimic quantum behavior on conventional hardware to improve learning and optimization:

- **Quantum-inspired evolutionary algorithm (QIEA)**: It represents solutions using probability amplitudes instead of fixed bits and updates them with rotation-like operators, improving diversity and accelerating convergence in high-dimensional searches.
- **Quantum-inspired particle swarm optimization (QPSO)**: These models particle positions probabilistically using a quantum delta potential concept, enabling broader exploration and reducing premature convergence compared to classical PSO.
- **Quantum-inspired Boltzmann machine (QIBM)**: QIBMs incorporate quantum tunneling–like effects into energy-based models, helping escape local minima and enhancing deep generative learning.
- **Quantum annealing–based learning:** Inspired by quantum annealing (e.g., in *D-Wave*), quantum-inspired annealing uses classical stochastic methods such as **simulated quantum annealing** (**SQA**) to efficiently approximate NP-hard optimization problems.

Comparative landscape

To better understand their differences, quantum-inspired algorithms can be compared based on the quantum concepts they imitate and the problems they address.

Quantum-inspired algorithms differ in how they adapt quantum concepts to classical computation, each offering unique advantages for specific problem domains.

The following table compares key algorithm types, highlighting their quantum analogies, computational strengths, and application areas:

Algorithm type	Quantum analogy	Computational advantage	Typical application
QIEA	Superposition and rotation operators	Enhanced diversity and convergence	Feature selection, clustering
QPSO	Quantum potential well exploration	Global optimization with reduced stagnation	Path planning, hyperparameter tuning
QIBM	Quantum energy landscape	Escaping local minima	Generative modeling, representation learning
SQA	Quantum tunneling and energy decay	Efficient global search	Scheduling, resource allocation

Table 16.3: *Comparative landscape of quantum-inspired algorithms*

This comparative view emphasizes how quantum metaphors—even when simulated classically—can yield practical improvements in adaptability and exploration.

Illustrative Python example of quantum-inspired optimization

Quantum-inspired optimization emulates quantum behaviors (e.g., amplitude rotation and interference) to improve search on classical hardware. The following code simulates amplitude rotation updates that steer a probability distribution toward higher-fitness regions:

```
import numpy as np
# Initialize population as probability amplitudes
population = np.random.rand(10)
population = population / np.linalg.norm(population)  # normalization
# Define a fitness function (maximize cosine curve)
def fitness(x):
    return np.cos(3 * x) * np.exp(-x**2)
# Quantum-inspired amplitude rotation update
for iteration in range(50):
    probs = np.abs(population)**2
    expectation = np.sum(probs * fitness(np.linspace(-2, 2, len(population))))
    rotation = np.sign(expectation) * 0.05
    population = np.cos(rotation)*population + np.sin(rotation)*np.roll(population, 1)
print("Final normalized amplitudes:", population)
```

Although purely classical, this snippet captures the essence of amplitude evolution—iteratively rotating probability distributions toward higher-fitness states, much like the constructive interference of a quantum search.

Hybrid AI-Quantum architectures

The integration of AI and QC reaches its most practical form through hybrid architectures, where classical and quantum systems collaborate within a unified computational workflow. Rather than attempting to replace classical

AI models, quantum processors are embedded as specialized accelerators that handle complex sub-tasks—optimization, sampling, or high-dimensional feature transformations—while the classical environment manages orchestration, data handling, and model evaluation.

This complementary design leverages the strengths of both paradigms: AI's adaptability and learning power with QC's representational richness and parallelism. Together, they lay the groundwork for what researchers now call **Quantum-Enhanced Machine Learning** (QEML).

These hybrid systems allow classical AI models and quantum circuits to work together within the same learning pipeline. While classical components manage training and optimization, quantum circuits contribute specialized transformations that can improve model expressiveness and computational efficiency.

Logic of hybridization

Hybridization is not a mere engineering compromise; it is an architectural necessity.

Quantum hardware, at its current stage, remains constrained by limited qubit counts, noise, and decoherence, whereas AI frameworks operate efficiently on classical systems with massive data throughput.

A hybrid model divides computational responsibility across these two realms:

- Classical components handle large-scale data preprocessing, normalization, and post-measurement analytics.
- Quantum components execute mathematically intensive operations that benefit from superposition or entanglement, such as kernel mapping, optimization, and sampling.

The bridge between them is typically established through PQCs, quantum analogues of neural network layers whose parameters can be trained using classical gradient-based optimization.

Hybrid workflow

Hybrid AI-Quantum models operate through an iterative interaction between classical algorithms and quantum circuits. Classical components manage data preparation and optimization, while quantum circuits perform specialized transformations that contribute to the learning process.

A hybrid AI-Quantum model follows a cyclic workflow that integrates classical processing with quantum transformation and optimization. The learning loop consists of four iterative stages:

1. **Data encoding**: Classical data are mapped to quantum states using schemes such as angle, amplitude, or basis encoding.
2. **Quantum processing**: A PQC transforms the state using tunable parameters, capturing learned correlations
3. **Measurement and extraction**: Measurement converts the quantum state into classical outputs, typically as probability distributions.
4. **Classical optimization**: A loss function evaluates results, and classical optimizers update circuit parameters.

These steps repeat iteratively, forming a hybrid loop that combines classical learning with quantum evolution.

Figure 16.3 illustrates this four-phase workflow, showing how classical intelligence and quantum mechanics interact in an iterative feedback loop to refine learning performance:

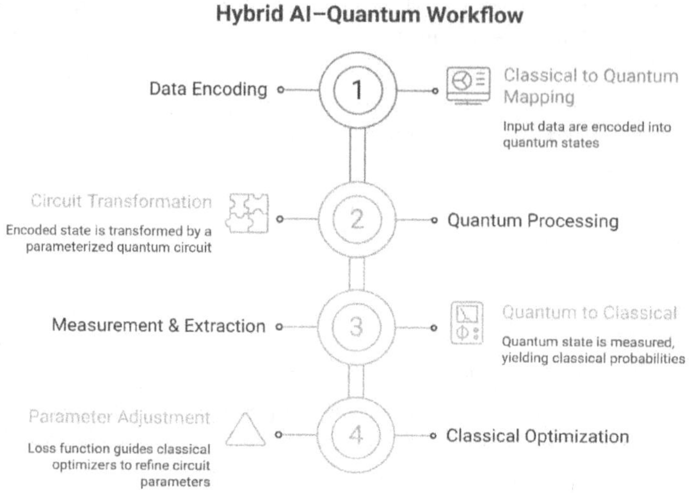

***Figure 16.3**: Hybrid AI-Quantum workflow*

Representative hybrid architectures

Researchers have proposed several hybrid models that integrate classical machine learning with quantum circuits. These architectures demonstrate how quantum components can be embedded within traditional AI pipelines to enhance learning and optimization.

Hybrid architectures combine classical and quantum components, assigning complementary roles to enhance learning, expressiveness, and optimization. The following models illustrate common hybrid frameworks:

- **VQC**: VQC employs a PQC to encode features and produce measurements, which a classical loss function evaluates. Classical optimizers update parameters, forming a closed hybrid learning loop.
- **Hybrid QNN (HQNN)**: HQNNs insert quantum layers into classical pipelines, where classical networks extract features and quantum circuits perform nonlinear transformations before returning results for classical decision-making.
- **Quantum autoencoder**: Quantum autoencoders compress high-dimensional quantum states into fewer qubits, supporting quantum data compression, noise reduction, and state discrimination.
- **Hybrid reinforcement learning agent**: Quantum circuits act as policy evaluators, leveraging quantum parallelism, while classical components manage environment interaction and reward optimization.

Example of minimal hybrid model using PennyLane framework

To better understand how hybrid AI-Quantum models operate in practice, the following example demonstrates a simple integration of a quantum circuit with a classical learning component using the PennyLane framework.

The following example demonstrates a hybrid quantum-classical model implemented with the PennyLane framework, where a quantum circuit acts as a trainable layer inside a neural network:

```
import pennylane as qml
from pennylane import numpy as np
# Define a single-qubit device
dev = qml.device("default.qubit", wires=1)
```

```
# Quantum node (trainable circuit)
@qml.qnode(dev)
def quantum_layer(x, weights):
    qml.RX(x, wires=0)
    qml.RY(weights[0], wires=0)
    return qml.expval(qml.PauliZ(0))
# Classical-quantum hybrid model
def hybrid_model(x, weights):
    q_out = quantum_layer(x, weights)
    return np.tanh(2.0 * q_out)  # classical activation
# Training step (simplified)
weights = np.array([0.3], requires_grad=True)
x = np.pi / 4
output = hybrid_model(x, weights)
print(f"Hybrid output: {output:.3f}")
```

This concise script illustrates how a PQC can be embedded within a classical nonlinear function, forming the smallest possible hybrid inference pipeline. In larger systems, such layers are trained using automatic differentiation to minimize prediction error.

Using PennyLane and PyTorch for Hybrid Quantum Models

Hybrid AI-Quantum models can be seamlessly integrated with modern deep learning frameworks such as PyTorch. PennyLane provides native interfaces that allow quantum circuits to function as differentiable layers within classical neural networks. This enables gradient-based optimization using standard deep learning workflows while incorporating quantum transformations as part of the model architecture.

In such hybrid models, classical preprocessing layers prepare input data, a quantum circuit performs nonlinear transformations in Hilbert space, and classical neural layers interpret the resulting measurements. Automatic differentiation allows gradients to propagate through both classical and quantum components, enabling end-to-end training.

The following example demonstrates how a PennyLane quantum circuit can be embedded as a PyTorch layer, forming a simple hybrid neural network:

```
import pennylane as qml
import torch
from torch import nn
# Define quantum device
dev = qml.device("default.qubit", wires=1)
# Define quantum circuit
@qml.qnode(dev, interface="torch")
def quantum_circuit(inputs, weights):
    qml.RX(inputs, wires=0)
    qml.RY(weights[0], wires=0)
    return qml.expval(qml.PauliZ(0))
# Convert quantum circuit into a PyTorch layer
weight_shapes = {"weights": 1}
quantum_layer = qml.qnn.TorchLayer(quantum_circuit, weight_shapes)
# Hybrid neural model
model = nn.Sequential(
    quantum_layer,
```

```
    nn.Tanh()
)
# Example input
x = torch.tensor([0.5])
output = model(x)
print("Hybrid PyTorch-Quantum output:", output.item())
```

This example demonstrates how a quantum circuit can be made trainable within a PyTorch model, enabling hybrid learning pipelines in which classical and quantum layers collaborate during optimization. Such architectures form the foundation of QML systems that combine classical deep learning with quantum computational primitives.

Architecture overview

Hybrid AI-Quantum systems consist of several interconnected components that coordinate classical data processing with quantum computation. Each component performs a specific role to support efficient learning and system integration.

A well-designed hybrid system relies on seamless coordination between classical and quantum components to ensure efficient data flow and learning stability. The following table summarizes the core components of a hybrid AI-Quantum architecture, outlining their roles and common technology implementations:

Component	Primary role	Technology example
Classical preprocessor	Data normalization, encoding, and loss computation	NumPy, PyTorch, TensorFlow
Quantum layer	Nonlinear transformation in Hilbert space	Qiskit, PennyLane, Cirq
Optimizer	Parameter update and gradient tracking	Adam, RMSProp, L-BFGS
Measurement interface	Converts quantum outputs to classical data	Expectation values, sampling

***Table 16.4**: Architecture overview of a hybrid AI-Quantum system*

The success of a hybrid system depends on the smooth data flow and gradient consistency between these layers ensuring that classical optimizers receive meaningful feedback from quantum operations.

Building advanced quantum neural networks

As AI and QC converge, one of the most promising outcomes is the emergence of QNNs computational models that combine the adaptive learning capability of neural networks with the probabilistic expressiveness of quantum mechanics. QNNs extend the logic of classical deep learning into the quantum domain, operating not on deterministic bits, but on qubits whose states can exist in complex superpositions.

The fundamental idea behind a QNN is simple yet powerful: *replace the linear algebra of classical neurons with the unitary transformations of quantum gates*, and train these transformations using methods inspired by machine learning. When constructed effectively, QNNs can represent exponentially large feature spaces with relatively few qubits, offering a new level of efficiency for pattern recognition, classification, and generative modeling.

Conceptual foundations

A classical neuron computes a weighted sum followed by an activation function, whereas a quantum neuron applies unitary rotations to qubit states. The trainable parameters are rotation angles, and the neuron's output is obtained by measuring the final qubit state.

The key components of a QNN include:

- **Quantum data encoding layer**: Transforms classical data into quantum states. Encoding schemes such as amplitude encoding or angle encoding ensure that data are properly mapped into the Hilbert space.

- **PQC**: Acts as the network's hidden layer. Quantum gates such as Rotation-X (RX), Rotation-Y (RY), Rotation-Z (RZ), and the Controlled-NOT (CNOT) gate, with tunable parameters, determine how qubits interact and evolve during the learning process.
- **Measurement layer**: Measures the qubits to extract classical information, usually in the form of expectation values of specific operators.
- **Classical optimization loop**: Uses gradient-based or gradient-free methods to minimize a cost function by iteratively adjusting gate parameters.

Anatomy of a quantum neural network

To understand how QNNs operate, it is useful to examine the main layers that structure the learning process within a QNN.

A QNN consists of sequential layers, each designed to encode data, establish entanglement, apply learnable transformations, and extract measurable outputs.

The following table outlines the core layers of a QNN, describing their functional roles and the quantum gates commonly used in each layer:

Layer type	Purpose	Typical gates used
Data encoding layer	Converts classical features into quantum amplitudes	RX, RY, RZ rotations
Entangling layer	Establishes correlations among qubits	CNOT, CZ, CRX
Variational layer	Contains trainable parameters for learning	RY(θ), RZ(φ) with learnable θ, φ
Measurement layer	Extracts observable results	Pauli-Z, expectation values

***Table 16.5**: Anatomy of a QNN*

During training, the output from the measurement layer is compared with the target label, and a cost function (e.g., mean squared error or cross-entropy) is computed.

Gradients with respect to quantum parameters are calculated using the parameter-shift rule, a technique unique to quantum differentiation.

Parameter-shift rule

Unlike classical systems, quantum gates are not differentiable directly; they are evaluated only indirectly. The parameter-shift rule provides a simple yet elegant solution—it estimates the gradient by evaluating the circuit twice with shifted parameters:

$$\frac{\partial f(\theta)}{\partial \theta} = \frac{f(\theta + \pi/2) - f(\theta - \pi/2)}{2}$$

Here, $f(\theta)$ represents the expectation value measured from the quantum circuit.

This rule enables QNNs to be trained efficiently using familiar optimization methods, such as gradient descent or Adam, and to be fully integrated into classical AI frameworks.

Illustrative example on two layer QNN in PennyLane

To illustrate how a QNN operates in practice, the following example builds a simple two-layer QNN using the PennyLane framework.

The following example demonstrates the construction of a simple two-qubit QNN using PennyLane. This hybrid model encodes classical data into quantum states, applies parameterized rotations, and outputs an expectation value:

```
import pennylane as qml
from pennylane import numpy as np
```

```
# Define a two-qubit device
dev = qml.device("default.qubit", wires=2)
# Quantum node representing the QNN
@qml.qnode(dev)
def qnn(inputs, weights):
    # Data encoding
    qml.RY(inputs[0], wires=0)
    qml.RY(inputs[1], wires=1)
    # Entanglement layer
    qml.CNOT(wires=[0, 1])
    # Variational layer
    qml.RY(weights[0], wires=0)
    qml.RZ(weights[1], wires=1)
    qml.CNOT(wires=[1, 0])
    # Measurement
    return qml.expval(qml.PauliZ(0))
# Example data and parameters
inputs = np.array([np.pi/4, np.pi/3])
weights = np.array([0.5, 0.8])
output = qnn(inputs, weights)
print(f"QNN output: {output:.4f}")
```

The explanation is as follows:

- Classical data are encoded using RY rotations, creating a superposed initial state.
- A CNOT gate introduces entanglement between the qubits, allowing information sharing.
- The variational layer applies trainable rotations that adjust during learning.
- Measurement returns the expectation value of the Pauli-Z observable, which forms the QNN's output.

Training and performance considerations

Training QNNs introduces unique challenges due to the interaction between quantum circuits and classical optimization methods.

Training QNNs involves both quantum uncertainty and classical stochasticity. Several key considerations arise:

- **Gradient vanishing**: As circuit depth increases, gradients may vanish due to random interference, a phenomenon known as barren plateau. Solutions include structured ansatz design and layer-wise training.
- **Hardware noise**: Real quantum devices introduce decoherence that can distort learning. Hybrid simulation and noise-aware optimization help mitigate this effect.
- **Scalability**: Although current qubit counts are limited, modular QNN architectures can scale through distributed or hybrid configurations.
- **Interpretability**: Understanding how quantum transformations encode decision boundaries remains an active research area, similar to early studies of deep neural networks.

AI for quantum system optimization

As quantum devices transition from theoretical constructs to operational technologies, their practical performance depends critically on optimization of circuits, control parameters, noise management, and hardware calibration. However, the sheer complexity of quantum systems makes manual tuning nearly impossible. A single-qubit's behavior can fluctuate due to environmental noise, electromagnetic interference, or drift in control electronics. This is where AI becomes indispensable.

AI offers adaptive and data-driven methodologies that can learn the behavior of quantum systems, predict performance bottlenecks, and automatically optimize experimental configurations. The result is a feedback-driven paradigm where quantum systems evolve under the supervision of intelligent learning agents: self-calibrating, self-correcting, and progressively more efficient.

By analyzing experimental data and system behavior, AI models can identify patterns that help improve the stability and efficiency of quantum operations. This enables more reliable and automated management of complex quantum systems.

Need for intelligent optimization

Traditional quantum control relies on physics-based models that work well for small systems but scale poorly to large, noisy qubit ensembles. Due to nonlinear quantum dynamics, even small control perturbations can cause significant outcome deviations.

AI circumvents these limitations by employing algorithms that learn directly from experimental data. By treating the quantum system as a black box, machine learning models can:

- Predict how qubits will behave under varying control settings.
- Identify error patterns and correlations across qubit networks.
- Propose optimal pulse sequences or circuit structures to enhance fidelity.
- Continuously adapt through reinforcement or Bayesian feedback.

This adaptive cycle transforms static control theory into a living optimization process that evolves with the hardware itself.

Core application areas

AI techniques are increasingly applied across different stages of quantum system development, helping improve control, reliability, and operational efficiency.

AI plays a key role in optimizing quantum systems by automating calibration, control, and performance improvement across multiple layers. The following areas highlight how AI enhances reliability, efficiency, and scalability in QC:

- **Quantum error correction and noise mitigation**: AI models detect and correct errors by analyzing noisy measurements. CNNs infer error syndromes, while **reinforcement learning** (**RL**) agents adaptively apply corrections, often outperforming rule-based methods in noisy environments.
- **Gate and pulse optimization**: Deep learning models such as RNNs and GANs design optimized control pulses for quantum gates, improving fidelity and reducing leakage without explicit physical modeling.
- **Resource scheduling in quantum clouds**: On shared platforms like *IBM Quantum* and *AWS Braket*, AI optimizes job scheduling and queue management to reduce latency and improve throughput.
- **Quantum compiler and circuit optimization**: GNNs and evolutionary algorithms reduce circuit depth and gate count while aligning layouts with hardware connectivity, minimizing decoherence during execution.
- **Quantum state estimation and tomography**: AI models such as **variational autoencoders** (**VAEs**) and neural density estimator's approximate quantum states efficiently, enabling faster and scalable state reconstruction from measurement data.

Case example on reinforcement learning for quantum control

Reinforcement learning enables quantum systems to improve control strategies through continuous interaction and feedback.

RL provides a natural framework for quantum optimization. An RL agent interacts with a quantum environment by sending control actions (e.g., gate pulses) and receiving rewards (e.g., fidelity or energy minimization). Over time, it learns a policy that maximizes performance.

A conceptual outline of the process is as follows:

```
# Pseudo-illustration of an AI-based control feedback loop
state = quantum_system.initialize()
agent = RLAgent()
for episode in range(1000):
    action = agent.select_action(state)
    new_state, reward = quantum_system.apply_control(action)
    agent.update_policy(state, action, reward, new_state)
    state = new_state
print("Optimized control policy learned by the agent.")
```

Although simplified, this representation captures the essence of adaptive control: AI continuously refines quantum operations through feedback rather than pre-defined formulas.

Integration loop of AI within the quantum stack

AI can be integrated across multiple layers of the QC stack to support intelligent control and system optimization.

AI enhances every layer of the QC stack, providing intelligent optimization and adaptive control across hardware, software, and user interfaces.

The following table summarizes how AI contributes to different layers of the quantum stack, detailing their optimization goals and commonly applied techniques:

Layer	Optimization objective	AI technique used
Hardware layer	Noise suppression, qubit calibration	Reinforcement learning, Bayesian regression
Control layer	Pulse shaping, timing correction	Deep neural networks, GANs
Compiler layer	Circuit depth minimization, mapping	Graph neural networks, evolutionary algorithms
Execution layer	Resource allocation, load balancing	Scheduling algorithms, predictive analytics
User layer	Job recommendation, error forecasting	Decision trees, ensemble models

***Table 16.6**: Integration of AI within the QC stack*

This vertical integration illustrates how AI functions not as an external tool but as an embedded intelligence permeating the quantum ecosystem.

Challenges and research frontiers

Despite major advances, AI-driven quantum optimization still faces challenges in scalability, reliability, and interpretability. Current research focuses on addressing these limitations by combining physical principles with intelligent learning frameworks to enable robust and scalable quantum systems:

- **Explainability**: Understanding why an AI model recommends specific pulse or circuit modifications is difficult because deep networks are opaque.
- **Generalization**: AI models trained on one hardware configuration may not transfer easily to others due to differences in noise characteristics.
- **Data scarcity**: Quantum experiments are expensive and slow to produce labeled data, limiting the number of training opportunities.
- **Physical constraints**: Optimization recommendations must always respect the laws of quantum mechanics—impossible actions must be automatically filtered out.

To address these issues, ongoing research explores **physics-informed neural networks (PINNs)** and hybrid physics–AI models that embed physical constraints into learning architectures, ensuring consistency with quantum principles.

Case studies and Python labs

The theoretical convergence of AI and QC takes on real meaning when observed in practical applications. This section presents a selection of case studies and Python-based laboratory exercises that bridge conceptual understanding with hands-on experimentation. Each case demonstrates how quantum principles can enrich AI workflows or, conversely, how AI can optimize quantum algorithms, reflecting the collaborative spirit of this new computational paradigm.

These examples are designed to be executed using readily available frameworks such as PennyLane, Qiskit Machine Learning, or TensorFlow Quantum, allowing students and researchers to replicate, extend, and adapt the experiments on standard classical hardware with simulator backends.

Case study 1: Quantum-enhanced support vector machine

Quantum-enhanced learning models leverage superposition and interference to expand feature representations, enabling more effective classification of nonlinear data patterns.

The following example demonstrates a QSVM implementation that leverages quantum kernels to achieve separability on complex datasets.

Objective: To demonstrate how quantum feature spaces can improve the separability of nonlinear datasets, using a QSVM implemented on simulated quantum hardware.

Conceptual background: Classical SVMs rely on kernel functions—such as polynomial or Gaussian kernels to project data into higher-dimensional spaces for classification. In the quantum variant, quantum circuits act as feature mappers, transforming classical inputs into quantum states whose inner products (or fidelities) define a quantum kernel. This kernel can sometimes separate data that classical functions cannot.

Python lab outline is as follows:

```
from qiskit import BasicAer
from qiskit.utils import QuantumInstance
from qiskit_machine_learning.kernels import QuantumKernel
from qiskit_machine_learning.algorithms import QSVC
import numpy as np
# Sample data: XOR pattern (nonlinearly separable)
X = np.array([[0,0],[0,1],[1,0],[1,1]])
y = np.array([0,1,1,0])
# Define a quantum feature map (ZZFeatureMap)
from qiskit.circuit.library import ZZFeatureMap
feature_map = ZZFeatureMap(feature_dimension=2, reps=2)
# Define quantum kernel and SVM classifier
backend = BasicAer.get_backend('qasm_simulator')
quantum_kernel = QuantumKernel(feature_map=feature_map, quantum_instance=QuantumInstance(backend))
classifier = QSVC(quantum_kernel=quantum_kernel)
classifier.fit(X, y)
print("Quantum SVM Predictions:", classifier.predict(X))
```

Outcome: The QSVM constructs a decision boundary derived from quantum interference patterns, often outperforming a classical SVM on small-scale, highly entangled datasets.

Case study 2: Reinforcement learning for quantum control

RL provides an adaptive framework for fine-tuning quantum system controls through continuous feedback and reward-based optimization.

The following simulation demonstrates how an RL agent learns optimal control actions to stabilize a quantum system by minimizing drift through iterative interaction.

Objective: To apply RL techniques for optimizing control parameters in a simulated quantum system.

Conceptual background: In quantum systems, pulse shaping and timing adjustments can significantly affect gate fidelity. RL agent can iteratively explore control strategies by applying actions (pulse updates), receiving rewards (based on system performance), and learning a policy that maximizes stability or accuracy.

The following is an illustrative simulation:

```
import numpy as np
# Define a simplified environment
class QuantumEnv:
    def __init__(self):
        self.state = 0.5  # initial drift
    def step(self, action):
        noise = np.random.normal(0, 0.05)
        self.state += action + noise
        reward = -abs(self.state)  # aim to keep state near 0
        return self.state, reward
env = QuantumEnv()
Q_table = np.zeros((10, 3))  # discrete approximation
alpha, gamma = 0.1, 0.9
# Basic Q-learning loop
for episode in range(500):
    s = np.random.randint(0, 10)
    a = np.random.choice([0,1,2]) - 1  # possible actions: -1,0,1
    new_s, reward = env.step(a*0.1)
    Q_table[s,a] += alpha * (reward + gamma * np.max(Q_table[int(abs(new_s*10)%10)]) - Q_
table[s,a])
print("Learned Q-table:", np.round(Q_table, 2))
```

Outcome: This simulation shows how an RL agent gradually discovers actions (control adjustments) that stabilize a dynamic quantum system, illustrating AI-assisted calibration loops.

Case study 3: Hybrid quantum neural network

HQNNs combine classical preprocessing with quantum computation to achieve expressive, high-dimensional mappings for complex learning tasks.

The code here illustrates a simple PennyLane-based HQNN, where classical inputs are encoded into a quantum circuit that performs entanglement-driven transformations for binary classification.

Objective: To construct a hybrid AI-Quantum model for binary classification that integrates a classical preprocessing layer with a PQC.

Conceptual background: Hybrid models leverage the best of both worlds: classical feature extraction combined with quantum nonlinear transformation in Hilbert space.

The classical component reduces data dimensionality, while the quantum circuit performs a compact yet expressive mapping before final classification.

Python lab (using PennyLane):

```
import pennylane as qml
from pennylane import numpy as np
dev = qml.device("default.qubit", wires=2)
@qml.qnode(dev)
def hybrid_circuit(x, params):
    # Classical-encoded features
    qml.RX(x[0], wires=0)
    qml.RY(x[1], wires=1)
    qml.CNOT(wires=[0, 1])
    qml.RY(params[0], wires=0)
    qml.RZ(params[1], wires=1)
    return qml.expval(qml.PauliZ(0))
# Example inference
x_input = np.array([np.pi/4, np.pi/3])
params = np.array([0.5, 1.0])
print(f"Hybrid model output: {hybrid_circuit(x_input, params):.3f}")
```

Outcome: The HQNN learns to encode classical features into quantum states and apply entanglement-based transformations, creating richer decision boundaries even with minimal parameters.

Suggested Python lab extensions

Hands-on exploration deepens understanding by turning abstract quantum–AI concepts into concrete skills. The following extensions offer practical pathways to broaden experimentation, from hybrid modeling to quantum-aware optimization and transfer learning:

- Implement a QVAE for learning low-dimensional representations of entangled states.
- Integrate TensorFlow Quantum with classical deep learning models for hybrid classification.
- Use AI-based optimizers (e.g., Bayesian or gradient-free methods) to tune variational parameters in QNNs.
- Compare quantum and classical kernel methods on noisy datasets to evaluate empirical advantages.
- Explore transfer learning where quantum-trained parameters are reused across related datasets.

Challenges and future research directions

The union of AI and QC stands at the threshold of extraordinary transformation. However, this intersection is not without profound technical, theoretical, and ethical challenges. While hybrid AI-Quantum systems have already demonstrated promising results in optimization, learning, and simulation, the field is still in its formative stage, limited by hardware maturity, algorithmic scalability, and interpretability constraints.

This section highlights the principal challenges confronting researchers today and the future research directions that are likely to define the next decade of AI-Quantum innovation.

Current challenges

Although significant progress has been made, several technical and practical challenges continue to affect the development and scalability of AI-Quantum systems.

Despite progress, AI-assisted quantum systems face challenges that limit scalability, efficiency, and interpretability. Key issues driving current hybrid and physics-informed research include the following.

- **Hardware limitations and noise sensitivity**: Current systems operate in the **noisy intermediate-scale quantum (NISQ)** regime, with qubits affected by decoherence, gate errors, and readout noise. In iterative AI training, noise accumulates and destabilizes learning.

Key issue: Noisy gradients can prevent convergence.

Mitigation: Error-aware cost functions, noise suppression, and AI-driven calibration are still computationally intensive.

- **Data encoding bottleneck**: Encoding classical data into quantum states can introduce significant overhead. Amplitude, basis, and angle encodings trade qubit count for circuit depth.

  Direction: Learnable encoders that adapt mappings to data and task complexity.

- **Gradient vanishing known as barren plateaus**: Deep parameterized circuits suffer exponentially vanishing gradients, hindering training.

  Approaches: Structured ansatzes, layer-wise training, and quantum-aware initialization.

- **Interpretability and explainability**: Quantum models operate in abstract Hilbert spaces, limiting visibility into intermediate states.

  Efforts: Explainable designs using observable decompositions and classical surrogates.

- **Integration complexity**: Integrating AI and quantum stacks remains fragmented. Bridging tools like TensorFlow Quantum, Qiskit Machine Learning, and PennyLane require standardized interfaces, differentiation pipelines, and hybrid APIs to ensure reproducibility.

Emerging research directions

Despite these barriers, the pace of discovery in AI-Quantum integration is accelerating.

The following domains outline some of the most compelling research frontiers for the coming years:

- **QFL**: Extends distributed learning to quantum settings, enabling privacy-preserving, collaborative training across quantum nodes without sharing raw data.
- **Quantum AutoML and architecture search**: Applies AutoML to automatically design efficient quantum circuits and variational ansatzes using reinforcement learning and evolutionary methods.
- **Neuromorphic–quantum hybrids**: Combines neuromorphic processors with quantum hardware to support brain-inspired, energy-efficient computation and probabilistic inference.
- **Quantum generative models**: Quantum GANs and quantum Boltzmann machines model complex probability distributions for data synthesis, molecular design, and cryptography.
- **AI-assisted quantum architecture search**: Uses AI to optimize qubit connectivity, predict noise, and guide fabrication, enabling scalable, industry-ready quantum hardware.

Ethical and societal implications

As quantum AI matures, it will influence sectors beyond science and engineering, including finance, healthcare, national security, and education. This raises questions about algorithmic accountability, data privacy, and quantum-enabled surveillance. Policymakers and ethicists will need to collaborate with technologists to ensure that quantum intelligence is guided by transparency, fairness, and global inclusivity.

The power of quantum intelligence lies not only in its speed or precision, but in its *alignment with human values.* Ethical stewardship must evolve in parallel with technological advancement.

Vision of the future

The long-term aspiration of AI-Quantum research is to create autonomous cognitive quantum systems, machines capable of self-learning, self-correction, and contextual decision-making that transcend classical boundaries. Such systems will integrate symbolic reasoning, neural learning, and quantum inference into unified cognitive frameworks.

These advancements hint at an era in which computation itself becomes an evolving, intelligent phenomenon, an ecosystem of interacting algorithms and physical processes that learn symbiotically.

As research progresses, these integrated systems are expected to unlock new possibilities in scientific discovery, intelligent automation, and advanced decision-making across complex computational domains.

Conclusion

This chapter explored the powerful convergence of AI and QC, highlighting how their integration is shaping the future of intelligent computation. We examined the bidirectional relationship in which AI enhances quantum systems through calibration, noise mitigation, and control optimization, while QC expands AI capabilities through high-dimensional representations and accelerated learning. Through discussions of quantum-inspired algorithms, hybrid architectures, and QNNs, readers gained insight into how classical and quantum models can collaborate to form adaptive, self-optimizing systems. The Python-based case studies using Qiskit Machine Learning and PennyLane demonstrated practical implementations from quantum feature mapping and hybrid optimization to reinforcement-learning-based quantum control. By bridging theoretical principles with hands-on experimentation, this chapter established a foundation for designing, simulating, and analyzing AI-Quantum workflows, paving the way for deeper exploration into next-generation cognitive and hybrid quantum systems.

Questions

1. **What is meant by the convergence of AI and QC?**

   Answer: It refers to the integration of data-driven AI techniques with quantum computational principles. AI provides adaptive models for learning and optimization, while QC offers exponential representational power and parallelism, creating a synergistic framework for intelligent computation.

2. **How does AI assist in improving quantum hardware performance?**

   Answer: AI models such as reinforcement learning and Bayesian optimization can calibrate qubits, tune pulse parameters, and predict system drift, enabling higher-fidelity, autonomous, data-driven quantum control.

3. **What is quantum-inspired algorithms?**

   Answer: These are classical algorithms that emulate quantum behaviors—like superposition and entanglement without using real qubits. Examples include QIEAs and SQA, which enhance classical optimization and search tasks.

4. **What is a hybrid AI-Quantum architecture?**

   Answer: It combines classical neural networks with PQCs. Classical layers handle preprocessing and optimization, while quantum layers perform complex transformations in Hilbert space for richer learning.

5. **What distinguishes a QNN from a classical neural network?**

   Answer: QNNs use quantum gates instead of linear weight matrices, operating on qubits in superposition. Learning occurs through interference and measurement rather than summation and activation functions.

6. **How does AI optimize quantum compilers and circuit design?**

   Answer: Techniques like graph neural networks and evolutionary search reduce circuit depth, align logical layouts with hardware connectivity, and minimize decoherence during execution.

7. **What are the common challenges in AI-Quantum integration?**

   Answer: Major issues include hardware noise, data encoding overhead, barren plateaus in gradient optimization, limited interpretability, and difficulties integrating diverse toolchains such as Qiskit, PennyLane, and TensorFlow Quantum.

8. **How can learners experiment with AI-Quantum systems using Python?**

   Answer: Frameworks like Qiskit Machine Learning and PennyLane enable users to build hybrid models, train QNNs, and test quantum feature mappings using simulators or real backends.

9. **Why are quantum kernels significant in machine learning?**

   Answer: Quantum kernels map classical data into high-dimensional quantum feature spaces, allowing nonlinear relationships to be captured more efficiently, improving classification and pattern recognition.

10. **What future directions are expected in Quantum AI research?**

    Answer: Promising areas include quantum federated learning, quantum AutoML, neuromorphic–quantum hybrids, quantum generative models, and AI-assisted quantum hardware design—advancing toward autonomous, cognitive quantum systems.

Exercises

1. Install Qiskit Machine Learning or PennyLane and verify the installation by running a simple PQC. Print the circuit diagram and describe how it represents data encoding in a QNN.
2. Implement a QSVM using Qiskit. Use a small nonlinear dataset (e.g., XOR pattern) and demonstrate how the quantum kernel separates the data in Hilbert space.
3. Create a hybrid quantum–classical model in PennyLane that includes one classical preprocessing layer and one PQC layer. Train it on a simple binary classification task and report the model accuracy.
4. Simulate RL loop for quantum control where an AI agent adjusts control parameters (e.g., rotation angles) to maximize a reward. Plot the learning curve showing performance over episodes.
5. Implement a QIEA in Python using probabilistic amplitude updates. Compare its convergence behavior with a traditional genetic algorithm.
6. Design a QNN with two qubits and a variational layer. Train, it using the parameter-shift rule and visualize the cost function across iterations.
7. Run an AI-assisted quantum calibration task by fitting a regression model (e.g., linear regression) to simulated qubit drift data. Predict the future drift and interpret how AI aids hardware stabilization.
8. Construct and analyze a quantum autoencoder circuit to compress a three-qubit state into two qubits. Discuss how this principle aligns with classical autoencoders in AI.
9. Compare quantum and classical kernel methods by implementing both on a noisy dataset. Evaluate their classification accuracy and discuss where quantum kernels show potential advantages.
10. Write a short reflection on how AI and QC form a feedback-driven ecosystem—highlighting how AI enhances quantum systems while quantum mechanics expands AI's representational capacity.

CHAPTER 17
Road Ahead for Quantum Computing

Introduction

The scalability of quantum computing is the field's greatest engineering frontier. Early prototypes have demonstrated the feasibility of quantum operations, but building large-scale, fault-tolerant systems demands far more than increasing qubit counts. Each additional qubit introduces new layers of complexity maintaining coherence, minimizing noise, synchronizing control electronics, and ensuring precise fabrication. Unlike classical scaling driven by transistor miniaturization, quantum scaling must preserve fragile quantum states under extreme environmental stability and timing precision.

This chapter explores scalability as a multidisciplinary challenge spanning physics, materials science, and intelligent automation. It begins by outlining the three pillars of scalability: qubit quantity, qubit quality, and control complexity and explains why progress depends on balancing all three factors simultaneously. The discussion then examines significant barriers, including decoherence, error-correction overheads, fabrication imperfections, cryogenic control limitations, and crosstalk between densely packed qubits.

Next, the chapter highlights emerging approaches toward scalable hardware, including topological qubits for intrinsic error resistance, neutral-atom and photonic systems for modular architectures, silicon spin qubits leveraging **Complementary Metal Oxide Semiconductor** (**CMOS**) compatibility, and hybrid quantum–classical designs integrating diverse technologies.

Finally, readers are introduced to the broader ecosystem supporting scalability—from open cloud platforms and standardization frameworks to global quantum initiatives and the expanding professional workforce driving this transformation.

By the end of the chapter, readers will understand how scalability defines the path from today's **noisy intermediate-scale quantum** (**NISQ**) devices to tomorrow's fault-tolerant quantum computers capable of reliable, large-scale computation.

Structure

The chapter covers the following topics:

- Scalability and hardware challenges
- Quantum cloud ecosystems
- Glossary of key quantum terms
- Industry trends in quantum computing
- Career paths in quantum science and engineering
- Further learning resources

Objectives

This chapter explores scalability and hardware challenges in quantum computing, where engineering precision, materials science, and intelligent control converge to build large-scale, fault-tolerant systems. Readers will understand how scalability depends on balancing qubit quantity, quality, and control complexity, rather than merely increasing qubit counts. The chapter examines key barriers: decoherence, error-correction overheads, fabrication imperfections, cryogenic limitations, and crosstalk and discusses how advances in **Artificial Intelligence (AI)**-driven control, cryogenic electronics, and materials innovation are addressing them. Learners will explore emerging scalable hardware paradigms: topological, neutral-atom, photonic, silicon spin, and hybrid systems, each offering unique pathways to stable, manufacturable quantum architectures. The roadmap from NISQ devices to **fault-tolerant quantum computing (FTQC)** is outlined, alongside evolving cloud ecosystems and global initiatives driving progress. By the end, readers will grasp how scalability transforms prototypes into reliable, large-scale quantum computers capable of powering the next era of computation.

Scalability and hardware challenges

The journey toward large-scale quantum computing is both exhilarating and demanding. Although the first generation of quantum processors has demonstrated experimental success, achieving true scalability, where systems perform billions of reliable quantum operations remains the ultimate frontier. Scalability is not merely a question of adding more qubits; it is the art of maintaining precision, coherence, and control as systems expand in complexity. As of now, quantum engineering stands at the delicate intersection of physics, materials science, and intelligent automation.

Essence of scalability

Scalability is a central challenge in practical quantum computing, involving expansion from a few qubits to large-scale systems while maintaining stability and precision. This is not simply about adding qubits, but an engineering problem that combines physics, materials, and control, with increasing demands on coherence, synchronization, and error management. A scalable quantum computer must balance three interdependent factors:

- **Qubit quantity**: The number of controllable **quantum bits (Qbits)**.
- **Qubit quality**: The coherence and error rate per operation.
- **Control complexity**: The efficiency of managing qubits through electronics and firmware.

Unlike classical transistors, qubits are highly fragile, requiring ultra-stable environments, often at millikelvin temperatures, and precise timing control. As systems scale, added hardware increases interference, calibration complexity, and energy dissipation, making large-scale stability challenging.

Key barriers to large-scale quantum systems

Achieving large-scale, FTQC is constrained more by engineering than theory. As systems scale beyond hundreds of qubits, maintaining coherence, precision, and control becomes increasingly complex, requiring coordinated advances in materials, control electronics, and error-correction. Several key technical barriers continue to limit the development of large-scale quantum systems. The most significant challenges include the following:

- **Decoherence and environmental noise**: Quantum states are highly sensitive to environmental disturbances, leading to decoherence. Superconducting qubits offer fast gates but short coherence, while trapped ions are more stable but slower. Scalability requires qubits that are both fast and long-lived.

- **Quantum error-correction (QEC) overheads**: Reliable computation demands error-correction, often requiring hundreds or thousands of physical qubits per logical qubit. Advances in surface codes and AI-assisted decoding aim to reduce this overhead through adaptive noise prediction and correction.

- **Fabrication and material limitations**: Atomic-scale imperfections introduce loss and unwanted coupling. Emerging materials such as silicon–germanium and diamond NV centers promise improved uniformity and scalable fabrication.

- **Control electronics and cryogenic bottlenecks**: Room-temperature control creates wiring and heat bottlenecks. Cryogenic control electronics placed near qubits—such as **cryo-CMOS controllers (e.g., Intel Horse Ridge and IBM cryo-controller prototypes)**, reduce latency and thermal load.

- **Crosstalk and connectivity constraints**: As arrays grow, crosstalk increases. Modular architectures and networked quantum nodes connected via optical links enable scalable, distributed designs similar to cloud systems.

Emerging approaches toward scalable quantum hardware

While current quantum systems are limited in scale, emerging hardware paradigms are redefining scalability by emphasizing error resilience, modularity, and integration with semiconductor and photonic technologies. The goal is not just higher qubit counts, but stable, manufacturable, and interconnected platforms for sustained quantum computation:

- **Topological qubits**: It stores information in non-local states that are naturally resistant to local errors, potentially reducing the need for active error-correction. Research efforts most notably by Microsoft on Majorana zero modes—aim to realize this approach experimentally.
- **Neutral-atom and photonic platforms**: Neutral-atom systems offer reconfigurable, highly connected qubit arrays, while photonic qubits operate at room-temperature and support fast, long-distance communication—making them well suited for distributed quantum architectures.
- **Silicon spin qubits**: Built on established CMOS technology, silicon spin qubits enable scalable fabrication, higher operating temperatures, and potential integration of quantum and classical logic on the same chip.
- **Hybrid systems**: Hybrid architectures combine multiple qubit types, such as superconducting, photon, or spin–phonon systems to balance coherence, connectivity, and scalability, representing a key direction in practical quantum hardware design.

Evolution roadmap from NISQ to FTQC

The current NISQ era focuses on exploring near-term utility from imperfect devices. The long-term goal, however, is FTQC, a state where algorithms can execute indefinitely without corruption.

The transition to FTQC will likely unfold in phases:

- **Noise-aware computation**: Mitigating errors through circuit optimization.
- **Partial error-correction**: Encoding selected qubits for critical operations.
- **Full fault tolerance**: Implementing logical qubits across universal processors.

Throughout this journey, hybridization with classical **high-performance computing** (**HPC**) and AI systems will remain essential, bridging today's limitations with tomorrow's breakthroughs.

Looking ahead

Scalability in quantum computing will be defined not by more qubits, but by smarter qubit systems that self-calibrate, adapt to noise, and co-design solutions with AI assistance.

Research is shifting toward quantum self-correction, neuromorphic control architectures, and error-aware compilers, all aimed at turning quantum devices into robust computational platforms.

In the coming years, progress will depend on the integration of advances across multiple layers of the quantum computing stack, including hardware engineering, algorithm design, and intelligent software frameworks. Collaborative research between physicists, computer scientists, and engineers will play a critical role in transforming experimental prototypes into reliable and scalable computing systems. As these technologies mature, quantum platforms are expected to move gradually from laboratory demonstrations toward practical tools capable of supporting complex scientific and industrial applications.

Industry trends in quantum computing

Quantum computing has transitioned from scientific experimentation to a vibrant and competitive technology landscape. Over the past decade, the field has evolved from isolated laboratory prototypes to globally connected quantum ecosystems, driven by cloud access, strategic investment, and industry–academia collaboration.

This section explores the significant trends shaping this transformation from hybrid computing models to government-backed initiatives and workforce growth.

This transformation has been fueled by rapid advances in quantum hardware, expanding software ecosystems, and unprecedented collaboration between academia, industry, and government agencies. Major technology companies, startups, and research institutions are investing heavily in developing scalable quantum processors, robust programming frameworks, and practical applications. As a result, quantum computing is no longer confined to specialized laboratories; it is becoming part of a broader technological movement aimed at redefining how complex computational problems are approached in science, engineering, and industry.

Quantum technology inflection point

Every emerging technology undergoes a period of skepticism before reaching adoption. In quantum computing, that turning point arrived when experimental devices demonstrated that practical algorithms outperformed classical baselines in specific domains, a milestone often called quantum advantage.

The field now stands at an inflection point similar to the early days of AI or semiconductor design. Global companies are transitioning from asking *can quantum work*, to *how do we integrate quantum into our workflows?*

The answer lies in three converging industrial trends:

- **Hybrid integration**: Blending quantum and classical computing.
- **Cloud democratization**: Universal access to real hardware.
- **Targeted commercialization**: Identifying domain-specific quantum advantage.

Hybrid quantum and classical integration

Quantum devices are still limited by noise and size, but classical systems can complement them through co-processing. This hybrid model, where quantum processors serve as accelerators within existing HPC frameworks, has become the leading paradigm for near-term applications.

The following examples highlight how major organizations are bridging theory and practice in scalable quantum–classical integration:

- IBM integrates Qiskit Runtime with its HPC clusters to perform iterative hybrid optimization.
- *NVIDIA Corporation* and *Oak Ridge National Laboratory* (*ORNL*) are exploring workflows that integrate **graphics processing units** (**GPU**) and **quantum processing units** (**QPU**) to accelerate quantum simulations.
- AWS Braket supports hybrid jobs that combine quantum sampling with classical gradient descent.
- Google's **TensorFlow Quantum** (**TFQ**) bridges AI and quantum models, allowing neural networks to train quantum circuits.

Rise of quantum as a service

In the past, accessing a quantum processor required proximity to cryogenic labs and specialized expertise. Today, through **quantum as a service** (**QaaS**), users can run quantum algorithms remotely through web portals and **application programming interfaces** (**APIs**). Cloud providers manage hardware complexity, allowing developers to focus purely on algorithmic innovation.

The following points summarize the core advantages of cloud-enabled quantum ecosystems:

- **Accessibility**: Global access via web interfaces and Python **software development kits (SDKs)** (Qiskit, Cirq, Braket).
- **Scalability**: Infrastructure upgrades and calibration are handled transparently by providers.
- **Cost efficiency**: Pay-per-use pricing enables experimentation without capital investment.
- **Collaboration**: Cloud platforms allow shared workspaces for academic and industrial teams.

The following platforms illustrate the leadership and distinctive focus areas of today's major quantum providers:

- **IBM Quantum Platform**: The pioneer of open-access cloud quantum computing.
- **Amazon Braket**: Multi-vendor integration under a unified SDK.
- **Microsoft Azure Quantum**: Enterprise alignment with Q# and hybrid resource estimation.
- **Google Quantum AI**: Research-oriented service integrated with TFQ.

Open standards and software interoperability

As quantum computing ecosystems expand, interoperability has become essential for sustained innovation. Open standards enable hardware-independent algorithm design, supporting collaboration, reproducibility, and long-term software stability across platforms.

The following table summarizes some of the most widely adopted frameworks and standards that are driving cross-platform compatibility and unifying the global quantum software ecosystem:

Standard/Framework	Purpose	Supported by
Open quantum assembly language (OpenQASM) 3.0	Standardized quantum assembly syntax enabling dynamic circuits.	*IBM, Qiskit*
Quantum Intermediate Representation (QIR)	Compiler-level abstraction based on **Low Level Virtual Machine (LLVM)**, promoting hardware independence.	*Microsoft, Quantinuum*
OpenPulse	Low level control protocol for pulse-level experimentation.	*IBM Research*
PennyLane	Hybrid **Machine Learning (ML)**–Quantum interface supporting PyTorch, TensorFlow, and JAX.	*Xanadu*
Cirq and TFQ	End-to-end ML integration with Google Cloud.	*Google*

Table 17.1*: Major open standards enabling quantum software interoperability*

National and global quantum initiatives

Quantum computing is now a strategic priority in national innovation agendas, with governments investing in research infrastructure, talent, and technological sovereignty due to its long-term impact on defense, communication, and industry.

The following table highlights key national and regional programs leading the worldwide quantum race:

Program/Region	Primary goals	Funding level
U.S. National Quantum Initiative (NQI)	Public–private partnerships, quantum centers, and education programs.	USD 1.2+ billion
EU Quantum Flagship	Hardware standardization, quantum communication networks.	EUR 1 billion (2018–2028)
India's National Quantum Mission (NQM)	Indigenous quantum computers, sensors, and encryption technologies.	₹6000 crore (~USD 730 million)
China's Quantum Laboratory	Quantum satellite communication and cryptography.	USD 10+ billion
Japan Quantum Technology Hub	Material innovation and hybrid photonic circuits.	Government-funded research alliance

Table 17.2*: Major national and regional programs advancing global quantum computing initiatives*

These initiatives ensure a distributed, collaborative global ecosystem that prevents the monopolization of quantum technologies by a single entity or nation.

Emerging application frontiers

The next phase of quantum computing will be defined not by hardware milestones alone, but by domain-specific breakthroughs, where quantum systems achieve measurable advantage over classical computation. Industries are beginning to identify problem classes ideally suited to quantum algorithms, particularly those involving complex optimization, high-dimensional data, or molecular-level simulations.

The following table outlines key application domains where quantum computing is poised to deliver transformative impact in the coming decade:

Domain	Example use cases	Quantum benefit
Finance	Portfolio optimization, risk analytics, fraud detection	Parallel optimization using QAOA, Monte Carlo acceleration
Pharmaceuticals	Protein folding, molecular energy estimation	Quantum simulation of molecular Hamiltonians
Logistics	Supply chain routing, scheduling	Combinatorial optimization on quantum annealers
Cybersecurity	QKD, post-quantum encryption	Unbreakable communication, secure random generation
AI	Quantum neural networks, generative models	Exponential feature mapping and faster convergence

Table 17.3: *Key industrial domains demonstrating emerging quantum advantage*

Investment and workforce dynamics

The quantum industry is attracting strong venture and institutional investment, with startups advancing hardware miniaturization, error-correction, and hybrid software. In parallel, universities are updating curricula to prepare future quantum engineers, emphasizing programming, linear algebra, and interdisciplinary skills.

Recent trends include:

- Rapid growth of quantum startups worldwide, surpassing 500 active companies.
- Increasing demand for quantum software engineers and algorithm developers.
- Rise of quantum education alliances, such as *QWorld* and *IBM Quantum Educators Program*.
- Expansion of academic–industry fellowships to bridge research and commercialization.

Road ahead

The quantum industry is maturing into an interconnected value chain where hardware providers, software platforms, and application developers co-evolve. We are witnessing the emergence of Quantum 2.0, a phase characterized by integration, standardization, and commercialization.

As hardware scales and algorithms improve, success will depend on collaboration rather than competition. Governments will fund, enterprises will operationalize, and universities will nurture the talent that powers the next decade of innovation.

Quantum cloud ecosystems

The rise of cloud computing has profoundly reshaped the quantum landscape. What was once accessible only to specialized research laboratories requiring cryogenic equipment, vacuum chambers, and high-precision lasers—can now be explored through a web browser and a few lines of Python code. This democratization of access marks a historic shift: quantum computing is no longer an exclusive scientific endeavor but a global cloud service.

Cloud platforms have therefore become the primary gateway for learning, experimentation, and collaboration in quantum computing. By lowering infrastructure barriers, they enable a broader community of students, researchers, and developers to engage with quantum technologies and contribute to their advancement.

Rise of quantum computing as a cloud service

Cloud delivery has solved two fundamental barriers in quantum experimentation—accessibility and scalability. By hosting quantum processors and simulators on the cloud, major technology companies now enable students, developers, and researchers to run algorithms without worrying about hardware maintenance or environmental stability.

Quantum cloud ecosystems typically offer:

- Hardware access to real superconducting, ion-trap, or photonic qubits.
- High-performance simulators for pre-testing and noise-free execution.
- SDKs and APIs (like Qiskit, Cirq, Braket, or Q#) to interface directly from Python.
- Hybrid workflow integration with classical computing and AI frameworks.

The result is a seamless bridge between quantum theory and practical implementation.

IBM Quantum Platform and the Qiskit ecosystem

IBM was the first to make quantum hardware openly accessible through the cloud in 2016, a milestone that transformed the field. The IBM Quantum Platform, powered by the Qiskit framework, remains the most mature public ecosystem for quantum learning and research.

The following components form the core foundation of IBM's quantum computing environment:

- **Qiskit SDK**: Open-source Python library for circuit design, simulation, and execution.
- **Qiskit Runtime**: Low-latency, cloud-native service for optimized quantum program execution.
- **Quantum Composer and Lab**: Interactive web interface for drag-and-drop circuit creation.
- **Hardware portfolio**: Devices ranging from 5 to 127 qubits, with transparent calibration data and real-time queue visibility.

Here is an example showing the execution of a Bell state circuit on IBM Quantum Simulator.

This simple Qiskit program creates and simulates a Bell state—the fundamental two-qubit entangled state:

```
# Example: Executing a Bell state circuit on IBM Quantum simulator
from qiskit import QuantumCircuit, Aer, execute
qc = QuantumCircuit(2)
qc.h(0); qc.cx(0, 1)
backend = Aer.get_backend('statevector_simulator')
result = execute(qc, backend).result()
print(result.get_statevector())
```

Google Quantum AI with Cirq and TFQ

Among the major contributors to the quantum cloud ecosystem, Google Quantum AI has focused on integrating quantum computing with machine learning frameworks and scalable software tools.

Google Quantum AI integrates hardware development with machine learning frameworks, emphasizing quantum AI synergy.

The following are the core features of Google's Quantum AI environment:

- **Cirq**: Python library for constructing and optimizing quantum circuits.
- **TFQ**: Combines TensorFlow's deep-learning capabilities with quantum models.

- **Sycamore processor**: The superconducting chip that achieved quantum supremacy in 2019.
- **Quantum Computing Service**: Limited research-access platform for real device execution.

TFQ enables developers to embed quantum circuits as layers within classical neural networks, thereby pioneering the quantum-enhanced AI paradigm.

Amazon Braket as a multi-vendor quantum gateway

Amazon Braket offers a unified, vendor-agnostic quantum environment through a single SDK, providing access to diverse hardware backends on AWS. By simplifying experimentation, hybrid workloads, and deployment, Braket reflects Amazon's scalable approach to quantum research and enterprise innovation.

The following table summarizes the core capabilities and design features that make Amazon Braket one of the most versatile ecosystems in the quantum cloud landscape:

Feature	Description
Hardware providers	IonQ (ion-trap), Rigetti (superconducting), Oxford Quantum Circuits (photonic).
LocalSimulator	High-speed, noise-free simulator for debugging and small-scale testing.
Hybrid jobs	Seamless integration of classical compute via AWS EC2 and SageMaker.
Security	AWS IAM ensures secure, credential-based quantum job submission.

***Table 17.4**: Core features of the Amazon Braket quantum platform*

The following example shows the of a building a simple quantum circuit in Amazon Braket.

This short program creates a Bell state circuit using Amazon Braket's Python SDK. It demonstrates how easily quantum circuits can be constructed and visualized within the Braket environment:

```
# Example: Building a simple quantum circuit in Amazon Braket
from braket.circuits import Circuit
bell = Circuit().h(0).cnot(0, 1).measure_all()
print(bell)
```

Microsoft Azure Quantum and Q#

Microsoft Azure Quantum focuses on enterprise integration and developer productivity. It provides a unified portal that connects users to multiple hardware vendors through the **Quantum Development Kit** (**QDK**) and its native language, Q#.

The following features summarize the core strengths of the Azure Quantum environment:

- **Q# language**: Strongly typed, domain-specific language for quantum algorithms.
- **Resource estimator**: Predicts logical qubit and gate requirements for scalable execution.
- **Hybrid integration**: Supports execution from Python notebooks and Visual Studio Code.
- **Hardware partners**: Includes *IonQ*, *Quantinuum*, and *Quantum Computing Inc.* (*QCI*).

This example demonstrates running Q# programs from Python using the `qsharp` package, highlighting Microsoft Azure Quantum's seamless hybrid integration between classical Python code and quantum operations:

```
# Example: Running a simple Q# operation from Python
import qsharp
from HelloQuantum import SayHello
SayHello.simulate()
```

Comparative landscape of major cloud providers

The race for quantum cloud dominance centers on innovation, accessibility, and integration. Leading platforms combine open ecosystems with enterprise-grade hybrid services, forming the foundation of QaaS and enabling scalable experimentation and collaboration across academia and industry.

The following table provides a comparative snapshot of the leading quantum-cloud ecosystems and their unique contributions:

Provider	Primary SDK/language	Hardware focus	Unique strength
IBM Quantum	Qiskit (Python)	Superconducting qubits	Education, transparency, and an open community
Google Quantum AI	Cirq/TFQ	Superconducting (Sycamore)	AI integration and algorithmic innovation
Amazon Braket	Braket SDK (Python)	Ion-trap, superconducting, photonic	Multi-vendor access and benchmarking
Microsoft Azure Quantum	Q# / QDK	Partner hardware (IonQ, Quantinuum)	Resource estimation and enterprise adoption

Table 17.5: Comparative overview of leading quantum-cloud providers

Each platform serves a distinct purpose: IBM focuses on education, Google on research integration, Amazon on flexibility, and Microsoft on enterprise alignment. Together, they represent a complementary ecosystem that ensures progress across all layers of the quantum stack.

Open communities and learning networks

Beyond hardware and SDKs, the real strength of quantum platforms lies in their learning ecosystems. Each provider actively cultivates global communities through workshops, hackathons, mentorship programs, and online forums nurturing the next-generation of quantum scientists and developers.

The following table summarizes the key community and learning initiatives that foster collaboration and skill development across major quantum platforms:

Platform	Community initiatives
IBM Quantum	*Qiskit Global Summer School, Educators program,* and community challenges.
Google Quantum AI	Cirq developer group and TFQ research forum.
Amazon Braket	*AWS Slack* and startup incubation events.
Microsoft Azure Quantum	Learn quantum track, certification badges, and GitHub repositories.

Table 17.6: Major community and learning initiatives across quantum cloud platforms

Road ahead for quantum cloud computing

Quantum cloud platforms are evolving from hardware-access services to integrated innovation environments. The next-generation will feature:

- AI-driven compiler optimization that automatically selects hardware based on workload.
- Cross-platform circuit portability, enabling users to run the same algorithm on any backend.
- Quantum containerization, similar to Docker for classical computing, ensures reproducibility across systems.
- Quantum app marketplaces, where researchers can publish pre-built circuits and workflows.

Career paths in quantum science and engineering

The quantum era is not only reshaping computation—it is reshaping careers.

As research transitions into commercialization, demand for quantum-literate professionals has grown exponentially. New roles are emerging that blend physics, programming, AI, and engineering into a single interdisciplinary language. Understanding these career trajectories helps learners map their academic and professional growth to the opportunities unfolding across the global quantum ecosystem.

To navigate this evolving landscape, it is important to understand how the quantum workforce itself is transforming. As quantum technologies move from experimental research toward real-world deployment, new interdisciplinary roles are emerging that connect scientific discovery with engineering implementation, software development, and industrial innovation. Examining these shifts provides valuable insight into how future professionals can position themselves within the rapidly expanding quantum ecosystem.

Evolution of the quantum workforce

In the early decades of quantum research, the field was dominated by theoretical physicists and experimental scientists exploring quantum phenomena in university laboratories. Today, the ecosystem has diversified: software engineers, AI researchers, material scientists, and data analysts are joining hands with physicists to build practical quantum technologies.

This transformation mirrors what happened in the early days of computing when mainframes gave way to personal computers, and programmers from varied disciplines became central to technological progress.

Major career domains

As quantum technology transitions from research to commercialization, the career landscape is expanding rapidly, spanning academia, industry, entrepreneurship, and education.

Professionals entering this field can choose from diverse pathways, depending on their interests in theoretical foundations, engineering design, policy, or public engagement.

What unites all these roles is an emphasis on interdisciplinary expertise, blending physics, computer science, and innovation management

Let us outline the four primary career domains shaping the global quantum workforce.

Academic and research careers

Research remains the foundation of quantum progress. Universities, national laboratories, and research institutions focus on algorithm design, hardware innovation, and fundamental physics.

Key roles include:

- **Quantum algorithm researcher**: Designs novel quantum algorithms and optimization frameworks.
- **Experimental physicist**: Develops and tests qubit systems in superconducting, photonic, or ion-trap setups.
- **Postdoctoral fellow/research scientist**: Works on hybrid simulation models and error-correction architectures.
- **Quantum educator/faculty**: Teaches and develops academic courses, fostering the next-generation of quantum professionals.
- **Skills required**: Strong foundations in quantum mechanics, linear algebra, and programming (Python, MATLAB, Julia). Experience with platforms such as Qiskit, Cirq, or Braket is increasingly expected, even in academic research.

Industry and engineering careers

Quantum technology companies are now hiring across multiple engineering verticals. The emphasis has shifted from proof-of-concept to product engineering, turning quantum prototypes into stable, scalable systems. The following table highlights key roles and skill sets defining the quantum industry landscape:

Role	Primary focus	Typical skills/tools
Quantum software engineer	Develops circuits, simulations, and SDKs.	Python, Qiskit, Cirq, TFQ
Quantum control engineer	Designs microwave control signals and pulse sequences.	Control theory, RF electronics, cryogenics
Quantum hardware engineer	Fabricates qubit chips and packaging.	Nanofabrication, superconducting materials
Quantum compiler developer	Optimizes code and error mitigation layers.	C++, LLVM, and quantum assembly languages such as OpenQASM and QIR.
Quantum data scientist	Integrates ML models with quantum simulators.	ML frameworks, optimization, hybrid workflows

***Table 17.7**: Key engineering roles and technical skill sets in the quantum technology industry*

Entrepreneurship and startups

Startups are driving innovation by specializing in niche segments such as quantum security, quantum cloud services, and quantum **software as a service** (**SaaS**).

The following list highlights prominent quantum startups and their areas of specialization:

- **Xanadu (Canada)**: Photonic hardware and PennyLane software for quantum-AI applications.
- **Rigetti Computing (United States)**: Superconducting quantum hardware accessible through cloud APIs.
- **Quantinuum (United Kingdom/U.S.)**: Trapped-ion hardware and algorithmic research.
- **QNu Labs (India)**: Quantum key distribution and communication security.
- **Pasqal (France)**: Neutral-atom processors for scalable architectures.

Entrepreneurial opportunities exist not only in hardware manufacturing but also in education, consulting, and application design. Venture-backed innovation hubs and quantum accelerators now support early-stage startups through funding and mentorship.

Education, policy, and communication roles

Quantum literacy extends beyond technology—it requires education, ethics, and policy alignment. As adoption grows, new interdisciplinary roles are emerging in education, outreach, regulation, and public awareness.

The following key roles illustrate the broader career opportunities emerging at the intersection of technology, education, and policy:

- **Quantum curriculum developer**: Designs academic modules and MOOCs for universities.
- **Science communicator**: Translates complex research into accessible media and content.
- **Policy analyst/strategist**: Advises on national security, data privacy, and intellectual property in quantum innovation.
- **Quantum program manager**: Oversees multi-institutional collaborations and grants.

These roles help ensure that quantum technology evolves responsibly, inclusively, and sustainably in the long term.

Skills and competencies in demand

As quantum computing becomes more interdisciplinary, required skills now extend beyond physics and mathematics to include software engineering, data science, and systems integration, with professionals expected to bridge theory, simulation, experimentation, and deployment.

The following table summarizes the core skill areas and representative tools that define today's quantum-ready workforce:

Skill area	Examples/tools
Programming	Python, Qiskit, Cirq, Braket SDK, PennyLane
Mathematics	Linear algebra, vector spaces, probability, tensor calculus
Quantum theory	Qubits, gates, superposition, entanglement, algorithms
Machine learning and AI	TensorFlow, PyTorch, quantum-AI hybrids
Hardware fundamentals	Cryogenics, superconductivity, laser control
Cloud computing	AWS Braket, Azure Quantum, IBM Quantum Platform
Communication	Technical writing, data visualization, and collaboration tools

***Table 17.8:** Core interdisciplinary skills and tools shaping quantum workforce readiness*

Career development pathways

Quantum computing careers can begin from multiple entry points, depending on background and expertise.

Learners can enter the field through different pathways, including academic study, research, or professional upskilling. Regardless of the starting point, continuous learning and hands-on experimentation remain essential for building expertise in quantum technologies.

For students

The following steps offer a practical starting point for students entering quantum computing:

1. Begin with foundational courses in quantum mechanics and linear algebra.
2. Practice coding circuits using free SDKs like Qiskit and Cirq.
3. Participate in *Qiskit Global Summer School*, *QHack*, or *Quantum League competitions*.

For researchers

The following steps help researchers advance and contribute to quantum research:

1. Focus on hybrid AI–quantum algorithms or quantum error mitigation.
2. Publish open-source notebooks and research articles in **https://arxiv.org/archive/quant-ph**.
3. Apply for international fellowships through programs such as *Quantum Open Source Foundation* (*QOSF*) or the *IBM Quantum Network*.

For professionals and engineers

The following steps guide professionals and engineers transitioning into the quantum domain:

1. Transition from classical computing or AI by taking short-term certification courses.
2. Experiment with cloud APIs for real hardware testing.
3. Build hybrid prototypes that showcase problem-solving using both classical and quantum logic.

Future of quantum careers

Industry forecasts by *McKinsey* and *Institute of Electrical and Electronics Engineers* (*IEEE*) suggest that by 2030, the global quantum workforce will exceed 300,000 professionals, spanning **research and development** (**R&D**), education, and enterprise deployment.

New hybrid roles are already emerging. The following emerging roles reflect the convergence of quantum computing with AI, cybersecurity, and systems engineering:

- **Quantum AI architect**: Designs neural quantum architectures.
- **Quantum security analyst**: Specializes in post-quantum cryptography.
- **Quantum DevOps engineer**: Manages quantum workloads across distributed systems.
- **Quantum product manager**: Bridges R&D and customer use cases.

This rapid diversification highlights an important truth: quantum computing is not replacing existing professions; it is redefining them. Professionals who adapt early by gaining cross-domain fluency will become the architects of this new technological era.

Glossary of key quantum terms

Quantum computing introduces an entirely new language—one that fuses physics, mathematics, and computer science into a unified conceptual framework.

This glossary serves as a quick reference and learning companion, reinforcing the vocabulary you have encountered throughout this book. Each term includes not just a definition but also its practical significance in programming and experimentation using Python-based quantum SDKs such as Qiskit, Cirq, and PennyLane.

The following table summarizes essential quantum terms and their applications in research and software development:

Term	Meaning and application
Amplitude	A complex number that defines the probability amplitude of a qubit being in a particular state. Its squared magnitude gives the probability of measurement outcomes. In code, amplitudes are stored as statevectors or density matrices.
Bell state	A maximally entangled two-qubit state (e.g., $\lvert\Phi^+\rangle = (\lvert 00\rangle + \lvert 11\rangle)/\sqrt{2}$). Used to test entanglement and teleportation circuits in Qiskit or Cirq.
Bloch sphere	A visual model representing all possible pure states of a single-qubit as points on a sphere. Qiskit's **`plot_bloch_vector()`** helps visualize qubit states during learning.
Circuit depth	The number of sequential gate layers in a quantum circuit affects noise and total execution time. Optimization tools in Qiskit and Braket help minimize depth for better fidelity.
Coherence time (T1, T2)	Duration for which a qubit maintains its quantum state before decoherence occurs. Displayed in calibration data for real hardware on IBM Quantum.
Decoherence	The process by which quantum information is lost due to interaction with the environment limits qubit reliability. Error mitigation techniques are designed to reduce decoherence.
Entanglement	A quantum correlation between qubits that causes their states to be interdependent. Essential for algorithms like teleportation, Grover's search, and QAOA.
Error mitigation	Software-based methods to approximate ideal results without full error-correction, including zero-noise extrapolation and probabilistic error cancellation.
Fault tolerance	The ability of a quantum computer to perform indefinitely despite errors is achieved through logical qubits and error-correcting codes—a key milestone on the road to scalable quantum computing.
Gate fidelity	A measure of how accurately a quantum gate performs its intended operation, typically expressed as a percentage. Higher fidelity means lower cumulative error during execution.

Hilbert space	The mathematical vector space representing all possible states of a quantum system. Each additional qubit doubles its dimensionality (2^n).
Measurement	The act of observing a quantum system, collapsing superposition into a definite classical outcome (0 or 1). Implemented using **`measure_all()`** in most SDKs.
Noise	Random fluctuations that distort quantum operations, caused by temperature, electromagnetic interference, or imperfect control pulses.
Quantum advantage	The demonstrated ability of a quantum processor to outperform classical systems on a specific computational task. Google's 2019 Sycamore experiment achieved this milestone.
Quantum algorithm	A structured series of gate operations that exploit superposition and entanglement to solve a problem (e.g., Grover's, Shor's, VQE).
Quantum circuit	The programmable representation of a quantum algorithm consists of gates, measurements, and registers. It is the fundamental object manipulated in Python SDKs.
QEC	The method of encoding logical qubits using multiple physical qubits to detect and correct errors without measuring the quantum data directly.
Quantum gate	A reversible operation that changes a qubit's state; analogous to classical logic gates. Examples: X, H, CNOT, and T gates.
Quantum register	A set of qubits that can be operated on collectively within a circuit. Acts as a memory space for quantum data.
Quantum volume (QV)	IBM's comprehensive metric combines qubit count, connectivity, and fidelity to benchmark usable computational power.
Qubit	The basic unit of quantum information that can exist in a superposition of 0 and 1, represented as $\mid \psi\rangle = \alpha \mid 0\rangle + \beta \mid 1\rangle$.
Superposition	The ability of a qubit to exist in multiple states simultaneously until measured. The H gate creates superposition.
Variational quantum algorithm (VQA)	A hybrid approach combining quantum circuits with classical optimizers to minimize cost functions (e.g., VQE, QAOA).
Wavefunction (Ψ)	A mathematical expression containing all information about a quantum system: its evolution follows the Schrödinger equation.

Table 17.9: *Key terms and concepts in quantum computing*

Building a quantum vocabulary

Learning quantum computing is like learning a new language. Each concept from entanglement to error-correction represents a grammar rule governing how information behaves in the quantum realm. As you continue exploring quantum programming, refer back to this glossary frequently. Over time, these terms will evolve from abstract definitions into intuitive, operational tools that guide your thinking as both a learner and a quantum engineer.

Reinforce terminology by experimenting with it: for every new concept, build a circuit that demonstrates it. For example, test entanglement with a Bell state or simulate decoherence using noise models in Qiskit's Aer simulator.

Further learning resources

Quantum computing is a fast-moving field. What was a theoretical possibility a decade ago is now a public cloud service, and today's research preprints can become tomorrow's industry standard.

To thrive in this dynamic environment, learners must adopt a culture of continuous learning, balancing foundational study, hands-on experimentation, and community participation.

This section curates key courses, journals, platforms, and global communities to help you deepen your understanding and stay connected to the forefront of quantum innovation.

To support this journey, a wide range of learning resources is now available through online courses, research journals, interactive platforms, and global communities. These resources allow learners to deepen their theoretical understanding, experiment with real quantum hardware, and connect with peers and mentors worldwide. Exploring them systematically can help transform curiosity about quantum computing into sustained expertise and meaningful contributions.

Online courses and learning portals

Quantum computing education is now globally accessible through digital platforms that integrate theory, simulation, and cloud-based experimentation, enabling learners at all levels to explore qubits, circuits, and hybrid algorithms using Python frameworks such as Qiskit, Cirq, and PennyLane. The following curated list provides reliable, up-to-date portals offering structured courses, labs, and certifications:

- **Comprehensive learning platforms**: A variety of global online platforms now provide structured pathways for learning quantum computing, from conceptual foundations to advanced research and hardware design. The following curated list includes university programs, professional portals, and cloud-based labs that support continuous learning and experimentation:

Course /Portal	Level	Focus area	Direct URL
IBM Quantum Learning Portal	Beginner – advanced	Qiskit SDK, quantum hardware access, runtime services	**https://quantum.cloud.ibm.com/learning**
MIT xPRO Quantum Computing Certificate Program	Intermediate	Applied quantum algorithms and practical applications	**https://learn-xpro.mit.edu/quantum-computing**
edX Quantum Computing Courses	Beginner – advanced	Quantum mechanics and algorithmic foundations	**https://www.edx.org/learn/quantum-computing**
SkillsBuild Quantum Computing Virtual Labs	Beginner	Foundational concepts and interactive cloud labs	**https://skillsbuild.org/students/course-catalog/quantum-computing**
Qureca Online Courses Catalog	Intermediate	Quantum algorithms, entrepreneurship, and business integration	**https://lms.qureca.com/catalogue/online-courses/**
KI Campus Quantum Machine Learning with Qiskit	Intermediate	Hybrid AI–Quantum models using Python	**https://ki-campus.org/en/learning-opportunities/courses/quantum-machine-learning-qiskit**
Ingenii Quantum Machine Learning Fundamentals	Intermediate	**Quantum Machine Learning (QML)** theory and hands-on implementation	**https://www.ingenii.io/qml-fundamentals**
CERN Quantum Technology Initiative Introduction to Quantum Computing	Beginner – Intermediate	Physics-based principles for computation	**https://quantum.cern/introduction-quantum-computing**
D Wave Training Quantum Programming Core	Intermediate – Advanced	Quantum annealing and optimization techniques	**https://www.dwavequantum.com/learn/training/**
Udemy QC101 Quantum Computing and Intro to QML	Beginner	Quantum physics and machine-learning concepts for developers	**https://www.udemy.com/course/qc101-introduction-to-quantum-computing-quantum-physics-for-beginners/**
FutureLearn Introduction to Quantum Computing	Beginner	Conceptual foundation for non-physics learners	**https://www.futurelearn.com/courses/introduction-to-quantum-computing**
Technical University Delft Quantum Academy	Advanced	Hardware engineering and error-correction strategies	**https://qutech.nl/**

***Table 17.10**: Leading online platforms and courses for learning quantum computing*

- **Recommended learning path**: The following roadmap suggests a tiered pathway that helps learners build competence step by step, aligned with their experience level and goals:
  - **Beginner**: Start with IBM Quantum Learning Portal, SkillsBuild, or FutureLearn for conceptual grounding and visual labs.
  - **Intermediate**: Move to edX, MIT xPRO, or KI-Campus for structured algorithm design and Python SDK practice.
  - **Advanced**: Explore D-Wave Training, TU Delft Quantum Academy, or Ingenii QML Fundamentals for specialization in hardware or machine learning.

Research journals and technical publications

Staying abreast of cutting-edge research ensures you remain aligned with the fastest-moving advances in quantum computing, hardware, algorithms, and applications. This section highlights leading journals in quantum computing and provides practical guidance on how to use these resources effectively for research and learning.

- **Key journals**: Publishing in reputable journals is essential for advancing visibility and credibility in the quantum research community. The following list highlights leading international journals that regularly feature breakthroughs in quantum computing, communication, and information science:

Journal	Scope/focus	URL
npj Quantum Information	Peer-reviewed, open-access journal by Nature, focused on quantum information science—from computing and communication to sensing and metrology.	**https://www.nature.com/npjqi/**
Quantum Science and Technology, IOP Publishing	Covers engineering, hardware, materials, and applied quantum technologies.	**https://iopscience.iop.org/journal/2058-9565**
Physical Review X Quantum	High-impact open-access journal covering broad quantum science and interdisciplinary work.	**https://journals.aps.org/prxquantum/**
Nature npj Quantum Information, Nature Publishing Group	A broader section within Nature Publishing covering quantum information research and developments.	**https://www.nature.com/subjects/quantum-information**

***Table 17.11**: Leading journals in quantum computing and information science*

- **Using the journals effectively**: In addition to identifying key journals, the following guidelines help make journal reading more purposeful and outcome-oriented:
  - **Breakpoint reading**: Focus on Review Articles first—they provide excellent overviews of sub-fields. For npj Quantum Information, review articles are indexed separately.
  - **Bridge theory and application**: When reading a theory-heavy paper (e.g., at Physical Review X Quantum), pause to think: *How could this translate into code or hardware?*
  - **Track engineering progress**: Use *IEEE Transactions on Quantum Engineering* to monitor hardware, control electronics, and system-integration advances—areas less covered by theory-focused physics journals.
  - **Focus on open access**: Many newer journals, including *npj Quantum Information*, are open access, allowing students and practitioners in regions with limited library access to read full papers for free.

Interactive platforms and simulators

Theory becomes meaningful when you experiment. While books and courses give you the ideas, interactive platforms and simulators provide the practice—allowing you to build, test, and refine quantum circuits in real-time. These environments bring quantum computing into your hands through cloud access, browser-based notebooks, and integrated toolkits.

These platforms allow learners and researchers to experiment with quantum algorithms, design and execute quantum circuits, and observe how quantum operations influence computational outcomes. By providing interactive environments with visualization tools, simulators, and cloud-based quantum processors, they help bridge the gap between theoretical understanding and practical implementation. As a result, users can gradually build intuition about quantum behavior while gaining hands-on experience with modern quantum programming frameworks and development tools.

Key platforms for hands-on quantum learning

Hands-on experimentation is central to mastering quantum computing.

Several platforms now provide cloud-based access to real hardware, simulators, and Python SDKs, enabling learners to explore circuits, algorithms, and hybrid quantum–classical workflows interactively.

The following table lists the most popular environments for practical learning and experimentation in quantum programming:

Platform	Focus	Direct URL
Qiskit/IBM Quantum Cloud	Full access to real superconducting quantum processors, Python SDK (Qiskit), and built-in tutorials.	**https://quantum.cloud.ibm.com/**
Cirq and TFQ, Google Quantum AI	Hybrid quantum–classical workflows for machine learning and circuit design.	**https://quantumai.google/cirq**
Braket SDK, Amazon Braket	Unified access to multiple hardware types (ion-trap, superconducting, photonic) via a single Python SDK.	**https://aws.amazon.com/braket/**
Q# and Quantum Development Kit, Microsoft Azure Quantum	Enterprise-focused environment with strong simulation tools and resource estimation.	**https://azure.microsoft.com/en-in/services/quantum/**
Open-source simulators and notebooks	Lightweight, no-hardware tools ideal for prototyping and learning (e.g., PennyLane Playground, Google Colab + Cirq).	**https://pennylane.ai/**

Table 17.12: *Key platforms for hands-on quantum learning*

Effective use of these platforms

The following best practices help learners and researchers use cloud-based quantum environments efficiently and productively:

- **Start with a simulator**: Prior to running on real hardware, test your circuits on noise-free or noise-modeled simulators.
- **Use cloud hardware**: Once you are confident, execute on real devices to observe the impact of real-world noise, calibration, and qubit connectivity.
- **Analyze calibration data**: Many platforms (especially IBM's) provide device calibration metrics (T1, T2, gate fidelity). Understanding these helps you refine circuits for better results.
- **Iterate with hybrid workflows**: Combine classical pre and post-processing with quantum circuits (e.g., machine learning kernels, variational algorithms) to exploit near-term quantum devices.

- **Share and reproduce work**: Save your notebooks, publish your experiments, and collaborate through open-source repositories. Reproducibility matters as much in quantum as in classical software.

Open source communities and global networks

In quantum computing, knowledge evolves fastest when shared. Beyond books and hardware platforms, the atmosphere of collaboration, open-source contribution, and global networking forms the backbone of innovation. These communities enable learners, developers, and researchers to connect, contribute, and grow together, accelerating their journey from users to creators.

These communities provide an environment where ideas, tools, and research outcomes can be openly exchanged and collaboratively improved. Through discussion forums, shared repositories, and community-driven projects, individuals gain access to collective expertise and practical guidance from experienced contributors across the world. Participation in such networks also encourages continuous learning, enabling members to stay informed about emerging tools, research breakthroughs, and evolving best practices in quantum computing.

Key communities to join

Active participation in professional and open-source communities accelerates learning, collaboration, and career growth in quantum computing. Joining such groups provides access to mentorship, global events, and project-based opportunities—bridging the gap between theory and real-world practice.

The following table lists some of the most influential quantum communities that welcome students, researchers, and professionals alike:

Community/Organization	Focus area and benefits	URL
QOSF	Promotes open-source quantum software, mentorship programs for hands-on projects, and standardization.	**https://qosf.org/**
Women in Quantum (WIQ)	A global network empowering women and underrepresented groups in quantum science and technology (mentoring, career board, events).	**https://onequantum.org/women-in-quantum/**
Girls in Quantum (GiQ)	A student-centered community offering free resources, workshops, and a global network for younger learners.	**https://girlsinquantum.com/**
Quantum Society/broader regional quantum interest groups	Regional meet-ups, hackathons, and local chapters are building quantum literacy globally.	—

***Table 17.13**: Key global and regional quantum communities*

Gains from participation

The following points highlight the key benefits of joining and actively engaging in quantum communities:

- **Mentorship and learning**: Programs like QOSF pair you with industry or academic mentors, helping you complete real open-source quantum projects.
- **Networking and careers**: Platforms like WIQ promote job boards, career fairs, and mentoring for underrepresented talent in quantum.
- **Collaboration and contribution**: Open-source projects from QOSF and affiliated organizations allow you to shift from consuming quantum code to contributing to it, an important transition.
- **Global exposure**: Many quantum challenges and hackathons are international, giving you access to peer networks in 30+ countries.

Getting involved

The following steps provide a practical roadmap for students and professionals to begin engaging with quantum communities and contributing meaningfully to open-source projects:

1. Create a GitHub profile and list a small quantum circuit, notebook, or algorithm demonstration.
2. Join the Slack/Discord channels of QOSF or your regional quantum community.
3. Attend an online mini-hackathon or open-source sprint—many events are free and virtual.
4. Submit your first pull request: fix a documentation typo, add a comment to a quantum library, or implement a small extension (e.g., demo circuit).
5. Showcase your contribution on your professional profile (LinkedIn/GitHub) and mention it in your quantum learning portfolio.

Building a personal learning plan

Quantum computing is not mastered in a semester—it is a continuous journey of exploration, coding, and reflection. Since the field evolves rapidly, learners must build a personal roadmap that keeps pace with new research while reinforcing fundamentals.

A structured learning plan ensures that theoretical insight and practical experience grow together.

Such a learning plan should combine foundational study with consistent hands-on practice. Learners can begin by strengthening their understanding of core topics such as linear algebra, quantum mechanics, and quantum algorithms, while simultaneously experimenting with quantum programming frameworks and simulators. Setting clear milestones—such as completing online courses, implementing small quantum circuits, or reproducing results from research papers can help maintain steady progress. Over time, this structured approach allows learners to deepen their conceptual understanding while gradually building the practical skills required to contribute meaningfully to the evolving quantum computing ecosystem.

Five-step learning framework

Mastering quantum computing requires a balance between conceptual study, practical coding, and community engagement. A structured learning process helps learners progress from understanding quantum principles to implementing and sharing real experiments.

The following table presents a five-step roadmap that integrates reading, experimentation, reflection, and collaboration for continuous growth:

Step	Focus	Action plan
1. Read and explore	Build conceptual clarity from trusted sources.	Begin with *Quantum Computing With Python by Dr. Muralidhar Kurni* for applied practice, and complement it with *Quantum Computation and Quantum Information by Nielsen and Chuang* for theoretical depth. Track the latest research on **https://arxiv.org/**.
2. Build and code	Reinforce concepts through implementation.	Recreate textbook examples from *Quantum Computing With Python using Qiskit, Cirq, or PennyLane*. Develop mini-projects such as Bell state generators, teleportation circuits, or Grover search simulators.
3. Experiment and analyze	Transition from simulators to real hardware.	*Execute circuits on IBM Quantum, Amazon Braket*, or *Azure Quantum*. Compare simulated vs. noisy results to understand decoherence and fidelity.
4. Reflect and document	Strengthen retention through metacognition.	Keep a *Quantum Learning Journal* summarizing experiments, insights, and questions. Reflection turns experience into intuition.
5. Share and collaborate	Expand learning through community.	Publish notebooks on GitHub, join *QOSF* or *Qiskit Community*, and participate in open-source projects or global hackathons.

***Table 17.14**: Step-by-step framework for developing applied expertise in quantum computing*

Designing a sustainable weekly routine

A consistent rhythm yields a deeper understanding than occasional intensity. The following sample routine demonstrates how learners can balance study, experimentation, and reflection throughout the week:

- **Monday**: Read one section from *Quantum Computing With Python* or revisit a chapter in *Nielsen and Chuang* (30 minutes).
- **Wednesday**: Build or simulate a new circuit (1 hour).
- **Friday**: Run the experiment on a real backend (45 minutes).
- **Weekend**: Reflect, update your notes, and share key learnings online.

Setting realistic milestones

Learning quantum computing is a gradual journey that benefits from structured progress tracking. Breaking the process into clear, quarterly milestones helps learners stay focused, motivated, and aligned with tangible outcomes.

The following table outlines a four-quarter progression plan that balances conceptual depth, coding proficiency, and community engagement:

Quarter	Learning focus	Expected outcome
Q1 foundations	Quantum principles, linear algebra, Qiskit basics	Build and visualize two-qubit circuits
Q2 algorithms	Grover's, Deutsch–Jozsa, VQE	Implement three canonical algorithms
Q3 applications	Quantum ML and hybrid models	Develop a working QML prototype
Q4 contribution	Open-source projects, hackathons	Submit a pull request or short paper

***Table 17.15**: Quarterly roadmap for developing progressive mastery in quantum computing*

Tracking progress and motivation

The following simple practices can help learners track growth and stay engaged throughout their quantum learning journey:

- Maintain a skill tracker sheet to log new gates, APIs, and algorithms learned.

- Join virtual study groups or local quantum clubs to stay accountable.
- Revisit earlier notebooks every few months to appreciate growth.
- Celebrate milestones, progress deserves recognition.

Conclusion

This chapter explored scalability and hardware challenges as critical foundations for advancing quantum computing from experimental prototypes to reliable, fault-tolerant systems. By examining the relationship between qubit quantity, qubit quality, and control complexity, readers gained insight into why true scalability depends on preserving coherence, precision, and synchronization as quantum hardware increases in size and sophistication. Key engineering challenges, including decoherence, error-correction overheads, fabrication limitations, cryogenic constraints, and qubit crosstalk were discussed alongside emerging solutions, including AI-driven calibration, cryogenic control electronics, and advances in quantum materials. By examining topological, photonic, neutral-atom, silicon-spin, and hybrid architectures, the chapter highlighted the diverse technological pathways currently shaping scalable quantum systems. The roadmap from the NISQ era toward FTQC also emphasized the growing importance of hybrid HPC integration, cloud-based platforms, and coordinated global initiatives in accelerating progress.

Beyond technological breakthroughs, the future of quantum computing will also depend on the strength of its broader ecosystem. Research institutions, cloud platforms, open-source communities, and skilled professionals must work together across disciplinary boundaries to translate experimental achievements into practical solutions. As quantum technologies continue to mature, collaboration among physicists, computer scientists, engineers, and industry innovators will play an increasingly important role. Educational programs, accessible cloud environments, and international research partnerships are already lowering barriers to experimentation and discovery, enabling a wider community to engage with quantum technologies.

Ultimately, scalability represents more than a technical milestone. It signifies the transition of quantum computing from an experimental research field into a transformative computational paradigm capable of reshaping science, industry, and technological innovation.

Questions

1. **What does scalability mean in quantum computing?**

   Answer: Scalability is the ability to grow quantum systems from a few qubits to very large numbers while preserving stability, coherence, and control accuracy, ensuring reliable performance and manageable error rates at scale.

2. **Why is scalability considered more difficult in quantum systems than in classical computing?**

   Answer: Unlike classical scaling through transistor miniaturization, quantum scaling must protect fragile quantum states from noise, temperature, and electromagnetic interference. Each added qubit increases the system's fragility, requiring extreme environmental stability and precise synchronization.

3. **What are the three main factors governing scalability?**

   Answer: Scalability depends on balancing qubit quantity (number of controllable qubits), qubit quality (coherence and fidelity), and control complexity (efficiency of electronics and firmware managing the qubits).

4. **What are the significant barriers to achieving large-scale quantum computing?**

   Answer: Key barriers include decoherence, QEC overheads, fabrication imperfections, cryogenic control bottlenecks, and crosstalk between qubits. Each of these issues affects stability, connectivity, or operational reliability.

5. **How does QEC impact scalability?**

Answer: QEC improves reliability but requires significant redundancy often hundreds of physical qubits to create a single logical qubit. This overhead increases the complexity, cost, and hardware demand for scalable systems.

6. **What role does AI play in enhancing quantum scalability?**

   Answer: AI assists in dynamic calibration, error prediction, and real-time optimization of qubit parameters through reinforcement learning. This adaptive control reduces noise, improves fidelity, and helps manage system complexity efficiently.

7. **Which emerging hardware technologies are promising for scalable quantum computing?**

   Answer: Promising scalability paths include topological qubits for fault tolerance, neutral-atom and photonic platforms for modularity, silicon spin qubits for CMOS integration, and hybrid systems that combine qubit types for balanced performance.

8. **What is the significance of the NISQ-to-FTQC roadmap?**

   Answer: It marks the transition from the NISQ era, where noise limits circuit depth, to FTQC, in which logical qubits operate reliably at scale, enabling practical large-scale computation.

9. **How do quantum cloud platforms support scalability?**

   Answer: Cloud platforms such as IBM Quantum, Google Quantum AI, Amazon Braket, and Microsoft Azure Quantum offer remote access to quantum hardware, simulators, and hybrid tools, democratizing experimentation and accelerating development through shared infrastructure and open standards.

10. **Why is scalability critical for the future of quantum computing?**

    Answer: Without scalability, quantum processors remain limited to laboratory demonstrations. Scalable, fault-tolerant hardware is essential to transform quantum computing into a reliable technology for real-world applications in science, industry, and AI.

Exercises

1. Simulate decoherence in Qiskit using a two-qubit Bell circuit with amplitude-damping and depolarizing noise; report fidelity and measurement distributions across noise levels to show scalability limits.
2. Build a three-qubit bit-flip error-correction code in Qiskit; inject an X error, perform syndrome measurement and correction, verify recovery, and note physical-to-logical overhead.
3. Create a cryo control/wiring diagram from room-temperature electronics to a millikelvin chip; label control lines, multiplexing, cryo-CMOS blocks, and explain wiring-bottleneck mitigation.
4. Run a Bell state experiment on IBM Quantum or AWS Braket and on a local simulator; plot results and relate differences to T_1, T_2, and gate/readout errors.
5. Prepare a comparison table of superconducting, trapped-ion, photonic, and silicon-spin qubits (advantages, limitations, applications), and justify the most practical NISQ scaling approach.
6. Implement a repetition/surface-code-style syndrome demo in Qiskit; sweep physical error probability p and plot logical error rate vs. p to illustrate thresholds.
7. Replace depolarizing-only noise with combined amplitude and phase-damping; compare logical fidelity and depth sensitivity under the same workload.
8. Vary gate and readout error rates in Qiskit Aer or Cirq; plot entanglement fidelity degradation and discuss error mitigation and control-electronics needs.
9. Research one scalability initiative (cryo-CMOS, neutral-atom arrays, photonic interconnects); summarize architecture, overhead reduction approach, and reported benefits.
10. Write a 200-word reflection on why scalability (qubit count, quality, control complexity) is central for moving from NISQ to fault-tolerant systems, noting AI control, cloud access, and hybrid integration.

APPENDIX
AI-assisted Programming for Quantum Computing

Introduction

AI-assisted programming is transforming the way developers build and experiment with quantum systems. By combining **artificial intelligence** (**AI**) with quantum computing, programmers can now move seamlessly from conceptual ideas to executable circuits using natural language prompts. Tools such as *GitHub Copilot, ChatGPT, and Code Llama* help translate human intent into structured code for frameworks like *Qiskit*, *Cirq*, *PennyLane*, and *AWS Braket*, reducing syntax complexity and accelerating circuit design.

A key strength of this approach lies in its end-to-end workflow support. The same AI assistant can generate circuit templates, suggest optimizations, identify syntax issues, and recommend simulators or transpilation levels. This makes AI invaluable in classrooms, research labs, and industry environments, offering beginners rapid feedback and enabling experts to focus on high-level logic and innovation.

AI-assisted programming also provides greater deployment flexibility. Developers may use cloud-based environments such as **Visual Studio** (**VS**) Code or Jupyter for instant prototyping, or adopt open-source models like Code Llama for private, offline projects requiring data confidentiality and local control. In every case, human oversight remains essential to ensure correctness, interpret results, and maintain scientific validity.

This appendix introduces the foundations and practical methods of AI-assisted quantum programming. It explains how AI tools generate, debug, and optimize circuits; how they integrate into hybrid workflows with PennyLane and PyTorch; and how ethical considerations guide responsible usage. By the end, readers will understand how to collaborate effectively with AI—coding faster, learning more deeply, and maintaining precision in quantum development.

Structure

The chapter covers the following topics:

- Introduction to AI-assisted programming for quantum development
- AI tools for quantum developers
- AI-assisted circuit design and simulation
- Debugging, testing, and optimization with AI support
- Case study: AI-guided Grover's algorithm and VQE implementation
- Hybrid AI-quantum workflows using PennyLane and PyTorch
- Ethical concerns and practical limitations of AI-assisted coding

Objectives

This appendix aims to equip readers with the knowledge and skills to apply AI-assisted programming in quantum software development, bridging automation and human expertise. Readers will explore how AI tools such as

ChatGPT, GitHub Copilot, and Code Llama simplify circuit design, debugging, and optimization across leading frameworks, including Qiskit, Cirq, AWS Braket, and PennyLane. The appendix demonstrates how AI accelerates each stage of the workflow, from generating parameterized circuits to visualizing simulation results and fine-tuning hybrid models that combine quantum layers with classical neural networks. In addition, readers will gain awareness of the ethical and practical dimensions of AI integration, including authorship, reproducibility, and responsible use of AI tools in research and education. By the end of this appendix, readers will be confident in leveraging AI as a collaborative partner to design, analyze, and optimize quantum algorithms effectively and responsibly.

Introduction to AI-assisted programming for quantum development

The integration of AI into quantum programming represents a transformative shift in computational science. As quantum technologies advance, AI-powered assistants help bridge the gap between complex mathematical abstractions and practical coding workflows. This section outlines how AI is reshaping quantum software development by accelerating circuit design, reducing syntax complexity, and enabling researchers to focus on conceptual innovation rather than repetitive coding.

By combining AI's pattern-recognition capabilities with the precision of quantum computing, developers can generate, debug, and optimize quantum algorithms more efficiently and accurately. The following subsections examine this paradigm by highlighting its foundations, tools, human–AI collaboration models, benefits, best practices, and the evolving ecosystem that defines modern AI-assisted quantum programming.

The increasing complexity of quantum algorithms and programming frameworks has created a need for intelligent development support. AI-assisted tools help developers design circuits, generate code, and identify errors more efficiently. By suggesting circuit structures and debugging solutions, these tools reduce coding effort and simplify complex workflows.

This support is especially useful in quantum computing, where concepts such as superposition and entanglement introduce unfamiliar abstractions. Integrating AI into development environments, therefore, makes quantum programming more accessible and enables faster experimentation.

Next frontier of quantum development

Quantum computing and AI are transformative technologies of the 21st century. Quantum computing exploits superposition and entanglement to solve classically intractable problems, while AI enhances computation and reasoning. Together, they reinforce one another: AI accelerates design, debugging, and optimization of quantum algorithms, and quantum computing enables new learning paradigms.

AI-assisted programming represents a fundamental shift in developer–code interaction. By collaborating with AI coding assistants, developers generate and optimize code for quantum frameworks, reducing syntax overhead and emphasizing algorithmic logic and conceptual correctness.

Understanding AI-assisted coding

AI-assisted programming tools use **large language models** (**LLMs**) trained on code, documentation, and research data to learn token relationships and generate contextually appropriate code suggestions.

When integrated into development environments such as VS Code, JupyterLab, or PyCharm, these assistants can:

- Auto-complete code structures, class definitions, and quantum gate sequences.
- Generate templates for circuits, algorithms, or data pipelines.
- Identify potential logic or syntax errors and propose corrections.
- Recommend optimized configurations or simulation parameters.

In quantum computing, AI-driven suggestions quickly scaffold quantum circuits—from qubit initialization to measurement—reducing effort caused by complex abstractions and verbose frameworks.

Benefits of AI for quantum developers

Quantum programming differs from classical programming in three fundamental ways:

- **Abstract representation of states**: Quantum programs manipulate qubits through linear-algebraic transformations, which are conceptually dense.
- **High error sensitivity**: A misplaced gate or measurement collapses an entire computation.
- **Rapidly evolving libraries**: Frameworks like Qiskit, Cirq, and Braket are continuously updated, often leading to version mismatches and deprecations.

AI assistants act as intelligent copilots, recalling library syntax and contextualizing user prompts to generate executable code. This leads to higher productivity, faster exploration, and reduced errors.

Here is an example scenario: a researcher asks ChatGPT:

```
Generate a Qiskit circuit implementing Grover's algorithm for a two-qubit system.
```

Within seconds, the assistant generates a functional, annotated template with oracle and diffuser components, enabling users to focus on verification and adaptation rather than construction.

Human–AI synergy

AI cannot replace human intuition. Quantum programming still requires conceptual mastery, and AI-generated code may not always ensure correct physical behavior or computational efficiency.

The most effective use of AI in quantum development is collaborative:

- The AI assistant serves as a fast, tireless partner for ideation, code generation, and troubleshooting.
- The human developer provides oversight, interprets physical meaning, and ensures fidelity to the mathematical model.
- This collaboration forms a human-in-the-loop workflow, one in which automation accelerates progress, while human reasoning ensures precision.

Emerging ecosystem

The AI-assisted quantum programming ecosystem is rapidly evolving, enabling efficient coding, debugging, and learning, and bridging human creativity with machine intelligence.

Key contributors to this expanding ecosystem include:

- GitHub Copilot integrates seamlessly with Python **integrated development environments** (**IDEs**) to provide inline code completions for Qiskit and Cirq **application programming Interfaces** (**APIs**).
- ChatGPT and Claude act as conversational research partners, capable of generating both code and explanatory text.
- Code Llama enables offline or private AI-assisted development for institutions emphasizing data confidentiality.

These tools are further supported by community-driven plugins, model fine-tuning, and open-source prompt libraries, creating a fertile environment for experimentation and education.

AI tools for quantum developers

The rapid progress of LLMs has transformed developer–code interaction, with AI-assisted tools now integral to modern workflows. For quantum developers, these tools reduce syntax complexity and enable greater focus on conceptual modeling, circuit optimization, and algorithmic experimentation.

In this section, we explore the three most widely adopted AI assistants, GitHub Copilot, ChatGPT, and Code Llama, and analyze their roles, capabilities, integration approaches, and best-use scenarios for quantum programming.

GitHub Copilot as an inline intelligence for quantum IDEs

GitHub Copilot, powered by *OpenAI Codex*, is an AI code completion tool integrated with major IDEs that provides context-aware line and block suggestions from comments and partial code.

AI-assisted tools simplify and accelerate quantum programming by enhancing accuracy and reducing manual effort. They offer:

- **Contextual autocompletion**: Suggests Qiskit or Cirq methods (e.g., `QuantumCircuit.h()` or `qc.measure_all()`) as you type.
- **Comment-to-code translation**: Developers can type comments such as `# create a 3-qubit GHZ state using Qiskit`, and Copilot auto-generates the full code block.
- **Error-aware suggestions**: Learns from syntax context to reduce typographical or API-related errors.
- **Customization**: Supports fine-tuned settings for code verbosity, multi-line suggestions, and language preferences.

For example:

```
# Create a 3-qubit GHZ state using Qiskit
from qiskit import QuantumCircuit, Aer, execute
qc = QuantumCircuit(3)
qc.h(0)
qc.cx(0, 1)
qc.cx(1, 2)
qc.measure_all()
```

In this example, typing the initial comment prompts Copilot to produce the complete GHZ circuit code automatically.

ChatGPT as a conversational partner for quantum programming

ChatGPT extends beyond line-by-line code assistance into dialogue-driven programming. Built on *OpenAI GPT-4* or *GPT-5* models, it allows developers to converse, brainstorm, and co-develop complete quantum solutions through iterative refinement.

AI assistants enhance quantum coding through intelligent automation and guidance:

- **Conversational code generation**: Accepts natural language prompts to produce circuits, algorithms, and annotated explanations.
- **Iterative refinement**: Developers can request modifications (e.g., `replace Hadamard with RX rotation` or `add noise model using AerSimulator`).
- **Debugging and error analysis**: Interprets Python tracebacks and suggests fixes for version mismatches or incorrect imports.
- **Learning and documentation aid**: Explains theoretical concepts (e.g., `difference between QAOA and VQE`) in an accessible form.

The following is an example dialogue:

User: `Write Qiskit code to demonstrate Bell state creation and measurement.`

ChatGPT: `Generates circuit code, includes qc.h(0) and qc.cx(0,1), adds measurement and visualization.`

User: `Add noise model simulation.`

ChatGPT: `Adds Aer noise module with depolarizing channel and re-runs circuit.`

This two-way iteration fosters a learning-by-dialogue environment, empowering developers to understand why the generated code works—not just how.

Code Llama for secure AI-assisted programming

Unlike cloud-based AI assistants, Code Llama can be deployed locally within institutional infrastructure. This makes it suitable for research environments where data privacy and algorithm confidentiality are important.

In quantum development workflows, Code Llama can assist with circuit generation, debugging, and code suggestions for frameworks such as Qiskit or Cirq. Its open-source design also allows researchers to fine-tune the model using specialized quantum datasets.

Code Llama is an open-source coding LLM that supports on-premise deployment, enabling secure AI code generation for sensitive quantum algorithms.

AI-assisted tools like Code Llama offer unique advantages tailored to quantum research and development:

- **Offline access**: Ideal for labs without cloud connectivity or those prioritizing IP confidentiality.
- **Fine-tuning capability**: Can be trained on custom quantum datasets, enhancing understanding of specialized APIs such as Qiskit Runtime and the Amazon Braket **software development kit** (**SDK**).
- **Integration with Jupyter**: Works via text-completion engines in Jupyter or Colab notebooks.
- **Transparency**: Open model weights support reproducibility and academic experimentation.

Role of prompt engineering

All three assistants rely heavily on prompt quality. In quantum programming, where symbolic notation and algorithmic precision are essential, clarity and specificity are crucial.

The following is a good prompt example:

```
Write Python code in Qiskit to simulate a 3-qubit QAOA circuit with a cost Hamiltonian for Max-Cut.
```

The following is a poor prompt example:

```
Make a quantum algorithm.
```

The former specifies the framework, algorithm type, qubit count, and target function, resulting in a more accurate and contextually rich response.

AI-assisted circuit design and simulation

The integration of AI tools into quantum circuit design is reshaping how developers create, test, and visualize algorithms. By translating natural language intent into executable code, AI reduces development time, improves learning, and supports experimentation across major quantum frameworks.

This section examines how AI simplifies the circuit development workflow, from automatic generation and framework-specific scaffolding to human validation and visualization highlighting the combined role of AI assistance and human expertise.

In practice, AI assistance streamlines the early stages of circuit development by quickly translating conceptual ideas into executable templates. Developers can then refine these drafts, validate physical correctness, and extend them for specific experiments or applications.

Shift toward intelligent circuit generation

Quantum circuit design traditionally demands deep knowledge of gates, qubit topology, and measurement, requiring manual translation of mathematics into circuits that is time-consuming and error-prone. AI-assisted tools shift this paradigm by converting natural language prompts into executable code for major quantum frameworks, reducing the learning curve and boosting developer productivity.

Instead of starting with a blank notebook, a developer can describe their intent:

```
Create a two-qubit Bell-state circuit and display its Bloch sphere visualization.
```

An AI assistant instantly scaffolds the corresponding Python program.

This prompt-driven workflow illustrates how AI tools convert conceptual descriptions into working circuit templates, allowing developers to concentrate on verification, optimization, and interpretation rather than initial code construction.

Using AI to scaffold circuits in Qiskit

Qiskit is one of the most widely used SDKs for quantum programming. AI assistants like ChatGPT and GitHub Copilot can automatically compose Qiskit circuits with initialization, entanglement, and measurement commands.

Through natural language prompts or code comments, AI assistants can generate circuit templates, recommend gate sequences, and suggest measurement strategies, enabling faster experimentation and learning.

Example 1: Generating Bell State circuit

The prompt is as follows:

```
Write Qiskit code to prepare and measure the Bell state |Φ⁺⟩.
```

The AI-generated output is as follows:

```
from qiskit import QuantumCircuit, Aer, execute
from qiskit.visualization import plot_histogram
# Create a 2-qubit Bell state |Φ+> = (|00> + |11>)/√2
qc = QuantumCircuit(2, 2)
qc.h(0)
qc.cx(0, 1)
qc.measure([0,1], [0,1])
simulator = Aer.get_backend('qasm_simulator')
result = execute(qc, simulator, shots=1024).result()
counts = result.get_counts()
plot_histogram(counts)
```

The assistant not only writes syntactically correct code but also includes measurement visualization—a subtle feature many beginners overlook.

Extending AI-generated designs in Cirq

Cirq, Google's quantum SDK, differs from Qiskit in how it defines circuits and gates. AI assistants can adapt to this syntax automatically if prompted correctly.

This capability allows developers to move between frameworks more easily, focusing on algorithmic logic while the assistant adapts syntax and library conventions.

Example 2: Prompt-based Cirq circuit

The prompt is as follows:

```
Generate Cirq code to build a 3-qubit GHZ state and simulate its measurement.
```

The AI-generated output is as follows:

```
import cirq
# Create 3 qubits
```

```
qubits = cirq.LineQubit.range(3)
circuit = cirq.Circuit()
# GHZ state preparation
circuit.append(cirq.H(qubits[0]))
circuit.append(cirq.CX(qubits[0], qubits[1]))
circuit.append(cirq.CX(qubits[1], qubits[2]))
circuit.append(cirq.measure(*qubits, key='result'))
# Simulation
sim = cirq.Simulator()
result = sim.run(circuit, repetitions=1000)
print(result.histogram(key='result'))
```

This highlights AI's contextual transferability—recognizing that GHZ state generation follows the same conceptual pattern across frameworks despite implementation differences.

Quantum circuit prototyping on AWS Braket

AWS Braket offers a unified platform for simulation and execution across multiple vendor backends. AI assistants can scaffold Braket scripts, reducing onboarding friction for cloud-based quantum execution.

AI-assisted scripting also simplifies interaction with cloud-based quantum services by generating ready-to-run code for simulators or hardware backends.

Example 3: AI-generated Braket workflow

The prompt is as follows:

`Write AWS Braket Python code to run a Bell-state circuit on the local simulator.`

The AI-generated output is as follows:

```
from braket.circuits import Circuit
from braket.devices import LocalSimulator
device = LocalSimulator()
# Create Bell state
bell = Circuit().h(0).cnot(0,1).measure(0,1)
result = device.run(bell, shots=1000).result()
print(result.measurement_counts)
```

This minimal code is typical of AI-assisted generation—compact, correct, and ready to extend with additional measurements or visualization utilities.

Debugging, testing, and optimization with AI support

As quantum software grows in complexity, ensuring accuracy, stability, and performance becomes increasingly challenging. AI-assisted debugging and optimization now play a vital role in addressing these challenges—helping developers identify, interpret, and resolve issues faster than traditional methods. By combining AI insights with human expertise, quantum teams can maintain high reliability while accelerating iteration cycles.

This section explores how AI assistants such as ChatGPT, GitHub Copilot, and Code Llama enhance every stage of the debugging and optimization process—from error detection and unit testing to transpilation, resource tuning, and continuous integration.

AI-assisted debugging tools complement traditional development practices by providing quick explanations, code corrections, and optimization suggestions. This guidance allows developers to diagnose issues more efficiently while maintaining focus on algorithm design and experimental objectives.

AI as a quantum debugging partner

Quantum programming introduces new categories of errors not typically encountered in classical software development—such as qubit misalignment, gate incompatibility, or simulation backend mismatches. Traditional debugging techniques are often inadequate because qubit intermediate states are probabilistic and cannot be directly observed without measurement collapse.

In this context, AI-assisted debugging emerges as an invaluable support system. Tools like ChatGPT, GitHub Copilot, and Code Llama can interpret error traces, infer probable causes, and suggest corrections, sometimes faster than manual debugging. They also help optimize code by reducing gate depth, identifying redundant operations, and suggesting performance-enhancing alternatives.

Common error types in quantum programming

Even with AI-assisted coding, quantum programs may encounter syntax, API, or conceptual errors; recognizing them supports efficient debugging and reliable execution across simulators and hardware backends.

The following table summarizes the most common error categories, their descriptions, and representative examples to help developers quickly identify and resolve these issues:

Error type	Description	Example
Syntax errors	Improper Python structure or function call.	Missing parentheses in `qc.h(0`.
Library deprecation	Using outdated API methods.	`Aer.get_backend('qasm_simulator')` is deprecated in later versions.
Logic errors	Incorrect gate sequencing or measurement order.	Using `cx(1,0)` instead of `cx(0,1)`.
Simulator/Hardware mismatch	Using an incompatible backend configuration.	Attempting to run `AerSimulator` on a device-only circuit.
Parameter errors	Wrong arguments in parameterized gates.	Using degrees instead of radians in rotation angles.

Table A.1: Common error types in quantum programming

Manually tracing these issues is tedious; AI assistants act as quantum-aware copilots, analyzing errors and context to propose relevant corrections.

AI-assisted error diagnosis

When a Qiskit or Cirq program raises a traceback, AI can interpret it in natural language. The following is an example:

Error message:

```
AttributeError: module 'qiskit' has no attribute 'Aer'
```

Prompt to ChatGPT:

```
Explain and fix this Qiskit error.
```

AI response:

```
The error occurs because Aer is now available under qiskit_aer. You can fix it by installing the qiskit-aer package and importing it as:
from qiskit_aer import Aer
```"
```

In seconds, the assistant identifies both the cause and the updated import syntax—something that would otherwise require manual reference checking.
```

Testing quantum circuits with AI guidance

Testing in quantum computing focuses on verifying results rather than on deterministic output comparison. AI can help generate unit tests that simulate expected measurement outcomes or verify properties like unitarity.

Here is an example prompt:

`Write a test function to verify that a 2-qubit Bell circuit outputs equal counts for 00 and 11.`

The AI-generated code is as follows:

```
def test_bell_state_balance():
    from qiskit import QuantumCircuit, Aer, execute
    from numpy import isclose

    qc = QuantumCircuit(2,2)
    qc.h(0); qc.cx(0,1); qc.measure([0,1], [0,1])
    sim = Aer.get_backend('qasm_simulator')
    result = execute(qc, sim, shots=1024).result()
    counts = result.get_counts()
    assert isclose(counts.get('00',0), counts.get('11',0), rtol=0.1)
```

The AI assistant can also extend this logic to Cirq or AWS Braket frameworks, showcasing multi-platform adaptability.

AI-driven optimization and transpilation

Optimization in quantum programming often involves minimizing gate depth, reducing noise sensitivity, or reordering operations to exploit hardware topology. AI assistants can assist in this process by:

- **Suggesting efficient gate substitutions**: For example, replacing H–Z–H with X when equivalent under a unitary transformation.
- **Advising transpilation levels**: Qiskit's transpiler accepts multiple optimization levels (0–3). A prompt like:

  `Optimize my Qiskit circuit for IBM's ibmq_manila backend." leads ChatGPT to generate:`

  ```
  from qiskit import transpile
  qc_opt = transpile(qc, backend=backend, optimization_level=3)
  ```
- **Recommending noise models or simulators**: AI can propose realistic Aer noise models to simulate hardware imperfections, guiding developers to test circuit robustness.
- **Performance hints**: Tools like Copilot suggest vectorized or parallelized operations, improving simulator runtime efficiency.

Integrating AI into continuous testing pipelines

For quantum research teams, AI assistants streamline testing, validation, and maintenance by automating repetitive checks and summarizing results, improving consistency, efficiency, and reliability across complex projects.

Key applications include:

- Copilot or Code Llama can auto-generate unit tests for every new circuit definition.
- ChatGPT can summarize test logs and highlight failed quantum jobs with explanations.
- Integration with GitHub Actions allows AI to recommend version control actions based on test results.

Typical workflow steps include:

1. Developer commits a new quantum algorithm notebook.
2. CI pipeline triggers test execution.

3. ChatGPT API analyzes test outputs and posts readable summaries:
   `Test for GHZ circuit failed—measurement imbalance observed beyond 10% threshold.`

This hybrid automation saves time and ensures consistent validation across projects.

AI for quantum resource optimization

In practice, AI assistants analyze circuit structure and backend requirements to recommend refinements that improve efficiency and reliability. By suggesting optimized gate arrangements or simulator configurations, these tools help developers create circuits that are better suited for real hardware execution.

AI assistants help improve the efficiency of quantum circuits by analyzing design choices and suggesting performance-focused refinements.

Key optimization areas include:

- **Qubit count**: Suggesting circuit re-encoding using fewer qubits.
- **Gate depth**: Reordering or merging gates to reduce decoherence risk.
- **Execution cost**: Estimating runtime credits on AWS Braket or IBM Q hardware.

A well-designed prompt, such as `Simplify this 5-qubit Qiskit circuit while maintaining entanglement fidelity`, allows the assistant to rewrite the code and, optionally, apply `transpile(..., optimization_level=3)` to achieve a leaner structure.

Limitations and human oversight

Therefore, AI should be viewed as a supportive development partner rather than a replacement for expert judgment. Developers must still evaluate the physical correctness of circuits, validate results, and ensure that suggested optimizations remain compatible with the intended algorithm and hardware constraints.

While AI-assisted debugging accelerates problem-solving in quantum programming, it still requires human verification to ensure correctness and physical validity.

Key limitations include:

- Generated fixes might rely on outdated library versions.
- Suggestions may optimize syntax but ignore physical gate constraints.
- Over-dependence can reduce conceptual understanding of circuit behavior.
- Thus, while AI dramatically accelerates correction and testing, human validation remains the ultimate checkpoint.

Case study: AI-guided Grover's algorithm and VQE implementation

The convergence of AI-assisted programming and quantum algorithm design marks a new phase in computational development. Tools such as ChatGPT, GitHub Copilot, and Code Llama support circuit construction, error detection, and execution optimization by converting natural language prompts into executable code, bridging theory and implementation. Human oversight remains essential to ensure alignment with algorithmic goals, hardware constraints, and physical principles.

This section highlights two examples: AI-guided Grover's algorithm and AI-assisted **variational quantum eigensolver** (**VQE**) demonstrating how AI and human expertise jointly streamline quantum programming and hybrid computation.

Together, these examples demonstrate how AI-assisted tools can accelerate algorithm development while preserving the need for careful human validation. By combining automated code generation with theoretical understanding, developers can implement and refine quantum algorithms more efficiently.

Case study 1: AI-guided Grover's algorithm implementation

Grover's algorithm illustrates the synergy between AI-assisted programming and quantum search optimization, offering a quadratic speed-up over classical search. This case study shows how AI assistants can generate circuits, detect errors, and suggest optimizations, while human developers ensure algorithmic validity and physical correctness.

In practice, AI assistants help developers translate algorithmic concepts into working circuits by generating templates and suggesting corrections. Human oversight then ensures that the resulting implementation accurately reflects the theoretical structure of the algorithm.

AI meets quantum search

Grover's algorithm demonstrates a quadratic speed-up over classical search, locating a marked item in $O(\sqrt{N})$ queries instead of $O(N)$. Traditionally, implementing it in Qiskit requires manual construction of the oracle, diffuser, and control logic, which can be challenging for beginners. This case study shows how AI-assisted tools can scaffold the algorithm, identify errors, and suggest optimizations, while human developers ensure conceptual correctness.

Defining the objective

Our goal is to:

- Design Grover's algorithm to find the target state $|11\rangle$ in a two-qubit system.
- Use AI to generate base code scaffolding.
- Verify and refine the implementation manually.
- Analyze output distribution to confirm amplitude amplification.
- This case illustrates human–AI collaboration—where AI accelerates code creation, and the developer ensures theoretical precision.

AI-generated baseline implementation

The following is the prompt to ChatGPT:

Generate Python (Qiskit) code for Grover's Algorithm to find |11⟩ in a 2-qubit system, including oracle, diffuser, and measurement.

The AI-generated code is as follows:

```
from qiskit import QuantumCircuit, Aer, execute
from qiskit.visualization import plot_histogram
# Step 1: Oracle for |11>
oracle = QuantumCircuit(2)
oracle.cz(0, 1)
# Step 2: Diffuser
diffuser = QuantumCircuit(2)
diffuser.h([0, 1])
diffuser.x([0, 1])
diffuser.h(1)
diffuser.cx(0, 1)
diffuser.h(1)
```

```
diffuser.x([0, 1])
diffuser.h([0, 1])
# Step 3: Grover circuit
qc = QuantumCircuit(2, 2)
qc.h([0, 1])
qc.append(oracle, [0, 1])
qc.append(diffuser, [0, 1])
qc.measure([0, 1], [0, 1])
# Simulation
sim = Aer.get_backend('qasm_simulator')
result = execute(qc, sim, shots=1024).result()
counts = result.get_counts()
plot_histogram(counts)
```

The generated code runs successfully and yields a high probability for `'11'`, verifying the AI's reasoning.

Human verification and refinement

Upon review, the human developer notices:

- The `oracle.cz(0, 1)` correctly inverts the $|11\rangle$ phase.
- The diffuser performs inversion about the mean, but can be simplified using built-in Qiskit methods.

To validate correctness, the developer adds circuit visualization and a **Statevector** check:

```
from qiskit.visualization import plot_bloch_multivector
from qiskit.quantum_info import Statevector
sv = Statevector.from_instruction(qc)
plot_bloch_multivector(sv)
```

This confirms that the final state has high amplitude on $|11\rangle$, consistent with Grover's search principle.

AI-assisted optimization

Next, the developer asks:

Optimize this Grover circuit for minimum gate depth.

The AI response is as follows:

Use transpile() with optimization_level = 3 and merge H-X-H patterns.

The assistant suggests:

```
from qiskit import transpile
qc_opt = transpile(qc, optimization_level=3)
qc_opt.draw('mpl')
```

It provides a reduced-depth circuit with fewer redundant gates. This showcases AI's awareness of transpilation and circuit simplification—a critical phase in deploying circuits to noisy hardware.

Debugging through dialogue

Suppose an error occurs due to deprecated syntax:

```
Aer.get_backend('qasm_simulator') -> AttributeError
```

When prompted, AI replies:

Use from qiskit_aer import Aer or from qiskit providers aer import Aer depending on your version.

This exchange exemplifies how conversational debugging reduces friction during development—especially for evolving frameworks like Qiskit 6.x and beyond.

Comparing simulation and hardware execution

AI can also guide hardware-ready deployment.

The prompt is as follows:

```
Modify this circuit to run on IBM Quantum real device ibmq_manila and include error mitigation.
```

The following are the AI-suggested steps:

1. `Replace Aer simulator with IBMQ.load_account() and backend selection.`
2. `Use transpile(qc, backend, optimization_level=3).`
3. `Add measurement error mitigation via CompleteMeasFitter.`

The assistant produces:

```
from qiskit_ibm_runtime import QiskitRuntimeService
service = QiskitRuntimeService()
backend = service.backend('ibmq_manila')
job = backend.run(qc_opt, shots=1024)
```

This bridges simulation and hardware execution while teaching a practical deployment workflow.

Performance and result interpretation

Running the AI-guided implementation yields measurement counts similar to:

```
{'11': 492, '00': 14, '01': 10, '10': 8}
```

This indicates successful amplitude amplification toward the marked state $|11\rangle$. The histogram shows the result clearly peaks at the target, validating the circuit's function.

Key takeaways

AI assistants streamline the quantum development workflow by converting natural language queries into executable code, generating circuit components, identifying syntax and import errors, suggesting optimization strategies, and adding visualization tools. Human expertise remains essential to ensure algorithmic accuracy, verify logical correctness, validate library versions, review physical constraints, and interpret quantum results. Together, this hybrid workflow combines AI efficiency with human theoretical rigor, ensuring both speed and correctness in quantum programming.

Case study 2: AI-assisted variational quantum eigensolver

The VQE shows how AI-assisted programming simplifies hybrid quantum–classical workflows. Tasks such as Hamiltonian definition, ansatz design, optimizer setup, and simulation management can be largely automated, converting high-level descriptions into executable code. This case study illustrates how AI tools support VQE construction, optimization, and visualization in Qiskit Nature, while human oversight ensures accuracy, parameter choices, and physical interpretation.

This example highlights how AI assistance can streamline hybrid quantum–classical workflows. By generating initial code structures and suggesting optimization strategies, AI tools reduce development overhead while allowing researchers to focus on interpretation and refinement.

Merging AI creativity with quantum optimization

The VQE is a key hybrid quantum–classical algorithm for estimating a Hamiltonian's ground-state energy using a parameterized circuit and classical optimization. Although conceptually simple, VQE implementation requires defining the Hamiltonian, constructing the ansatz, optimizing the parameters, and managing the backend. AI-assisted programming reduces setup time by generating boilerplate code, tuning parameters, and suggesting optimizers, while human oversight ensures physical correctness and convergence stability.

Case study objective

In this case study, we aim to:

- Implement a simple VQE for the **hydrogen molecule** (H_2).
- Use ChatGPT or GitHub Copilot to generate code scaffolding.
- Optimize and interpret results under human supervision.
- Demonstrate how AI accelerates the hybrid workflow between Qiskit and classical optimizers (e.g., COBYLA, SPSA, L-BFGS-B).

AI-generated baseline implementation

The prompt to ChatGPT is as follows:

```
Write Qiskit code to compute the ground-state energy of H₂ using VQE with COBYLA optimizer.
```

The following is the AI-generated code:

```
from qiskit import Aer
from qiskit.algorithms import VQE
from qiskit.algorithms.optimizers import COBYLA
from qiskit.primitives import Estimator
from qiskit.circuit.library import TwoLocal
from qiskit_nature.second_q.hamiltonians import MolecularHamiltonian
from qiskit_nature.second_q.drivers import PySCFDriver
from qiskit_nature.second_q.mappers import ParityMapper
# Step 1: Build molecular Hamiltonian for H2
driver = PySCFDriver(atom='H .0 .0 .0; H .0 .0 .735', basis='sto3g')
problem = driver.run()
hamiltonian = problem.hamiltonian
# Step 2: Mapper and ansatz
mapper = ParityMapper()
ansatz = TwoLocal(rotation_blocks='ry', entanglement_blocks='cz', reps=2)
# Step 3: Initialize VQE
optimizer = COBYLA(maxiter=200)
estimator = Estimator()
vqe = VQE(estimator, ansatz, optimizer)
# Step 4: Compute ground-state energy
result = vqe.compute_minimum_eigenvalue(hamiltonian.second_q_op())
print(result.eigenvalue.real)
```

The AI correctly identifies the `PySCFDriver`, `ParityMapper`, and `TwoLocal` ansatz—common components in Qiskit Nature's VQE pipeline, illustrating strong contextual awareness of specialized quantum APIs.

Human validation and enhancement

The human developer refines and validates the circuit by:

- **Confirming imports**: Updating to current Qiskit Nature APIs if necessary (`from qiskit_nature.second_q.drivers import PySCFDriverV2`).
- **Visualizing the Ansatz**: `ansatz.decompose().draw('mpl')`
- **Benchmarking energies**: Comparing results to the theoretical −1.137 Hartree ground-state value.

The expected output is as follows:

```
Estimated Ground-State Energy ≈ -1.135 Hartree
```

AI-driven parameter tuning and optimizer suggestions

After observing convergence speed, the developer asks:

Suggest a different optimizer to improve VQE accuracy.

The AI response is as follows:

Try L_BFGS_B or SPSA optimizers for faster convergence and noise resilience.

The generated code snippet is as follows:

```
from qiskit.algorithms.optimizers import L_BFGS_B
optimizer = L_BFGS_B(maxfun=300)
vqe = VQE(estimator, ansatz, optimizer)
```

AI further suggests hybrid strategies combining SPSA for noisy backends and COBYLA for noiseless simulations demonstrating a nuanced understanding of practical trade-offs.

Error analysis and debugging assistance

When running the AI-generated code, a typical error may appear:

```
ImportError: cannot import name 'MolecularHamiltonian'
```

Upon re-prompting, the assistant clarifies:

MolecularHamiltonian is deprecated; use

qiskit_nature.second_q.hamiltonians.ElectronicEnergy instead.

Such conversational correction saves extensive documentation lookup and encourages iterative learning through guided repair.

Visualization and result interpretation

AI can add visualization automatically:

Prompt:

Plot energy convergence of VQE iterations using Matplotlib.

Generated code:

```
import matplotlib.pyplot as plt
energies = result.optimizer_history['energy']
plt.plot(energies, marker='o')
plt.xlabel('Iteration')
plt.ylabel('Energy (Hartree)')
plt.title('VQE Convergence for H₂ Molecule')
plt.show()
```

This yields a clear plot showing monotonic energy minimization toward ≈ −1.13 Hartree, confirming proper convergence of the hybrid loop.

AI support for noise modeling and backend selection

To extend realism, the developer prompts:

Modify the VQE code to run on a noisy simulator using Aer NoiseModel.

The AI-generated addition is as follows:

```
from qiskit_aer.noise import NoiseModel
from qiskit.providers.fake_provider import FakeManila
backend = FakeManila()
```

```
noise_model = NoiseModel.from_backend(backend)
sim = Aer.get_backend('aer_simulator')
result = vqe.compute_minimum_eigenvalue(hamiltonian.second_q_op(), noise_model=noise_model)
```

The AI automatically integrates noise realism, helping developers anticipate hardware imperfections.

Key takeaways

AI assists quantum algorithm development by generating problem setup, execution logic, optimizations, debug fixes, and visualizations, while human expertise ensures validation, stability, context-aware choices, and physical interpretation. This collaboration accelerates experimentation, replacing extensive setup with an interactive workflow.

Hybrid AI-quantum workflows using PennyLane and PyTorch

Hybrid AI-quantum workflows combine deep learning adaptability with quantum computational power, using classical networks for data and optimization and quantum circuits for nonlinear, high-dimensional transformations. Frameworks like PennyLane enable end-to-end differentiable programming with PyTorch and TensorFlow, while AI-assisted programming accelerates design, training, and optimization without manual gradient coding.

This section outlines how AI tools support hybrid model construction, quantum backpropagation, and human–AI collaboration to streamline workflow design.

In practice, AI-assisted tools simplify the development of hybrid quantum–classical models by automatically generating circuit templates, linking them with classical neural networks, and suggesting training configurations. This support enables developers to focus more on model design and interpretation while reducing the effort required to integrate quantum layers with classical machine learning frameworks.

Rise of differentiable quantum programming

The next frontier in computational intelligence lies in hybrid AI-quantum workflows, where classical deep learning models and quantum circuits collaborate in a unified framework. The classical component handles large-scale data preprocessing and gradient-based optimization, while the quantum component captures high-dimensional feature correlations or performs nonlinear transformations in Hilbert space.

Frameworks like PennyLane bridge this divide by seamlessly integrating with PyTorch and TensorFlow, enabling end-to-end automatic differentiation across both quantum and classical layers. When paired with AI-assisted programming tools, developers can now design and train complex hybrid models faster without deriving gradients or manually rewriting circuit structures.

Understanding hybrid AI-quantum models

Hybrid AI-quantum models integrate classical neural networks for feature extraction and optimization with quantum circuits for non-classical transformations, creating a unified architecture that addresses problems beyond the reach of either paradigm alone.

A typical hybrid quantum–classical model includes the following components:

- **Classical neural network**: Processes input features or learns post-measurement data.
- **Quantum layer**: Encodes data into qubits, applies parameterized gates, and returns measurement outputs.
- **Optimization loop**: Trains both the classical and quantum parameters together using gradient descent.

In essence, the hybrid model performs:

$$\text{Output} = f_{classical}(Q_\theta(x))$$

Where Q_θ is the **parameterized quantum circuit** (**PQC**) and $f_{classical}$ is the classical neural layer.

AI assistants like ChatGPT and Copilot can automatically generate the scaffolding for such workflows, define differentiable cost functions, and link the forward and backward passes between PennyLane and PyTorch.

AI-assisted construction of a hybrid model

Building hybrid quantum–classical neural networks is traditionally complex and time-intensive due to the integration of frameworks. AI-assisted programming automates much of this workflow covering device setup, circuit definition, training, and evaluation, while allowing human refinement. The example demonstrates how AI constructs a PennyLane–PyTorch hybrid model that enables seamless coordination between quantum feature extraction and classical learning within a unified, trainable architecture.

The prompt to ChatGPT is as follows:

`Create a hybrid quantum-classical neural network using PennyLane and PyTorch for binary classification of two data points.`

The AI-generated code is as follows:

```
import pennylane as qml
from pennylane import numpy as np
import torch
from torch import nn, optim
# Step 1: Quantum device
dev = qml.device("default.qubit", wires=2)
# Step 2: Parameterized Quantum Circuit (PQC)
@qml.qnode(dev, interface="torch")
def quantum_circuit(inputs, weights):
    qml.templates.AngleEmbedding(inputs, wires=[0, 1])
    qml.templates.StronglyEntanglingLayers(weights, wires=[0, 1])
    return [qml.expval(qml.PauliZ(0))]
# Step 3: Define hybrid model
class HybridModel(nn.Module):
    def __init__(self):
        super().__init__()
        self.q_weights = nn.Parameter(0.01 * torch.randn((1, 2, 3), requires_grad=True))
        self.fc = nn.Linear(1, 2)
    def forward(self, x):
        q_out = torch.stack([quantum_circuit(xi, self.q_weights) for xi in x])
        return torch.softmax(self.fc(q_out), dim=1)
# Step 4: Training
model = HybridModel()
criterion = nn.CrossEntropyLoss()
optimizer = optim.Adam(model.parameters(), lr=0.05)
# Dummy dataset
X = torch.tensor([[0.1, 0.2], [3.1, 2.9]], dtype=torch.float32)
Y = torch.tensor([0, 1])
for epoch in range(30):
    optimizer.zero_grad()
    output = model(X)
    loss = criterion(output, Y)
    loss.backward()
    optimizer.step()
```

```
    if epoch % 5 == 0:
        print(f"Epoch {epoch} Loss: {loss.item():.4f}")
```

This hybrid model demonstrates how a quantum circuit acts as a nonlinear feature extractor within a PyTorch pipeline, allowing the entire network, including quantum parameters to be trained via gradient backpropagation.

Human refinement and visualization

While AI can generate hybrid quantum–classical model structures, human oversight is essential to ensure correctness, interpret training behavior, and maintain physical validity through visualization, performance analysis, and parameter inspection.

Common human refinements include:

- **Quantum circuit visualization**:
  ```
  qml.draw(quantum_circuit)([0.1, 0.2], model.q_weights)
  ```
- **Loss trajectory plotting**:
  ```
  import matplotlib.pyplot as plt
  plt.plot(loss_values)
  plt.title('Hybrid Model Training Loss')
  plt.xlabel('Epoch')
  plt.ylabel('Loss')
  plt.show()
  ```

Parameter inspection to ensure weights evolve meaningfully during training.

AI-assisted optimization and experimentation

AI tools automate model construction and support architecture and hyperparameter refinement. Through iterative prompting, developers can explore alternative configurations, improve convergence, and simulate realistic hardware conditions with minimal manual effort.

Typical AI-driven optimization strategies include:

- **Optimizer switching**: Suggesting RMSProp or SGD when Adam shows oscillation.
- **Layer depth adjustment**: Recommending `reps=2` or `reps=3` for improved expressive power.
- **Activation choice**: Advising replacement of softmax with sigmoid for binary targets.
- **Noise integration**: Adding `qml.NoiseModel()` to simulate real hardware behavior.

The following is a prompt example:

```
Add Gaussian noise to circuit parameters to simulate noisy training.
```

The AI output is as follows:

```
noise = 0.02 * torch.randn_like(self.q_weights)
self.q_weights = nn.Parameter(self.q_weights + noise)
```

Understanding backpropagation across the quantum layer

A key advantage of frameworks like PennyLane is the ability to perform differentiable quantum programming.

The AI can explain:

```
Gradients flow through quantum nodes because the QNode is wrapped as a differentiable function
compatible with PyTorch's autograd system.
Mathematically:
```

$$\frac{dL}{d\theta} = \frac{\partial L}{\partial Q_\theta} \cdot \frac{\partial Q_\theta}{\partial \theta}$$

This allows hybrid models to be trained using standard deep learning optimization routines, an area in which AI assistants can provide theoretical support or gradient equations when asked.

Practical demonstration quantum XOR learning

A powerful example of AI-assisted hybrid modeling is the recreation of the classic XOR learning problem, a benchmark for testing nonlinear decision boundaries. With a simple natural language prompt, AI can generate a complete PennyLane–PyTorch workflow that integrates quantum entanglement and classical optimization.

The following is a prompt example:

```
Implement a hybrid model using PennyLane and PyTorch to learn XOR behavior.
```

AI generates code using two qubits, an entangling layer, and a binary classifier. After training for 100 epochs, the hybrid model accurately maps XOR truth table inputs to outputs demonstrating quantum nonlinearity in action.

Human–AI collaboration in hybrid workflow design

Hybrid quantum–classical model development relies on a balance between AI automation and human insight: AI speeds coding, integration, and troubleshooting, while humans ensure theoretical accuracy, stability, and interpretability, accelerating experimentation and deepening understanding across both components.

The table summarizes how AI and human roles complement each other across hybrid workflow stages, from circuit creation to analysis and visualization:

Task	AI contribution	Human role
Circuit creation	Writes parameterized templates (`AngleEmbedding`, `StronglyEntanglingLayers`).	Adjust layer depth and structure.
Model integration	Connects the quantum node to the PyTorch forward pass.	Inspect gradients and convergence.
Debugging	Detects tensor shape mismatches.	Fix complex tensor–array conversions.
Experimentation	Suggests optimizers and learning rates.	Select optimal training hyperparameters.
Visualization	Adds plots or state diagrams.	Interpret the learning trajectory.

***Table A.2**: Human–AI roles in hybrid workflow design*

This human–AI co-design model dramatically reduces coding complexity and accelerates innovation cycles in hybrid quantum machine learning research.

Future scope of AI-quantum integration

As AI and quantum computing converge, future hybrid systems will feature self-optimizing, adaptive pipelines, blurring the line between algorithm design and execution as AI increasingly creates and refines quantum models.

Key trends shaping this evolution include:

- **Dynamic PQC generation**: LLMs such as ChatGPT will automatically design PQCs tailored to specific datasets and objectives.
- **Autonomous structure tuning**: **Reinforcement learning** (**RL**) agents will iteratively refine circuit architectures for improved accuracy and noise resilience.

- **Quantum-aware compilation**: Future AI compilers will integrate hardware calibration, error mitigation, and software optimization into unified workflows.

Together, these advances point toward a future where AI not only writes quantum code but co-evolves it, continuously testing, adapting, and optimizing architectures to achieve efficient, hardware-specific performance.

Ethical concerns and practical limitations of AI coding

The integration of AI-assisted programming into quantum software development has transformed research and education by enabling faster experimentation, automated optimization, and broader access, while also introducing ethical responsibilities and practical constraints. As AI becomes an active collaborator, concerns around authorship, transparency, data security, and scientific integrity grow.

This section examines these implications, addressing ethical boundaries and technical limitations that affect reproducibility and reliability, and emphasizing the need for human oversight, clear documentation, and ethical accountability.

As a result, developers and researchers must adopt responsible practices when using AI-assisted tools. While these systems improve productivity and accessibility, their outputs must be carefully validated to ensure that scientific accuracy, transparency, and ethical standards are maintained throughout the development process.

Balancing innovation with responsibility

AI-assisted programming has accelerated the pace of quantum software development, empowering researchers to experiment, iterate, and deploy quantum algorithms faster than ever before. However, with this acceleration comes a new set of ethical responsibilities and practical challenges.

As AI becomes an active collaborator in code generation and problem-solving, questions arise about authorship, reliability, data privacy, **intellectual property** (**IP**), and academic integrity. In quantum computing, where precision, reproducibility, and verification are critical these concerns become even more pronounced.

Responsible adoption therefore requires clear guidelines on how AI-generated code is used, verified, and credited. Developers must treat AI suggestions as supportive inputs rather than authoritative solutions, ensuring that all implementations are critically reviewed and validated.

Double-edged nature of AI assistance

AI systems like ChatGPT, GitHub Copilot, and Code Llama are trained on vast amounts of public code and text data. While this enables them to generate versatile and contextually rich outputs, it also raises ethical questions:

- **Attribution and authorship**: Code suggested by AI may have originated from open-source repositories. Failing to credit original developers can unintentionally breach licenses.
- **IP**: AI-generated code may reproduce copyrighted fragments or mimic proprietary algorithms, leading to potential IP disputes.
- **Transparency and accountability**: Developers must ensure that any AI-generated code included in research or publication is verifiable and acknowledged transparently.

Data privacy and security risks

Quantum research environments often involve proprietary simulators, experimental setups, or sensitive datasets, such as chemical, cryptographic, or optimization data. Using AI assistants in these contexts requires careful consideration of data exposure risks:

- **Cloud dependency**: Most AI assistants process queries remotely, meaning user input may leave the local environment.
- **Proprietary algorithms**: Uploading internal or unpublished code to a public AI service may violate institutional confidentiality policies.
- **Security assurance**: Offline models, such as Code Llama (local) or GPT on-premises, provide safer alternatives for sensitive research.

Hallucinations and reliability issues

These limitations highlight the importance of combining automated assistance with careful human evaluation. Developers must review generated code, confirm library compatibility, and test results thoroughly to avoid unintended errors in quantum experiments.

While AI assistants are competent, they are not infallible.

They may generate:

- Nonexistent API functions (`qc.apply_oracle()`).
- Incorrect parameter types (`rotation_angle=90` instead of radians).
- Deprecated or syntactically invalid code.

These hallucinations can mislead beginners or introduce subtle logical errors into simulations. In quantum programming, even minor errors—such as a swapped control / target qubit—can invalidate results.

Best practices include:

- Always run and verify AI-generated code in simulators.
- Cross-check generated explanations with official SDK documentation.
- Treat AI outputs as first drafts, not final authority.

Over-reliance and skill atrophy

An emerging risk is over-reliance on AI tools for routine coding and problem-solving.

While these assistants can reduce time spent on boilerplate code, they can also discourage deep learning of mathematical and algorithmic fundamentals.

Quantum computing demands:

- Understanding of linear algebra and Hilbert space.
- Familiarity with quantum gates and measurement theory.
- Competence in error mitigation and hardware noise modeling.
- If developers rely solely on AI without cultivating conceptual mastery, they risk producing code that works but lacks scientific validity.

Reproducibility and research integrity

Scientific reproducibility is a cornerstone of academic credibility requires transparent reporting of how code and results were generated. With AI tools in the mix, maintaining reproducibility becomes more complex.

Key challenges include:

- AI models evolve continuously; future versions may produce different code for identical prompts.
- The generated code is non-deterministic and depends on model randomness.
- Lack of prompt documentation can obscure the developmental process.

Recommended mitigation strategies include:

- Archive prompts alongside results and code versions.
- Record environment details (AI model version, quantum SDK version).
- Use version-controlled notebooks (e.g., Jupyter with Git) to maintain traceability.

Ethical use in education and assessment

Establishing transparent policies helps ensure that AI tools support learning rather than replace it. When used responsibly, these tools can enhance understanding by assisting with debugging and explanation while still requiring students to develop their own algorithmic reasoning.

In academic settings, AI assistance raises concerns of academic honesty and fair assessment. When students use AI tools for assignments in quantum programming courses, clear boundaries must be set:

- **Permitted uses**: Syntax correction, debugging help, and conceptual explanation.
- **Restricted uses**: Direct code generation for graded assignments without acknowledgment.
- **Encouraged practice**: Collaborative learning help students compare AI suggestions with manual logic to deepen understanding.

Computational and practical limitations

Despite its advantages, AI-assisted quantum development faces several technical constraints that impact efficiency, adaptability, and accuracy. These challenges stem from current limitations in model memory, hardware integration, and evolving software environments.

The following table outlines key technical limitations and their implications for developers working on AI-driven quantum workflows:

Limitation	Impact
Model context window	AI may forget earlier code context in long quantum scripts.
Hardware awareness	AI lacks dynamic awareness of available qubit topology or backend calibration data.
Performance cost	Frequent API calls or suggestions increase latency and computational overhead.
Version drift	Generated code may use outdated functions as SDKs evolve rapidly.

***Table A.3**: Technical limitations in AI-assisted quantum development*

These factors highlight that human intervention remains crucial for maintaining operational reliability in production-level quantum projects.

Towards responsible AI-quantum synergy

Responsible innovation requires a balance between efficiency and ethics.

A sustainable framework for AI-assisted quantum development should emphasize:

- **Transparency**: Document AI involvement in all stages of development.
- **Accountability**: Validate all results before publication or deployment.
- **Privacy**: Avoid sharing sensitive or unpublished datasets with cloud-based tools.
- **Education**: Promote understanding of both AI's capabilities and its fallibility.
- **Ethical principle**: AI should augment human reasoning, not replace it.

The fusion of AI and quantum computing must uphold the same scientific rigor that defines classical computation and physics.

Conclusion

This appendix introduced AI-assisted programming as a transformative approach to quantum software development, demonstrating how AI enhances efficiency, creativity, and precision in the development of quantum applications. Through detailed discussions and case studies, we explored how tools such as ChatGPT, GitHub Copilot, and Code Llama automate circuit generation, debugging, and optimization across leading frameworks like Qiskit, Cirq, AWS Braket, and PennyLane. We also examined the integration of AI within hybrid quantum–classical workflows, where quantum circuits and neural networks collaborate to solve complex learning and optimization problems. Practical examples illustrated how AI accelerates the design and refinement of such systems while human insight ensures physical accuracy and interpretability. Finally, the appendix emphasized the importance of ethical responsibility, reproducibility, and human oversight in AI-driven development.

Looking ahead, the collaboration between AI and quantum computing is likely to become an essential component of future scientific and engineering workflows. As quantum hardware continues to evolve and software ecosystems mature, AI-assisted tools will increasingly support researchers in exploring new algorithms, optimizing resource usage, and simplifying complex experimental setups. However, the effectiveness of these technologies ultimately depends on thoughtful and responsible use. Developers must combine the speed and automation offered by AI with rigorous validation, conceptual understanding, and adherence to scientific standards. When applied in this balanced manner, AI-assisted programming can significantly accelerate discovery while preserving the integrity and reliability that underpin quantum research and innovation.

Questions

1. **What is AI-assisted programming, and why is it important in quantum development?**

   Answer: AI-assisted programming uses tools such as ChatGPT, GitHub Copilot, and Code Llama to generate, debug, and optimize code. In quantum development, it simplifies the creation of complex circuits and algorithms, reduces syntax errors, and accelerates experimentation allowing developers to focus on conceptual design rather than repetitive coding tasks.

2. **How do AI tools assist in building quantum circuits?**

   Answer: AI tools convert natural language prompts into executable Python code, automatically adding initialization, entanglement, measurement, and often visualization, making circuit creation faster and more accessible for learners and researchers.

3. **Which AI tools are most commonly used for quantum programming?**

   Answer: The three primary AI assistants are GitHub Copilot, ChatGPT, and Code Llama: Copilot provides inline IDE completions, ChatGPT supports conversational problem-solving and debugging, and Code Llama enables offline, secure coding.

4. **What role does AI play in hybrid AI-quantum workflows?**

   Answer: In hybrid workflows, AI links classical neural networks with quantum layers, generating PennyLane–PyTorch models, differentiable circuits, and suggesting optimizers or noise models to enable smooth training and testing.

5. **How does AI improve debugging and optimization in quantum programming?**

   Answer: AI can interpret tracebacks, detect deprecated APIs, and suggest instant fixes, while recommending transpilation levels, gate simplifications, and backend-specific optimizations to reduce circuit depth and improve runtime performance.

6. **What are the main limitations of AI-assisted coding in quantum development?**

   Answer: Limitations include context-window constraints, limited hardware awareness, API overhead, and SDK version drift, underscoring the need for ongoing human oversight.

7. **What ethical concerns arise from using AI in coding and research?**

   Answer: Ethical challenges include authorship, IP, data privacy, and transparency. As AI-generated code may reuse open-source patterns, researchers must document AI involvement and verify originality.

8. **How can developers maintain reproducibility in AI-assisted quantum research?**

   Answer: Reproducibility is ensured by archiving prompts, recording AI model versions, documenting quantum SDK details, and using version-controlled Jupyter notebooks with Git, keeping results traceable as tools evolve.

9. **Why is human oversight essential despite AI's capabilities?**

   Answer: While AI accelerates coding and debugging, it lacks physical intuition and domain judgment. Human developers ensure alignment with quantum logic, hardware constraints, and scientific validity, preserving accuracy and reliability.

10. **What is the key takeaway from AI-assisted quantum programming?**

    Answer: AI and quantum computing together form a new frontier where automation meets scientific reasoning. Used responsibly, AI acts as a collaborative partner, boosting productivity, innovation, and deeper exploration in quantum algorithms and hybrid models.

Exercises

1. Use ChatGPT or GitHub Copilot to generate Qiskit code for a two-qubit Bell state, run it on Aer **quantum assembly language** (**QASM**) with 1024 shots, and plot a histogram to confirm entanglement; explain how the AI interpreted the prompt and structured the circuit.
2. Create a Qiskit circuit with an intentional syntax error, ask an AI assistant to identify and fix it, verify the corrected code runs, and describe the fix.
3. Use ChatGPT to generate a PennyLane–PyTorch hybrid quantum–classical model for binary classification of two data points, train it, plot loss per epoch, and discuss the quantum layer's role.
4. Implement Grover's algorithm for a two-qubit system using AI-generated code, run it on Qiskit Aer, plot the histogram, and explain amplitude amplification that leads to a peak at $|11\rangle$.
5. Ask ChatGPT to optimize a three-qubit GHZ circuit by reducing gate depth or improving performance, compare the results with the original, and explain the effects on accuracy and runtime.
6. Use Code Llama (offline) to autocomplete a partial Qiskit Bell state script, run it, and evaluate its support for secure, private development.
7. Generate a PennyLane–PyTorch hybrid workflow with AI assistance, visualize the training curve, and explain how classical and quantum layers interact during optimization.
8. Ask ChatGPT to add a depolarizing noise model in Aer, run the Bell circuit under noise, compare with the ideal case, and discuss the impact of noise on entanglement fidelity.
9. Write a ~150-word reflection on ethical AI use in quantum research, covering authorship, reproducibility, and human oversight.
10. Develop a Jupyter Notebook containing AI prompts, generated code, and outputs; use Git or Colab version history to document changes and explain how version control supports reproducibility.

Index

A

B

C

R

www.ingramcontent.com/pod-product-compliance
Lightning Source LLC
LaVergne TN
LVHW060543061126
851857LV00017B/1879
9789378543609